Empowerment Practice with Families in Distress

Judith Bula Wise

Columbia University Press

New York

Columbia University Press

Publishers Since 1893

New York   Chichester, West Sussex

Copyright © 2005 Judith Bula Wise

Library of Congress Cataloging-in-Publication Data
Wise, Judith Bula.
Empowerment practice with families in distress / Judith Bula Wise.
      p. cm.—(Empowering the powerless)
Includes bibliographical references and index.
ISBN 0-231-12462-7 (cloth : alk. paper)
ISBN 0-231-12463-5 (pbk. : alk. paper)
1. Family social work. 2. Social work with people with social disabilities.
    3. Problem families—Services for. 4. Power (Social sciences). I. Title. II. Series.
HV697.W57 2004
362.82′532—cd22   2004055134

♾

Columbia University Press books are printed on permanent and durable acid-free paper.
Printed in the United States of America
c 10 9 8 7 6 5 4 3 2 1
p 10 9 8 7 6 5 4 3 2 1

In the struggle for the soul of our families … we need to give children a reflection of themselves they can be proud of. We need to give them this message of love if we are to mend the gashes in our world.

Now by love I don't mean indulgence. I don't mean sentimentality. By love *I mean a condition that we are capable of and desperate for, which envelops and sustains and supports and encourages and doesn't even have to touch. I mean love that recognizes that if we are the source of all humanity, then we are sisters and brothers to those in Afghanistan and in Tel Aviv and in Kyoto and in Lagos.*

Yes, absolutely.

I mean love that says, I free you.

Because only when we are free can we do the work of mending the world.

Maya Angelou, "Great Expectations"

This book is dedicated in memory of my parents, Fay Elizabeth Haeckel Bula and Ralph Elmer Bula, with deep gratitude for their constantly sustaining, encouraging, and freeing love.

Contents

Editor's Note

Empowering Practice with Families in Distress is the sixth book in the social work series Empowering the Powerless, published by Columbia University Press. Social work practice with families can be traced back to the beginnings of the Charity Organization Societies and Settlement House movements. While each movement's focus and emphases were different, both were committed to family practice. Writing in the traditions of these social work movements, Professor Wise brilliantly uses empowerment theory and practice principles to capture the uniqueness of this social work approach. Most important, she creatively applies these concepts to family practice.

Early in the book, Professor Wise introduces the reader to three complex family cases. Each family case represents a separate chapter in which a family suffers from some form of oppression such as poverty, discrimination, violence, and addiction. Professor Wise captures overt family patterns as well as the subtler nuances of day-to-day family transactions. She vividly describes how family members relate to each other and how the family as a unit relates to its community. In subsequent chapters, Professor Wise uses the backdrop of phases in the helping process (beginnings, middles, and endings) to teach us through these cases about the principles and skills of family work with a particular sensitivity to cultural factors.

I present the series's sixth book, *Empowering Practice with Families in Distress*, with special pride. Professor Wise, a friend and a former colleague, is a gifted family practitioner, teacher, and writer. She makes a profound contribution to our understanding of both family and empowerment practice.

Alex Gitterman, Series Editor

Acknowledgments

The "web of relationships" informing and supporting these pages reaches from past to present and from professional to personal. To all, I offer my deepest gratitude and appreciation.

First, to the families whose stories inform and inspire with grace and courage. Your names have been kept in confidence, but your lives are open on the page so that others may learn from your experiences. To each of you, my deepest gratitude.

To Dr. Alex Gitterman, series editor and "writing mentor." The following quote could have been written with you in mind: "To write is human; to edit is divine" (King 2000:13). Thank you for your empowering support, encouragement, and enlightening editing every step of the way.

This book could not have come into being without the discerning eye of John Michel, senior executive editor at Columbia University Press, and his administrative staff, Barbara Storey and Jeanie Lu, as well as editors Irene Pavitt and Jan McInroy. I also appreciate the astute perceptions of the reviewers.

I thank my colleagues at the University of Denver. To Dean Catherine Alter and Provost William Zaranka, thank you for your support of this work through the granting of the Sabbatical Leave as well as the Provost's Enhancement Award. I stand on the figurative shoulders of several DU scholars who have written in the area of empowerment thinking in recent years. Drs. Susan Manning, Enid Cox, Jean East, Ruth Parsons, and others in this respected group of colleagues have all influenced this work. I thank Drs. Cox, Manning, and East for reviewing portions of the manuscript. I am deeply grateful for the time and effort you gave, as well for as your valuable contributions. A special thanks to Jean East and Sue Kenney, codirectors of Project WISE, for opening your doors to enrich and enliven the community focus with your remarkable and dedicated service to families in need. Appreciation also goes to Neysa Folmer for your support, willingness, and patience in working with the diagrams and genograms.

I am surrounded with an incredible support network of friends: Margot Schoeps, Sally Purvis, Susan Trucksees, Pam Metz, Susan Manning, Helen and Joe Rodgers, Jean McLendon, Sandy Novak, Joan Winter, Michele and Bud Baldwin, Maria Gomori, Ken Block, Jonathan Stolzenberg, Becky and Bob Spitzer, Maria Yellow Horse Brave Heart, Lani Tolman, Nancy Sugden, Jane Westberg, and Jack Lavino. Our ongoing friendships blur the line between friend and family. Thank you for your decades of support and encouragement.

I have been extremely fortunate to have two wise long-term mentors whose influence I gratefully acknowledge in these pages. The first is Dr. Dennis Dailey, teacher, guide, coach, skilled listener, who over the past thirty years has always been responsive. I thank you for the way you look at life, for being an example of what it means to base one's choices on strength, competence, enjoyment, passion, compassion, and possibility. I gratefully acknowledge your review of the earlier drafts of this manuscript.

The second mentor I wish to acknowledge is Virginia Satir, dissertation committee member, model teacher, inspiration, colleague, friend, "professional mom." Her writing first introduced me to the possibility of working with families. I am grateful to have served as a member of Dr. Satir's training staff, where many of my thoughts about family of origin and the role of parents in the well-being of their children were shaped and refined. She was by far one of the most empowered persons I have ever known.

To practicing "family" specialist social workers, I wish to acknowledge your balancing act between professional attention to many families and personal attention to your own family that is a part of each day. You are the ones who best understand that to interweave personal family experience with professional choice is the only way to approach this work with integrity. Your perspectives are evident in these pages.

To my own families, who have created the backdrop for my professional life in working with families for the past thirty years, I offer my deepest thanks. There are four families to be acknowledged: my family of origin; my family and extended family of my first marriage of twenty-two years; my six-year intergenerational and multicultural "family of choice" while single; and my present family and extended family of my second marriage.

To my parents and brothers, Ralph and Fay, Mick and Joe, who all have been examples in their lives of reaching out beyond oneself to serve others—physician, dietitian, teacher of self-defense and water-survival skills to infants and children, participant with the I Have a Dream Foundation, Peace Corps volunteer, inner-city English and literature teacher—I am grateful to know enough about our ancestors to know that we share the normal sprinkling of rogues and outcasts as well as true legends in their own time. From the hundreds of families I have come to know over the years, I often wonder, How is it possible to have been so fortunate as to be with you? I offer a tribute in memory of both my parents and my deepest thanks to my brothers, Mick and Joe. You have shaped the ways I look at family in all of its awesome complexity.

In between family of origin and my family of today are two other families that deserve acknowledgment. The family and extended family of my first marriage provided many experiences of being family together that bring fond memories and respectful acknowledgment of the ways in which similarities bring families together and the ways in which differences can carry family members apart. I thank you and am grateful for the times we had together as family. And I also acknowledge my wonderful multicultural and multigenerational "family of choice," which came together before I heard of Maggie Kuhn (the founder of the Gray Panthers) and her active promotion of the importance of multigenerational households in our lives. During six and a half years of being single, I invited graduate students from area universities other than DU—students of various ages, ethnicities, religions, sexual orientations, classes, abilities, and interests—to share my living space. I can truly affirm Maggie Kuhn's wise words that "the generations have much to learn with and from each other." This was a delightful experience in the meaning of "family of choice," one that I can highly recommend to others if and when the circumstances present themselves.

Finally, to my beautiful family today. To my husband, Chip, this project could never have seen completion without your gentle patience, loving and steady encouragement. In every way, mentioned and unmentioned, I will always be so grateful to you and for you. To my stepchildren, Annah, Parker, and Connor, the complex and uncertain transition of watching a "stepmom" enter the picture of your lives is one I hope never to take for granted. Thank you for handling that transition with such grace, acceptance, and welcoming. You each are such a gift to me in your individual and collective ways. And to a most amazing "new" extended family of in-laws, who, much to the surprise of all of us, claims the same place of origin in the late nineteenth and early twentieth centuries as my own family of origin, I am grateful to each one of you for open, welcoming arms, breathtaking laughter, fabulous food, and shared holidays. Our common roots provide convincing evidence that we all are truly connected as family in more ways than we may realize.

Empowerment Practice with Families in Distress

Introduction

Social work services with families in distress and need in the United States can be traced to 1818 and the volunteer "visitors" to homes of the poor, one of the programs on the agenda of the New York Society for Prevention of Pauperism. The New York Association for Improving the Condition of the Poor (AICP), established in 1843, "served as a model for many general relief societies in the 1840s and 1850s" (Lubove 1977) and actively served the needs of families in financial, health, emotional, and other forms of distress. Social work "owes its beginning as a profession to the multiproblem family" (Wood and Geismar 1989:45). In 1890 a family-oriented approach was promoted by Franklin B. Sanborn, chairman of the National Conference on Charities and Corrections: "The family must be taken as a whole, otherwise the strongest social bond will be weakened" (quoted in Pumphrey and Pumphrey 1961:220).

From the beginnings of both the Charity Organization Societies and the settlement houses, the ideas of which had been borrowed from England and most of which were established in the 1870s and the 1880s, one can see a debate echoing concerns about approaches that would be empowering through sharing with the families served rather than bestowing charity upon them. Even though "friendly visitors" were encouraged to establish nonpaternalistic relationships with the families they served, their efforts were still seen generally as "paternalistic and condescending" by settlement house workers who chose to "bring together the privileged and the underprivileged for sharing...rather than giving" (Reynolds 1963:29). Whether to define problems environmentally, as the settlement house workers did, or as personal deficiencies, as the charity workers tended to do (Germain and Hartman 1980), continues as one of the lively debates in services to families to this day.

Agreement was evident, however, that the family rather than the individual was the unit of attention from the beginnings of both organizations. In 1880 Josephine Shaw Lowell recommended that volunteers meet conjointly with both parents when possible (Siporin 1980:12). Ten years later, in 1890, Zilpha Smith emphasized that every person seen "cannot be removed from family relations. We deal with the family as a whole" (quoted in Rich 1956:4). By the turn of the century, the voice of Mary Richmond was being heard, with her encouragement for establishing training courses. The first social work course ever taught was "The Treatment of Needy Families in Their Own Homes," at the New York Charity Organization Society's Summer School of Applied Philanthropy, which later became the Columbia University Graduate School of Social Work (Wood and Geismar 1989:49). When member agencies of the Charity Organization Societies were asked by one of their organizers, Francis McLean, "whether the family or the community should be the peculiar unit of charity organization," the reply came as "their own interest and special competence...was casework with 'disorganized families'" (Leiby 1978:126).

World Wars I and II, the Great Depression, unprecedented numbers of immigrants to the United States, massive epidemics, the connection between social work's acceptance of external pressure for professional legitimacy, and the tempting, and for some irresistible, popularity of Freudian thought resulted in a dizzying pendulum swing for those who sought deeper understanding of the roots of compassion for families in poverty and need. Mary Richmond was one of the first to posit the two extremes of variation as a focus on the environment as the source of social ills faced by these families and a focus on deficits identified within the individuals. Over time the pendulum swing between these two points was characterized by person-or-environment with emphasis on the person, person-or-environment with emphasis on the environment, person-and-environment inclusive of the transactions between them, person-in-environment (PIE) (still found in many social work texts today), and the most recent configuration—person: environment, with emphasis on the inseparable link in the transactions between persons and their contexts.

The ecological perspective has been identified as one approach that offers "some bridging concepts" (Wood and Geismar 1989:56), finally recognizing that in the lived experience of families and individuals the people and their environment are never separate. Advances in systems theory and the ecological perspective lead to "person WITH environment," which is the perspective used in this text, a perspective congruent with empowerment thinking and the theories supporting it, as well as one that seeks to describe active transaction "with" rather than the more passive "in." One does not simply reside "in" one's family. Words are frustratingly inadequate much of the time when describing human complexity, and few human structures are more complex than the family. However, the constant movement and flow of interactions and complex transactions "with" other family members and "with" surrounding dynamics of extended family, groups, community institutions and organizations, and beyond demand a refinement in the use of language to achieve a closer fit with the realities we seek to describe.

Social work theory has been through many versions of the relationship between individuals and their environments. "Person AND environment" with the source of the "problem" believed to be in *the person*, "person AND environment" with the source of the "problem" believed to be in *the environment*, then on to "person IN environment" or P-I-E, as it has been known for several decades. The advent of the metaphors of systems thinking and their applications to social work practice settings raised creative and critical questions about the passive connotations of persons IN their environments, particularly as we became more informed about such concepts as "dynamic flow" and the "constancy of transaction and change."

Empowerment thinking as well, with its vital role of action, calls the use of passive connotation into question. In response, the use of "person WITH environment" began to appear more frequently in social work literature, and its implications took practice into additional layers of understanding. Certainly as we emphasize the mutuality inherent in empowering practice and speak about "power WITH" our clients and client families, about learning WITH them, about connecting WITH others as a central form of coping, and as we seek to understand how family members use their power WITH each other, the use of "person WITH environment" provides the clearest picture of the transactions represented in the core ideas of this text. Another approach is to briefly consider the opposite. It is well documented that isolation from others can be one of the most disempowering realities for many of our clients. Connections with family and community can help erase such isolation.

This same integration was promoted by Ada Eliot Sheffield in the 1920s and 1930s. Sheffield admitted that she viewed a dualistic stance as merely piecemeal, "whereas a psychosocial whole operates as a system which like an organism conditions the very nature of its interdependent elements" (Sheffield 1937:265). To debate whether social workers should change people or change environments made no sense to her. Instead she saw a system of interactions as the focus and the key components of that multilevel system as what needed the change. Family members and the family as a group were included in this process, but it was the entire "web or network of interactions" that one worked with "so that the problem no longer existed, or at least was as ameliorated as much as was realistically possible" (Wood and Geismar 1989:57–58). Sheffield may have found herself marching to a different drummer than were the dualistic thinkers of the 1930s, but social workers who continued the traditional commitment to impoverished families facing multiple problems and oppressive circumstances were marching to her drummer as well. Over the next several decades their voices were not necessarily the loudest, nor the longest-winded, nor the most often published. But like Sheffield, they stayed very close to the lives and the experiences of the families they served. Their voices were never lost entirely, and the roots of a reemergence were steadily forming, a growing recognition that these ideas always hold a rightful and well-deserved place among the evolution of ideas that we call social work today.

Another early exception to the individual focus was M. Robert Gomberg. In 1944 he wrote that the focus of casework was the family as a whole. In 1951 he and Frances Levinson published *Diagnosis and Process in Family Counseling*. These writings have been credited as predating and greatly influencing the person who was later, in 1958, labeled "the father of family therapy," Nathan Ackerman. Historical descriptions of the family therapy movement written by psychiatrists (Bowen 1978; Guerin 1976) do not mention social workers' lengthy history of work with families in poverty and distress or the earlier theoreticians of family practice in family agencies in New York and Chicago. The only social worker mentioned in these historical summaries is Virginia Satir, whose *Conjoint Family Therapy* continues to be one of the classics in the field today.

Simultaneously in the 1950s, a focus on the "multiproblem family" emerged with the recognition that medically oriented psychodynamic thought provided inadequate guidelines for this population. Family-centered social work (Overton and Tinker 1957) recaptured the "interdependence of family positions and roles as well as society's responsibility for aiding the socially deprived" (Wood and Geismar 1989:66).

In the early 1960s Reynolds joined Gomberg in resisting emphasis on work with individuals, saying, "It is only by an artificial abstraction that we ever think we are dealing with individuals alone.... We isolate an individual for treatment only temporarily and with great risk that what we thought was excellent work will be undone in the complex of family relationships" (Reynolds 1963:203–204). Group workers also acknowledged the abstraction of seeing individuals separately from their contexts, yet paid only minimal lip service to "the template for all group process," the family (Wood and Geismar 1989:64).

The family-centered positions of the late 1950s were largely overlooked until much later (e.g., Hartman and Laird 1983), however, and the pendulum continued to be propelled back and forth in the works of Reynolds, Hamilton, Hollis and Woods, and Perlman. Textbooks of the 1960s emphasized the individual. When the medical perspective was predominant in the agency setting, family stressors were "treated as if they were the individual problem of the individuals involved. Information about other family members and family relationships was obtained vicariously if at all" (Wood and Geismar 1989:60).

Family-centered home-based services did gain prominence in child protection during the 1970s in response to child abuse and neglect and family violence and in response to President Jimmy Carter's commitment to work for a strengthening of families in the United States. In the 1980s family-centered home-based services were also seen as part of Family Preservation units and Homebuilders services. Social work authors such as Stein (1960), Hearn (1969), and Siporin (1970, 1972, 1975) continued emphasizing the importance of the role of the environment in work with poor families, and Hearn was one of the first to present the usefulness of systems thinking for these purposes. The role of the social worker was recognized as a comprehensive one (Goldstein 1970; Pincus and Minahan 1973; Middleman and Goldberg 1974), one that was capable of responses at the multiple levels of the system, and "one that went beyond the narrow role of psychotherapist only" (Wood and Geismar 1989:68). Ecological metaphors applied to human systems (Bronfenbrenner 1979) closely mirrored the person-in-environment configuration and added to the descriptive clarity of family dynamics: "goodness of fit" between needs and resources; problems in living pointing to the need for increased skills and coping capacities or to the need for additional resources in the systems outside and surrounding the family. It is respectfully noted that these ideas are reminiscent of Ada Sheffield's work of 1937.

Family-Centered Social Work Practice (Hartman and Laird 1983) is an important contribution that should be mentioned because of its tribute to early family social workers, its use of general system theory and the ecological perspective for contextual understanding of the family, and its comprehensive applications of the family-centered approach to social work practice with families. Hartman and Laird's text serves as valuable groundwork for this text, with similarities in theoretical base and focus. The addition of an emphasis on empowerment thinking grows systematically from these roots.

To summarize this brief history of family social work, the beginnings of social work with families can be placed at approximately 1820. The family therapy movement that is currently said to have originated primarily among physicians and within the medical profession shows its earliest influence in the 1950s, one hundred thirty years later. Today's social workers can easily see that the roots of many of the ideas seen among today's family therapists are embedded in the work of the early social work leaders and their "competence in casework with disorganized families." As social workers, we can continue to give this credit to the women and men who shaped our social work heritage in working with families. The empowerment approach, both historically and as presented here, and the family therapy approaches of today—structural, strategic, communication, contextual, and experiential, for example—work together to enhance and strengthen each other. One example, developed further later in the book, is the overlap between middle-phase dynamics in the empowerment approach—dynamics related to increasing coping skills, providing information and educational tools, and participating with others—which can also be seen as interventions of choice by practicing family therapists.

With conscious awareness of the uniqueness of the social work approach and, for this volume, its meaning for empowering practice *with* families (rather than *upon* them), we will serve our predecessors well. Constraints of space and time do not permit an extensive elaboration of the "family therapy" approaches and their respective theories, concepts, and applications. Such information is widely available in other sources. Similarities abound between empowerment thinking, the social work history of serving impoverished families in their contexts, and several of the family therapy approaches used today. This book is built upon, and pays tribute to, the social work approach consistent with the practicing family social workers of the 1800s and the 1900s. Its uniqueness lies in its selective focus and use of empowerment theory and practice principles for work with families in distress.

Themes of empowerment have persistently occurred within the research, writings, and practice of social workers for more than a century (Simon 1994). Within the past twenty-five years alone, the literature on social work practice with families using an empowerment perspective has expanded far beyond that of earlier decades. This volume is the sixth in the social work series Empowering the Powerless. The purpose of the series is to "provide perspectives on empowerment strategy in social work, which seeks to help clients draw on personal, interpersonal, and political power to enable them to gain greater control over their environments and attain their aspirations" (Gitterman, quoted in Simon 1994). The uses of empowerment thinking are diverse. Proponents of empowerment thinking today begin at a very different point than did our predecessors of a century ago, thirty years ago, even five years ago. The pervasiveness of empowerment thinking in nearly every aspect of human growth speaks to its wide acceptance. This same pervasiveness has also been viewed as contributing to its potential demise (Weissberg 1999). If it can be applied anywhere, anytime, to nearly every situation, then what unique meaning can be derived from such an inclusive term? Both acceptance and criticism are extensive. Social workers have particular affinities with empowerment theory, as well as particular cautions to heed. With its root in the word *power* and all that that word implies for work with oppressed populations, it is no wonder that many social workers come to empowerment thinking kicking and screaming, as I did myself. Social workers who work from an empowerment perspective and who remain committed to stances of social justice, equality, and mutuality must be especially sensitive to the actions that can result from such a theoretical stance and refrain from automatically assuming that it is the most beneficial for clients. Carefully hearing and critically assessing the many challenges directed at empowerment thinking, however, can refine and strengthen our effectiveness in applying its principles to work with families.

Empowering simply for the sake of empowering is not enough. Professionals must be held accountable for acknowledging the ends to which our empowerment efforts have led. Sometimes those ends have served the researcher, the scholar, and the practitioner far better than they have served the people to whom the empowerment strategies were supposedly directed in the first place (Weissberg 1999), though there are significant exceptions to this claim in social work scholarship and practice.

One could argue, for example, that if empowerment strategies are applied to families, the adolescent who gains knowledge about how to steal from parents or siblings might be "empowered" to commit robbery at more criminal levels later on. The alcoholic whose family members continue enabling behaviors can be "empowered" to continue the cycle of addiction and substance abuse. Questions regarding the purpose and the result must be asked. Goals for the use of an empowerment stance with client families—sustaining, enhancing, and helping to create family well-being, as defined by the family—are discussed in greater depth in chapter 1. At this point, however, the source of these goals can be identified.

The mission statement of the National Association of Social Workers Code of Ethics (1996) includes this objective: "To enhance human well-being and help meet the basic human needs of all people, with particular attention to the needs and empowerment of people who are vulnerable, oppressed, and living in poverty" (1). Clarifying what is meant by "human well-being" and, for purposes here, "family well-being" is no small task, however. The goal of wellness and family well-being (Duncan and Chase-Lansdale 2002; Longres 2000; Robbins, Chatterjee, and Canda 1998; Shriver 2001), the supporting strengths perspective (Saleebey 1997), and how a focus on strengths applies to practice with families (Kaplan and Girard 1994; Saleebey 1997; Walsh 1998), have been promoted and advanced to varying degrees in the social work literature. All reflect, support, and advance empowerment thinking. A partial answer to the question "Empowerment for what purpose?" then is to help social workers as they assist in strengthening families, particularly those who are "vulnerable, oppressed, and living in poverty," by helping to meet basic needs and by enhancing the families' own sense of what family well-being means to them.

As long as these efforts remain within the individual or family system, however, our task as social workers is unfinished. The family as a system exists at the intersection between the individual and the community. Any action in our practice with families, and with the individuals in those families, must include practice efforts directed toward the well-being of the wider community as well before our work is truly complete. The well-being of families cannot occur and be sustained over time if the context within which families live is not also one of support and well-being. Ecology and systems, two pillars of the theory base for the work of this book, help to structure the purpose of "helping people and promoting responsive environments that support human growth, health, and satisfaction in social functioning" as well as focusing on "the reciprocity of person-environment exchanges, in which each shapes and influences the other over time" (Germain and Gitterman 1996:5, 7).

Empowerment authors have been essential in establishing a framework and giving words to the ideal for which we aim. This volume builds upon those ideas and those visions. It is needed, not to add to the visionary statements but rather to increase depth in our approaches to working with families in particular. The beliefs about where social workers are headed when working with families, the theoretical perspectives and practice choices shaping the structure of the book, were all selected using one criterion. They had to be known to work—that is, they had to have been empirically derived from observation and experience and to have been used with results defined as effective by the family members themselves. Each must have contributed to that which is known to work with the complex, often deemed hopeless, situations of the families most frequently seen by social workers today.

"It works! People respond well to this. When people are treated like sick, dependent children, they tend to respond in a similar manner. When people are treated like capable, responsible adults, they also respond in a similar manner" (Howie, in Carling 1995:xvi). Howie, who spent several years in a psychiatric institution, includes "freedom of choice, independence, self-determination, and empowerment" when he makes the above reference to what people are responding well to. He goes on to say, "Sure we need supports, and not everyone can achieve at the same level of independence. But we should each achieve the level and type of independence that WE choose, using the supports that WE choose" (xv). Hearing the voices of family members like Howie is one of the essential ways to discover what works from an empowering stance. Over time families and professional helpers have worked together to mutually respond to each other regarding what works for families and how helpers can best participate in those efforts. Three major actions repeatedly show up: providing relevant information and learning; enhancing coping skills; and participating with others (e.g., Bernheim and Lehman 1985; Gutiérrez and Lewis 1999; Hatfield and Lefley 1987; *Our Fight* 1999). A few words to provide background can ground these three key actions within the helping context.

As recently as two generations ago, the idea of taking one's family's stresses or conflicts to a stranger outside the family was a completely foreign idea in the United States. In many parts of the world, it still is. During the intervening decades, this choice became more acceptable in the "developed" world.

Though seeking support and counsel from trained professionals is not completely out of the question in current times, it continues to be an enormous decision or, if required by others, perhaps an agonizing event. Difficulties reach far beyond the capacity of one family to move on to their own self-defined goals. The most essential source of information about what needs to occur to move beyond the trauma, the pain, the sense of powerlessness, is always within the family. Yet when this information is not enough and the family members' desired results seem frustratingly out of reach, additional knowledge, the support of others facing similar situations, and help in learning how to cope with the vast complexity of the situation—tools that are also referred to as "empowering"—can go a long way toward the realization of those self-stated goals:

> They [survivors of trauma] possess a special sort of wisdom, aware of the greatest threats and deepest gifts of human existence. Life is simultaneously terrifying and wonderful. Their traumatic experience was undeniably agonizing, and yet, having successfully struggled to rebuild their inner world, survivors emerge profoundly and gratefully aware of the extraordinary value of life in the face of the ever-present possibility of loss. (Janoff-Bulman 1999:320)

During the writing of the first draft of the middle chapters of this book, the terrorist attacks of September 11, 2001, took place. With an event that so rearranged the collective human psyche for many in the United States, each family and each individual faced the shock and the realization that the way violence had been dealt with in the past would not necessarily serve as guidance for how to respond to this level of violence. Earlier lessons in coping seemed inadequate to the task at hand.

Yet the response to the horror had begun even as the travesty of the destruction continued to unfold. Rescuers, community supports, and medical assistants were all on the scene doing what they do best, even though they clearly realized that the "best" they could offer was woefully inadequate to the task at hand. On an individual level, across the nation and beyond, the message came through, "Go about the business of living your lives." What had once been taken for granted now became an act of courage and defiance. Taking the elevator in the building where one worked. Flying on airplanes. Picking up the mail. People were coping.

As I returned to the work on the manuscript, I, too, found that the relationship with the material and with you, the readers, had changed in significant ways. First, I realized that everyone in this audience of readers, rather than only a certain number, could "get it" about the oppression of violence on some level. True understanding of the daily tyranny faced by families for whom domestic violence, the violence of poverty, the violence of addictions, the violence of prejudice and discrimination underlying crimes of hate, for example, can be difficult or filled with misinformation for those who have not personally experienced such horrors day after day. As this one act in a historical and global cycle of violence took shape, the emissaries of the tyrant arrived on our soil, crossed the boundary into this homeland, and used members of our own national "family" to kill other members of that family. In families who live with domestic violence and who are victims of battering, in families where addictions rule and poverty and discrimination determine the next step, the tyrant lives in the same house, the home has been violated many times over, and the people who reside there describe being held hostage by threats, uncertainty, and panic. They know there is more to come but are not sure when, so they live on constant alert. The element of surprise, the shock and numbness, the confusion, the fear, the determination to act anyway, the enormous courage to attempt to seek safety for oneself and one's children—all these are the same dynamics. They are simply occurring on different levels, whether globally in nations that have been living with such terror and oppression for centuries or in the home where the instigators of the terror and oppression are members of the family itself.

Second, in the aftermath of the devastation, the same actions that support empowerment practice—that is, providing information relevant to present needs, enhancing coping skills, and strengthening avenues of participation with others—were evident at every turn. Following the events of September 11, information and the clarification of misinformation were provided constantly and repetitiously and could be absorbed to the point of saturation and beyond if desired. From the people responsible to those who were victims, from the religion of Islam to the topography of Afghanistan, from the signs of trauma to the signs of courage and hope—information was provided.

Models of coping were available. Stories emerged about the passengers on the hijacked flights. The voices of their family members were heard, reporting final conversations, grieving, and honoring those who had died. Countless numbers put words to their own reactions while, in the next breath, assisting others who needed support. The lines between receiving help and giving help were blurred. Hundreds of thousands gave blood and, while waiting in long lines to do so, helped each other attempt to comprehend what was happening. Tension and compassion were running high. Friends and neighbors protected people who were targets for discrimination and harassment by others. As time went on, the rebuilding of physical structures mirrored the rebuilding of the human spirit. This was not just a rebuilding of what had been. The building of structures and spirit now included the intertwining of lands of plenty and lands of scarcity, the peoples who grieved and those who supported them, the "wide awake" reminders of the preciousness of human connections because of actions that can instantaneously destroy them. On one airplane over Pennsylvania, those who chose to give their lives to save other lives and those who chose to give their lives to destroy other lives came together, not unlike the way the heroic and the diabolic come together within each person as two parts of the same human spirit, not unlike the way the heroic and the diabolic are seen in the families we serve.

Examples of people participating with one another, of being surrounded by support networks, of coming together to mourn their loss and to help ground each other were apparent from the earliest moments after the disaster. Memorial services brought together adherents of more than twenty different religions. Community and religious leaders joined to create opportunities for participation. The meaning of the term *global family* took on new dimensions, as it became known that the lives lost at Ground Zero touched families in sixty-three countries around the globe. Alliances extended from family networks to the alliances of nations.

The similarities of dynamics on global and familial levels, responses that include information-seeking, coping, and participation with others, and the choices to be made each day between actions that enhance, sustain, and create versus actions that destroy are aspects of the underlying structure of this book. These levels of empowerment, empowering actions, and the purpose of empowering practice receive further explanation and illustration in the chapters to come. The starting point of all empowering practice with families is with the words and the voices of the families themselves.

Family members do know what they need in order to feel "empowered," though they seldom use that particular word to describe it. We may hear "I need a job," "We need a program for my son, who has dyslexia," "I want to know where our next meal is coming from," "I want to get off drugs." A statement like "I want to be empowered to find my next meal" is seldom heard—and would sound ludicrous if it were. It is important to look closely at this term *empowerment*, what its uses are, what it can and cannot do, what expectations arise when using it as part of our professional jargon.

This scrutiny is part of the text to follow. In the meantime, we can look at what we know from strong and powerful families who long predate the attention given to them by academicians, researchers, and helping professionals. Families of today are connected with the pragmatic and utilitarian functions of families from earlier centuries. Families with perseverance, strength, resilience, compassion, and great wisdom have existed since the beginning of the family unit as a primary link in our societal web. Our understanding is still evolving, the understanding of what it is, for example, that makes Family A strong and supportive to its members and able to contribute to the well-being of its community while Family B seems to be inundated with perpetual crises. Our well-meaning theories are further confounded when five years later, Family B appears to be functioning from a place of strength while Family A is facing crisis after crisis.

All families go through times of harmony and times of distress, and they have different ways of making sense of those experiences and of coping with them. For social workers and other helping professionals, the first meeting with families in need often occurs at the time of greatest crisis and confusion. It is less evident that this is also a time of strength, coping, and resilience.

Social workers bring their own family histories into their transactions with client families. Earlier personal events and memories play a key role in our efforts to assist others. At the same time, we cannot rely on our experience alone if we are to help families in need today. The enormous complexities of form, structure, life events, barriers to resources, and a multiplicity of other factors create daunting challenges for anyone who hopes to serve in a helping role.

Essentially, this book is built around four tasks: (1) to synthesize information about social work with families from an empowerment perspective; (2) to identify and encourage a new step in our use of empowerment thinking for practice with families; (3) to respond to the question "What works?" with today's families in need; and (4) to offer possibilities for moving with these ideas about empowerment into the future, when the words in these pages will be left behind for even more concise, more responsive, and more useful approaches.

This book supports the practice approach that encourages beginning with, ending with, and throughout the work staying mindful of client strengths and resources. This approach does not eliminate the need for understanding the stresses, distresses, and life events being faced, but such factors are viewed as one part of the whole picture, rather than as the central focus of the work to follow. We have learned over the years that a problem focus at the beginning often leads unfortunately, even though unintentionally, to a greater problem focus during and after the work. Even a solution focus needs a problem to solve. In the strengths approach, problem-solving skills are instead viewed as one among many of the skills used in practice; they are not the primary focus of the work. Many of the social worker's short-term settings do not permit time to focus at length on the problem with the eventual hope that we will, at a later time, arrive at a solution to that problem.

The strengths approach is believed to be more congruent with an empowerment perspective than approaches that begin with the problem: a problem-focused approach, a problem-based approach, or a problem-solving approach. These thoughts reiterate those of social work scholars who encourage a shift in how we have historically viewed our use of the word *problem* (Germain and Gitterman 1996:ix ; Saleebey 1997:42; Weick and Chamberlain 1997). Why do some call an event a "problem," while others call the same event a "life stressor"? Psycholinguists inform us of the power of language to influence our own responses and the emotional responses of the recipients of our words. Scholars of trauma response also inform us of the frequent auditory and visual distortions that can lead to distortions of language and meaning in the post-traumatic experience. Social workers often witness highly distressed, at-risk clients at the point of post-trauma interpreting the phrase "work on the problem" as meaning that they themselves ARE the problem, not that they HAVE a problem. For the person who is trying to recover from trauma, it can be cognitively and emotionally impossible to separate the two.

But what happens if we do redefine what we have called "problems" and call them "events and stressors that are part of life"? Trauma is part of life? Illness is part of life? Rape and incest are part of life? Global terrorism is part of life? Poverty and homelessness are part of life? Divorce is part of life? Murder and suicide are parts of life? Battering and domestic violence are part of life? Cancer is part of life? Hate crimes are part of life? Student massacres of other students are part of our lives? Certainly these events are not a part of everyone's life. Or are they?

These events are life. Our connectedness as a human family, a global human family in an information and technological age, underscores the daily reminder that what affects one of us affects us all. We especially, as social workers with the commitment to expose the bruises, violations, acts of discrimination, and horrors of our society, do not have the luxury of minimizing or denying that these realities exist. If we remain consistent with our focus on strengthening, empowering, and being well/well-being, we will consider the shift of our main focus from "problem" to "events that are part of life." This in no way minimizes the horrors that our client families face; nor does it eliminate the necessity of understanding the difficulties as interpreted by them. It does, however, set the stage for a way to move beyond the unwanted situation. This view closely resembles the framework of the *Life Model of Social Work Practice* (Germain and Gitterman 1996) with its use of transitions, interpersonal relationships, and the environment as areas for focus. Life events, yes, but whether they remain crises or become opportunities is determined by how coping happens.

This book is divided into four parts. Part I provides an overview of empowerment theory, followed by an integration of those ideas with approaches to practice with families. Chapter 1 recounts the history of the concept of empowerment, states the definition used in this book, and explores the nature of empowerment as a response to oppression. The language of empowerment is identified, a language that helps to shape a distinct difference in approaches to practice. Some recent criticisms of its use are presented and analyzed. Dynamic transactions occur at three levels of empowerment practice: the personal, the interpersonal, and the social/community (Gutiérrez and Lewis 1999). Empowerment practice takes place at the intersection of these three levels.

This discussion brings us to new standards of accountability as we go on, in chapter 2, to describe the many variations in form and structure of today's families from this perspective. Social workers and other helping professionals work with foster families, adoptive families, blended families, immigrant families, lesbian and gay families, multilingual families, poor families, homeless families, families with several generations under one roof, families with one parent in the home, and cross-cultural families, among others. Many families have sufficient resources to meet the needs of their members on an ongoing basis. Many other families, however, experience the expectations for socialization, education, nurturing, and care as overwhelming and far beyond their available resources. Social workers and others are called to respond to these family stresses, pressures, conflicts, and contradictions. The chapter concludes with the identification, description, and illustration of seven key principles of empowering practice with families.

In part II, chapters 3 through 5, readers are introduced to the Laurencio-Smiths, the Williamses, and the Brown-Wileys. These three families were selected for several reasons. First, practice is not empowerment practice without an emphasis on diminishing some form of major oppression. Therefore, families who were challenged by major oppressions such as poverty, violence, addiction, and discrimination were given priority. Second, these families were selected because of the degree of complexity of their situations, complexity perhaps related to their family structure or to the number and intensity of situations that they were facing. These families include a variety of ethnicities, socioeconomic classes, religions, sexual orientations, abilities, geographical locations, and languages. They have multigenerational realities that play a role in how they face the challenges before them. The helping agencies and personnel involved in addressing the events in their lives add to the complexity as well. Third, these families fit the definition of "families facing multiple problems" (though that is an inadequate phrase, simply because the family with only one or two "problems" is nonexistent). These families must deal with so many life challenges simultaneously that there is no time to resolve one before the next demands attention; they find that earlier coping skills do not work in the present situation; and they have come to the attention of multiple community agencies (Kaplan 1986:1–3). The fourth reason these families were selected was because multicultural understanding is expanded in some way in the transaction between the family and the social workers with whom they worked. Multicultural understanding is one of the categories of Lee's (2001) multifocal vision for the empowerment approach to social work practice. This volume builds upon that work and goes on to identify and develop multicultural respect as one of the seven principles of empowerment practice.

Part III focuses on how the use of an empowerment frame of reference helps families. Chapter 6 presents the three phases of work—beginning, middle, and ending—and the specific roles and skills used at each phase. The three core actions of empowering practice—providing relevant information and learning, enhancing coping skills, and offering choices for participation with others—are discussed and illustrated through specific examples from the three families mentioned above. An integration of the major concepts of the strengths perspective provides theoretical support.

Practice examples are used throughout the text to deepen understanding of multicultural variables, tools and techniques for assessment, family structures, dynamics of self-referred or mandated clients, developmental stages, and learning styles in work with families. Empirically based qualitative data gathered over thirty years of practice, supervision, teaching, consultation, and research with families supports the practice narratives presented. All identifying characteristics of the families and their members have been changed to protect confidentiality.

Part IV broadens the empowerment lens to include the transactions that occur between families and their communities. Whereas earlier chapters looked at dynamics from the "inside out"—that is, from families outward toward their communities—chapter 7 moves the spotlight from the "outside in," from the wider community inward, highlighting the impact of the nature and activity of the community upon the well-being of families. External resources can help to anchor changes made internally in the family. Support groups are drawn from a cross section of the community. It is in the community that families can receive feedback about which coping skills are most effective. An expansive understanding of community resources available for families is one of the essential skills for empowering and competent social work practice. Just as early family social workers challenged the illusion of helping an individual apart from her or his family, it is now equally important to confront the illusion that we can help families without grasping how interconnected they are with their communities.

One community project, Project WISE (Women's Initiative for Service and Empowerment), based upon empowerment principles from its origin, illustrates what empowering practice with families, integrated with community support, can look like. Project WISE, under the directorship of Jean East, Ph.D., M.S.W., and Sue Kenney, M.S.W., has been serving families in the Denver metropolitan community since 1993. Their narratives about the rewards and struggles in seeing empowerment practice come alive among the families they have served exemplify and illustrate every aspect of empowerment practice as set forth in this text.

Nationally, the many programs that serve the needs of distressed families all need additional exposure, not only to extend awareness about how much is really happening through the use of the empowerment perspective in practice, but also to enable individuals involved in these programs to learn together how best to serve the needs of our most at-risk families.

Chapter 8 offers a discussion of two major supporting theories: general system theory and ecological theory. These theories have served empowerment thinking in the past and continue to serve it at present. Both theories have grown and changed since the early days of their integration into work with families. Therefore the chapter also includes a discussion of recent advances in both systems and ecological thought and how those advances now set the stage for additional possibilities in future work with families in distress.

This book is intended for social workers in training. It can be used effectively as a text at the undergraduate level or as a supplemental text at the graduate level. At the present time, most master's programs in social work use generalist or integrative practice texts with a companion volume on families. Only a few texts are available with a specialized focus on practice with families; this is a helpful reference in any practice setting where families are served. One of its greatest strengths is its commitment to serving the well-being of all families, a commitment that makes the volume a valuable tool for family practitioners who share this empowering purpose.

Part I

A Family-Centered Empowerment Framework

1

Empowerment Then and Now

Empowerment Then

For nearly two centuries, social workers have been familiar with empowerment thinking as it relates to work with families in distress. It has been known by different names across that span of time, as noted in the introduction's historical overview of social work services to families since the early 1800s. The widely used concepts and actions of those times were grounded in the work of Karl Marx, Susan B. Anthony, Emma Goldman, Mahatma Gandhi, Martin Luther King Jr., Malcolm X, and Paulo Freire (Simon 1990) and shaped the empowerment theories that "give philosophical preference to the views of the oppressed, so that they can be given voice and power in overcoming...domination of some groups over others" (Robbins, Chatterjee, and Kanda 1998:115).

Themes of empowerment have also occurred within the research, writings, and practice of social workers for more than a century (Simon 1994). Since those days of the earliest family social workers, empowerment thinking has been found in the human rights movement, political psychology, feminist theory, and community organization principles. Empowerment has been defined as a goal, a strategy, a process, a state of being, a practice approach, an intervention, a program, and a worldview (Jacobs 1992). Claims of what empowerment can do have included reducing the powerlessness inherent in being a member of a stigmatized group (Solomon 1976); increasing power in order to take action to improve personal, interpersonal, and political situations (Gutiérrez 1990); gaining power and resources to shape our worlds and reach full human potential (Shriver 2001); and "convey[ing] the hope of the fullness of life for all people" (Lee 2001:4). According to Shriver, "The purpose of empowerment is in essence the purpose of social work: to preserve and restore human dignity, to benefit from and celebrate the diversities of humans, and to transform ourselves and our society into one that welcomes and supports the voices, the potential, the ways of knowing, the energies of us all" (2001:29).

Empowerment, both concept and action, comes alive as an ongoing, reciprocal process from conceptual understanding to visible action. One cannot assume that understanding theoretical concepts alone automatically leads to helpful choices. Choices of theory are guided by a sense of purpose—that is, a "critical consciousness" (Freire 1998) about where the work is headed—and by what result is anticipated. As the topic of this volume in the Empowering the Powerless series of practice texts for social work, the empowerment perspective is preselected as the framework for thinking about practice. From that starting point, supporting theories must have some level of congruence with empowerment thinking. Parallels between empowerment thinking and the strengths perspective, for example, have been extensively discussed in the social work literature (Compton and Galaway 1999; Saleebey 1997; Weick and Chamberlain 1997). Empowering families by emphasizing strengths (while understanding the stressors) almost seems redundant. Yet because of a historical, culturally embedded, pathology-oriented tendency to emphasize problems, this approach must be stated explicitly.

The strengths perspective does not imply, however, that problems are to be overlooked in our work with families; on the contrary, they are faced directly and thoroughly. It does imply that in the work itself the emphasis is on the strengths and resources that families have available to them to help them address and move beyond the distress. By focusing on strengths, we become our strengths; by focusing on problems, we become our problems. "Putting problems in their place" (Weick and Chamberlain 1997) is essential, and that place is in acknowledging that persons and families are so much more than the problems they face. Acknowledging that *having* a problem and *coping with* that problem are no more than two steps in a life process is an essential aspect of empowering practice. Problem-solving skills are seen in this perspective as *one* of several sets of coping skills. In empowerment thinking one problem solved, even several problems solved, does not an empowered family make. Turning attention to resources and strengths can, at the very least, bring into view choices and possibilities for transforming a challenge into actions for moving on.

Empowering and strengthening families occurs within a complex web of transactions, and theories that can serve as containers for this complexity are needed. Systems theory and the ecological perspective have historically been used for this purpose, both in thinking about families as complex systems and in viewing them as part of the natural and biological social order. The helping process is embedded within this framework.

Empowerment has not stood still as its influence has grown over the years. The uses of empowerment today are not the uses of empowerment fifty years ago, or even twenty years ago. Nor should they be. Refinements, conscientious critique, and gains in knowledge have all resulted in a different, and in some ways more mature, empowerment perspective for today's work with families.

Empowerment Now

What exactly is empowerment now? First, we must consider what empowerment is from a societal standpoint at this time in history, for it is within this society that today's families exist and do their best to make it from one day to the next, whether from positions of strength or from points of distress.

At its most basic, *empowerment* is still simply just a word, and therefore a symbol or metaphor for the reality it attempts to describe. Sociolinguists (Chambers 2003; Gee 1996; Markee 2000) inform us of the vivid internal images created by all words. Indeed, this is an essential step in the way the brain learns language, through visual identification with what the word represents in the world. *Empowerment* is no exception to this process of image-making and attaching meaning to images. It is a word with *power* as its base. With that one act of dropping both prefix and suffix momentarily, to understand the root, the inquiry opens to connotations of the contrast between the lighter and the darker sides of power. Therefore, one step taken in this section will be that of understanding power in families: power over, power under, power with; power within, power between, power among. Because of this multifaceted nature of power, the word *empowerment* has been seen to inspire and to infuriate, to bring hope and to bring skepticism. Its strength comes from the need out of which it arises: to refuse to stand silently by in the face of oppression and abuses of power that exist around the globe, and around the neighborhood, and within our own families. And one of its weaknesses also comes from the need out of which it arises: its use has become so pervasive, in nearly every discipline and walk of life imaginable, that its effectiveness is called into question. "Empowerment is everywhere," says Weissberg (1999):

> Business gurus advise employee empowerment as the assured path toward greater profitability and client satisfaction. Prestigious foundations such as Rockefeller and Ford bestow their blessings with financial generosity. Commerce embraces it—one travel agency offers an "Empowerment Cruise" departing from Miami, Florida, to Cozumel, Mexico, complete with gourmet food and Las Vegas–style gambling. A quick Yahoo website tour reveals some 167 organizations embodying empowerment doctrines: myriad health groups

(mental disorders, sickle cell disease, families of children with Down's syndrome), endless sexual orientation societies (including cross-dressing), business assistance ventures galore, plus clubs for nearly every racial-ethnic segment of society, to mention merely the highlights of the highlights. (1–2)

And for the dog lovers of the world, there is *Too Proud to Beg: Self-Empowerment for Today's Dog* (Olson 1997) including chapters titled "Dogs Proclaim Their Independence from Oppressive Masters," "The Canine Bill of Rights," and a fifteen-page section titled "Canine Empowerment" (9). Perhaps this has gone far enough in making the point that the use of the word *empowerment* has indeed reached absurd proportions.

Social work students, scholars, and researchers share this concern as well. Laurie was in her first-year internship at a women's shelter when Betty, a member of the group she was leading, "let her have it" after she mentioned the word *empowerment*. Betty, in her early thirties, directed her message right at the student:

> What kind of fancy word is that? Is that something out of your books or something? You think I don't already have plenty of power myself? Well, let me tell you something, honey. Do you have any idea how much power it takes to plan for months to get away from someone who holds a knife to your neck and threatens your kids? When was the last time you had to make ends meet using food stamps? Don't get me wrong. I want to hear what you have to say. I can use all the help I can get. But just don't go assuming that you are going to EM-power me before you have asked me what kind of power I already have. Hell, I bet I could EM-power you just as much as you think you could do it to me.

To Laurie's credit, she heard the message in Betty's words and brought this quote to class so that others could benefit as well. Laurie phrased her learning in this way: "This is not a word to use casually. It may be that just doing it speaks louder than words, but doing it has to be grounded in an understanding about the framework."

"If I hear another social worker talk about empowering others, I think I will scream." These are the words of one seasoned and highly respected social work professor who has been educating social work students for more than thirty years. He places the passion of this statement in the following context:

> Your questions about power are interesting. See, the issue for me is not one of having or not having power. The issue is how we live our power. One question is really about warranted power. I do not apologize for those powers earned or achieved. It is the ones that are granted because of my maleness that make me crazy. The real challenge is to embrace only those powers earned and not to internalize or accept those powers granted.

We don't empower others. We risk being in very intimate relationships in which both we and our clients discover our power. To grant others power seems so condescending to me. Does this make any sense to you? Obviously I am still chewing on the whole business. What I do know for a certainty is that embracing the genuineness of one's power is not easy in a world that has scripts for us to follow, yet it is in the embracing of the genuine power that we reach a sense of wholeness. (Dailey 1997:1–2)

And, finally: "I am concerned about the current popularity of concepts like resilience and empowerment. In desperate times, the profession's language is becoming more romantic and flowery" (Gitterman 2001:xviii). These sentiments are mirrored in a similar observation: "Inflated claims about what works are the norm rather than the exception in the helping professions" (Allen-Meares and Garvin 2000:52).

Such cautions, seen through the eyes of the critical thinkers, the skeptics, the realists, serve a function that any user of empowerment thinking cannot ignore. These views hold us accountable and place the ethical considerations of our work constantly before us. They will not allow us to ignore the grinding realities faced by the families with whom we work. This feedback helps avoid the dangers of "group think" (Brookfield 1995) and getting pulled along by the swift current of the popular and the trendy. As social workers, we do live with a long and honorable history in empowerment thinking, a history with solid foundations that welcome refinements offered by the critical eye.

One of today's most well-researched criticisms of empowerment thinking is by Robert Weissberg (1999), who offers words of caution in three key areas:

1. Stay realistic about what empowerment can do and what it cannot do, and avoid placing our expectations in the realm of its being an answer to all social ills. Stay modest in our definitions and recognize that, for the most part, we are "playing to our own audiences" (236). It is legitimate to raise questions about day-to-day effectiveness when the claims of what empowerment can do are so far-reaching: "The glorification of empowerment as today's Messiah is but a harmful and totally unnecessary illusion. We can do better.... It is not a question of relishing misery as preordained; it is a matter of carefully and honestly attending to what is possible" (236).

2. Hold any "self-designated empowerment experts occupying academic or professional positions" accountable in the sense that their claims must match their outcome (certainly true for a number of social work authors), for the "inescapable conclusion" reached by Weissberg's perusal of countless documents was that "gaining professional advancement constitutes the endeavor's primary purpose" and that it is the "researchers, not the homeless family...who [secure] empowerment via the building of well-compensated records" (230).

3. Recognize that "empowerment theorizing is still in its infancy stage" (235) and that the term *empowerment* has been "expropriated well beyond its intended use" (233), but the *action* associated with empowerment thinking "everyday, no doubt, works wonders and it deserves recommendation for many of our ills. . . . Successes have been noted (Andrus and Ruhlin 1998; Manning 1998; Olasky 1992; Woodson 1987). There are modest efforts everywhere that have commendable records" (Weissberg 1999:233). The *action* of empowerment has been a part of social work practice since the beginning of social work as a profession. We are not dealing with anything new here. "We should not quickly abandon our historical storehouse of proven remedies. We have lots of admirable solutions waiting to be applied" (236).

We must, however, ask, "Empowerment for what purpose?" Empowerment approaches cannot be all things to all people. Weissberg helps us to stay realistic, prevents us from jumping on the "bandwagon" for the wrong reasons, and provides grounding for differential applications of empowerment practice. We cannot follow these helpful guidelines, however, without a sense of purpose about our use of empowerment thinking in the first place. For the work of this text, I have selected "family well-being" from the NASW Code of Ethics as the answer to the question "Empowerment for what purpose?" Current research on well-being in general with application to family well-being is identified and described. Empowerment, systems, ecological, strengths, and family well-being form a conceptual base, with family well-being serving as the main purpose and direction of the work. Along with the conceptual base, empowerment sustains, enhances, and creates family well-being for families not only during their times of distress but beyond those times as well.

Empowerment Defined

To "carefully and honestly [attend] to what is possible," to stay realistic and modest, assuring that claims match outcome, to include the "voice" of those who seek empowerment, and to build on historical empowerment practice that has withstood the test of time, the definition of empowerment used here is "the freedom to choose" (Howie the Harp, in Carling 1995:xiv–xvi) and "the ability to make things happen" (Giddens 1994:15), to move on with living enhanced by well-being (from the 1996 social work Code of Ethics). Succinct enough to be usable, general enough to be widely applicable, this definition also intentionally removes the juxtaposition of "power and control" as sometimes used in earlier definitions of empowerment. Additional support for this definition will be discussed in the upcoming section on power as the root of empowerment thinking.

To support a family's freedom to choose how, when, where, and with whom to make things happen to move on with their lives in a context of well-being, there must be comprehension of empowerment as a concept as well as clarity about how it translates into action. Theory and practice are continuously intertwined in professional practice. We consider one at a time in the written word simply because writing and speaking occur in linear fashion, one word at a time. The reciprocal relationship between concept and action determines how concept continually informs action and action, in turn, continually informs and sharpens concept.

Making Things Happen with Freedom to Choose . . . Toward What Purpose?

The purpose for our practice is clearly identified through the mission of the profession: "the enhancement of individual well-being" and the "attention to the needs and empowerment of people who are vulnerable, oppressed, and living in poverty" (NASW Code of Ethics 1996:97, 135). Empowerment practice is defined through this purpose. *Enhancing* a family's well-being requires, first of all, that the family integrity be preserved so that their well-being can be continued or enhanced. Empowering practice, therefore, is guided by a purpose realized through actions that *sustain* families, ones that *enhance* strengths they already have, and ones that assist in their continuing efforts to *create* themselves as the family they want to be (figure 1.1). This purpose informs the information we gather on behalf of the families. At the same time, it determines the quality of our actions as we work with them and the distressing situations that they are facing.

Clarity about the family's picture of what the outcome of the work is and the purpose for getting there is essential to help the social worker avoid the temptation to jump too quickly into such actions as "problem-solving" or "goal-setting." Even though these are relevant skills to use along the way with appropriate timing and when they are responsive to the families' needs, such actions also may be misguided by the belief that a problem solved or a goal reached will result in an "empowered" family. The families typically seen by social workers live with multiple, complex, and ongoing sets of intensely distressful situations; they are families for whom there is no time to recover from one traumatic event before they are confronted with the next; they are families who are surrounded with an entire network of helping systems and the individuals who serve them. In such families, a focus on solving one problem without awareness of the wider impact on the entire system may create several other problems.

So we must ask: "Empowerment for what?" "Empowerment is not inherently virtuous; seeking inappropriate control can be ruinous" (Weissberg 1999:235). En-

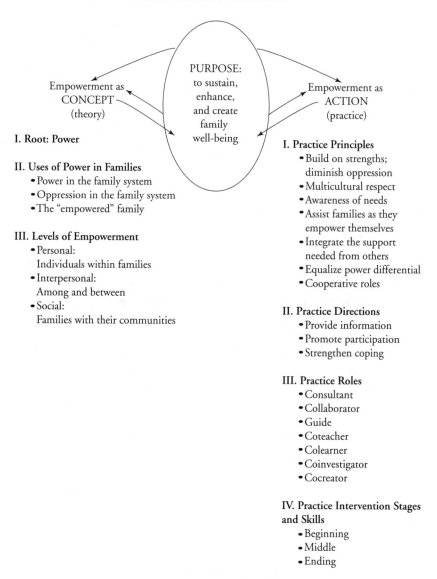

FIGURE 1.1 An empowerment approach for practice with families.

hancing family well-being may be our destination for empowering practice, but discerning what that looks like for each family is the task for this section and for work with families in distress.

For the families who are the subjects of this book, the enhancement of family well-being cannot be separated from the enhancement of "individual well-being" for each individual member of the family, nor can it be separated from the well-being of the wider communities within which they reside. In fact, the uses of the term *well-being* in the NASW Code of Ethics refer to "individual well-being in a social context" and "the well-being of society." The purpose guides practice at every level of empowerment—the personal, the interpersonal, the social (Lee 2001)—through practice principles, directions, roles, and stages. The practice arena is where empowering transactions come to life. Purpose, theory, practice, and the integration of all three shape the following discussion (see figure 1.1), which begins with a closer look at family well-being.

Family Well-being

Well-being has been equated with happiness (Argyle 1999; Kahneman 1999; Nozick 1989); with satisfaction, good fortune, and fun (Kahneman 2001); with pleasure (Berridge 1999; Kahneman, Diener, and Schwarz 1999; Kubovy 1999); with "the good life," enjoyment, and quality of life (Kahneman, Diener, and Schwarz 1999). It has been correlated to factors of age, education, social class, income, marriage/partnership, ethnicity, employment, leisure, religion, life events, and competencies (Argyle 1999), as well as gender (Nolen-Hoeksema and Rusting 1999), personality (Diener and Lucas 1999), life task participation (Cantor and Sanderson 1999), self-regulation (Higgins, Grant, and Shah 1999), emotion (Berenbaum et al. 1999; Frijda 1999); and personal control (Peterson 1999). It has been related to social factors of close relationships (Myers 1999), the workplace (Warr 1999), welfare (van Pragg and Frijters 1999), and national differences (Diener and Suh 1999). Even biological perspectives of well-being have been pursued in physiology (Sapolsky 1999; Ito and Cacioppo 1999), neurobiology (LeDoux and Armony 1999), and brain stimulation (Shizgal 1999). Relevant for understanding family well-being are competencies, close relationships and marriage/partnership, life events and life task participation, and employment and welfare. The chapters that follow will account for each of these issues. Competencies will be addressed as we begin with strengths and build on those strengths to respond to a family's needs. Close relationship and marriage/partnership will be addressed at the interpersonal level of empowerment practice. "Hearing the story in their own voices" provides the picture of life events faced by the family. Life task participation plays a role in the design of actions that can be empowering for the family members, given their particular strengths and needs. And finally, employment and welfare are relevant to one of the major oppressions faced by these families, the oppression of poverty.

"Social networks are perhaps the critical component of well-being" (Carling 1995:250). The family is often, but not always, the first, the primary, and a life-long social network for its individual members. Depending on the nature of the relationships between and among family members, it can be a source of well-being. Ongoing abuse, violence, criticism, ridicule, and destructive relationships also occur frequently in families and are common dynamics in families seen by social workers. The social networks that support the family as a whole are, there-fore, also key factors in the well-being of the family as a unit. Social approval and acceptance may be more present for the teenager among his or her peers than at home. Appreciation for work contributions may come on the job but not at home. Multiple levels of support, simultaneously available to individuals, to families, and to communities, make the possibility of well-being at any one level much more attainable. Components have been identified that contribute to this quality of life for families: physical and material well-being; relationships with other people (including family and close friends); social, community, and civic activities; personal development and fulfillment; and recreation (Flanagan 1978). Empowering practice integrates these components of well-being, not in a general sense but in the highly particular and unique way in which each of them finds its expression in the day-to-day life of each family (Longres 2000).

Creating a helping environment in which a family's well-being is the primary objective also means carefully listening to what well-being means to them individ-ually and as a family. Some of the above responses may fit for a particular family. All are culture bound and class bound, some are shaped from earlier traumas and successes. For each family, the well-being they have, hope for, or wish to regain is a mutual discovery process that becomes a very important part of setting the direction for empowering work together.

The Language of Empowerment

Current uses of *empowerment* are surrounded with a vocabulary that stands in marked contrast to the language of pathology-focused practice. Such language has been a part of the helping professions for more than a century. Competence-based practice (Maluccio 1981) and the strengths perspective (Saleebey 1997) have added significantly to this changing vocabulary. Table 1.1 identifies some of the terms currently found in the language of empowerment.

This is not an exhaustive list of empowerment language, but it is enough to set the stage for a different way of approaching the work. Sociolinguists and psycho-linguists remind us of the power that words have in creating vivid mental images. Strengths-based language and deficit-based language create different images for the transactions that take place between social workers and the families they meet. It is possible to believe that we are committed to empowering practice and yet to have our pathology-based training reveal itself in the subtleties of the vocabulary we use. Family members easily identify and respond to such discrepancies.

TABLE 1.1 The Language of Empowerment

Choice	Skills
Freedom of choice	Involvement
Capabilities	Well-being
Capacities	Options
Support	Respect (mutual respect)
Resources	Access
Voice	Mobilized
Listen	Diversity
Strengths	Equalizing
Competence	Cooperation
Resilience	Collaboration
Potential	Opportunities
Integration	Possibilities
Quality of Life	Sustain
Enhance	Create
Allies	Consumers/citizens/participants
Independence/interdependence	

Choice + Information = Informed Choices

The history of empowerment thinking in social work has been briefly traced and the overwhelming societal enthusiasm for its major ideas has been recognized. Criticisms and challenges have been welcomed to refine earlier uses of empowerment thought and to assist in coming to the present with modesty, more realistic expectations, and a critical consciousness. A definition has been shaped from these perspectives. That definition has been placed within an explicit purpose to guide decision making and direction. And from all of these contributions a language of empowerment has emerged and has been identified. It is time now to look beneath the surface to the root of empowerment, to look directly at "power" and how it plays out in the lives of families.

Understanding Power in Family Systems

Understanding power and using it for constructive purposes and growth purposes in the family system can create pathways for enhancing and strengthening family connectedness and well-being. Abuses of power, on the contrary, immobilize, numb, and destroy those connections. When power is used abusively through violence, discrimination, perpetuation of poverty, as part of an addictive cycle, or in other forms of oppression, empowerment provides a framework to enact changes in the distribution of that power (Shriver 2001:29).

> A sense of power is critical to one's mental health. Everyone needs it. . . . For power is a systemic phenomenon, a key factor in functioning, from the individual level . . . to the levels of family, group, and social role adaptation. Internal power is manifest in the individual's sense of mastery or competence. The power relationships between people determine whether their interactions are characterized by dominance-subordination or equality. (Pinderhughes 1989:110)

Individuals and the systems within which they exist are inseparable. There is no way to understand a family apart from the individuals who are in it; there is no way to understand individuals in a family without looking at their dynamics as part of the whole unit. In similar fashion, the ways in which families use community resources and respond to community concerns are intertwined with how they help define the character of their community.

The family plays a key role in the emotional and mental health of its members, a role based in part upon how power is addressed, either through expectations of dominance and submission— that is, power over and power under—or through manifestations of mutuality—that is, power with or "power sharing" (Pinderhughes 1989:142). Different roles in the family, such as the role of parent or the role of child, require different age-appropriate tasks, experience, and abilities.

There is a close association between how power gets used in the family and the individual's sense of competence and mastery, a sense of her or his strengths and assets. From an empowerment perspective, competence by one family member never excludes other family members from having their own experiences of competence and strength. This is often not the case, however, in families where there is a one-up, one-down use of competition. Such competition requires someone to accept a one-down position when someone else in the family has taken a one-up position. When efforts to exert competence are made despite family or societal expectations to the contrary, enormous costs in depression, eating disorders, and illness can result (Silverstein and Perlick 1995). By comparison, in an empowering context of "power with," the competencies of all can be valued and combined to strengthen the competence of the entire family.

Access to power is another aspect of empowering or oppressive uses of power within the family. Would it be ethical, for example, to increase access to power to persons who have, in the past, been abusers of power? In order to use an empowerment perspective for practice, understanding power, powerlessness, and access to power, as well as the relationships among these three, is essential as we consider choices for action. Understanding differences between "power over," "personal power," and "power with" as tools or pathways to accessing power is also significant. Access to power refers not only to resources available within communities and those enhanced by policy decisions. Access to power and resources, or a lack of such access, can also be observed in families and individuals. Each person can access forms of power that enhance and forms of power that inhibit; each person has learned from being in positions of powerlessness and powerfulness. Within each interpersonal relationship and each family, powerlessness and powerfulness have been experienced. The same is observable in organizations and in communities. Power and powerlessness are interconnected and often define each other. A single mom can access a sense of personal power in the afternoon while presenting a plan of action to her colleagues in the workplace only to return home to a violent spouse or teenager and an immediate sense of her powerlessness to know what to do next. Georgia talks of her pride and appreciation of herself when she once again "makes ends meet" on food stamps and $450 a month for herself and her three children. However, facing "the Look" given by those who take her food stamps brings on an instantaneous withering of any sense of accomplishment she might have had before walking in that door.

Families living with domestic violence have an important lesson for empowerment thinkers. These clients of safe houses and battered-women's shelters (as well as the professionals who work with them) have reacted to the phrases "access to power" and "gaining control over one's life." These phrases have frequently shown up in some of the definitions of "empowerment" in the past. While shaken, fear-filled, and vulnerable following a battering incident, attempting to cope with the cognitive and emotional distortions that come with post-trauma, just hearing the words *power* and *control* used in any context spells nothing short of extreme danger for many of these clients. Caught in an overwhelming sense of powerlessness, they think it inconceivable that they might one day regain strength for themselves and their children, even though it was exactly that strength that got them to the shelter or the safe house.

Domestic violence scholars and practitioners alike have long been aware of "power and control" issues as being at the root of oppressive violence within families (e.g., Dutton 1995; Hamberger and Renzetti 1996; Lystad 1986; Pence and Paymar 1993; Roberts 1998). Empowerment approaches stand against intimidation, emotional abuse, isolation, minimizing, denying, blaming, using children, privilege, economic abuse, coercion, and threats that are the realities in violent homes. By contrast, behaviors indicative of "equality" are similar to empowerment thinking: nonthreatening behavior, respect, trust and support, honesty and accountability, responsible parenting, shared responsibility, economic partnership, and negotiation and fairness (Pence and Paymar 1993:3, 8).

Raising consciousness about "coercive" and "exploitative" power (Germain and Gitterman 1996) is essential in our use of empowerment thinking today and crucial in our understanding of how power gets used (and abused) in families.

Coercive power is defined as the "withholding of power by dominant groups from other groups on the basis of personal or cultural features" (Germain and Gitterman 1996:23). Application to the family system brings coercion into the home. All family members possess strengths and power relative to individual abilities and stages of development, development that is physical and emotional as well as intellectual and spiritual. When information essential to well-being is withheld, coercive power is being used. When resources needed for growth and creativity are withheld, coercive power is being used.

Exploitative power is defined as the "abuse of power by dominant groups that creates technological pollution around the world, endangering the health and well-being of all people and communities and, most especially, poor people and their communities" (Germain and Gitterman 1996:23). Even though this definition focuses on groups and communities surrounding the family system, its meaning is significant when considering exploitation in families. The exploitation of children for financial gain and for the emotional needs of adults, for example, has a long history (Pieres 2003). Child protective services and adult protection services speak to the abuses of power and the exploitations that exist across the life span. Not only do these services raise awareness about the ageism in our societal fabric but they also increase awareness about racism, sexism, homophobia, religious and ethnic prejudice, language exclusivity, and geographic supremacy, all of which can be toxic in families.

Technological gain at great cost to the poor is identified in this definition of exploitative power; gain that ignores pollutants contaminating the water we drink, the air we breathe, and food we eat. The impact of technology in the daily lives of families must be acknowledged, both for the advantages it offers and for the ways in which it creates more distance between family members. Digital cameras, e-mail, and conference calling can be used as tools that decrease geographical distance for many of today's families. Conversely, the television, cellular phones, and video games, possibly with their own individual headsets and earphones, can all be used to create seemingly impenetrable "bubbles" around individual family members and cut off family interactions in unprecedented ways, creating "technological pollution."

The "digital divide," a term coined by the National Telecommunications and Information Administration in 1999, defines differential access to technological advantage, with greater accessibility for those with wealth than for those who are poor. "Who has access to technology and who is equipped to use that technology are increasingly determining social and economic well-being, a central concern for social workers" (Shriver 2001:322).

In families, the interpretation of power that strengthens and power that oppresses varies from person to person. Assertiveness, for example, is one characteristic applauded in some families as a positive quality. And it can be—in certain contexts. However, in a family with the expectation that everyone be verbally assertive, there may be much talking but very little listening. If there is one family member who processes information at a different rate or who recognizes the importance of listening and therefore is less verbal, this "quiet one" may have been labeled at fault for not meeting the family expectation of (verbal) assertiveness. The reality from that person's point of view usually centers around issues like lack of air time, "can't get a word in edgewise," having their sentences finished by someone else, or not being heard when they do speak. The silence required for listening, a logical response to that individual, may then become the catalyst for an even more frantic pace in the verbal exchange of the other family members. The cyclical and escalating pattern becomes evident when looking at the whole transaction, but it is a pattern that could remain hidden if only individuals were seen, one at a time. The longer one exists in an environment where one's voice cannot be heard, the more likely the oppression of that silencing will have an impact on the individual's health as well as that of the whole system.

As this example illustrates, uses and abuses of power in a family occur within a context of communication patterns, verbal and nonverbal, and the behaviors that accompany them. These forms of communication can stop oppressive forces and transform them into more empowering possibilities. Communication patterns can also give life to oppressive forces, perpetuating poverty, escalating violence, reinforcing scripts of addiction and discrimination. Power struggles and the "power over/power under" relationships that exist within families are maintained through communication patterns (Haley 1959; Satir 1967). Assumed power in families is communicated through different roles (parent, child), different ages (older, younger), different genders (male, female), and different abilities (money management, social skills, level of education).

One of the most pervasive forms of oppression in family communication, use of "power over" in the attempt to force others into experiences of powerlessness, is verbal abuse. Other terms used include *psychological abuse* and *emotional abuse*. Recognition of "distress signals" related to verbal, psychological, and emotional abuse is a necessary skill for social workers to have in order to do empowering practice with families. Often these signals are expressed nonverbally rather than with words. In chapter 5, when readers are introduced to the Brown-Wiley family, a family living with domestic violence, examples of verbal and emotional abuse will be provided in greater detail. At this point it is sufficient to note that among those who have suffered both physical and verbal abuse, the vast majority report that the effects of verbal abuse are far worse than those of physical abuse (Evans 1992). Yet the impact of verbal abuse is more likely minimized when compared to physical abuse. All workers seek to protect the safety of their client families. To do so within the framework of providing empowering practice requires attention to the devastating and debilitating oppression of verbal abuse. Facing the dark sides of power in families requires reminding ourselves that we do so in order to help transform those events into a past that is over. We do so to help families move toward "getting things done" and strengthening resilience. We use communication that offers a different picture, one of verbal and emotional support and encouragement.

Uses and abuses of power in family dynamics exist side by side and may be observable literally in the same breath. In the presence of the social worker, it is likely that family members want to be seen at their best. Unfortunately, this can mean that they attempt to exaggerate shared power or that they minimize power abuses. Professional skill includes reading and hearing all messages, verbal and nonverbal, to piece together an overall picture of the family's uses and abuses of power. The expressions of power are unique to each family. Table 1.2 summarizes the empowering and oppressive uses of power identified in this discussion. These lists are intended to provide only a beginning vocabulary for the uses and abuses of power as observed in families; this vocabulary will be expanded through the discussions and illustrations of practice situations that follow.

Understanding Oppression in Family Systems

The empowerment perspective also includes an informed perspective of oppression. Different forms of oppression share common elements. These common elements are described in the following discussion, with particular attention to how they can shape family life. Four specific expressions of oppression—poverty, violence, addictions, and discrimination—are then emphasized with particular relevance for families.

Oppression is present when power is abused, when expectations for relationships of dominance and submission (power over and power under or powerlessness) predominate among family members. Exploitation, marginalization, and powerlessness are "faces of oppression" that refer to relationships that "delimit people's material lives, including the resources they have access to and the concrete opportunities they have or do not have to develop and exercise their capacities" (Young 1990:44).

Oppression in the family is evident when there is an absence of mutuality (power with), an absence of respect, and an absence of concern to preserve, sustain, enhance, and create relationships. Family members know when they are being treated as objects, as means to ends, as "appliances" to meet the needs of others:

> It is virtually impossible to view one oppression, such as sexism or homophobia, in isolation because they are all connected: sexism, racism, homophobia, classism, ableism, anti-Semitism, ageism. They are linked by a common ori-

TABLE 1.2 Empowering and Oppressive Uses of Power

Empowering Uses	Oppressive Uses
Power sharing	Power over/power under
Respect	Insult, minimize, marginalize
Focus on strengths	Focus on pathology
Resilience	Abuses
Inherent skills and resources	Isolation
Inherent dignity and worth	Intimidation
Encouragement of uniqueness	Discouragement of uniqueness
Right to self-determination	Coercion
Development of capacity to learn, cope, and participate	Exploitation
Mutuality/shared roles	Dominance/submission
Trust and support	
Fairness	
Commonality	
Competence	
Well-being	

gin—economic power and control—and by common methods of limiting, controlling and destroying lives. There is no hierarchy of oppressions. Each is terrible and destructive. To eliminate one oppression successfully, a movement has to include work to eliminate them all or else success will always be limited and incomplete. (Pharr 1988:53)

Pharr identifies common elements of all oppressions: the existence of a defined norm and institutional and economic power; maintenance of control through the use of violence and threats of violence, rendering the victim invisible, distortion of events, stereotyping, blaming the victim for the oppression, isolation, and emphasizing individual solutions over group support and cooperation; and further breaking down of the victim's autonomy, seen through behaviors that indicate internalized oppression and horizontal hostility. *Defined norms* can be identified in families as we listen to their "shoulds," the formal and informal rules they have defined for themselves—for example, "You should be more enthusiastic," "You should get better grades," "We should invite your parents," "You should stop drinking." Family *economic power* becomes evident through inquiries about who has access to the money in the family, who makes the decisions about how money is disbursed and how it gets spent, whether there are both individual and joint arrangements with equality and "power with" when it comes to the family's financial resources.

The *use of violence* is discussed in greater detail below as one of the major forms of oppression within and surrounding families. *Threats of violence* (directed toward physical or emotional violence), *rendering the person invisible* (speaking as if the person is not present), *distortions of events* (including either minimizations or exaggerations), *stereotyping* (placing the person within categories and generalities rather than acknowledging uniqueness), *blaming the victim* (making the conditions of the oppression the fault of the other person and refusing to take responsibility for oppressive "power over" behaviors), and *isolation* (actively placing barriers between the person and her or his natural sources of support and interaction) are all forms of verbal and psychological abuse (Evans 1992; Murphy and Cascardi 1993). Emphasis on *individual solutions rather than group support* serves an abuser's purpose of cutting off support systems and further isolating victims from assistance and help when the abuse escalates to proportions beyond one individual's capacity to respond. Behaviors indicating *internalized oppression* can include self-imposed actions of any of the categories just described, tentativeness and silencing, and lack of self-esteem and assertiveness. *Horizontal hostility* is observable in families when peers, siblings for example, act out upon each other the anger and hostility they feel toward someone in the family who is perceived as having "power over" them.

Other "insights about oppression" from the Present Time Report to the World Conference (1981) are helpful. "Each particular oppression has certain features in common with all other oppressions" (69), "eliminating any one oppression requires eliminating all oppressions" (72), "oppression can be and is internalized" (65), which the authors of the report view as the most damaging form of oppression. They assert that "oppression operates, and can only operate, through distress patterns" that are instilled in early childhood: "No person would ever agree to or submit to being oppressed unless a pattern of oppression had first been installed, in the first place by adultism in our early childhood. Adultism, and the installation of patterns of oppression through adultism, is the foundation that allows other oppressions to be installed" (63). "Adultism" is defined as the oppression of young people by adults, and it is seen as the "training ground for all other oppressions" (70). Social workers who work directly with families have unique opportunities to observe behaviors between adults and children in the family. The worker's awareness about her or his potential for "adultism" toward children in client families can help prevent actions that perpetuate the oppression of young people by adults: "If adults did not install powerlessness patterns early in the life of each young person, if the young person's submission was not enforced during this early time of physical smallness, insufficient information, dependence on others, and naïve expectations of good treatment from surrounding humans, then later oppressions would be difficult or impossible to install" (70–71). Oppression does not happen apart from the context of the relationship between oppressor and oppressed. From early family patterns, all persons receive experiential learning about both roles.

Time and space limitations do not permit an exhaustive look at every form of oppression that occurs in and upon today's family. Guided by the social work mission to address the needs of those who are vulnerable and living in poverty, by several decades of working with and observing families in distress, and also by the voices of the families who are part of the practice presented in part II, I have selected four major oppressive processes for further attention: poverty, violence, addictions, and discrimination.

Family Poverty

"It is a cruel paradox that crisis may be the only constant in the lives of poor families" (Walsh 1998:238). Family poverty in the United States is increasing. Poverty plays a key role in family stress, domestic violence, malnutrition, homelessness, juvenile delinquency, gender and ethnic inequalities, and physical and emotional illness (Rank and Hirschl 1999). Though not true globally, in the United States poverty has been publicly perceived as something that happens to other people (Gans 1995), even though more children are living in poverty in this country than in any other industrialized nation (Schorr 1997). However, when Rank and Hirschl (1999) adopted the view of looking across the life span, they demonstrated that poverty touches a clear majority (approximately 60 percent) of people in the United States at some point in their lives. One of the criteria for inclusion in this majority was living below the poverty line for at least one year. One third of the group, however, experience dire poverty. "Rather than an isolated event that occurs only among what has been labeled the 'underclass,' the reality is that the majority of Americans will encounter poverty firsthand during their adult lifetimes" (211). Rank and Hirschl's comparison between black Americans and white Americans revealed that "by age 75, 91 percent of black Americans will have experienced at least one year in poverty, and 68 percent will have encountered the stark experience of extreme poverty. Among white Americans, poverty is an event that will eventually touch more than half the population" (212). One conclusion of this research is that the poverty among us can no longer be perceived as a condition of marginalized groups, families, and individuals only. It is a "mainstream event experienced by the dominant racial group" also (212). Poverty is systematically embedded in our capitalistic economic structure.

In 1992 the rate of poverty for African American children was 46 percent and for Latino children, 40 percent. At that same time, the rate of poverty for white children was 16 percent (Corcoran and Chaudry 1997). "Children born poor run the risk of long-term poverty" (Lee 2001), at least seven to ten years. Almost 90 percent of the long-term poor children were African American in 1992 (Corcoran and Chaudry 1997). In 1996, when the United States ranked seventeenth out of eighteen industrialized nations studied by Rainwater and Smeeding (1996), 14.5

million children lived in poverty in the United States. In 2000 the National Survey of America's Families conducted by the Urban Institute identified family poverty as cutting across ethnicities but in highly differential patterns. "Whites are less likely than other groups to be poor. African American and Hispanic heritage families are about three times more likely to live in poverty than white families" (AmeriStat 2000).

Predictors of family poverty include a lack of or a low level of education (Lewit, Terman, and Behrman 1997), ethnic-based differences in housing segregation as well as ethnic- and gender-based differences in earnings, plus single-parent family structures (Corcoran and Chaudry 1997).

> Poor children have higher incidents of infant death, low birth weights, and inadequate prenatal care. They have a greater chance of repeating a grade or being expelled from school. They are one-third less likely to attend college and one-half as likely to graduate from college. They have less access to all material resources and less access to community resources such as good schools, safe neighborhoods, and adequate governmental services than do children raised in families with adequate incomes. Clearly, life chances and options are diminished by poverty. (Sherman, quoted in Corcoran and Chaudry 1997:41)

"Families headed by women are characterized by poverty" (Germain and Gitterman 1996:196). Women continue to earn less than men, from sixty-three to eighty-seven cents on the dollar. Because of the demands of child care and often simultaneous care of an aging parent, many women are not in the workforce and are, instead, dependent upon welfare programs. Many employers still lack an understanding of the needs that parenting and caregiving responsibilities create for support and flexibility in scheduling and for on-site day care centers. Often, even when women do try to maintain employment to support their families, they are penalized by outdated job policies when home life and work life conflict. Child support from children's fathers is an unpredictable source of income for families headed by women, even though there has been some improvement in recent years resulting from various legal measures to enforce these obligations in certain states.

Family Violence

Domestic violence was declared as this nation's number one health problem in 1984 (U.S. Surgeon General's Task Force, quoted in Gelles and Loseke 1993). The information leading to that conclusion continues to hold twenty years later. Family violence is receiving more attention today than in the past, but it has been a part of family dynamics throughout history and universally, in all parts of the globe. Violence has been used as a means to keep those labeled as subordinates "in their place," and within the family context those subordinates have included women and children. Violence between siblings (physical, sexual, emotional) has received less attention, even though its impact and consequences are equally as devastating to its victims and survivors (Gelles and Loseke 1993:1). For same-sex couples who experience violence, power imbalances were reported by half of the lesbians interviewed as the reason the violence had occurred. Seventy percent cited jealousy and non-monogamy as reasons for the abuse. Gay men are more likely to reciprocate violence than are women (Rutter and Schwartz 2000).

Elder abuse has been estimated as affecting between 4 and 10 percent of today's older adults. Because older adults are so often isolated, however, it is believed that most of the cases of abuse go unreported, with the estimate being that only one in six is reported. Because older adults are also marginalized in the United States, even if they do attempt to report the abusive behavior, their observations often are questioned as possible imaginings or memory problems or confusion. They often choose to remain silent because they are aware that they may be removed from their homes if they do report the abuse.

Adult-to-adult domestic violence is experienced or witnessed by more than 15 million women, men, and children each year. Three out of five U.S. households experience parents hitting their children, and one-half of all U.S. households experience some form of domestic violence each year. Medical costs from family violence and related incidents total approximately $7 billion annually. When lost wages, sick leave, absenteeism, and diminished or non-productivity are factored in, additional costs of another $110 million are estimated.

Violence is one of the most widespread forms of oppression found in families. "Violence, like charity, begins at home" (J. Gilligan 1996:5). The dimensions of empowerment require an examination of the connections among personal, interpersonal, and societal levels of any phenomenon. Family violence has characteristics at all three levels that are important for social workers to understand as we work with families in distress.

Personal

Violence against oneself—self-harm, substance addictions, suicide attempts—or an individual's violence against others—physical, sexual, verbal—are inward and outward manifestations of personal characteristics seen as preconditions for violence or, in their most extreme form, death by suicide or homicide. Three preconditions for violence within the person have been identified: (1) deep, chronic, and acute shame is hidden because it is accompanied by a belief that the cause of the shame is very trivial; (2) nonviolent means of warding off the feelings of shame and low self-esteem are perceived as not being available; and (3) thoughts and emotions capable of inhibiting violent impulses are lacking (J. Gilligan 1996:111–113).

Shame-based self-talk originates in interpersonal transactions in families. At the base of manifestations of violence are messages that result in humiliation, disrespect, or dishonoring and are accompanied by an intensity "to the point that it threatens the coherence of the self, or when they find themselves in a specific situation from which they feel they cannot withdraw nonviolently except by 'losing face' to a catastrophic degree" (J. Gilligan 1996:114).

These responses relate to personal powerlessness that can be traced, in part, to a lack of acceptance of feelings when the person was a child. Referring to subsequent verbally abusive behaviors in adulthood, "feelings of pain and powerlessness, harbored since childhood, are never dispelled. They only increase and so, also, does abusive behavior.... [The] need to keep the overwhelming pain that 'must not exist' at bay is an underlying dynamic force which compels [the person] to seek Power Over, control, dominance, and superiority" (Evans 1992:164). The lack of acceptance may first have been experienced in the family and then later internalized by the person. Surrounding that internalization, however, is the fear that "it may be true. At my core I may truly be unacceptable and not valid as a person." Believing that one is unacceptable leads to the belief that one must be controlled in order to behave in acceptable ways. If this has been part of the climate in the family of origin, the person internalizes this belief and responds intrapersonally toward himself or herself, through an inner conversation or "self-talk," using the same dynamics of power over, control, dominance, and superiority. These dynamics carry over into interpersonal relationships.

Interpersonal

Violence between family members, interpersonally, occurs both intragenerationally—spouse to spouse, partner to partner, sibling to sibling—and cross-generationally—parent to child, child to parent, adult child to elder parent, elder parents to their adult children, grandparent to grandchild, grandchild to grandparent. "In family violence, everyone is victimized" (Lystad 1986:ix). Family violence is physical, sexual, and/or emotional-psychological-verbal violence as well as social and economic.

More than half of all women experience some form of spousal violence during marriage and women in the United States are more likely to be assaulted in their homes than anywhere else (Kaplan and Girard 1994:73). Two to 4 million women are battered each year in the United States, and approximately "one third of severe injuries to women are inflicted by male partners or ex-partners" (Jacobson and Gottman 1988; Rutter and Schwartz 2000:74). The actual rates of battering are difficult to determine, not only because battering tends to occur in private settings but also because each victim knows only too well that reporting an incident without the possibility of getting away and remaining away from the relationship can mean an escalation of the batterer's violence to even more severe proportions. This is viewed as a risk too great to take, especially when support from extended family, the police, and the court system may be uncertain and when access to resources, financial and otherwise, may have been thoroughly cut off.

Social/Community

"The United States has by far the highest rates of criminal violence of any Western democracy or, for that matter, of any economically developed nation on earth" (J. Gilligan 1996:24). The social component of family violence includes social conditions and institutionalized forms of violence that reinforce and promote violence as well as minimize or allow violence against victims. A continuum of physical violence includes behaviors that range from slapping and shoving to homicide and suicide. A continuum of sexual violence includes behaviors ranging from minimizing sexual needs and criticizing the victim's sexuality to rape that accompanies murder. A continuum of psychological, emotional, and verbal violence includes jokes, insults, and yelling, as well as threats, enforced isolation, homicide, and suicide. And a continuum of social abuse includes the use of socially reinforced degrading stereotypes, degrading victims' culture/religion/ethnicity/age/sexual orientation/socioeconomic status/language/abilities, destroying the other's belongings, threats, making the victim financially dependent, and eliminating support systems to complete isolation and homicide or suicide. When lesser forms of violence are ignored or left unattended, escalation into more lethal forms occurs. When social workers work with families in which violence is suspected or observed at any point, we work with a potential for death that cannot be minimized or underestimated.

The interrelatedness of all oppressions is evident in the relationship between family violence and family poverty. As Gandhi said, "The deadliest form of violence is poverty" (quoted in J. Gilligan 1996:xiii), and Hollingsworth (1998) also stressed the connection:

> Children from families with annual incomes below $15,000 were 22 times more likely to experience maltreatment than children from families whose incomes exceeded $30,000. They were 18 times more likely to be sexually abused, almost 56 times more likely to be educationally neglected, and over 22 times more likely to be seriously injured. Children of single parents had an 87 percent greater risk of being harmed by physical neglect and an 80 percent greater risk of suffering serious injury or harm from abuse and neglect. (113–114)

Addictions and Their Impact on Families

Addictions oppress family members and block the full possibilities of relationships characterized by intimate connection and family well-being. When a family member is under the influence of an addictive substance, for example, all interactions of family members occur with the substance acting as a shroud over the person, who gazes through its numbing effects. Addictive behaviors include the use and abuse of various substances such as alcohol and drugs but also extend to other behaviors such as compulsive gambling, compulsive cleanliness, sex addiction, anger addiction, compulsive overeating, compulsive shopping, workaholism, and addictive use of television and computer or Internet games, to name a few.

Addiction is defined as "a physical, psychological, social, emotional, and spiritual disease characterized by continuous or periodic loss of control" of one's behaviors, preoccupation with and use of the addictive substance or behavior "despite adverse consequences, and distortions in thinking, particularly denial" (Brown and Lewis 1999:13). Sociocultural context has been identified as the most influential factor in determining the use or non-use of addictive substances and behaviors. The family climate is one of the most influential sociocultural factors. Preexisting attitudes and tendencies toward the use or non-use of drugs, attitudes potentially located in the family of origin, are exaggerated when there is increased access to drugs. Therefore, the preexisting tendency to *not* use drugs is exaggerated when ease of access is increased for those who have a preexisting attitude of *non*-use. And the tendency to use drugs is, in similar fashion, exaggerated when ease of access is increased for those who have a preexisting attitude of use (Hanson 2001:72).

Strong family connections and support protect many persons from addictive behaviors (Turner 1997). One of the strongest indicators for successful outcomes in addictions treatment is a person's family stability (Smyth 1998). When parents model forms of stress management that result in learning and growth rather than turning to substances to numb the tension, children and adolescents are less likely to choose drug use as a method of managing their own stress (Rhodes and Jason 1988).

A family in which one or more members are engaged in addictive behaviors may be a family who denies or ignores potentially destructive outcomes. Drinking alcohol, for example, may be seen as an integral part of celebrations, or its effects may be minimized through labels such as "social drinking." Denial can also be the response to earlier addiction-related experiences that have been so painful that they want "to forget about them as soon as possible and just pretend it never happened." Sometimes family members view these events as so horrible that they do not know how to raise the issue with the family member who has the addiction. At other times, family members believe they are choosing the most loving path by adopting martyrlike behavior. "It is my role to forgive. It does no good to blame her for my pain, so I'll just go on loving her and hoping that one day she will see the error of her ways."

A family reaches the point of oppression by the addiction when their daily life becomes dominated by the anxieties, tensions, and chronic trauma of active substance use or participation in other addictive behaviors. The addiction progresses to eventually "control and dictate core family beliefs and influence all aspects of behavior as well as cognitive and affective development" (Brown and Lewis 1999:4). Brenda, age 17, was so humiliated the last time she brought a friend home and found her mother passed out at the kitchen table that she vowed she would never bring her friends there again. William Bending Tree was on the verge of losing his job as a construction worker because when he drank too much he lost all ability to control his anger, and he had assaulted a coworker. Paula Simpson, age 20, faced her second year of college with the "emotional equipment of a twelve-year-old." She began organizing her life around her dual drug and alcohol abuse when she was 12, and she placed that as the time when her emotional growth had "come to a screeching halt" as well.

When such behaviors exist in the family, family members report a distinct sense of being replaced, of having to compete with the addiction for "relationship time." Family members frequently report uncertainty about whether they are truly relating to the person, to the substance, or as one spouse phrased it, to the person "through the fog of the chemical of the moment, which for John is either alcohol or marijuana, sometimes both. These show up as three different personalities. If there was a way I could keep the John I love and divorce the two chemical personalities, I would do it in a flash. It makes me so sad to know it can't work that way."

John's dual, and perhaps multiple, addictions describe the more common scenario than does addiction to a single substance or behavior. Multiple addictions may occur for only one member in the family, or they may occur for several members. Parents sometimes introduce their children to addictive substances, directly or by example and modeling. Jason and his dad, for example, were not only "drinking buddies" but, on Jason's sixteenth birthday, after all but a handful of his friends had left, his dad supplied Jason and three of his friends with "joints of the finest mary jane I had ever smoked." Jason's dad continued as their supplier of "very fine and not so fine" marijuana through their remaining high school years. Jason spoke clearly about how this example from his father set the stage for his later use of heavier and more lethal substances. Most users of legal (alcohol, cigarettes, caffeine, prescription) drugs and "gateway" drugs, such as marijuana, however, "do not progress to more serious drug involvement," nor do "most experimental users of any drug develop destructive and addictive patterns of use" (Hanson 2001:71).

Family members' denial may work in subtle ways around these multiple addictions, prioritizing addictions from most to least dangerous as an attempt to justify their acceptance of less lethal behaviors. With a smile of affection on her face, Sharon reported, "Sure, he watches television sometimes six or eight hours each evening but, hey, at least that's not killing him the way the cigarettes and alcohol were." It did not take her long to realize, however, that this "replacement" behavior of John's was truly killing their relationship.

Addictions frequently interact with other forms of oppression. Parents who abuse alcohol or drugs are three times more likely to resort to violence and abuse their children and four times more likely to neglect them (Reid, Macchetto, and Foster 1999). Poverty is a major risk factor for drug abuse (Chilcoat and Johanson 1998; Hawkins et al. 1992; Turner 1997). Communities with poorly developed schools and institutions create an environment linked with addictive behaviors (Cohen et al. 1996).

Addictions are culturally embedded. Multicultural and demographic variations are important considerations when evaluating a family's oppression by addictions. Addictive behavior occurs in all age groups, in both genders, across all socioeconomic strata, and in all ethnic groups. Women and older adults abstain from alcohol more than young men. Women do, however, experience more adverse consequences associated with drinking than do heavy-drinking men (Straussner and Zelvin 1997). Latinos and African Americans drink less and have lower rates of heavy drinking than do whites. While Asian Americans have some of the lowest rates of alcohol use, American Indians, especially men ages 25 to 44, have higher rates of alcohol use than do members of other ethnic groups. Some researchers, such as those just mentioned, cite impoverished communities at greater environmental risk for drug use. Other investigators, however, who have expanded their scope to an international arena, a comparison between the United States, the United Kingdom, France, and Germany, have concluded that "alcohol consumption is generally a product of growing prosperity, not an index of social misery" (J. Roberts 1997:118). Historical perspectives include changing social conventions, among them family norms that permit or encourage the use of alcohol and other substances. Such social conventions include family celebrations, religious holidays, events related to rites of passage, and leisure activities. Even with the cultural embeddedness of addictive behaviors, some perspectives still point to individual choice based on costs and benefits of consumption as the key factor. Such a conclusion, however, seems to ignore a core characteristic of addictions—that the behaviors continue despite the consequences.

Discrimination in Families

The impact of discrimination upon families occurs through dynamics that are both external and internal to the family and the extended family. To date, literature on family discrimination has focused predominantly on forms external to the family, with the view that "internalized" variations carry over into the internal reality of family life. Societal discrimination is perpetuated through the media, through social policies, through lack of information, through institutionalized forms of racism, sexism, ageism, homophobia, and through discrimination against those who live in poverty, who are immigrants, who are mobile with the help of wheelchairs or who live with other physical, mental, or emotional challenges, and against those who practice certain religious or spiritual beliefs. Even when children receive family messages and guidance about acceptance of others, it is extremely difficult, if not impossible, to prevent the impact of this barrage of prejudicial messages when participating in one's life in the community, school, workplace, and other institutions.

Intrafamilial discrimination is not simply a translation of societal definitions of discrimination directly into any particular family system. Discrimination, by definition, is the action of making a "distinction in favor of or against a person on the basis of a group or class to which the person belongs, rather than according to merit" (Costello 1992:384). Also, discrimination is an "action or policy based on prejudice," with prejudice meaning "an unfavorable opinion or feeling formed beforehand or without knowledge, thought, or reason" (Costello 1992:1064).

Discrimination in families reflects these definitions and goes beyond them. It reflects these definitions when individual family members are scapegoated by other family members; when older adult family members are marginalized and excluded from the lives of their offspring; when women are ridiculed, put down, or blocked from opportunities that are available to their brothers and fathers; when men are stereotyped into a "provider" role to the exclusion of relationship needs and wants; when communication between parents and children or between spouses is characterized by name-calling, threats, trivializing, accusing, discounting, denial, and criticizing (Evans 1992:77–78), as well as coercion, intimidation, isolation, economic abuse, and blaming (Miller 1995:110).

Intrafamilial discrimination also creates a qualitatively different experience for each family. Parents may share discriminatory beliefs against people who are different from themselves in some way—ethnic background, sexual orientation, or religion and spiritual beliefs, for example. They may expect that their children will assume these same opinions and beliefs. Some families carry implicit or explicit "rules" that "if you think like we do, the way we want you to, you are considered a member of this family, and if you don't, then you are not a member of this family."

Carol's parents used every stereotype and label they could think of for her fiancé, Eduardo. They tried humiliation of her in front of their friends and refused to participate in plans for the wedding. Finally, three days before the wedding they called to tell her not to expect them at the ceremony. Carol's brother, Neil, however, gave the couple his full support. He had known Eduardo for two years before Carol and Eduardo decided they wanted to marry. Neil played a unique role the day of the wedding. As Carol's only brother and because Eduardo's siblings were four sisters, Neil escorted Carol down the aisle, then stepped into position as Eduardo's best man.

Ginny's story provides another illustration of the impact of intrafamilial discrimination. Ginny was rejected by her father and "written out of the will" when she came out as a lesbian to her parents. He told her that he never wanted to see her again. When she returned home to attend the high school graduation of her younger brother, her father "looked right through" her but "got up and moved to the other side of the auditorium," so she knew he had registered that she was there. After the graduation ceremonies, Ginny was sickened that her brother was used as a messenger to tell her that she was not welcome at the party that would be held at their family home.

In these examples, family members are being treated differently, not on merit but because they have been "prejudged" (the act of prejudice) according to group membership—older adult; lesbian; labeled by ethnicity; or according to gender—woman or man, male or female, girl or boy. The empowerment stance claims the commitment to build on strength and diminish oppression. To see strengths and recognize many differing abilities in people of all ages, of all sexual orientations, of all ethnic backgrounds and genders, of all economic strata is a beginning. As one African American caregiver reminds her interns, however, "Discriminating on the positive side is still discrimination and stereotyping. Some of these folks see that as just plain insulting. Take Harriet. Last week, one intern told her that her people are so wise. Well, Harriet set her straight. She said, 'Yeah, my grandmother was a very wise person but my uncle, her son, was one of the most stupid, selfish, and greedy people I've known.'" In other words, build not on your own ideas of what a strength is for this person but first reach for those qualities that they define as strengths and build from there. The same holds true for the way in which oppressions are identified. Know the person. Respect the characteristics held in common with others (ethnicity, gender, sexual orientation, age), but remain open to learning how each person's expression of those characteristics is "one of a kind," unique. Our work must include each family member's perceptions about strength and oppression, about "their right to define and describe their own experiences in the world" (Allen, Fine, and Demo 2000:6).

Oppressions and abuses of power extend throughout multiple generations. Other oppressive experiences such as chronic illness, mental illness, or responses to traumatic events are specific to individual family units. These experiences are not mutually exclusive, for example, a family living with violence may also be living with substance abuse and chronic illness. Oppressions cannot be removed overnight; some cannot be conquered even in a lifetime. Through the empowerment lens, however, we recognize that the strength in these families is often BE-

CAUSE of, not in spite of, the oppressions with which they are confronted. Such a family is identified as "empowered" because of their response to oppression. Oppressive forces may interrupt, redirect, or slow their progress toward sustaining, enhancing, and creating their well-being as a family, but they do not prevent a path toward empowerment. The keys to empowerment are found in responses to oppression.

Levels of Empowerment: Personal, Interpersonal, and Social/Community

All three levels of empowerment are in a continual dynamic flux, simultaneously affecting each family and the individual members in it. These three levels are inseparable in the actions of the day-to-day life of a family.

Personal

Personal empowerment includes self-esteem, self-respect, self-worth, and self-efficacy (Gutiérrez and Lewis 1999; Gutiérrez, Parsons, and Cox 1998; Lee 2001). External oppressive forces can destroy these sources of strength and direction. Internalized oppression is an even more formidable foe of building strong foundations of self-respect and self-efficacy. The first step in identifying personal power with each individual member in a family is that of recognizing the power each already has (Gutiérrez, Parsons, and Cox 1998). Personal empowerment can originate within the person, from family members, or from those in the person's wider social context. Subsequent steps for enhancing self-efficacy include "personally mastering a new activity, seeing a similar person master the activity, being told one is capable of mastering the activity, and experiencing manageable levels of anxiety while attempting the new activity" (Gutiérrez and Lewis 1999:9). One indication that people are living from a position of personal empowerment is the refusal to accept or tolerate devaluation of themselves or of others (Evans 1992).

Interpersonal

Equally important are the interpersonal contexts of the family members' relationships with each other and the helping relationship between the family and the social worker. Surrey (1987) defines interpersonal empowerment as "the motivation, freedom and capacity to act purposefully, with the mobilization of the energies, resources, strengths, or powers of each person through a mutual, relational process. Personal empowerment can be viewed only through connection—that is, through the establishment of mutually empathic and mutually empowering relationships. Thus, personal empowerment and the relational context through which this emerges must always be considered simultaneously" (3). Surrey's definition makes clear the relational process of empowerment. There is a constant, dynamic, ever-changing transaction that defines the context of both personal and interpersonal empowerment, as well as empowerment in the wider social arenas. Relationship is primary in Surrey's view of the empowerment process: "The alternative model of interaction that we are proposing might be termed [the] 'power *with*' or 'power *together*' or 'power emerging from *interaction*' model. It [suggests] that all participants in the relationship interact in ways that build connection and enhance everyone's personal power. What is required is a recognition that relationships are the source of power and effectiveness, not of weakness or inaction or a threat to effectiveness" (1987:4–9).

Relationships that "build connection" and "enhance personal power," *everyone*'s personal power. Thus, the relationships among and between the individual members of the family are an additional focus for understanding empowerment within the family system. Likewise, in practice the relationship with the social worker must also be taken into account. Whether actual or perceived, there may be a discrepancy regarding the power in the relationship between clients and their social workers. Potential biases may interrupt efforts to build connections and may serve, instead, to disempower client families rather than to empower them. For example, traditional nuclear families, though no longer the norm in the United States today, may still occupy the status of "norm" and therefore "privilege" in attitudes relevant to social work practice.

Attitudes that stereotype women or men according to traditional sex-role biases may act as a barrier toward their achievement of personal power. Attitudes that stereotype lesbian and gay couples can result in a similar barrier. So also can stereotypes of multicultural families, couples without children, families in which the parents are unmarried, families who are multilingual, families with several generations under one roof, families who are homeless, foster families, adoptive families, blended families. The specific tasks of any helping professional working with families include separating stereotype from fact, examining one's personal values and making responsible decisions from them, and being aware of one's degree of acceptance toward variations in family structures. "Through our diversity we find our strengths" (Katz 1988:3). A diverse society "must be built on strength, not weakness; on contribution, not limitation; on opportunity, not deficiency. A society built on deficit, weakness and limitation finds itself in collapse. A society built on strength, contribution, and opportunity is empowered" (Katz 1988:3).

Social/Community

A "society built on strength, contribution, and opportunity" defines the third level of empowerment. Empowerment practice is not complete without attention to the needs of families that result from inadequacies in their social context. Nor is it complete without accessing the resources available in the community to answer those needs. When a social worker helps family members to access resources in their community, empowering opportunities will continue to exist for that family long after the relationship with the social worker has ended. The family, as one of the primary social institutions in all cultures, serves as a microcosm of the wider social dimensions of empowerment. Lessons of social and community empowerment and oppression are first learned in one's family. These are lessons that never leave us. Children are astute observers, and they discern emotional environments built on strength, contribution, opportunity, mutuality, cooperation, and respect from those built on weakness, limitation, deficiency, domination, and lack of respect.

As social workers assist families in building on strengths and accessing resources in their social and community environments, multiple social systems create and enhance supports to meet each family's needs. The need for community-based empowerment practice recognizes how environments shape families. The social dimensions of poverty, violence, addictions, and discrimination are evident in inadequate housing, malnutrition, lack of health care, unemployment and underemployment, to name only a few. Community-based empowerment practice addresses these concerns through collaborative relationships, capacity building, extended-family networks, and non-kinship networks (Hodges, Burwell, and Ortega 1998).

Empowerment Principles for Practice with Families

Work with families from an empowerment perspective occurs through principles, practice actions, roles, and stages in the process of working with families. The identification of these intertwining factors is based upon a rich history from social work scholarship and practice. For example, the key role of the family in the development of the individual's sense of confidence and competence in social interactions and in performing in valued social roles (Solomon 1976), empowering treatment skills in helping African American families (Gray, Hartman, and Saalberg 1985), and aspects of empowerment found in the interactions between social workers and their clients (Pinderhughes 1983) all contribute to empowering practice with families. Additionally, empowerment is seen as a practice goal that avoids polarization of social action and individualized perspectives (Furlong, as cited in Payne 1991:225). The complexity of the connections between relationship and empowerment (Surrey 1987), empowerment-based practice with the homeless (Fabricant 1988) and in public child welfare (Hegar and Hunseker 1988), similarities and differences in enabling and empowering families (Dunst, Trivette, and Deal 1988), working with women of color from the empowerment perspective (Gutiérrez 1990), and empowerment themes for social work practice with couples (Jacobs 1992) help establish this foundation for practice. Social workers must also carefully assess the sense of power they have or lack in their own families (Pinderhughes 1989), as these experiences will influence helping roles with client families. Empowerment has been designated as "the cornerstone of all family-based programs" (Kaplan and Girard 1994:40). "True empowerment comes when families influence their environment" (54), a statement that supports the importance of community-based empowerment practice with families mentioned earlier.

With the contributions of these authors as a foundation, principles for practice with families are identified as a summary to this section. Elaboration of these principles and an integration of them with practice actions, roles, and the stages and skills of practice are part of the content of chapter 2. The unique set of actions selected for each family reflects this framework plus the situational realities faced by the particular family.

Social workers who use an empowerment perspective for work with families will

1. Identify and build on strengths and resources while simultaneously identifying and diminishing oppressive factors.
2. Establish a relationship of mutual, multicultural respect with all client families, supporting all ethnicities, ages, gender, sexual orientations, differing abilities, languages, religions/spiritual beliefs, developmental stages, socioeconomic strata, geographic backgrounds, levels of education, and family structures.
3. Include an awareness of individual, interpersonal, and community needs as well as the transactional needs between these three levels and the impact of those needs on the family system.
4. Work from the premise that, with sufficient resources, family members have the capacity to empower themselves (Lee 1994), to "make things happen" (Giddens 1994:8) according to their own choices, goals, and sense of family well-being.
5. Recognize that family members need each other and the support of other families and community organizations to find empowerment as a family.

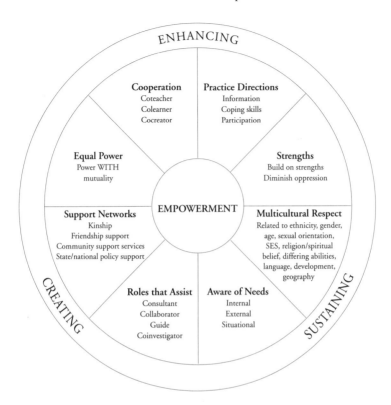

FIGURE 1.2 The Empowerment Wheel. (Adapted from Ellen Pence and Michael Paymar, *Education Groups for Men Who Batter: The Duluth Model.* Copyright © 1993 by Springer Publishing Company, Inc., New York, 10012. Used by permission)

6. Establish and maintain a "power WITH" relationship to equalize the power differential between client family members and worker, engaging in self-reflection and evaluation when needed, and defining a helping relationship that is empowering for family members.
7. Serve families through roles that support and assist family members and reflect these empowering principles.

These seven principles are also represented in the Empowerment Wheel (figure 1.2).

Two qualifying factors help shape the context in which these principles can be used most effectively: (1) dynamics that enhance empowerment and (2) differential application of empowerment principles according to need, ability, and readiness. They help deepen the use of empowerment thinking, sensitize us to the specific qualities in each family's situation, and help maximize usefulness of these approaches.

Dynamics that Enhance Empowerment Practice with Families

Factors that inhibit empowerment have been identified (Conger and Kanungo 1988). Their opposites serve as guides for identifying dynamics that enhance empowering environments for families:

- Transitions that are anticipated and planned when possible, discussed, and described, taking place in supportive climates with other family members and including understanding of both endings and beginnings
- A personal climate with accurate and supportive communication
- A flexible rule structure
- Parenting styles characterized as positive, appropriate to the adult role, with clear reasons given for actions and the outcomes of those actions
- Rewards and supports given in ways that reflect individual developmental stages, that are respectful and responsive to specific context, and that acknowledge specific areas of age-appropriate competence
- Clear definition of roles
- Multiple opportunities for participation
- Frequent and regular contact with parents
- Realistic goals and expectations

These enhancers to family strength and well-being are observable in family illustrations of later chapters. Examples of working with these factors from an empowerment perspective are also presented.

Differential Application According to Need, Ability, and Readiness

Client families will be at different places in their need, ability, and readiness to accept empowerment approaches. The needs of a family facing poverty and homelessness are different from the needs of a family seeking assistance in changing communication patterns. Following crisis or trauma, family members will have different abilities to comprehend information and a different sense of readiness to move forward than they would have if no recent traumatic event had been experienced. Assessing and intervening according to a family's level of need ensures that interventions are need-centered, not agency-centered. Kilpatrick and Holland (2003) identified four levels of needs.

Level I needs are essential for survival and well-being. They include food, shelter, protection from danger, health care, and provisions for at least minimum standards of nurturance. Work with families at this level builds on strengths and resources and mobilizes support (2). Level II needs are defined by necessities of the family's organization and structure. Setting limits and ascertaining whether those who are in positions of authority are the ones who, in fact, hold the authority are tasks for the Level II family. A foundation of focusing on strengths and coping is a significant part of work with these families. Additionally, clear expectations regarding task assignments and behaviors, plus strengthening alliances between those who are in charge, are effective interventions with Level II families (5).

Families assessed with Level I and/or Level II needs benefit most from a major focus on strengths, resources, and coping skills. The authors present a contrast for families assessed with Level III and/or Level IV needs, stating that these families benefit when there is a focus on problems. Even though this text uses empowerment's focus on strengths, resources, and coping (Levels I and II), an understanding of the characteristics used in Kilpatrick and Holland's model can be helpful at the other two levels as well.

Level III families are those families who face issues related to space. How much privacy is allowed? How accessible are family members to each other? Who is allowed to cross whose boundaries and who is not allowed? Are boundaries permeable, impermeable, semipermeable? Rules and "shoulds" around dominant and submissive behavior are often rigid and nonnegotiable. With families at all four of the levels, these patterns may be part of a multigenerational pattern or a culturally/ethnically embedded pattern, and it becomes imperative to grasp what the "ideal" family structure is for each family at each level. Boundary definition between generations is another indication of the family's structure and organization, and clarification of boundaries that may be confusing for some family members is a helpful intervention

Level IV families are most often recognized by their goals related to improving their quality of life together, of concerns around "the fine art of living fully and growing toward actualization of each member's potential" (8). They may wish for a stronger sense of self in the family or in the marriage/committed relationship. They may seek support for traveling through a major life transition such as the birth of a first child, a change in employment, or planning for retirement. Spiritual needs and the need for greater meaning may also be issues that are part of work with families at Level IV.

Empowering interventions can be used at all four levels of need. Some overlap exists between the recommended interventions listed by Kilpatrick and Holland and those of the empowerment approach—that is, strengths and resources, examining communication and the power structure, flexibility. It serves an assessment well to recognize the client family's ability to use empowerment interventions related to need and readiness.

Trauma and the response to trauma change the ability of clients to use empowering interventions. Traumatic events lead to numbing, confusion at the cognitive and emotional levels, and distortions in time and space (Everstine and Everstine 1993; Herman 1992; Waites 1993). These responses occur to help the healing process. Any attempt to label the subsequent behaviors as a "disorder," such as posttraumatic stress disorder (PTSD), will be avoided in the context of an empowering response. Even though it may be premature to offer educational material and group support immediately following a traumatic event, "coping" still fits as an appropriate identification of what is occurring (Snyder 1999). How these supports for coping are offered makes the difference. The helper may need to literally show the person actions that will assist in coping: "Hold on to this railing." "Take a deep breath." "Focus your eyes here." Concrete, specific, concise. As steps toward recovery from trauma take place, the helper becomes less and less directive. As time elapses, other interventions, such as information about what happened and about support networks with family and others facing similar circumstances, are appropriate.

Readiness applies to both the social worker and the family members. The social worker can have a greater sense of readiness in sharing power with clients following a careful analysis of the power dynamics that she or he brings to practice (Pinderhughes 1989). Client families bring readiness to acknowledge power struggles, readiness to use outside supports, readiness to take action on their own behalf.

Some client families have been facing ongoing crises for months or years. Physical, emotional, psychological, and verbal abuse; child or elder or spouse or partner abuse; incest; chronic unemployment; addictions; long-term physical and mental illnesses all fit this description. In such situations, deeply ingrained denial is often seen as one primary coping behavior or as the first step in the grieving and loss process. To utilize empowerment methods of growth and change, families are guided to recognize their oppression and, additionally, to reach a point of wanting to do something about it. Awareness precedes readiness. Gutiérrez and Lewis (1999) recognize that many women are not aware of their oppressed status. Victims of abuse are often not aware that they do not have to take the abuse. Among oppressed populations, powerlessness has sometimes been learned as expected behavior and, if they have known nothing else, it may have become internalized and may have taken on a distorted aspect of normalcy.

Even more delicate are the situations in which an increase of personal power, and the behaviors that go with it, may place the clients at further risk—for example in a violent family situation. Escalation of abuse tends to occur when the victim takes a stand against the abuse. Readiness is a key factor for victims' advocates who know too well the reality that it takes an average of seven attempts for a victim to permanently leave an abusive relationship. When a victim feels "empowered" to leave, the lethality of that relationship increases by 200 percent and can continue at that level sometimes as long as two years. Readiness to accept information about the cycle of abuse (Walker 1984), to hear how others are coping, and to participate in the support offered at the local shelter can spell life-threatening possibilities for the victim.

These three factors—need, ability, readiness—are significant in the context of using empowerment. Differential application is tailored on the basis of the families' situations related to these factors. Along with factors that inhibit empowerment and differential meanings of "access to power," need, ability, and readiness help to shape the context for the seven principles for empowering practice with families. As with any approach to practice, there is a context, a time and place, with multiple factors involved that demand an awareness of when to use empowerment vocabulary and methods and when to refrain. Empowerment practice is not indicated for all people in all situations at any time. It is one perspective, one approach, among many, and knowing when and where to call on its helpful aspects is essential for using it effectively.

2

Seeing Families Through an Empowerment Lens

Blended families, foster families, adoptive families, families with one parent in the home, multigenerational families, multilingual families, lesbian and gay families, common law families, traditional nuclear families, dual-occupation and dual-career families, homeless families, immigrant families, multicultural families, polygamous and polyandrous families—these are some of the families that social workers meet. These families represent only a portion of the diversity in structure observed among families in the United States today. Their complexity includes factors of socioeconomic strata, age, gender, religion and spiritual beliefs, sexual orientation, differing abilities, languages, geography, ethnicity, and developmental stages, and stages in the family life cycle (Carter and McGoldrick 1989), as well as the individual developmental stages of each family member. All of these factors are interrelated, each adds a facet to the designs we see as we look through an empowerment lens to view the kaleidoscope of today's families in the United States.

The Many Faces of the U.S. Family Today

At the time of this writing, many of the results of the 2000 Census on "household and family characteristics" still await publication. Therefore, we will call upon slightly earlier statistics. In March 1998, there were 102.5 million households in the United States, and 69 percent of those were family households. The U.S. Census Bureau uses several terms—*family households* is one of them—to define the variations in family form and structure. In order to understand what this statistic means, and who those other 31 percent are, these terms and their definitions are listed in table 2.1.

TABLE 2.1 Census Bureau Terms for Family Forms and Structures

Family. A family is a group of two people or more (one of whom is the householder) related by birth, marriage, or adoption and residing together; all such people are considered members of one family.

Family group. A family group is any two or more people residing together, and related by birth, marriage, or adoption. A household may be composed of one such group, more than one, or none at all.

Family household. A family household is a household maintained by a householder who is in a family (as defined above) and includes any unrelated people (unrelated subfamily members and/or secondary individuals) who may be residing there.

Subfamily. A subfamily is a married couple with or without children or a single parent with one or more own never-married children under 18 years old. A subfamily does not maintain their own household, but lives in the home of someone else.

Related subfamily. A related subfamily is a married couple with or without children, or one parent with one or more own never married children under 18 years old, living in a household and related to, but not including, the person or couple who maintains the household. One example of a related subfamily is a young married couple sharing the home of the husband's or wife's parents.

Unrelated subfamily. An unrelated subfamily (formerly called a secondary family) is a married couple with or without children, or a single parent with one or more own never-married children under 18 years old living in a household. Unrelated subfamily members are not related to the householder. An unrelated subfamily may include people such as guests, partners, roommates, or resident employees and their spouses and/or children.

Stepfamily. A stepfamily is a married-couple family household with at least one child under age 18 who is a stepchild (i.e., a son or daughter through marriage, but not by birth) of the householder. This definition undercounts the true number of stepfamilies in instances where the parent of the natural-born or biological child is the householder and that parent's spouse is not the child's parent, as biological or stepparentage is not ascertained in the *CPS* for both parents.

Source: Department of Commerce, Bureau of the Census, *Current Population Survey (CPS)—Definitions and Explanations.* Washington, D.C.: Department of Commerce, 1988.

Perceiving families according to these definitions or by household structure leaves many gaps and questions. Foster children who live temporarily with foster parents or an extended-family relative, lesbian and gay couples and their children, family members working in other countries, children who go back and forth between parents who have joint custody, family members who are in prison or who have been hospitalized because of mental or physical illness or who have entered, perhaps, an assisted-living residence—all are examples of families who do not fit the above definitions or whose boundary extends beyond the household. These situations, in fact, help identify that other 31 percent not covered by the definitions given in table 2.1.

One answer to the need to broaden our definitions of family is the concept of "familiness." "Familiness includes the traditional functions and responsibilities assigned by societies to families, such as childbearing, child rearing, intimacy, and security. It also recognizes the great diversity in structures, values, and contexts that define family for different people. In addition to traditional concerns when thinking about family, such as structure and function, *familiness* includes consideration of culture, gender, sexual orientation, age, disabling conditions, income, and spirituality" (Shriver 2001:317). Such a definition joins an empowerment frame of reference through multicultural respect and strength, historical strength that the social unit of family fulfills as part of society, extending across generations to include its essential functions in present-day society.

Several trends increase awareness of the changing structure of familiness. From 1970 to 1990, there was a sharp decline in married-couple households with children, sometimes referred to as the "traditional American family," from 40 percent to 26 percent. This trend then slowed dramatically in the next seven years, dropping only one percentage point, to 25 percent, by 1997. The decline of 15 percentage points from 1970 is evident in the statistics of *Current Population Reports* of the Census Bureau, but for families who seek the services of social workers, these traditional forms may still be held as an ideal. One important task for family social workers is to normalize the diversity of family forms and structures found among today's families. As recently as 1997, single parents with their own children under 18 were at 27.3 percent, exceeding the 25 percent statistic of married-couple households. From 1970 to 1997, the number of female-headed households jumped 133 percent, from 5.5 million to 12.8 million, and the number of male-headed households jumped 213 percent, from 1.2 million to 3.8 million. By contrast, the number of married-couple families grew only 20 percent during that same time period. The number of single mothers remained constant at 9.8 million during the three-year period 1995–1998. The number of single fathers during that same time period, however, grew 25 percent, from 1.7 million in 1995 to 2.1 million in 1998. Men now account for one-sixth of the 11.9 million single parents in the United States (U.S. Department of Commerce 1997, 1998).

Another statistic adding to the diversity of family forms is the 51 percent of all families who have none of their own children under 18 living in the home. These families are not necessarily without children. Related grandchildren, nieces, or nephews may be present. Foster children may live in the home. Greater numbers of adult (over 18) sons and daughters live in their parents' homes (14.4 percent of family households in 1998). Also included in this 51 percent are the families whose adult sons and daughters are living away from home. The trend of young couples to delay marriage and childbearing also plays a role in this statistic.

The trend away from marriage also helps to account for the increase of single mothers who have never been married and who have children under six:

> In 1997, 58 percent of Black female householders with own children under 18 and no spouse present had never been married. Comparable proportions were 42 percent for Hispanics and 25 percent for Whites. Among single mothers who had own children under 6 only, 85 percent of Blacks, 73 percent of Hispanics, and 56 percent of Whites had never married. Percentages of never-married mothers with own children 6 to 17 only, were 44 percent of Blacks, 30 percent of Hispanics, and 14 percent of Whites. (U.S. Department of Commerce 1997:5–6)

In the March 1998 update, it was noted in the mother-child families of all ethnicities combined, 42.2 percent of the mothers had never married (U.S. Department of Commerce 1998:1).

Demographically diverse characteristics contribute to the complexity of today's family forms and structures as well. Mothers who maintain their own households in mother-child families usually have been married and are older (median age 41.2 years) than mothers who do not maintain their own households but may live with parents or other relatives. Young (under 25) unmarried mothers often find added emotional and financial support for themselves and their children in the homes of their parents and relatives. Divorced mothers are also found in a family structure with other divorced mothers as roommates, boarders, or live-in employees. From any of these joint living arrangements, these parents may go on to establish their own households at some point in the future.

The net result of the decrease in the percentage of the married-couple households and the increase of the percentage of households without a married couple, plus the changes overall in delaying marriage and childbearing, divorce, and re-marriage, is a noticeable expansion of diversity in family forms and structures nationwide. There would be an even clearer picture if the data were available to calculate percentages of stepparent families, lesbian and gay couples and their children and families, and multiethnic families. Additional information about adoptive families, polygamous and polyandrous families, cross-generational partners (e.g., a mother in her fifties and a father in his twenties, for example) with children, cross-globally located families, and time since leaving homeland (for our immigrant families) would also be helpful information as we work with a widely diverse cross section of families in the United States today.

In light of these statistics, several points are clear for social workers. The families we see will not necessarily fit one of the categories of what a family is from census definitions, from stereotypes or traditional norms, or from our own family backgrounds. Nonjudgmental acceptance must extend to all of the diverse forms and structures, sizes and shapes, of today's families. Stereotypes must be recognized and evaluated in relation to fact. We may be tempted to base our work with families upon our own family experiences, family rules, family expectations, but yielding to that temptation can prove to be highly limiting, for these statistics also tell us that family forms and structures are historically embedded. The responses of families to their historical, social, and structural expectations in the 1970s took place in a noticeably different context than the context of the early 2000s.

To approach our work with families, we need an understanding of familiness that includes diverse forms and diverse structures. How is a family distinguished from other social groups? Family theorists Klein and White (1996) have identified several clarifying characteristics:

1. Families are intergenerational.
2. Families last for a considerably longer period of time than do other social groups.
3. Families contain both biological and affinal (legal, common law) relationships between members.
4. The biological and affinal aspects of families link them to a larger kinship network (20–23).

The definition of family used here includes each of these characteristics and goes beyond to include, from the definition of empowerment, the characteristic of choice. An open and accepting definition, one that remains flexible to what we see and hear from the families themselves, is more responsive to an empowerment framework of practice. The following definition paraphrases an earlier one by Hartman and Laird (1983): When two or more individuals decide they are a family, they become a family. They share living space, which may be a house or a hallway, a mansion or a shelter, on the top floor or under a bridge. In the ways they know, have learned, or wish to try, they seek to meet emotional, physical, life course, spiritual, intellectual, social, economic, and other needs arising in the intimate closeness of family life. They understand and seek to fulfill their roles in their families, performing tasks that reflect those roles.

Over the course of one life, a person often lives as part of several different family forms and structures. Most people spend some time with a parent or a family of origin, from a few minutes to eighteen or more years. Some families form on the basis of commitment. These may occur after one leaves the family of origin or much later. Increasing numbers of young adults are choosing to be single for several years before entering a committed relationship. Young heterosexual couples and lesbian, gay, bisexual, and transgendered couples alike are delaying the entrance of the first child into their families. Divorce and the endings of committed relationships are not necessarily seen as "in between" relationships, since more people are choosing to remain single into their later years. Single persons fashion their own family forms, sometimes with other people or with pets, a "family of choice," and sometimes they remain alone. In March 1998 people living alone accounted for 83.2 percent of the 31.6 million households where a person either lives alone or with others who are not biologically related or related by legal contract. If a recommitment or remarriage does occur, stepfamily and blended-family life may be another experience. As the life course progresses, family networks increasingly include single elderly adults. Among those who live alone, most are women (55 percent), and of that group 46 percent were 65 or older. Eighteen percent of the men living alone or with other unrelated individuals were 65 or older.

Multiple family forms and structures over the life course do not occur one at a time. Even after divorce, the previous family structure continues as part of the emotional and often physical reality for children and former spouses. And while living alone, each person is still part of a network of younger and older relatives, those who have died and those still living. One never completely leaves behind any family structure of which one has been a part. As we work with families, it is helpful to keep in mind these multiple realities and their impact on present functioning. Working from an empowerment perspective requires the recognition of resilience and strength, of risk-taking and creativity in such changes and diversity. The uniqueness of the actions of each family and their ways of coping with distressing events are grounded in these experiences, both as individuals and as a family.

The simple and the complex come together to create the many faces of today's families—simple in that all families are, in one sense, just families, a recognizable social form with continuity across centuries; complex because of the levels of personal, interpersonal, and social/community involvement along with the transactions among and between these levels; because of power and oppression as they exist in the family of attention; because of a view of these transactions as part of a wider natural order, one that includes identifiable patterns of coping and of adaptation; and because of a web of multicultural factors. To offer the most effective support and assistance possible in the midst of this shifting complexity, social workers need theories that have withstood the test of time as well as those that integrate responses to present-day needs. As the empowerment lens is placed among the family social worker's theoretical options, it plays a key role in work with families.

When We Look Through the Empowerment Lens at Today's Families, What Do We See?

One of the first things noticed when a helping professional using an empowerment lens meets a family is that the worker acknowledges the strength of the social unit we call "family" in every aspect of the work. There is a seriousness of purpose in this decision, for it is exactly upon this strength that the work together will be built. All recognition of strength is done within a context that is culturally attuned to the family's unique history as well as the coping experiences they have had before their contact with a social worker.

As Margaret Mahoney noted in 1986, "The endurance and universality of the concept of family testify to its strength and vitality. Family patterns vary and compositions alter, but the need to belong to something larger than oneself is innate and compelling. This need is demonstrated over and over again by groups that refer to themselves as 'family.' . . . Children play 'family,' and elders reinvent it when it does not exist" (quoted in Scanzoni 2000).

Ever since social workers began working with whole families as well as extended families, in the early and mid-nineteenth century, they have worked toward the improvement of the life and environmental situations of those families. A progression of terms has been used to describe families along the way. Three and a half decades ago Feldman and Scherz (1964) wrote about the "adequate" family:

> This family generally has made reasonably mature adaptations to the various life tasks confronting all families. It is a family likely to come to the attention of a social agency when some externally-created problem presents aspects that are more severe or disturbing than the family's usual coping ability can handle. . . . These families are able, with a minimum of intervention by the worker, to mobilize themselves and their resources, and regain or establish a new adequate level of independent social functioning. (47–48)

Their classification framework appears to go from adequate to worse, as the other three classifications are chaotic, neurotic, and psychotic (48–51). Does the idea of "adequacy" really capture what we seek to understand when we say "empowered"? Being "empowered" as a family who has been "living on the margins of society is an incremental process, not an absolute outcome; empowerment is also described as a "concept that conveys the hope of the fullness of life for all people" (Lee 2001:4–5). Later family research also gets us a bit closer to the goal.

Healthy families (Lewis et al. 1976), strong families (Stinnett et al. 1981; Stinnett et al. 1982; Rowe et al. 1984; Stinnett, Sanders, and DeFrain 1981; Van Horn and Matten 1984); normal or well-functioning families (Walsh 1982), nurturing families (Satir 1988), successful families (Beavers and Hampson 1990), and resilient families (Walsh 1998) are some of the contributions and characteristics that draw closer parallels to our understanding of empowered families. Yet the empowerment perspective calls for an adjustment in our approach, seemingly small but with major implications: to *put people first*, not characteristics. Families are families, period. We work with

- Families with health...and with illness
- Families with strengths...and with vulnerabilities
- Families with normalcy and well-functioning abilities...and with chaos, stress, and struggle
- Families who are nurturing...and who are abusive
- Families who know success...and who know barriers to their success
- Families with resilience...and with immobilization

Social workers are encouraged to "learn from people who cope effectively with the inevitable stressors in life and from those who nurture their children well" (Germain and Gitterman 1996:25). Therefore, it is important to build upon that which can be learned regarding the *characteristics* of health, strength, nurturing, success, and resilience as we create a kaleidoscope of families who are empowered and empowering. Table 2.2 summarizes some of what these authors have said.

Repetitive themes are evident: love and respect, expressive and open communication, parents who function in a clearly defined leader role, individual members who are able to take the others into consideration. *Adversity and conflict are not denied but are used in ways that **sustain** and **enhance** the family and add to their ability to **create** who they are rather than in ways that diminish and weaken it.* These characteristics are useful as well when imagined on a continuum. Each family brings differing degrees of resilience, strength, and health, for example. Their experiences of success are unique to their own histories, struggles, and talents. These descriptive terms are culturally and contextually embedded. For example, individual autonomy and choice stereotypically express values closer to a Western view and are more likely to be seen in some Euro-American families. "The concept of 'normal' is a social construction. Without understanding context, we cannot make meaning of people's concerns and behaviors" (Okun 1996:11).

TABLE 2.2 Characteristics of Families with Health, Strengths, Nurturing, Success, and Resilience

Health. Caring and supportive interactions with other family members; love and respect for those around them, old and young; respect for one's own worldview as well as that of others; expressive and empathetic; willing to explore numerous options; initiative; flexibility; parental relationship meets the needs of both parents; reciprocity in parental relationships; respectful negotiation; individual autonomy; low reliance on external authority; feelings seen as human; conflict faced openly; quality of tenderness viewed as preparation for future intimacy beyond the family of origin (Lewis et al. 1976:206–216).

Strengths. "Clients were closer to a strengths orientation than the workers" (Saleebey 1997:16). Looking to the families for answers about what makes a family strong: consideration, appreciation, respect, empathy, doing things together, good communication, loyalty, spiritual orientation, tradition (Horn and Matten 1984:450–451). Love, individuality, commitment, good parent image, sharing (Stinnett, Sanders, and DeFrain 1981:35). Every family has strengths and resources; the injury of trauma and abuse, illness and struggle are openly acknowledged and seen as sources of challenge and opportunity (Saleebey 1997:12–15).

Nurturing. Members listen to and hear one another; openness in expression of feelings; an environment of safety and support; comfort in showing affection; able to make plans and be flexible with them; incidents are used as learning opportunities; parents seen as empowering leaders; change is accepted as part of life; problems come along because life offers them and they get used to add to opportunities for nurturing (Satir 1988:13–17).

Success. Capable negotiation; clear expression of feelings, attitudes, and beliefs; respect for individual choices; affiliative attitudes toward one another; each member appears competent and is acknowledged as unique; spontaneity, enjoy each other, and mutual respect; conflict is handled directly and usually efficiently; parents are clear leaders who support and care for each other and provide models of respect and intimacy for the children (Beavers and Hampson 1990:30–31, 48).

Resilience. The process of regaining functioning following adversity; the power of recovery; having protective factors that cushion blows; making meaning of adversity; positive outlook; transcendence and spirituality; flexibility; connectedness; social and economic resources; clarity in communication; open emotional expression; collaborative problem solving (Gitterman 2001:xvi; Walsh 1998:24).

Our understanding of each family begins from this point of uniqueness, and the working relationship builds from that point, not from a comparison with other families who have managed similar circumstances. A family's health, strength, nurturing, successes, and resilience are intertwined in unique ways to create their own picture of the "empowered" family. Resources from one experience have an impact on later experiences, and coping skills used earlier are recalled to serve the present.

We can add other descriptions as well: families who persevere in the face of overwhelming odds; families who are natural helpers in their communities; families who are heroic in quiet, unassuming ways. All that is unique about each family comes to bear in answering the question "What does an 'empowered' family look like?" Strengths emerge as challenges are faced. Each family's challenges are unique to person, place, time, and context. Each family's strengths have their own story. It is only through hearing that story, both what is said and what is left unsaid, that an understanding of their version of empowerment can emerge.

The competence model of family functioning (Waters and Lawrence 1993) deserves special mention as part of this discussion. It has also been used for examining family strengths and represents an overlap with empowerment. This model "focuses on family strength as the *primary* factor to be assessed and utilized by the practitioner" (Shriver 2001:379). Once all possible strengths within the family system have been discovered, the distress signals presented are redefined as manifestations of the drive for competence that have gone off course rather than as some form of pathology or dysfunction. This model was used in an empirical research study of parenting strengths among African American families. The report of trends and parenting patterns found among these families serves as one model of using the language of empowerment and strengths: (1) substantial parental involvement in the lives of their children, (2) plentiful support for parenting from external caregivers, and (3) considerable male involvement in the lives of African American children. In similar fashion, themes of self-perceived values emerged: connection with extended family and relatives, emphasis on achievement and effort, recognition of the importance of respect for others, cultivation of spirituality, ability to foster self-reliance, recognition of the importance of education, acceptance of life's pain and instruction in coping skills, and recognition of the importance of self-respect and racial pride (Hurd, Moore, and Rogers 2001:381–386).

These factors can be added to the list of family strengths, increasing our understanding of what it is that we see when we look through an empowerment lens at today's families. These findings, in particular, provide an illustration of hearing the qualities observed and valued from families' voices. Comparison reveals characteristics that are similar to those found in earlier research as well as some that are unique to a particular strength of heritage, history, and background.

Are All Families Empowered? Are All Families Distressed?

Yes, at times empowered, and yes, at other times distressed. Both stress and distress are givens in the process of living. Times of distress are not without their qualities of strength and empowerment. Times of strength are not without their moments of stress and distress. In many ways, empowerment derives its meaning from the nature of the distress (i.e., oppression) being faced and, reciprocally, the distress derives meaning from empowerment in the context. The inseparability of these two creates a context for families' growth and change when facing trauma, oppression, and crisis. Opportunities for enhancing well-being, as well as for the demise of well-being, are present in this same context.

All families encounter times of distress—illness, loss of a family member, loss of job among them. Many families are able to recover and move forward with their lives. Distressed families have sometimes been identified in terms of their deficits—that is, by what is lacking. Empowerment thinking requires a different approach:

> It is most important to see vulnerable families as being overloaded and undersupported; as having many past and ongoing challenges and unmet needs; and as being at high risk for future serious problems and breakdown. We need to view them not as "problem families," but as families struggling with many problems, which are largely beyond their control and often not of their own making. Crisis situations are often embedded in problems in the community and the larger society, which must be addressed. Crises may also be fueled by reactivation of past traumas, which need to be understood and integrated for greater resilience. (Walsh 1998:238)

When the times of stress are ongoing and chronic and when familiar coping skills are not working, when situations are both internal and external to the family system, and when the families face multiple challenges all at the same time and have no time to recover from one before the next one strikes, then the families are "in distress" in the sense used here (Kaplan 1986:1–3). Also, these are families who are "overwhelmed by oppressive lives, and by circumstances and events they are powerless to control," they are frequently confronting "desperate life circumstances" and highly "stressful life events," and "community and family supports are weak or unavailable" (Gitterman 1991:1–2). Families facing times of profound distress have also been referred to as "high-risk families" (Kaplan and Girard 1994), "multiproblem families" (Kaplan 1986), "families in perpetual crisis" (Kagan and Schlosberg 1989), and from the People First commitment, "families facing multiple problems" (Kayser 1999).

When a family faces profound distress, trauma imposes its numbing and disorienting characteristics on every member of the family, on their interactions and patterns of communication, and on their ability to think and act. Steps toward trauma recovery are ever-present among the families who have shared traumatic experiences and who see their family as a protective element in such recovery. From a different vantage point, family members themselves are sometimes the source of the trauma, the perpetrators of oppression and violence, toward other family members (Blumenfield and Schoeps 1993; Everstine and Everstine 1993; Van der Kolk, McFarlane; and Weisaeth 1996; Waites 1993; Williams and Sommer 1994). Whether the trauma faced by the family is internal or external to the family unit, an empowerment stance helps workers to stay in touch with the family's strengths, coping skills, resources, and capacity for family well-being.

Seven Principles of Empowering Practice with Families in Distress

The integration of empowerment-based practice with the unique needs of families in distress is expanded through the seven principles of empowering practice with families, introduced at the end of chapter 1. A social worker's commitment to working with families from an empowerment perspective is grounded in empowerment theory and based upon an open and compassionate acceptance of families in all their forms and structures. Ethical guidelines emphasize the importance of separating fact from myth, and multicultural respect is an ever-present part of each transaction. "The concept of empowerment is the cornerstone of all family-based programs. Empowerment encompasses a way of thinking about families. It's a conviction that families deserve respect, have strengths, *can* make changes in their lives, and are resilient, and it means helping families gain *access* to their power, not giving them power" (Kaplan and Girard 1994:40).

The helper has no capacity to give power. We do not "empower" other people; they already have personal and collective power. When oppressive forces cut off access to that power, helpers assist in removing or diminishing the effects of those oppressive forces. Social workers using empowering practice help remove barriers to the family's ability to access their own power.

Client families do not automatically know that we believe in their strengths and resilience. I am reminded of the words of one father: "We have just spent so much time talking about the problems in our lives right now and what to do about them, but do you understand that this is just not all of who we are? We have everything we need to make it through this time. We just appreciate hearing that we are on the right track." Helping professionals need to acknowledge the family's capacities in concrete and specific ways. Oppressive forces can remove a family's sense of their own capacity to function. If not addressed, the sense of vulnerability and self-doubt can be overwhelming. When these issues are addressed, however, the family uses its own skills and mutual supports, strengths and resources, to meet its needs.

Practice approaches that exclude a family's strengths and resources, or position them as an afterthought, do not offer maximum assistance and, in some cases, may even contribute to the oppressive forces experienced by the family members. A worker using an empowerment approach assumes that facing life stresses is common to all families. The perceived degree of distress at any given moment will be different for each family, but distress is a universal experience. This commonality builds mutuality and credibility in the helping context.

With these comments, the stage is set to expand the discussion about the seven principles of empowering practice with families in distress.

Principle 1. Build on Strengths and Resources; Diminish Oppressive Factors

The two parts to this first principle, one that builds (strengths and resources) and one that diminishes (oppression), are closely related and complementary to each other. By adding actions that strengthen and by continuing them over time, less time and energy are available for actions that weaken. Eventually, earlier barriers are no longer needed. Environmental barriers that appear to be immovable in the short term (e.g., addictions, poverty, discrimination, violence) are met with coping skills that diminish their impact. Family members consider choices, they exercise their ability to make things happen, and they become able to move on with their lives.

Building on Strengths and Resources

To build on a family's strengths requires, first of all, identification of those strengths. This begins before the first meeting with the family, found in the mind-set we bring with us into the practice environment. Our mind-set is grounded in our social work beliefs and values, diminishing oppression and promoting social justice through access to resources. We come to our work believing that it is more beneficial for us to see this family, and for them to see themselves, as persons with much more to their lives than distress and pain. It is exactly the "much more" that helps them through this time of distress and pain. Placing strengths and assets in the foreground from the beginning moments of our contact results in an ending to the work that supports them as they move forward. This is not a technique. Beginning with strengths and resources and building on them does not mean ignoring the stresses and oppressions the family brings. It does mean putting those stresses and oppressions "in their place" (Weick and Chamberlain 1997)—that is, in a place where they will not continue to be a barrier to the well-being of the family members.

More than twenty years ago, Anthony Maluccio's (1979) study on the perceptions of clients and their social workers about the key elements of the helping process revealed that the clients were far ahead of the workers on their use of the strengths perspective. In this study, clients saw themselves as "able to enhance their functioning" by the use of services. They identified their "resources operant within themselves and their social networks." Their social workers, in contrast, saw the clients as having "continuing problems, weaknesses, and limited potentialities" (399). It is time to catch up with our clients, to hear what they have been saying about their needs and their wealth of possibilities.

Before the past ten years, social workers were surrounded by literature, research, and training models that emphasized pathology and deficit, a stance adopted from a medical model. Since then, we have finally confronted the tragic awareness that "people become their designation" and that the words we use do, powerfully, direct the quality and outcome of our work, we have seen more and more strengths-based approaches develop in many fields of practice (Saleebey 1999:14–15). The shift to a growth-development model means an emphasis on strengths and competencies. The worker's focus is on shoring up and amplifying families' strengths and resources (Kaplan and Girard 1994:48).

Strengths can be acknowledged from the first moments of contact. Entering practice from the strengths perspective helps to operationalize empowerment. Three methods of discovering strengths are used: (1) using highly tuned-in observation skills; (2) listening to client stories; and (3) letting people know we are interested in their capacities, talents, hopes, and dreams (Saleebey 1999:19–20). The *use of observation* tells us there is no need to wait until the verbal narrative of their story of distress and coping begins. For example, if the family has arrived at an agency for the first meeting, it can immediately be acknowledged that they made it. Navigating transportation, directions, and parking, not to mention what it can take to get several family members all in the same place at the same time, especially in highly chaotic situations, is no small undertaking for any family. For a family with the added layer of distress, fear, ambivalence, confusion, pain, exhaustion, depression, grief, and trauma, just getting to a social worker requires enormous strength and fortitude. There is a distinct statement of strength in the arrival of a family seeking help, and many of the resources exercised to make that arrival happen are evident in the first interaction. These are coping resources. After individual attention is given to each family member for introductions, their account of how they all got there together can be an excellent way to begin. The course of their day, as it would have proceeded had this time of help not been necessary, has been interrupted.

As we *listen to clients' stories*, we have a choice of where to place the emphasis. Family members may have been living with their stress for many years, months, or days before seeing a social worker. In a crisis situation the event may have occurred in the past few hours. The pain and confusion may have surrounded them so completely that they can think of nothing else. Denial may be so complete that they have no idea what they are doing there with a social worker. Each member's experience of the event or the crisis is unique, unlike the experiences of the other family members with regard to the same situation. Traumatic events greatly change a person's capacity for empathy. Some have the empathy to reach out to their siblings, children, or partner, understanding that they are not seeing things in the same light. Others experience such shock that they are immobilized, not able to address their own needs let alone those of other family members. "Stories—especially stories of survival—are often the richest source of clues about interests, hopes, strengths, and resources" (Saleebey 1999:20).

An empowering stance also includes *communicating interest in the family's capacities, talents, hopes, and dreams.* The information that they give us at this point helps us gain a sense of direction for the next steps in our work with the family. Family members provide vivid examples of their own and one another's capacities and talents from PAST experiences. Observation in the PRESENT plus hearing about their hopes and dreams for their FUTURE provides glimpses of potentially unrealized capacities. The hopes of one family member may directly mirror those of another family member. Family members may discover that their hopes block or interfere with someone else's, but they are hearing it for the first time. Taking time to emphasize a family's views of their own capacities, talents, and hopes sets the stage for empowering practice between worker and family. When past resources can support present work, the family is more likely to reach their goals for the future.

Building upon these strengths, as this first principle calls upon us to do, requires recognition of the transition from then to now—that what worked then might also work now, and that it might not. As the worker guides such a discussion, there is a close connection with Principle 4, knowing the family has the capacity to empower themselves. Strengths already present can be sustained and enhanced. When strengths to address the present distress appear to be lacking, the worker and the family members can turn to the core actions of empowering practice: gaining more information, learning additional coping skills, and possibly participating in a support group or in new efforts with members of the extended family. Strengths are created where they did not previously exist.

Diminishing Oppression

As strengths are sustained, enhanced, and/or created, oppressive forces frequently fall away, no longer needed to maintain a shaky balance in the family dynamic. As families who face the challenge of one or more family members' addiction to alcohol, for example, increase their involvement in AA, Al-Anon, and Alateen, a new and different support network develops, eventually replacing earlier networks of "drinking buddies." In another example, a couple changed the way they handled conflicts and explained to their children what they were doing and why. One day soon after this, the father overheard the older son working out a swap (basketball for the bike) with their younger son instead of using his former dominance and aggression tactics. Two months later, the younger son had his "assessment of progress" at school. The parents were told their son could be moved out of special education classes and that his diagnosis of "developmentally delayed" no longer applied. His ability to focus had returned, and he was consistently working up to his grade level.

Oppressive forces faced by families are not always so responsive to increased strengths, however. People with power, or with perceived power, are not typically willing to give away the power they believe they have. Poverty is deeply ingrained in a capitalistic structure. Violence is not only allowed or overlooked but is condoned, minimized, or glorified, all equally lethal to the victims of its perpetrators. Addictions are surrounded with misconceptions, misinformation, and myths promising or faking the "beautiful" life with one hand while delivering the proverbial stab in the back with the other. Bigotry is passed from generation to generation, founded on propaganda that destroys both bigots and their targets of prejudice and discrimination. Many of the families welcomed by social workers face all of these oppressions simultaneously.

When oppressive forces are this overbearing, the core actions for empowering practice allow family members and social workers to respond at personal, interpersonal, and social/community levels, to have a focus and direction with specific actions, and to respond creatively to address each family's needs in effective ways. One additional way to address oppressive forces—one that must be carefully assessed for effectiveness and potential outcome for everyone involved—is for family members to face their oppressors, holding them accountable for their actions and seeking reparative behaviors. One father and employee chose to confront his boss about inadequate child care services at his place of work. Two sisters, both incest survivors, made the decision to confront their father and uncle about the abuse perpetrated by these two men and the men they invited to join them in their "sex parties" with young teenage girls. Four families living in an apartment building that had become increasingly dangerous because of faulty electrical connections joined together to confront their landlord about the unrealistic increase in rent when the building was in such drastic need of repair. Confronting the oppressor as one action toward empowerment for families is a viable option in many situations. However, it is not beneficial in all situations, and thorough preparation must occur before the action takes place.

The following "story of survival" (Saleebey 1999:20) comes from a practice recording of a social worker, Susan, in her first year of professional practice as a child protective services worker. Joan is the mother in this family, and she has two daughters, Hildie and Linette.

While preparing for her first supervised visit with Joan, age 21, and her two daughters, ages ten months and two years, respectively, Susan could see from the intake form that three months earlier one of Joan's neighbors had discovered two-year-old Linette sitting unattended on the sidewalk in front of their apartment building at 10:15 p.m. The neighbor knew the little girl and tried to help her get back into her mom's apartment, but there was no answer when she knocked. The neighbor took Linette home with her and phoned the police. When the police entered Joan's apartment, they found her unconscious on the floor next to Hildie's crib and, unable to revive her, took her to the nearest hospital, where it was determined she had suffered a diabetic coma. Linette and her sister were placed with an aunt, one of Joan's sisters, the next day.

While preparing to see this family Susan wondered when Joan's daughters would be allowed to live with her again. Stabilization in managing her diabetes had been the priority in the weeks since the incident, but it appeared that was in place now and Joan had returned to her regular work hours. Susan knew she needed to set aside any quickly formed assumptions about the decisions at the time of the reported incident and look at the bigger picture, at Joan's place in her entire system. At 23, Susan did not have children of her own yet, and even though she found herself identifying strongly with Joan and with the needs of the children in this family, she reminded herself that she really knew nothing about raising children. Joan would be the authority on that one here. One strength identified. Susan chose to see it as a strength, even though the incident was labeled "neglect" in the police report. Susan noted that this was the first time Joan's parenting had come to the attention of the neighbors, police, and human services. Also, the intake report gave no indication of physical abuse, developmental delay, or lack of food and clothing for the children. Until factual evidence told her otherwise, Susan made the choice to see this as a single incident.

Susan was also reminded to locate potential strengths and resources within Joan's entire system. This immediately brought to mind several people: the neighbor who had protected

Linette and called for help for Joan, Joan's sister who was currently serving as caregiver for the two girls, potentially the father of the two girls, if available, and other extended family. Friends, coworkers, and babysitters might be other possibilities.

As Susan considered steps to diminish oppressive factors in Joan's and her daughters' situation, she considered factors of poverty, violence, addictions, and discrimination that the family might have faced. These directly related to the need to gather information about financial resources, including medical insurance, about the accuracy of the charges made against Joan, and about the program in place for Joan's diabetes management. Reviewing the reports from the past three months, Susan learned that Joan did have medical insurance through her work at the Department of Motor Vehicles. However, financial strain was a major factor in Joan's ongoing well-being as a result of erratic child support payments from the children's father, Joan's ex-husband, Frank. According to Joan, Frank "has a drinking problem" and when he drank too much he was physically abusive toward Joan and Linette. When Joan was pregnant with Hildie, Frank had struck her in the stomach, causing Joan to fear for the unborn child's safety as well as her own and Linette's. This escalation of her fear was her reason for seeking a divorce from Frank after only three years of marriage. Susan also saw this decision as one that took enormous strength and courage on Joan's part and was aware of the significant risks involved in making such a move. With the nature of Frank's possible alcohol addiction and the related violence as part of this family's picture, Susan recognized the urgency of determining their safety at the present time, making that the highest priority for their work. Finally, Susan found herself questioning the label of "neglect" in the report, wondering if some type of discrimination might be at work here. The answer to this question emerges as the illustration of her work with this family continues in the discussion of the empowerment principles to follow.

Awareness of strengths and oppressions in each family is key as the social worker enters the work. Without that awareness, we can unintentionally undercut or diminish a strength or, equally unfortunate, we may inadvertently support an oppressive force. Minimizing verbal or emotional abuse by saying it is not as significant as physical abuse is one example of how we might allow an extremely destructive oppression to continue rather than taking active steps to diminish it. Building on each family's strengths and diminishing their unique set of oppressions shape the content of every step of the work to come.

Principle 2. Multicultural Respect

The term *multicultural* has been defined as "simultaneous loyalty to and embracing of more than one culture (i.e., not simply the presence of two or more races or cultures)" (Williams 1992:281). Multicultural factors have been identified as including ethnicity, gender, age, socioeconomic class, religion/spiritual belief, sexual orientation, differing abilities, and language (Schniedewind and Davidson 1997). Definitions for each of these factors share language in the literature: ·

• *Ethnicity:* "Connectedness based on commonalities (such as religion, nationality, region, etc.) where specific aspects of cultural patterns are shared and where transmission over time creates a common history" (Pinderhughes 1989:6)

• *Gender:* "A social, not a psychological, concept denoted by the terms 'femininity' and 'masculinity,' which refer to a complex set of characteristics and behaviors prescribed for a particular sex by society and learned through the socialization experience" (Ruth 1990:14)

• *Age:* Number of years since birth or conception, noting that some ethnic and religious groups begin counting at the time of conception rather than at the time of birth

• *Socioeconomic class:* "Class is more than just the amount of money you have; it's also the presence of economic security" (Langston 1995:101)

• *Religion/spiritual beliefs:* "In most societies it is the basis for morality and for all human relationships, especially where it is believed that there is divine law controlling all things, and it gives meaning to life" (Allen et al. 1993:626)

• *Sexual orientation:* One's feelings of sexual attraction to people of the same sex, to people of the opposite sex, or to people of both sexes (Marcus 1993:6)

• *Differing abilities:* Having abilities that differ from the established social norm, some of which may include living with impaired sight or hearing, needing to use a wheelchair, having intellectual capacity that exceeds that of one's peers, or utilizing different patterns of learning and processing information

• *Language:* Includes one's first and primary language as well as later learned languages, not necessarily spoken (i.e., sign language), with emphasis on bilingual and multilingual skills as a definite strength

These eight do not constitute an exhaustive list of possible factors, but they do reflect the ones that are current and consistently appear in the literature. One aspect of the work conducted by members of the National Association for Multicultural Education (NAME) is a continuous inquiry about what factors to include on the list and what meanings to attribute to them. Several other factors that have appeared, less consistently, are race, developmental stage, geography, and family form.

Arguments against the inclusion of race on the list include "its ambiguous meaning as a measure of difference referring to culture," that "racism is often equated with prejudice and . . . raises to the level of social structure the tendency to use superiority as a solution to discomfort about difference," and "the confusion and misunderstanding it creates among people" (Pinderhughes 1989:89). "Races are not biologically differentiated groupings but rather social constructions. . . .

'White' does not denote a rigidly defined, congeneric grouping of indistinguishable human beings. It refers to an unstable category which gains its meaning only through social relations" (Lopez 1996:xiii–xiv). Critical race theorists recognize that "race" is a legal as well as a social construction. In fact, critical race theory begins with the premise that "race" is not fixed but is buffeted by an ever-fluctuating political and social environment, that it has been used to feed the fear at the roots of bigotry, prejudice, discrimination, hatred. Barbara Flagg (1993) has exposed the tendency of many whites not to see themselves in racial terms. She calls it the "transparency phenomenon" and asserts that it is a major barrier that must be overcome by whites in their development of racial self-awareness. This is an essential core task for all people, all families, who live where their race is defined as the norm, a norm that creates blindness. Lopez (1996) and other critical race theorists call on the socially committed of today to acknowledge the "falsity of race" (32). The strength of history, expression, ritual, language, celebration, music, food, and family gathering enables families to connect with a richness of heritage, ethnicity, and culture that is their own. Multicultural theorists do not ignore the complexities of the concept of "race." They do, however, encourage a critically conscious response (Freire 1998) that promotes strength, resilience, respect, freedom to pursue well-being, and celebration of diversity.

Those who argue for the inclusion of developmental stage as a multicultural factor recognize the frequent discrepancy between age and developmental stage (Bula 1998). This can refer to the difference between chronological age and the corresponding developmental stage, or it may refer to a person's emotional age as compared with her or his developmental stage. It can include those with developmental delays as well as those who are developmentally advanced. The developmental stage of "middle age," for example, contains certain "values, norms, beliefs, attitudes, folkways, behavior styles, and traditions that are linked together to form an integrated whole that functions to preserve the society" (Leighton 1982, quoted in Pinderhughes 1989:6), which is the earlier definition given to the term *culture*. It is helpful to bear in mind the addition of "life course" to the conceptual framework of the Life Model (Germain and Gitterman 1996) with its base in ecological thinking. This concept challenges the stage model and promotes greater flexibility than earlier, more linear, models could provide.

Acknowledging geography as an important multicultural factor has, in part, been exemplified at the NAME meetings through increased involvement of international presenters and participants. Inclusion of geography recognizes not only a person's place of birth but also the impact of transitions from one geographical location to another. Historically, the significance of forced geographic moves echoes across the generations: Africans forced into slavery; American Indians forced from familiar ancestral lands onto reservations; Jews forced into concentration camps; Japanese Americans forced into similar camps on U.S. soil. Loss of homeland leaves unmistakable marks on family members as they struggle in strange locations, often separated from one another for long periods of time, uncertain about when and how they will reunite. Voluntary transitions from one geographical location to another, such as those for immigrant families, or families who move from one section of a country to another, or those who make the transition from a rural environment to an urban one, all have major implications for individuals and families.

Family forms and structures can also be considered as a candidate for the list of multicultural factors (Bula 1998). Blended family, single-parent family, nuclear family, dual-career family, gay and lesbian family, multigenerational family, and others all have their own traditions, beliefs, behavioral styles, and attitudes that form a whole to preserve society. Each provides an early context in which children learn how to communicate, how to be in a relationship, how to be members of the larger society. All point to the evolving and emerging nature of the definition of the term *multicultural.*

Multicultural awareness takes on its unique shape through family stories of survival and coping, through the narratives of ancestors and the history of transitions, crises, rituals, and celebrations. The social worker's multicultural characteristics brought into the helping relationship interact with those of the family members and promote mutuality in multicultural respect and understanding. A conscious "use of self" in our work with families, a use of our "multicultural self" (Bula 2000:167–189), requires a critically conscious awareness of privilege and oppression, of values, beliefs, and attitudes. For it is in the intersection between the worlds of social worker and family members, the intersection of the many distinguishing aspects of each person that the stage for multicultural respect is set.

A unique multicultural picture exists for the family as a unit, but another set of multicultural pictures exists for each individual in the family. In many families, individual family members differ from each other in a variety of ways already discussed. In all families, members will be of different ages—even twins and triplets frequently emphasize who was born first and who came after. We cannot assume that family members come to us from the same geographic location or that they are at a developmental stage that matches their chronological age. Even gender distinctions are not always what they may appear to be, as the increasing number of families with members who have changed sexes reminds us. Stereotypes fall away as unhelpful attempts to categorize or condense a richness and diversity that defies such simplification. Instead, practice that invites the diversity present in the family builds upon a base of multicultural respect.

Multicultural counseling competencies (appendix A) include: (1) counselor awareness of his or her own assumptions, values, and biases; (2) an understanding of the worldview of the culturally different client; and (3) development of appropriate intervention strategies and techniques (Sue, Arredondo, and McDavis 1995:624–641). The first is a crucial step in the worker's preparation for seeing a family. The last two can be enhanced through the ethnographic approach (Leigh 1998).

The ethnographic approach is essential for working with distressed families from a position of multicultural respect. Its main objective is "to learn about cultural behavior, values, language, and worldviews of the person who is representative of the cultural group" (Leigh 1998:79). Stated in this way, this objective is based upon the premise that the social worker lacks this knowledge or, at the very least, lacks knowledge about how a particular family behaves, what values they hold, what language or languages they speak, and what their particular worldview is. A "lack of cultural congruence that affects the communication process" (39) has been identified as the major barrier in forming a relationship across cultures. In essence, the social worker is a stranger to this family and to the meaning they give to their world, and this being a stranger, lacking familiarity with their worldview and its meaning, is the role the social worker is called upon to fill.

Ethnographic information is used to determine directions for practice that are "congruent with the cultural demands of the person" (Leigh 1998:79) and the cultural demands of the family. In order for this to happen, the client family is also asked to assume the role of a cultural guide or teacher about their culture. Social workers must let go of the expectation that families will learn the culture of the helping process and instead must be willing to take on the role of learning from the family members.

There are several steps to the ethnographic interview: considerations before contact with the family (tuning in with cultural empathy); setting the stage through friendly conversation; explaining the model through expressing ignorance of their culture and inviting them to be the worker's "cultural guide"; assessment of the situation using global questions (broad questions leading to cultural understanding), descriptive questions, and reaching for explanation of cover terms (words that cover a range of ideas and meanings, often symbolic meaning); reaching consensus through negotiation for plans about how to address the distressing situation; selecting interventions that are culturally relevant; and ending the interview in a manner respectful of the family's cultural patterns regarding endings.

Empowering practice with families, as defined here, means that the multicultural respect takes place mutually, that the social worker can also inform the family members if stereotypic beliefs or attitudes are evident on their part regarding the multicultural background of the worker. Families often come with generalized information about agencies and agency personnel that may or may not be accurate and may or may not act as a barrier to the work. Allowing the family to hear the worker's unique and personal way of interpreting how the work can happen between them as individuals facing a distressing situation together can serve the ongoing nature of relationships between families, workers, agencies, and communities.

Principle 3. Recognizing Needs at the Three Levels of Empowerment (Personal, Interpersonal, Community)

Families know what they need. They tell us what they need individually and interpersonally as well as what is needed in their communities to better respond to the events and challenges that they must face. However, in the aftermath of traumatic events, in the face of challenges to earlier coping methods, or in light of overwhelming situational factors, they may not be able to articulate those needs verbally and they may experience a sense of hopelessness, imagining that having their needs met is beyond their grasp. Pride and the wish to avoid shame may prevent family members from expressing their needs to an outsider, especially if that outsider is met with suspicion rather than trust.

It may be difficult to determine what families need personally, interpersonally, and from their communities in the moment, yet it will always be important to listen to and to hear the unique needs of the family members in each situation. Listening to the voices of the families is key to empowerment practice. Responses to family needs, personally and interpersonally, must be sensitive to timing and cultural influences, the latter often originating in the community. In addition to specific needs, however, there have been clear reports from families regarding what is most helpful for them in a general sense as well. These responses fall into two categories: responses to their immediate and concrete needs and responses to ongoing needs.

Families have frequently reported that responses to concrete needs have been the most useful services received (Barthel 1992a, 1992b; Fraser and Haapala 1988; Morton and Grigsby 1993). Some authors (Kaplan and Girard 1994) have placed this response as the worker's first priority. Effectiveness in our work with distressed families means addressing both concrete and emotional needs plus relational and interpersonal needs, as well as needs that arise from participation as citizens in their communities. These levels of need, coinciding with the three levels of empowerment, are not separate. When concrete needs are addressed, there is always an emotional and relational component involved. When relational and emotional needs are addressed, there may also be the need for involvement of concrete community resources at the same time. Beginning with concrete needs helps to lay a foundation for meeting the variety of needs that may arise throughout the course of the work.

Families tend to be more open in allowing a worker to assist with concrete needs in the earlier phases of the relationship. Concrete needs are more often seen as needs that all share. Offering a glass of water or a place to sit can be seen simply as common courtesy between two persons, yet such gestures can also create the beginning of a relationship that can progress to more delicate or sensitive collaboration later on. When different languages make it difficult to understand the more subtle nature of emotional and relational needs, participation in concrete tasks, such as providing a change of clothing or fixing a meal, unites people around a common need, one that can be met without words.

Needs, both concrete and ongoing, will be met differently for different members of a family. When the Ramirez family stood on the front lawn of their burning apartment building, each expressed the need for support. Mrs. Ramirez anxiously gazed down the street at oncoming cars, looking for her husband's van to come around the corner. Her teenage daughter asked the social worker if she could borrow a cell phone to call her best friend to come be with her. And the four-year-old just needed to be held by his mother. This example shows how important it can be to understand developmental characteristics for each family member in the expression of her or his need.

In the midst of trauma, family members may not be able to handle more than one need at a time. Also while standing beside the Ramirez family, a worker from the Salvation Army delivered a message about temporary shelter—that is, the need for a community resource. This message, however, appeared not to register in Mrs. Ramirez's thinking. She was still looking for her husband at the time. The social worker, aware of the shock and numbing of senses (in this case, hearing) that can occur following a trauma, was able to provide the information about the temporary shelter at a later time, after the family had been reunited. Multiple needs of children may overwhelm parents at the time of crisis as well. Sometimes a social worker can assist in meeting these needs and explain to the children about the parent's inability to respond in the usual way.

In families who are experiencing distress and trauma, it helps to address concrete and ongoing needs in terms appropriate to the emotional ages (not necessarily the same as chronological ages) of the individual family members. One result of experiencing high stress is that people often call on earlier forms of coping in the attempt to provide reassurance, comfort, or stability. Robert, 29, a recovering alcoholic for twelve years, found himself reaching for a drink after hearing about his father's death in a car accident. Instead, he reached for the telephone and his social worker's number. In concrete, immediate terms, Robert needed to get rid of the alcohol he had purchased, which he did with the social worker listening on the phone, then he needed his AA sponsor's presence. Recognizing that at the moment Robert might be functioning at an emotional age comparable to his age when he was drinking (17) and that one of the behaviors he had reported struggling with was follow-through on his own behalf, the social worker offered to contact the AA sponsor for Robert. He accepted the offer, and the AA sponsor was at Robert's home twenty minutes later.

Finally, when recognizing needs, it is helpful to use incremental steps in meeting those needs. After the death of her husband, Marjorie, age 83, found that the task of trying to pay her bills was completely overwhelming. When the social worker showed her how to separate the receipt for payment, write the account number on her check, fill in the check for the correct amount, sign her name, make sure the address showed through the window, enclose the check, then seal and stamp the envelope, Marjorie became exhausted and confused. However, when they discovered together how much of the task Marjorie could complete at one time (such as signing her name three times) and agreed to divide this task and include it with other, lighter activities, her bills were ready to go in one afternoon.

Families have also reported responses that are most helpful to ongoing needs (Bernheim and Lehman 1985; Lee 2001; Hatfield and Lefley 1987). These are (1) information about what is happening, (2) increasing skill for coping with the situation, and (3) support from others who have faced similar experiences. These three are consistent with methods of practice identified as empowerment approaches to practice: enabling, linking, catalyzing, and priming (Solomon 1999:352–353). As the discussion progresses into a closer look at the middle phase of work, each of these approaches will be considered in greater depth.

Principle 4. With Sufficient Resources, Families Can Empower Themselves

How do we know when client families have sufficient resources to do the work necessary, to make things happen that will enable them to move on to a greater sense of well-being? This fourth principle of empowerment practice with families includes ongoing observation of available resources. Since the assistance of the social worker is a primary resource in the work together, it is vital to make the distinction between assistance that supports and assistance that interferes with a family's desired direction.

Where do we find the balance between helping through participation and collaboration and helping by stepping into the background? When will helping efforts sustain, enhance, and help create the family's picture of what is needed for their well-being? If we find we are guessing about the answer to this question, it is time to ask. Ask about what personal, interpersonal, and community resources are available. Ask the family members if they have what they need to proceed on their own. These are familiar questions that have also been stated in other forms, such as checking the person–environment fit (Germain and Gitterman 1996) or determining the balance of self-other-context (Satir et al. 1991). Environmental fit and importance of context are the third element of the strengths-based approach. These are the foundation for incremental change as each family works toward increased well-being.

Sometimes families are unable to empower themselves, when they do not yet have sufficient resources to proceed. One example is the post-trauma response that immobilizes and numbs. When we see exhaustion, shock, confusion, and fear, when they are doing their best but it is not getting them where they had hoped, the social worker's response is one of "doing for" the family until they can do for themselves again.

What are some of the indicators that a family is not yet ready to move forward on their own? Their verbal messages to that effect are, perhaps, the clearest indication. Information also comes to us nonverbally. When families are caught in cycles of abuse or addiction or both, if doors to opportunities are closing rather than opening, when isolation and loneliness have diminished the will to live, when they are holding on to a victim stance, when they are immobilized by fear or depression—all are indicators that additional resources are needed.

The Cline family had insufficient resources to change their father's addictive cycle. The social worker, Jim, knew that the father in this family, Hugh, was adamant about following the course his alcoholism was taking. Hugh's doctor had diagnosed liver damage and had insisted that the drinking stop immediately. Jim recognized that there was no way to change Hugh's mind about this, yet the needs of the other family members also required attention. Hugh's wife, Sylvia, was greatly relieved to hear someone else say that she could not change Hugh's decision, nor did she need to try to do so any longer. When asked about what information, coping skills, and support groups she wanted for herself, however, she was very clear about wanting to attend Al-Anon. Their teenage daughter spoke up and asked for information about Alateen. Jim informed them about the likelihood of change in the family as a result of their attendance at these meetings. The familiar scripts that they had used to survive the addictive cycle would no longer serve their purposes. They also had talked about the progression of Hugh's drinking inevitably leading to other crises in the future, medical or financial ones, for example, where he might be forced to consider another direction. Both Sylvia and her daughter believed that their respective groups and their support of each other could add resources that would allow them to face whatever happened with clearer understanding of what their options would be.

The Clines provide an illustration of a family in which some of the members seek to make choices toward a greater sense of well-being, while other family members do not choose this direction. Denial is an enormous force contributing to the oppressive power of addictions. Even though Hugh would not move beyond his denial, the other family members were supported to make changes toward more empowered positions. Skills of working with families such as the Clines include assisting the family as a unit, assisting individual members of the family, and addressing both levels simultaneously. Further illustration of these skills appears in later chapters.

Principle 5. Support Is Needed from Each Other, from Other Families, and from the Community

All people need the support of their parents, their siblings, and their extended-family members. Yet often what social workers are called upon to witness is exactly the opposite of support. For families facing extreme distress, showing support to each other can be overshadowed by intense personal pain. Responses to stress and trauma often involve withdrawal and pulling in or lashing out in flashes of emotion designed to keep people away rather than being able to manage one's own stress. At the times when family members need each other the most, they may have the least to give.

In practice with families in distress, sometimes the most empowering efforts are those that reconnect one family member to the others. Family members may have blamed one of their own in their efforts to make sense out of incomprehensible situations. The three guidelines for empowering practice—normalizing behavior as ways of coping, providing information or reminders about available skills, and offering support groups—can guide the worker toward useful responses. Whole-system distress calls for a whole-system response, and empowerment practice offers one way of providing such a response. With a commitment toward personal, interpersonal, and social/community dynamics; an emphasis on strengths, multicultural respect, awareness of needs, resources and supports (internal and external to the family unit); encouragement to look at uses of power; and experimentation with cooperative roles, empowerment practice offers a multilevel approach for these families.

In practice with families in extreme stress, the social worker may find that the source of that stress comes from within the family itself. When abuse and violence are present, this fifth principle of empowerment practice confronts a distinct variation: the need for the love and support of family members, particularly parents, never goes away, but when there is any expression of violence or abuse among or between family members, those needs for love and support may have to be met through other relationships and supportive connections in the community. Efforts to reconnect abusers and perpetrators of violence with their victims must always be approached with caution. Contact with the abuser, even in the presence of a social worker or other helping professional, may place the victim at further risk both during and after the meeting. Victims often do not feel they can speak freely while the abuser is in the room because what they say may increase the risk of further violence. Many victims also do not feel they can speak freely when the abuser is out of the room. In severe abuse situations, there may have been extreme threats of increased violence or death if the victim reveals any of the behaviors of the abuser to anyone outside the family. For these reasons, many researchers have spoken out against seeing couples and families together when violence and abuse are known to be present (Bograd 1992; Hansen and Harway 1993; Kaufman 1992; Pressman 1989).

The first concern is always the safety of the victims. The lack of safety is related in part to the forced isolation that often surrounds them. By "widening the circle" of people to protect all family members (Pennell and Burford 1994, 1997, 1999) and by building "communities of concern" (Braithwaite and Daly 1994:192), both of which are directions promoted through family group conferencing (Burford and Hudson 2000; Macgowan and Pennell 2001), the oppression of such isolation can be diminished.

One way of widening the circle is through the support of other families. In speaking about what they need most during times of extreme difficulty, families have asked for guidance from others who have faced similar circumstances. Even though there may be variations on the theme—families who have lost a child, who have a member with a mental illness, who are coping with addictions, who are immigrants—all benefit from hearing the stories of others who have been through similar challenges. Other families demonstrate the credibility of having survived their experiences. The stories about how their lives have changed, how they have survived and coped, and what they would offer to others come from someone who has been there. Families draw inspiration from one another in a way that is not available when they interact with professionals. When family members see that someone else, facing even greater difficulties than their own, has made it through the experience, they feel more hopeful that they may be able to do the same.

Charlotte said her turning point came after hearing from another mother of a child with Down's syndrome that she could have permission to "wrap yourself up in self pity…you bet, give yourself eight minutes of solid wailing and moaning self-pity whenever you feel you need it, then get on with your life." It was from her group that she also learned about opportunities with cooperative child care with other parents. This joint effort allowed her daughter to play with peers, gave her and her partner a chance for respite from the care of her child, and helped financially since she could decrease the number of hours when outside assistance was required.

And families need the support of their communities. Families in distress require a "dual focus" (Turner and MacNair 2003:219), an integration of work with the family and work with their community, which then responds to the needs of the family. Vulnerable families are alert to physical and social threats in the community that present barriers. Especially for poor families, families that are living with violence, those who are controlled by addictions, and those who face discrimination on a daily basis, the neighborhood and community may not be helpful or healthy places to live. Extended-family networks, natural helpers or non-kinship networks, and religious institutions frequently serve as resources for these families.

Lack of access to resources often frustrates families and those supporting them. Providing information about resources, going with families to where resources are available, and staying with them through the process until they do have access to the resource may be necessary actions for the worker. "Hands-on," concrete service to families is especially required with immigrant families and those who do not speak English, as well as those who live with sight or hearing impairment or developmental or mental challenges. All families who have experienced a recent trauma require such services as well.

Low-income families often hesitate to approach institutions that appear intimidating and overwhelming. When a family worker can gain familiarity with these institutions and serve as a guide and consultant for families, the likelihood that they will access services increases. Many agencies are doing their best in a variety of ways to follow their mandates for "integrated services." They are extending outreach to families in distress and easing the process of connecting with needed resources. Creative forms of networking that are being used include "case-finding programs that put outreach workers on the streets to discover hidden but responsive clients"; family preservation programs with workers in the home to strengthen home management and parenting skills; and "family resource centers, which combine interconnected social agencies with the resources of the school system and the mutual self-help resources of parenting groups" (Turner and MacNair 2003:224).

Principle 6. Establish and Maintain a "Power WITH" Relationship

Family members need to exert their own power and to obtain needed resources (Pinderhughes 1983). Workers come to the practice setting with three kinds of power: power from their expertise, power from their interpersonal skills, and power related to the resources to which they have access and that the clients need (Hasenfeld 1987). Client families come with these three kinds of power as well. Beginning with their strengths and resources (Principle 1) assures that their power is recognized from the outset, at the beginning contact with the social worker. Power WITH doubles the areas of expertise, interpersonal skill, and resources available in the work; the power of both the worker and the family members is essential.

In the ideal "power with" working relationship, a back-and-forth, reciprocal nature exists. Social worker and family members are mutually influencing each other as the process between them unfolds. "Power with" describes the transaction when there is a balance in what is given and received by the social worker and what is given and received by the family members; when the family guides the social worker in understanding their situation, history, recent methods of coping, and the like and the social worker, in turn, guides the family in learning about resources available to meet stated needs; when cooperation and collaboration characterize exchanges between family members and social worker.

"Power with" has also been identified as "power sharing" (Pinderhughes 1989). Power sharing moves the relationship with family members away from dominant and submissive roles into roles of participating as equals and relieves the pressure of "power over" or "power under" positions. There is a "greater readiness to consider treatment alternatives that focus on the use of external systems as supports for clients" (144). Power can be shared with external resources, with schools, with hospitals, with employers, and with support groups, resources that can better meet the needs of the family than the social worker alone can.

Establishing a "power with" or "power sharing" relationship with all the family members, some family members, or even one family member is easier said than done. All practitioners who have worked with families in distress know very clearly that not all family members welcome the idea of seeing a social worker. Families enter the helping relationship with ambivalence, hoping to receive the help they need but also suspicious about relationships that may either enable or frustrate the process of moving toward their goals. As Pinderhughes notes, "Clients challenge practitioner power all the time" (1989:142). In fact, such challenges may paradoxically be one way in which clients are seeking to establish their own sense of power in the relationship. Before power sharing can be demonstrated and explained as part of the working relationship, clients view their social workers as extensions of the institution. It is likely that they have experienced dominance and submission relationships in other institutions and, at least initially, they may see no reason to believe that something different would occur with this social worker. Unresolved power issues in families also carry over into the relationship with the social worker.

The steps and skills of the empowerment approach provide ways to address these challenges. When the family tells their story at the beginning, the social worker can glean clues from hearing about their previous experiences with other helping professionals and discern what they found to be helpful and not helpful. Those earlier efforts are respected and at the same time a picture develops of what may need to happen differently with the family at this time.

Principle 7. Using Cooperative Roles that Support and Assist Family Members

Many roles have been identified as congruent with the empowerment approach to practice. Teacher/trainer, resource consultant, and sensitizer (awareness raiser) (Solomon 1976); facilitator, advocate, and ally (Kaplan and Girard 1994:40); planner, colleague/monitor, catalyst, outreach, and researcher/scholar (Miley, O'Melia, and DuBois 2001:15–19); and partner, collaborator, coteacher, coinvestigator, dialogist, critical question poser, bridge builder, guide, ally and power equalizer, cobuilder, coactivist, and coworker (Lee 2001:61). Multiple roles are necessary, and each one adds to the creativity and responsiveness of intervention choices. The prefix "co-" identifies many of these roles as shared and makes explicit the cooperative and mutual nature of roles congruent with empowerment thinking. "Role sharing is a coping device well suited to the complexity of modern family pressures" (Lee 2001:171–172). Thus, as the worker participates in role sharing with family members, she supports the role sharing that the family already uses. Role sharing can also be modeled as an effective coping skill for the family once the work in the social work setting has been completed.

In empowering practice, role sharing means that no role works in only one direction. A role assumed by the worker to assist the client may, at another time, be a role assumed by the client to assist the worker's understanding. Any role can be filled by family members and by social workers. Individual skills and experience, as well as specific contexts and needs, determine when different people fill different roles and when one role is more appropriate than another.

Thus the worker and family members serve as *coconsultants* for each other as they work together to address the issues and stresses faced by the family. The worker and the family seek to *collaborate* with each other. The family sometimes *guides* the worker and the worker sometimes guides the family. The worker can serve as a *teacher* with the family members assuming the role of learners; then the reverse occurs with the family members being teachers to the social worker as *learner. Coinvestigators* and *cocreators* are the final two roles considered here. Descriptions of these roles are presented here, with additional illustrations in the chapters that follow.

Coconsultants

As coconsultants "workers and clients confer and deliberate together to develop plans for change." Coconsultants acknowledge "that both social workers and client systems bring information and resources, actual and potential, which are vital for resolving the issue at hand" (Miley, O'Melia, and DuBois 2001:14).

Collaborators

As collaborators, social workers who are working from an empowerment perspective serve more as team players with the clients. Factors contributing to the client family's sense of powerlessness may be considered within the context of the initial assessment of strengths and resources. Balancing perceived or actual powerlessness with available resources provides immediate avenues for action, and that action can contribute to the goals of diminishing oppressive factors and increasing a sense of efficacy and accomplishment. Collaboration involves attending to the relationships with family members, both individually and together, while simultaneously attending to the tasks related to planning, setting goals, and taking steps to reach those goals.

Guides

Sometimes the family has more information to guide, and at other times the worker has the greater information or experience. Families, for example, guide the worker in understanding who they are individually and together, how they face challenges, what works and does not work for them. Social workers guide family members by providing information about available services, how to access them, and how to use them. The role of guide can be one where hierarchical assumptions about power or unresolved issues around power in the worker's own family may emerge. One step in the worker's preparation, the Family Power Analysis (see appendix B) helps to ensure that these earlier family issues do not interfere in the helping process. The balance and the equal distribution of the role become the focus of an empowering process, each family member and each worker serving as guide where she or he has the information and experience to do so.

Coteachers and Colearners

The roles of teacher and learner are presented together to emphasize their inseparability. From the empowerment vantage point, which includes the reciprocal transactions among and between the members of the family and the social worker, it is considered impossible to separate these two roles. In the process of teaching, one is also learning. In the process of learning, one is also teaching others. The dynamics of the teaching-learning process will be further discussed in part II, which considers the providing of information as one of the methods of empowering practice.

Coinvestigators

The act of investigating is required when there is some gap in the information, when there is some curiosity, when there is a contradiction in facts or perceptions, when the worker and the family seem to be stuck in their process. Working together as coinvestigators acknowledges that certain members of the family will have easier access to answers, or to people with the answers, in the investigation than will other members of the family or the social worker. When social workers seek information to assist the family in reaching their goals, family members can be invited to participate in that search. Thus, coinvestigating can add valuable interpersonal time for clients and workers and further strengthen their working relationship.

Cocreators

Family members usually have a long history of cocreating themselves as a family before they ever come to the attention of a social worker. Patterns developed over time, unique to each family, play a key role in addressing the stressors that the family is facing at the time of the intervention with a social worker. A cocreator role with a client family is different from the cocreator role with an individual client. Each family member helps create the family as a unit and also creates himself or herself as an individual within the context of the family system. The creative process supporting all aspects of the work between worker and family is a key component of the purpose of empowerment practice: to help sustain, enhance, and create family well-being.

The wide diversity of today's families speaks to the strength, the resilience, and the creativity of each family who has moved beyond the structures, organization, rules, and roles of their families of origin. Such creativity is a valuable asset when the time comes for each family to face the challenges and stressors that are part of daily living, particularly those families for whom oppressions of poverty, violence, addictions, and discrimination are ever-present. All families have enormous repertoires of strengths, and all families face distress and challenges. Together with helpful supports within their families, in extended families, and in social and community networks, families can access their capacity to respond to distress as a joint effort rather than a solitary or isolated task.

Part II

![gray bar separator]

Three Family Profiles: The Journey from Oppression to Empowerment

The families whose stories shape the next three chapters exemplify remarkable strength in response to overwhelming odds. Drawing strength from adversity is a universal human experience. The strength in families is often not fully evident until they are called upon to face daunting challenges. This is only one of the reasons, however, that each of these families was selected. A second reason was to illustrate the empowerment framework in a variety of situations, at the personal, interpersonal, and social levels of practice, and in the broad diversity of the population served.

Empowerment, by definition, focuses attention on oppressions experienced by the families with whom we work. Each of the families whose stories are told here faces multiple oppressions. Their experiences clarify the interrelatedness among and between various forms of oppression: how discrimination feeds poverty, violence, and addictions; how poverty in turn feeds violence, addictions, and discrimination; how violence and addictions each feed the other forms of oppression. These are, of course, not the only oppressions familiar to social workers. The list is carefully selected but by no means exhaustive. Confronting these major oppressions in the illustrations to follow, however, can provide examples of the possibilities available to professionals as they assist family members.

In addition to these characteristics in the families selected, consideration was also given to what would be most helpful to readers. Therefore, the principles, roles, and actions used by social workers in response to the oppressions were key factors in the selection process. Is the practice congruent with empowerment principles? What roles does the social worker use in her or his work with this family?

Core actions (providing information, enhancing coping skills, participation with others) are supported by a variety of other actions. The selection process aimed to accomplish two objectives: to show how the core actions of empowerment practice can be sufficient and complete for some families and to show how they can serve as a foundation for practice that includes other interventions.

Finally, each family narrative was reviewed to assess whether the purpose of empowerment practice had been served: Was the worker aware of the qualities of well-being brought to the practice setting by each family and were those qualities acknowledged and *sustained* during their contact? How was the well-being of the family *enhanced* as a result of the work with this social worker? In what ways did the worker assist the family in *creating* new avenues of well-being that were responsive to the crisis presented and that would contribute to the family's strengths, coping, and well-being in the future?

Sometimes families become involved with social workers by their own choice. They reach out voluntarily for the assistance a social worker can provide. At other times, meeting with a social worker is the last thing that a family wants to do, for the social worker may be the person who determines if their children stay in the home, if they must leave, or if they can stay but must "be invaded by all kinds of unnecessary, ridiculous training," as one mother phrased it. The social worker may be the person who the families fear will assign some kind of label to them. When work with a social worker is mandated—ordered by the court or a program meant to help the family—the resulting practice environment carries a set of dynamics that can, initially at least, be quite different from those at work when the family comes to the social worker by their own choice. In the following chapters, the first family, the Laurencio-Smiths, voluntarily sought services from helping professionals; the second family, the Williamses, included family members who sought services and one family member who was mandated to services; and the third family, the Brown-Wileys, were mandated to services.

Each chapter in part II follows roughly the same format. A description of the event, or series of events, that brought the family to the attention of the social worker is followed by a description of personal, interpersonal, and social/community factors that interact in the dynamics of each family. This information sets the stage for the phases of work: the beginning, the middle, and the ending. Empowerment practice begins with strengths, and a section on "strengths in response to oppressions" is part of the description of the beginning phase of work with each family.

Excerpts from the beginning, the middle, and the ending phases of work are included. The description of the beginning phase includes examples of worker preparation, setting the stage, early contacts before meeting the family members face-to-face, consideration of referral source material, tuning in to differences between strengths-based and deficit-based uses of language, and anticipatory empathy. At the time of the first meeting, these excerpts provide variation in initial greetings, discovery of the help desired through hearing each family's story, how offers of service are made, the social workers' skills in lowering anxiety and managing stress and ambivalence, and the effective timing of the entry into the middle phase of the work. The middle phase emphasizes the interplay among the three primary empowering actions: providing information, enhancing coping skills, and promoting participation. This work sometimes leads to other supporting interventions that can further enhance the family's response to their trauma. In the ending process, several key tasks lead to completions: dealing with feelings related to experiencing endings, both the immediate one between social worker and family members and those that occurred at earlier points in time; consolidating gains; confirming connections with the community; hearing the family members' own words about gains in strengths, skills, resilience, empowerment; and undertaking a mutual evaluation process that acknowledges the work completed and the next steps to which it leads; and, finally, saying good-bye.

I respectfully acknowledge and thank each family and each social worker represented in these pages. Names have been changed to preserve confidentiality, yet much in these stories is identifiable and familiar in general terms. Facing adversity and distress is familiar to all families. Searching for choices and possibilities in the midst of uncertainty is familiar to all families. Being changed by the adversity, yet moving on with life, is familiar to all families. Wondering how best to be present and when to take our leave as we briefly, or not so briefly, enter and exit a family's life is familiar to all social workers.

3

The Laurencio-Smith Family: Our Differences Saved Us

Suspicious bruises, cuts, welts, and burn marks immediately caught the eye of Danny's father, Jorgé Laurencio (age 35), and his partner, Lydia Smith (age 28), when they were helping Danny (age 4) get ready for his nap that Tuesday afternoon in March. Danny had just returned from a visit with his biological mother, Maria, who lived in an apartment in a nearby town, about a twenty-minute drive through the Connecticut countryside. Jorgé recalls feeling both horrified and furious. His worst fears were becoming reality. When he and Maria were still living together, he had seen her come close to hitting Danny when she was drunk and angry, but she had always managed to leave the room before harm had come to the child, at least as far as he knew. Now he wondered.

When Jorgé and Lydia asked Danny about what had happened, his response was, "Mommy loves me today. She just wants me to be good," but he climbed into Lydia's lap as he said this and clung to her, seemingly for reassurance and safety. Jorgé called Maria to find out what had happened, but there was no answer. He contacted the community emergency crisis line, informed the worker on duty what had happened, and said that Danny was safely at home. After a "brief conversation that was somewhat reassuring," Jorgé requested a meeting with a worker. The crisis line worker gave him the number for the local Family and Children's Services agency, which he contacted immediately and gave the required intake information. The intake worker informed him that Barbara, one of the social workers, would receive the information about his family that day and would be contacting them as soon as possible. The result of Barbara's phone call was a conversation with Lydia and the scheduling of an appointment for the next morning.

Personal, Interpersonal, and Social/Community Levels

Personal

Jorgé was born and raised in Campos, a town just north of Rio de Janeiro, Brazil. He describes his ethnic background as Brazilian (paternal side) and French (maternal side) (figure 3.1).[1] His family of origin began with two parents but after his parents separated, it became a family with one parent in residence (his mother) plus three generations of extended-family members (maternal side). Jorgé is the oldest of two sons; his younger brother lives in Brazil, works for an uncle on a cattle ranch, and has remained single. In Brazil his family is viewed as very wealthy, but he quickly adds, "The wealth in Brazil is not the wealth in the United States."

Jorgé emigrated to the United States from Brazil with his first wife, Maria, also of Brazilian heritage, eight years before this intake at the Family and Children's Services agency in his community. Jorgé's dream had been to come to a U.S. university for training in business management. His parents provided some financial backing for his transition to the United States, enough to support several months of living expenses while the young couple got settled in their new community. Both Jorgé and Maria found employment within six months after their arrival. In order to meet their expenses, however, Jorgé needed to work two jobs, as a courier for a local advertising company during the day and as a part-time convenience store attendant in the evening. He could begin his course of study in a weekend program at a local college, but this left little time for family, especially when family concerns began to require more of his attention. Maria was hired as part of the housekeeping staff of a local hotel on a part-time basis.

Lydia, age 28, is of British descent, the youngest of three. She grew up surrounded by the "trappings of poverty" in London. She knew her father only "through the love and sadness I saw in my mother's eyes." Her father committed suicide when he was twenty-four and when her mother was six months pregnant with Lydia. After his death, her mother turned to alcohol and became addicted. She remained partially functional, just enough to maintain custody of the children. "Most of the places we lived were just filthy, dirty pits. That's the only way I can describe them to you. My mum counted on us kids to do the beggin' and the stealin'. I'm not exactly sure what she did with her time, other than drinking, I mean. She would set out in the morning with high hopes, but she was always drunk by the time we got home from school. The only thing that saved my brother and sister and me was spendin' weekends with our grandmother." By the time she reached her later teen years, Lydia was looking for a way to get out of London and to do something with her life. Several of her friends were applying to be nannies in the States, and

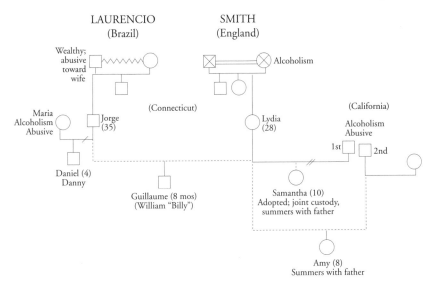

FIGURE 3.1 The genogram of the Laurencio-Smith family.

they encouraged her to add her name to the list. She decided to lie about her age, and six months later she was on her way to New Jersey.

Danny attends preschool and had changed from half to full days only two weeks before this meeting with the social worker. His teacher had already called Jorgé with concerns about Danny's aggressive behavior toward other children. At the age of four, he had experienced the tension between his parents, their separation, shuttling back and forth between their two different places, with multiple caregivers and teachers in both locations. The entrance of Lydia into his life, though she is seen as a loving and nurturing person, also has caused some confusion for Danny. He worries about his loyalty to his own mother and wonders if he is still "number one" with his father. Danny has also experienced the birth of a half brother with whom he now must compete for the attention of his father and Lydia. Jorgé reported that he could tell when Danny was working out some of his feelings by the way he physically expressed himself at a playground near their apartment.

Interpersonal

Lydia and Jorgé met in a local park adjacent to both of their workplaces. After they had seen each other several times over a four-month period, Jorgé introduced himself. Maria's absence of more than a year and the unsettled visitation schedule for her to see Danny were on his mind daily, and he found that Lydia was willing to listen to these concerns and help him think through what to do. Their relationship continued to grow, and one year after meeting in the park, they began living together. At the time of the meeting with the social worker, Lydia and Jorgé had lived together as partners for three years. This was her third committed relationship, his second. They fill the parenting role for four children: Samantha (age 10), Amy (age 8), Danny (age 4), and Guillaume (age 8 months). Samantha was born to one of Lydia's nieces who was too young to care for her infant daughter. Lydia was present at Samantha's birth and adopted her that day. Amy was born during Lydia's second committed relationship. Danny's biological parents are Jorgé and Maria. And Guillaume is Lydia and Jorgé's biological child. Guillaume is his Brazilian name, William is the British rendition, and at home he is known as "Billy."

Lydia and Jorgé are both U.S. citizens and currently live "on the edge" (Lydia's words) between poverty and lower-class existence. With four children, Lydia stopped working but has child support payments for Samantha and, sporadically, from Amy's father, and Jorgé now works one job rather than two. They have considered moving to a different part of the country where the cost of living is lower but are unable to cover expenses for such a move and, until recently, have felt that Danny still needs to have contact with his mother on a regular basis.

Considering extended-family members, neither Lydia nor Jorgé came into this relationship with examples from their families of origin of how to live as the common law blended family that they are today. Both are simultaneously filling the roles of parent and stepparent. For both, extended-family members are geographically on other continents. Jorgé's family would come in a crisis, as would Lydia's sister, but Lydia's mother has died and she has not seen or communicated with her brother in more than ten years. She heard from her sister that he had become "a vagabond-type person, roaming the countryside somewhere in Wales."

Other interpersonal relationships include the parent-to-child relationships, the siblings, and the ex-spouses and ex-partners. Even though Jorgé and Lydia do not fit the legal definition of stepparents, they still function in these roles in an emotional way with three of the children. Only Billy lives with his two biological parents. Both Jorgé and Lydia emphasize that "they are all *our* children" while at the same time, respecting the primary bond each has with her or his own biological children. Samantha has let Jorgé know several times, for example, "Thanks, but I just need my mom to help me with this one." When the children struggle with the differences between the adults in their lives, Lydia and Jorgé define this as "lucky" for the children because they "will always know there is more than one way to do things." No two children in this family have the same two biological parents. Lydia noted that her two daughters had had several conversations about this, and she, wanting to ensure an interpretation that would "make Danny feel good about himself," encouraged Samantha and Amy to think of these differences as what makes them unique and interesting to each other.

Sibling relationships reflect the dynamics in the parental/spousal relationship. Similar patterns between family members can be seen at different levels of that system. As tensions increased between Lydia and Amy's father, for example, Samantha and Amy had many more conflicts as well. With the recent suspicion of abuse of Danny by his mother, allegedly because of her anger at Jorgé for his relationship with Lydia, aggressive behavior was emerging in Danny toward his younger brother, Billy. For Danny, Samantha, and Amy the chance to develop their relationships together as siblings has been subjected to frequent interruption. Danny had been going to his mother's on weekends, and Samantha and Amy each spent summers with their respective fathers. The sibling subsystem is also characterized by two units related through age and gender: the older unit of two girls two years apart and the younger unit of two boys four years apart.

Ex-spouses and ex-partners form the final group of interpersonal relationships. At the time of the contact with their social worker, Jorgé and Maria had been separated for nearly five years but had not completed a divorce agreement. Maria and Jorgé still had regular contact, but Jorgé limited that contact to their parenting of Danny. Lydia's contact with her former partners was twice a year by phone with each one, at the beginning and ending of each summer to coordinate transportation for Samantha and Amy. Child support payments arrived on a predictable schedule: a lump sum once a year in September for Amy and "always approximately ten days late each month for Sam."

Social/Community

Contacts through work, friendships, the neighborhood, and their church formed the key components of Lydia's and Jorgé's social and community network. Lydia had resigned from her position as an assistant conference coordinator at a local hotel (a different hotel from the one where Maria worked) nine months earlier, in preparation for Billy's birth, but she still maintained regular contact with the friends she had made while working there. Jorgé was respected and appreciated at the advertising agency and had recently been offered an opportunity to further his education—"my dream come true." Both Jorgé and Lydia highly valued the friendships that they had formed, and they often referred to their friends as "being like family." This friendship network was definitely a strong resource upon which they could rely during a time of crisis or need. The support of neighbors was described as "a mixed bag." They lived in an ethnically mixed neighborhood, but they were the only couple of different ethnic backgrounds, and some people "just can't get their heads around that fact, though once they get to know us it usually changes." Jorgé explains that in Brazil, family arrangements are permitted to exist outside legal marriage arrangements. And the programs available at Lydia's church, such as the Here in Times of Need Committee, "gave me some reassurance that if things got worse, we could call on these people to help us out."

The Beginning Phase

Barbara, the social worker at the Family and Children's Services agency where Jorgé had phoned, first learned about Lydia and Jorgé from her on-site supervisor, who had taken the initial telephone information from Jorgé. This family was assigned to Barbara that same day, and she called Lydia and scheduled an appointment for the following day. One surprise for Barbara was Lydia's British accent. Barbara recalled seeing Jorgé's ethnicity identified as Brazilian, but now she faced her own assumptions that had caused her not to ask about Lydia's ethnic background. She found it difficult to understand Lydia's pronunciation, and she was not accustomed to being called "luv" with such frequency. It would be important to consider Jorgé's use of the language as well. This helped her tune in to an additional strength in this family: all three, and especially Danny, were likely to be at least bilingual and very possibly multilingual.

There was a second surprise as well for Barbara during the phone conversation with Lydia. She learned that Lydia and Jorgé had been living together for three years but were not married, as the intake report had indicated. Maria had refused to sign divorce papers, though both Lydia and Jorgé were hoping that this would eventually take place. Barbara was reminded of the importance of confirming information presented by secondary sources.

As they were talking, Barbara noted the "concern in Lydia's voice" and asked if she could be helpful. Lydia wondered if there was anything else they should be doing for Danny before coming for the appointment. Barbara referred to Danny's cuts, bruises, and burns and explained the importance of a physician's examination, not only to ensure that Danny would heal properly but also because the physician's report would serve as an important source of information if there was an investigation by Child Protective Services (CPS).

"It is one of those situations," Barbara continued, "when time is of the essence because, even after several hours, bruises can begin to fade."

"Thank you, luv. Yes, you know, we talked about taking Danny to his pediatrician. One of the marks just doesn't look right at all. So I'll call straightaway."

Barbara went on to ask Lydia if she was familiar with the requirement for social workers, physicians, and other professionals to report any suspicion of child abuse or neglect that came to their attention. Lydia mentioned that she had faced a similar situation when her daughter, Amy, was younger. Barbara said they would be talking further about reporting this incident during their meeting the next day.

"Is there anything else that would be helpful for you, Lydia?"

"Could you just pray for us, pray for this dear child?"

"I will do that. Until tomorrow, then?"

"Yes, we will see you tomorrow."

Social Worker's Preparation to See the Family

As Barbara prepared to see the Laurencio-Smiths the next day, two factors were immediately apparent. First, she herself had had an experience similar to Danny's. When she was four, her parents were separated, yet they lived close enough that she was taken back and forth between them. For Barbara's work with this family, she tuned in to the possibility that she might overidentify with Danny. At the same time, she could use this to increase her empathy, and she viewed that as one of her resources in this case.

Second, she was aware of her assumptions about Jorgé's and Lydia's ethnic backgrounds. She noted similarities with her own French Canadian background as well as differences that might play a role in their work together—for example, role stereotyping of the genders. This was a family with whom she would definitely want to request that they serve as her "cultural guides" (Leigh 1998) and with whom she would use the other guidelines of the ethnographic interview.

Barbara also realized the importance of carefully tuning in to other multicultural factors in addition to the information that she had so far about the family. Lydia had requested prayer, which could indicate that their (or at least her) religious beliefs might be a resource and that they might have access to a supportive group of people in the community. The intake information provided their place of residence and source of income, which led to an assumption about a lower-middle, or upper-lower, socioeconomic stratum, but this too would need to be confirmed. Their transitions from Brazil and Great Britain might point to different degrees of assimilation into their present community. As they were both U.S. citizens, immigration status, at least officially, did not appear to be an issue of concern. Barbara would keep this, as well as sexual orientation and differing abilities, in mind during the upcoming meeting.

What were the *strengths and resources* that helped them face the threat of further violence? And how was four-year-old Danny trying to make sense out of what was going on? Where were his fears and worries, and how was he coping? With anticipatory empathy, Barbara wrote: "The pain, sadness, and adrenaline related to fears around the violence could quickly consume me. I could feel that. So I knew it was time to try to step back from it or I would never be able to help. I had to remind myself about how much they have done already to deal with this. That is what we will build on."

Even though the *strength-based language* had seemed quite evident up to this point, Barbara checked for *deficit-based language* as well. She checked these uses of language in her own thinking, in that of her supervisor's report, and in Lydia's and Jorgé's interpretations. Many of Maria's behaviors were being described in deficit, pathology-based language. She also saw some indication that Jorgé might be attempting to take the blame himself. At one point, for example, Lydia mentioned that he had commented, "I was so stupid not to see this coming."

Barbara considered these deficit-based interpretations while also reaching beyond them to strengths. What might be the "underlying positive intentions" of these actions? What expressions of these same intentions could be *sustaining, enhancing,* and *creative* for this family rather than adding to their pain and oppression from the violence?

First Meeting: Arrival, Greeting, Use of Names, and Seating

To prepare for the arrival of the Laurencio-Smith family, Barbara reviewed her notes from the intake information, particularly next steps: to ask about Jorgé's friendship network, Danny's strengths, and Billy, Samantha, and Amy. When she approached the family in the waiting area, Jorgé was already on his feet, extending his hand. Danny was seated on Lydia's lap as they looked at a book. Barbara noticed their comfort together. Billy, Samantha, and Amy, though invited, were not present.

Taking the time to hear and repeat each person's name, asking about nicknames, showing interest in the origins of the name, can have a major impact on the first moments of interaction with a family. It is a natural way to establish the one-on-one connection with each member of the family, a crucial step for the work to come. It provides something familiar upon which the family members can focus, thereby helping to *diminish anxiety* related to the beginning. Asking about names is one way to proceed with the "friendly conversation" as recommended by the ethnographic interview. Introduction of names is also a universal *ritual of respect* in every culture.

Rather than guess about what Lydia preferred to be called, Barbara asked. She got the following response: "Cawlin' may Lid-ya is jess fine, luv, an' 'ere's our Danny." Danny hid behind Lydia and reached for his dad's hand. Both Jorgé and Lydia respected his need for reassurance, comforting him with their touch and their words. Neither of them made a request of Danny that he act or speak in a way different from his response. Children often experience the sheer size of adults as intimidating, but for children who have been physically abused, this reality often carries overwhelming fears and uncertainty. Barbara moved to where she and Danny could have direct eye contact, hoping to minimize that threat and *equalize the power* a little, letting him know she was pleased to meet him and glad that he had come. "I notice that your name on my form says Daniel. Do you like to be called Daniel?" He looked up at his dad and raised his eyebrows as if to say, "Now what?" It was significant to Barbara that Jorgé encouraged his son to answer for himself rather than answering for him.

"I like Danny because it fits me better."

"Okay, then, Danny it is. Thanks."

Rising, she invited them into her office.

Danny was fascinated with the fish in the aquarium in Barbara's office, and this became the subject of the "friendly conversation" at the beginning of their time together. Barbara asked about the absence of the other children. Billy had a slight temperature, and they had decided to leave the other children with a friend and neighbor. "The girls" were involved in play practice and had been given permission to do that instead of attending this meeting. Jorgé invited all to sit, "with *respeto* to Miss Warren." (Use of Spanish noted by Barbara.) Danny climbed up on the sofa next to Lydia, and Jorgé sat on the other side of Danny.

Barbara saw Jorgé's use of Spanish as her opportunity to inquire about what language would be most comfortable. Portuguese? Spanish? English? Jorgé explained that even though Portuguese was typically the language used in Brazil, Spanish was the language common to his parents and he sometimes still "fell into it." His mother was French, but when she met Jorgé's father, the only language they had in common was Spanish. With Lydia, Danny, and "the girls," however, the common language was English, and that would be fine here. This gave Barbara a natural opportunity to ask if they would be willing to act as her "cultural guides" when other information pertaining to cultural backgrounds would be helpful in their work together. They both smiled, saying they had learned a lot about doing this with each other over the years and appreciated that Barbara was open to their suggestions. "Our differences have saved us in many cases. When my ways don't work, we use his ways. When his ways don't work, we use mine," said Lydia.

Discovering What Help Is Desired: Hearing Their Story

Friendly conversation enables the transition to a greater sense of comfort as the session begins. Sometimes readiness to begin the work becomes evident through nonverbal behaviors. Lydia removed her sweater. Jorgé assumed a more relaxed position. Danny kept a close eye on his dad's and Lydia's behaviors and followed their lead, folding his legs underneath his body.

Jorgé then described a "new wrinkle" that had developed since Lydia's initial conversation with Barbara. The time for Danny to return to his mother's for the weekend was approaching, but Jorgé and Lydia wanted to keep Danny with them for his own safety. The immediacy of this need prompted Barbara to ask if Jorgé would like to use her phone to call the CPS worker to discuss the options with her. This seemed to be a relief for both Jorgé and Lydia (lowering anxiety and ambivalence). As they were responding, however, Barbara was aware of Danny's expression. The inclusion of children in discussions that have a direct influence on their lives is key to an empowering stance in practice, helping to *diminish oppressive* "power over" qualities in adult-to-child relationships, *equalizing power differentials*, and providing important modeling of *respect* for all persons in the family and how to use the needed *support of others.*

"Danny, do you know why your dad and Lydia want you to be with them this weekend and not visit your mom?" Barbara asked.

Nodding, Danny replied, "Cuz she hurts me sometimes."

JORGÉ: Yes, Lydia and I want to be sure that you are safe.
DANNY: I know. But when will I get to see her again?

Jorgé looked at Lydia, then they both looked to Barbara. Barbara recognized how important it was for Danny to hear the answer from his dad, so without speaking, she offered a hand gesture of support and encouragement to Jorgé.

JORGÉ: Danny, I don't know what to tell you about that today, but this is why we are here to talk with Miss Warren. We need her help to know when you can see your mom again. Is that okay with you?"
DANNY: Good.
BARBARA: Right now, we will call a person who can tell your dad about what will be best in the next few days. How does that sound?
DANNY: Good.

This exchange is an encapsulated example of addressing an immediate need, discovering what help is desired, offering that service, and in doing so helping to lower anxiety and ambivalence. An alternate way to proceed, one that could have served to equalize power even more effectively, would have been for Barbara to ask Jorgé and Lydia how they wanted to handle the weekend instead of offering her own solution—that is, making the phone call to CPS. The decision about engaging in this way is based on assessment of the degree of self-sufficiency or confusion seen in the family. It is not unusual to see higher levels of confusion in the earlier sessions, but Barbara observed that Lydia and Jorgé seemed able to manage the phone call without her help.

Jorgé did reach the CPS worker and received support to keep Danny with them over the approaching weekend. Jorgé also received some "coaching" on how to speak with Maria if she protested the change in plan. Even at this early stage in the beginning work with Jorgé, Lydia, and Danny, Barbara had assisted in integrating the support needed from others.

Once the immediate concern had been addressed, Barbara briefly summarized the picture she had so far of the situation they were facing, emphasized strengths and resources, checked for accuracy of her perceptions, and asked all three of them to go on "telling the rest of the story." Information from their responses was summarized earlier. When Barbara asked if there were other ways she could be helpful, Jorgé asked what could be expected from the investigation. This seemed to spark Lydia's memory about her phone call to the pediatrician, and she informed Barbara that they had an appointment with that doctor later that afternoon.

Barbara *provided information* about how the doctor would be able to look for specific signs to help her assess whether the injuries had been accidental or not. She might ask Jorgé, Lydia, and Danny about taking pictures, because such documentation could be very helpful later. Barbara also informed them about other aspects of the investigation: visits to their home and to Maria's home, as well as possible questions they might be asked.

> BARBARA: They [the CPS investigators] will be required to report on how the home is cared for, the level of cleanliness that is apparent, any safety concerns that they may notice. They will be asking about the food and clothing available for Danny, and they might ask how his recreational and learning needs are being met. They will ask about parental supervision, who is home with him and when. They may ask about his bedtime and will want to see that his bedroom, or where he sleeps, is adequate to his needs.

Jorgé asked, "Will Danny be required to answer questions?"

> BARBARA: They will want to speak with you, Danny, yes. These folks have talked with other kids like you, and they will want to take time to get to know you first. Your dad and Lydia will be right there with you. These people want do everything they can to make sure you don't get hurt again. How does that sound?
> DANNY: Okay, I guess.

(Danny had retrieved one of his books from Lydia's bag and was giving his attention to that. Though he was still attentive to what was going on, Barbara noticed, he was also letting the others know that he was ready to get on to other things.)

> JORGÉ: How long do we have to wait to know the results of the investigation and what we are supposed to do next?
> BARBARA: Sometimes investigations require more than one interview, so it can be difficult to give an exact time before the investigation starts. But we can continue meeting together as things proceed. Would that seem helpful for you?

Both nodded.

BARBARA: Jorgé, you had another question about what to do next, I think meaning after the investigation. Is that right?

JORGÉ: Yeah, but it may be too soon for that. I guess we have to wait to see what the report says first and then go from there. Is that right?

BARBARA: Yes, for the most part. Danny is fortunate to have the home you and Lydia provide for him. He can be safe even if he does need to stop the visits with his mom for a time or to have those visits supervised. Recommendations usually include what will be least disruptive for the children. It is likely that a plan will include a structured way of helping Maria receive additional supports so that she can correct her behaviors and better understand Danny's needs.

Strengths in Response to Oppressions

Family members often do not realize their true strength in coping until they face oppressive forces, such as Maria's suspected violence. Both Jorgé and Lydia were discovering strengths they had never had to call on before this experience. Barbara explained that looking closely at strengths and resources in the beginning is important because "in the end, they are what will get you through this experience with the best results possible." From an empowerment perspective, beginning with strengths is also one of the clearest ways to convey acceptance and to help lower anxiety and ambivalence.

For example, Barbara noted Jorgé's sense of urgency about the protection of his son. His response was immediate—no waiting for when he might be able to reach Maria, no waiting for how long it might take her to respond to him. This indicated strength in moving into an unpleasant, possibly frightening, situation rather than avoiding it. Jorgé could have reported only negative or damaging behavior of Maria's. Instead, he chose to report a past strength, her capacity to leave the room before hitting Danny, even though it now seemed possible that this self-control had broken down. Jorgé had offered to participate in getting the help Maria needed, recognizing that the "quality of my son's relationship with his mother in the future will depend a lot on what happens right now." Finally, Jorgé's ability to look ahead and anticipate complications for the upcoming weekend as well as to request assistance to manage those circumstances for Danny's safety indicated foresight, planning, and an openness to suggestions and feedback.

Barbara also noted Lydia's expression of support for Jorgé and her clarity about her role as second wife and stepmom. Lydia had mentioned her years of living single as helping her grow stronger in self-reliance, in developing a strong friendship network, and in learning about money management. Barbara also mentioned Lydia's interaction with Danny. "It is your lap he wants to be in. He seems to find comfort there." Lydia receives credit for the ways in which she has included Danny as an integral part of her relationship with Jorgé. There is no doubt that she is one of Danny's key resources at this time.

Danny's responses are common ones for children of his age who have been abused. The protection of the abusing parent appears to be based on survival messages: negative and painful attention is better than no attention at all; no attention at all means death. There is also a sense of loyalty to Maria that comes through and shows Danny's strength in wanting to let others know that she has good parts as well. Danny's expressiveness was noted, especially his expression of a worry about when he would see his mother again. Sometimes children receive silencing messages when their concerns arise—for example, "children are to be seen and not heard." Danny's behavior indicated that his sense of freedom to speak, "having a voice," about his concerns outweighed any messages he may have been given about remaining silent.

Even though Amy and Samantha had not attended the initial session, Barbara asked if they, too, were supports for Danny. "They are very much, you know, into their own little worlds most of the time, but they are both wonderful with Danny, too," was Lydia's response. "I think when they 'ear what's goin' on, they will be very upset at first but 'specially Amy will understand. She will know what to do 'cause she went through a similar thing with her dad. These girls have knowledge beyond their years, I tell ya. Usually I have regretted that this is the way things are for them. But now I see maybe they can use it, use it to help this little one."

Strengths were also evident in their interaction as a family unit. They spoke to each other directly, and both parents used age-appropriate language with Danny, making sure he understood what was being said. Supportive touching was part of their nonverbal communication with each other. Attentive listening and respect for different viewpoints were observed. Both Lydia and Jorgé placed Danny's needs ahead of their own needs.

Jorgé responded, "We can provide for our family. Things are tight, but I have a good job right now and other family who would help, too. Anything it takes to make sure this gets worked out, so that all the kids can get off to a good start in life, we will do it. We have limited financial resources, that's what I want you to know."

Oppressions

One result of witnessing violence or experiencing violence directly is powerfully oppressive fear. It is the death fear. The fear that ensues when one sees the violence an adult imposes upon a child can bring with it a fury that grows out of that fear. Exposure to violence leads to feelings of depression and anxiety, higher levels of antisocial and aggressive behaviors, lower school and work achievement, increased risk-taking, low self-esteem, and post-trauma symptoms such as nightmares, intrusive memories, and flashbacks (Gitterman 2001:15–16; Marans, Berkman, and Cohen 1996:106). For Jorgé, as one of the adults responsible for his son's safety, while he was simultaneously unable to reach Maria, the suspected source of the violence, the frustration and concern were almost more than he could bear.

Questions arose regarding the reported abuse against Danny. Were Danny's unsupervised contacts with his mom still continuing? The intake notes indicated a recent incident when Maria had picked up Danny at his day care and taken him to her sister's in a nearby community. The panic and uncertainty of those hours when Jorgé and Lydia did not know where Danny was were clearly stated in the report. In Jorgé's words: "It scared me to see the way she made excuses for what she had done. She can put on the charm, and I'm just afraid those people who investigate might fall for it. You know when they say 'behind closed doors,' well, that's what's going on here and I just don't know what to do about it." Barbara heard the helplessness that can come from such oppressive circumstances. This would become an area to pursue with Lydia, Jorgé, and Danny as the work continued.

The interlocking nature of oppressions makes it essential for the social worker to be curious about other oppressions as well. Even though violence was the most obvious oppression faced by the family, for example, Jorgé's explanation about financial resources might indicate that struggles with *poverty* also existed. Lydia had described them as living "on the edge" financially, and it was she who brought experience of poverty in England when she was a child. What *addictions* played a role in the dynamics of this family? There was a clue from Jorgé about Maria's drinking. If she was addicted, how did this place Danny at a higher risk when he was with his mother? Was Maria drinking when she was pregnant with Danny and, if so, had he been assessed for any complications related to fetal alcohol syndrome? Would Lydia's memory of her mother's addiction to alcohol play a role in how she saw Maria? Was anyone in the family being *discriminated* against in the extended family, in the workplace, in the community? Jorgé, Lydia, and Maria had been in the United States for eight years. They described a distance with some neighbors due to their not being married and living in a cross-cultural relationship. Were they experiencing any other barriers to creating an environment that provided safety and well-being for their family?

Barbara continued to listen for information pertaining to the empowering principles in addition to resources and strengths in response to oppressions: multicultural factors, needs, how they have strengthened themselves during other times of distress, support from others, how power is handled, and how roles are designated to achieve cooperation. The assessment also accounts for the family's process (both observed and reported), the family's structure (drawing the genogram together), family history (including historical oppressions such as slavery, the holocaust, or racial discrimination), further information about the individuals in the family, and physical and social factors of the surrounding environment (Lee 2001:209). The assessment is ongoing; information at one meeting may have shifted in another direction by the next meeting. Possibilities for action strategies for the middle phase of work begin to take shape when assessment information is still incomplete.

The Middle Phase

Between sessions Barbara reviewed the assessment information, noting gaps as well as strengths and resources at all three levels of the system—personal, interpersonal, and social/community. She found the information requested by the family and thought about additional information that they might need. What guidelines could she offer to extend or strengthen necessary coping skills? What groups might provide support, education, or mutual aid for this particular family? Would it be helpful to invite extended-family members or members of a non-kinship network to become part of the work with this family at some point? Barbara turned to the cross-cultural literature to learn more about British and Brazilian families. It seemed clear that Jorgé and Lydia saw this combination as a strength for them, and even though Barbara knew she would hear more from them about the uniqueness of this relationship, she also wanted to gain as much information as she could to support their observations and experiences.

The middle phase of empowering practice with families is characterized by three primary actions: providing information that the family requests or that the worker determines might be helpful, calling on coping skills seen in the work with the family, and considering possibilities for participation with others. In Barbara's initial work with Jorgé and Lydia, for example, she answered their request for information about what an investigation would involve. Danny asked for information about when he would see his mother again, and parents and social worker provided a mutual response. Their social and community networks indicated that they had resources for ongoing support and participation. All of these factors contributed to the family's capacities for coping.

Differential uses of these three core actions for family members occur at personal, interpersonal, and social/community levels. For example, all members of the family may need similar information about their involvement with the Child Protective Services investigators, but because of different developmental stages and different learning modes, that information will be delivered in person-specific ways. Coping actions for four-year-old Danny will look quite different from those needed by Samantha and Amy and by Jorgé and Lydia. Cross-generational participation within the family can be called upon as a resource, as well as same-generation participation. The social and community networks that are part of the life of the whole family can be engaged for support or buffered against if they are unsupportive.

The middle phase of work with the Laurencio-Smith family took place over nearly eight months. During that time several key events overlapped the investigation of Maria's behaviors with Danny and contributed to the complexity of their family life and to their need for ongoing work with Barbara. The first of those events happened in their third meeting, which took place at Jorgé and Lydia's home. Lydia reported that there was a "suspicious-looking mass" on her left lung and surgery was scheduled to remove it. Her sister, Maggie, had arrived the day before to help with the children's care while Lydia was recovering.

The second event occurred during the week after Lydia's surgery. Jorgé did not receive the promotion he had been anticipating at his work, but he did receive the first bill from Lydia's doctor and the hospital. The shock that his insurance would not cover her surgery because they were not married, on top of the realization that he would not be receiving the extra income that would have come with the promotion and the shock of how close he had come to losing Lydia were, in his words, "about to send me right over the edge."

And the third major event during this middle phase of work occurred approximately ten weeks after the beginning of their work with Barbara. After a series of threatening and, to Lydia, "frightening" phone calls from Maria, Jorgé decided that they would change their number to an unlisted one. One afternoon while Jorgé was still at work and Maggie had gone out to shop for food, Lydia responded to loud knocking at the door and discovered Maria standing in front of her. Maria began screaming immediately as she pushed her way through the door and into the living room of their apartment. "You took away my husband, and now you are trying to take my boy away from me. Well, you are NOT going to get him." They both could see Danny standing in the doorway to the kitchen. Maria began to move toward him, and Lydia found herself blocking Maria's path. The smell of alcohol on Maria's breath was "very overpowering" as she began beating Lydia with her fists.

Danny's shock at witnessing this scene had frozen him in place. Lydia was relieved to see Samantha put a firm arm around his waist, move him away from the door, and reach for the phone. Lydia learned later that Amy held and rocked Danny, "the same way Samantha had held and rocked Amy when my first husband got into his drunken rages." Samantha called 911. "Two police arrived within eight minutes of Sam's call." Samantha and Amy "did the best they could" to answer the questions asked by the police officers, but Danny was unable to speak at that time. He did not see the officer handcuff his mom, nor did he see her escorted out of their apartment building.

After this incident, Amy's schoolwork dropped off and Samantha began "acting like she thinks she's one of the parents around here rather than just being a ten-year-old" (Jorgé's words). Danny had nightmares, became afraid of going to bed, and would hide in the closet whenever there was a knock at the front door.

Lydia, who was still not fully recovered from her surgery at the time of Maria's attack, "just couldn't muster the oomph to defend" herself and had several bruises on her face and arms.

Empowering Responses

Barbara's responses to these events utilized the empowerment framework in consistent and creative ways. Her availability to the family during and after each of these pivotal events was responsive to their needs at the time. Sometimes contact was on a daily basis, sometimes every few days, until it gradually tapered off to once a week or longer as the family's ability to use their own resources diminished their need for Barbara's presence.

When Barbara learned about the mass on Lydia's lung and the upcoming surgery, the entire content of the "tuning in" she had done on the drive to their home "went right out the window. Maria had been evading the investigation by the CPS workers, and I was preparing to hear the most recent facts from Jorgé and Lydia and do some brainstorming with them about next steps if Maria was continuing to avoid contact with authorities. But all that got set aside when Lydia began telling me about the medical report."

As Barbara listened, she became aware that Lydia was uncomfortable because she lacked some information about what was going to happen during and after the surgery. (Awareness of needs.) "I think I got what she [the surgeon] said about what happens the day before surgery but then she lost me. I just couldn't follow after that and Jorgé said she talked so fast that he missed it too." (Personal need for information; interpersonal relationship with surgeon.) Barbara learned that they had hesitated to phone the doctor, assuming that she would be too busy to speak with them. Lydia and Jorgé's assumption was preventing them from getting the information they needed. Barbara "invited them to consider the difference between having the information they wanted and not having it. I offered what I knew about the connection between a person's emotions and the healing process."

Lydia decided that she did want the information (i.e., could she see the x-rays of her lung, what were the side effects of the anesthesia, would she have a scar, how soon could she go home, how long would the recovery take) before going into surgery. "But I do so much better face-to-face," she said, "that I think I'll wait to ask after I get to the hospital." So they chose to phone their doctor's assistant to make sure Lydia and Jorgé could have time to speak with the surgeon before the operation. In addition, they requested that Barbara go over their questions with them before that meeting and that she be there with them during the conversation with the doctor, "an extra pair of ears, you know" (Lydia's words). Barbara agreed to these requests and later identified this as "one of the many ways this couple took charge to empower themselves." Maggie was there to help take care of the children and to help out around the house while Lydia was recovering. Barbara remembered the committee at Lydia's church, the Here in Times of Need Committee, and asked if they had been contacted. They had not been, but at the mention of their name, Lydia remembered a friend on that committee that she wanted Maggie to meet. "When those two put their heads together, I won't have a thing to worry about." (Connecting family member with social/community network member; participation and support.)

Lydia and Jorgé did have the conversation with the surgeon the day before surgery, and Barbara was there with them. The doctor showed them the x-rays of Lydia's lung, explained what would be happening during surgery, and answered the rest of their questions to their satisfaction. Barbara "only had to interpret two or three times." After the conversation with the surgeon, Lydia commented, "I can do this now with all of me. Ya get what I mean here? Part of me was fightin' the whole thing before, I think. Now that part's ready to go along for the ride." Lydia's tumor turned out to be "malignant but contained." To be "on the safe side" she would receive a series of eight chemotherapy treatments, two times a week over the next four weeks, but additional surgery or treatment was not anticipated after that, at least not in the near future. She could anticipate experiencing a very low energy level, especially for at least a day or two immediately following each treatment.

The second major event that took place during the middle phase of work with this family occurred soon after Lydia's second chemotherapy treatment. Jorgé came home "angry, agitated, and scared." He had just found out that one of his younger coworkers had been given the position that he had hoped would mean a promotion for him. Barbara was scheduled to arrive for their next meeting at their home in about an hour.

Jorgé was still pacing when she arrived. Maggie was feeding the older children while Lydia was sitting in her rocking chair giving Billy his bottle. "I just don't get it," Jorgé said. "What happened? I deserve some kind of explanation for this. How are we supposed to pay all the bills? I can't believe this is happening on top of everything else that's going on." Reminders from her empowerment framework took Barbara to the importance of clarity and simplicity in her responses to the complexity faced by this family.

What was at risk? Jorgé's greatest fear was that he would not be able to provide for the needs of his family, that his income would not be enough to cover all the expenses, especially with Lydia's medical bills. Was it manageable? That was the unknown. All agreed, however, that some action needed to be taken to address these concerns.

Barbara invited ideas about what might help. Maggie was the first to speak, saying that she would be willing to stay until they felt they were on firmer ground. "I would just love to take care of your little ones, get to know them better, spoil 'em a bit if you'll let me. Besides having my room and board here in the States for a couple months sounds almost like a vacation to me." Both Jorgé and Lydia initially protested, aware that this would interrupt Maggie's life, something they were not willing to do. "What's there to interrupt, doll? I'm only part-time at my work and they can get along fine without me for a while and Johnny will probably be glad to have me out of his hair for a bit, too. What's family for, eh?" They accepted her offer.

"Well, I guess that puts one big piece in place then" (Lydia's observation).

Jorgé was shaking his head. "If only there was some way to tap into my insurance."

LYDIA: Well, I know a way.
JORGÉ: Yeah? What's that?

There was a moment of silence before Jorgé noticed the smile on Lydia's face.

JORGÉ: I get what you're thinking, Lyd. Let's get married. Huh? I'd love that, but you know what we're up against. Any ideas…anybody…how we get around that [meaning Maria]?
MAGGIE: What does she want from you? What is she afraid of if she signs those papers?
JORGÉ: At this point, I think she would go along if she knew she had enough money to live on. We had that conversation about a year ago, but then I couldn't pay her what she wanted. But I've had a raise since then and I think she did, too…
LYDIA: And I could go back to work…
JORGÉ: Oh, Lyd, we just need to get you healthy first.
LYDIA: Sure, but after that, well, there's no reason I couldn't at least do something part-time and maybe even from home so I can be here for Billy. You know it's not impossible.
BARBARA: Jorgé, has Maria indicated that she understands how alimony would work?
JORGÉ: Hm. No, I don't think so. It works differently in Brazil, and usually the woman has to be supported by her own family if there is a divorce. I bet that is what she's thinking. No wonder. She has no contact with them, except one brother. Tell me, if I did give her alimony, how long would that have to last?
BARBARA: That is something that could be worked out in the agreement, but it might include enough time for her to get some training to do something that would increase her earning potential so that she could support herself.
JORGÉ: Makes sense. What do you think, Lydia?
LYDIA: Would she agree to that? Worth a try, I guess.

Barbara offered information about additional options that could be made available to them through TANF (Temporary Assistance to Needy Families) and Emergency Family Assistance.

Jorgé noted, "That does take some of the pressure off if this alimony thing doesn't work, but I think we would like to see if we can make this work first."

A discussion followed regarding the additional expense that this would mean for Jorgé and Lydia. They were willing to try it, since it could lead to the marriage they had hoped for for so long and, in turn, to health insurance coverage for the medical bills.

Next, they considered the contact with Maria. Jorgé felt that he needed to be the one to speak with her, but because of the investigation by Child Protective Services, it was important to consider the timing of the request. Jorgé and Lydia both agreed that it would be better to ask Maria about the arrangement for alimony before she got the results of the investigation if that could happen. Barbara had a telephone number for Legal Aid and gave that to them, explaining what information would be required to compile the necessary documents. The process took several weeks. It did overlap with the results of the CPS investigation (supervised visits and alcohol addiction recovery classes for six months), but, somewhat of a surprise for Jorgé, this overlap seemed to have a beneficial effect in the relationship with Maria. Jorgé had been correct about Maria's worry about money. When she heard that she could receive a set amount each month for the next five years, she did agree to proceed with a divorce. She changed her mind a few times about the amount she wanted, but for Jorgé the end result of the signed agreement was "not as bad as it could have been."

In the midst of these occurrences and decisions, Barbara arrived at their home one evening to find an envelope on the table with her name on it. This was "the first thing on the agenda," they said. She opened it to find a handmade invitation to the marriage of Jorgé Laurencio and Lydia Smith the first week in June. "We wanted to make sure it happened while the girls are still here, before they leave for the summer. Can you come?" Barbara, without hesitation, said that nothing would please her more. She would definitely be there. It was to be a small ceremony in the chapel at Lydia's church. All four children, Maggie, Barbara, and two friends from the Here in Times of Need Committee were the attendees.

One week before the wedding, the third major event of this middle phase of work occurred. Maria's relapse into drinking and her arrival on the doorstep of Jorgé's and Lydia's apartment has been described above. In the hours and days that followed, Barbara once again was called upon to act as support, guide, and consultant. Lydia placed an emergency call to her immediately after the police left. Barbara, Maggie, and the victims' advocate from the local Safehouse program, who had been contacted as a routine part of the police response, arrived about the same time. They introduced themselves to each other, welcomed the advocate, and she explained her role to Jorgé, Lydia, and Maggie, telling them what services the Safehouse could offer to Lydia and the children and how to make contact if the need arose. Acknowledging the ongoing support provided by Barbara and Maggie, the advocate thanked them and left.

Emotions were high. Everyone was frazzled and upset, the children crying and holding on to one of their parents or Maggie. Barbara was holding and rocking Billy. Again Barbara recognized the importance of providing a time and space for those emotions to be heard and understood. As they responded to each other's support and as the tone began to calm, the questions began pouring out. Barbara actively assumed her role as guide by recommending that they all try to sleep and saying that they would meet again in the morning to begin answering the questions and concerns they had and to make decisions after that about what they could do to protect themselves from a similar incident in the future. They agreed that this would be best. Barbara said good night and left.

By the next morning, the three older children's responses to the violence of incident from the day before had already begun to manifest. Amy refused to get dressed for school, Danny ran to hide in the closet when Barbara knocked on the door, and Samantha was rushing to comfort and protect them both. As Barbara entered, beginning where the family was meant hearing their concern about Amy's refusal to go to school. What was at risk?

"Well," said Lydia, "nothing really is at risk with the school, but I'm afraid if we don't listen to Amy and what she needs this time, we might risk her not trusting us later on. She could miss a day or two and it would be okay. We can just call the school and let them know there's been a family emergency or something like that. Jorgé's already done that this morning for his job. I think Amy could do the same today, don't you think? Sam, do you want to take a day off, too?"

Samantha replied, "Well, Mum, if I could it would be better, I think. I'm not going to be thinking very clearly if I went to school anyway."

Considering what was at risk and whether it was serious enough to require action led to actions that helped the family members get back on track in a way that could address the emotional needs as well as set the stage for the planned work of their being together that morning. Danny seemed relieved by the decision as well and climbed up on the sofa to sit between Amy and Samantha. It occurred to Barbara that his two sisters were not about to leave him that day. She checked in with them about this, and they confirmed her observation. (Strength within the family upon which to build.)

Safety was the primary concern. Unfamiliar and angry people (the police, the Safehouse advocate, and Maria) had entered their home, adding to the uncertainty of the past several weeks and the disturbing conversations about other life-threatening events (Lydia's illness and surgery and Jorgé's job disappointment).

The fear was noticeably present in the room. Barbara used her awareness of the family's need and their strengths to help diminish the oppression of that fear.

Again, the first step was to listen. Barbara soon realized that each member of the family had given different meaning to the experience of Maria's violence, and this was resulting in each one needing a different way to restore a sense of safety. Jorgé wanted information about restraining orders. Lydia asked the children what they needed to feel safe. Samantha wanted more locks on the doors, and she needed to tell Lydia, "Don't ever open the door to her again." Amy was afraid to walk alone to her school three blocks away. All were talking at the same time, multiple requests being put on the table with no opportunity for others to respond. Danny began to cry, and everyone grew quiet as Samantha held him.

Guiding distressing feelings to a useful conclusion can be one of the most delicate and important tasks with which a social worker helps a family. Further steps in planning, decision making, and implementing are highly unlikely to occur until this happens. During the silence Jorgé and Lydia turned to Barbara.

> BARBARA: Danny, can you tell us what it is for you?
> DANNY: (Silence, and then...) She's my mom. When she's mean, she's scary. When she's nice...I love her when she's nice.
> BARBARA: I see. For you, it must feel wonderful to be with your mom when she's nice.
> DANNY: Oh, yes.
> BARBARA: And you would like to be somewhere else when she's mean?
> DANNY: Yes, but...I don't know how.
> BARBARA: If we could find a way for you to be somewhere else until your mom isn't mean to you anymore, would you feel good about that?
> DANNY: Yes, like when we go to that building by the lake? [The Family and Children's Services agency where the supervised visits with Maria took place.]
> BARBARA: Yes, like that.

Using words Danny could understand, Barbara explained the reasons someone else was present when he was with his mom, and she also explained some of what Maria was trying to learn in alcohol awareness classes and anger management classes. Months, as a matter of time, do not carry much meaning for a four-year-old. So Barbara explained that "later this year when the weather turns cold and the leaves fall off the trees, some people will see how your mom's doing. If she can be nice to you for the whole time you are together, then you can maybe spend more time with her."

Danny nodded. "But she hasn't learned it yet."

"That's right. But she will keep working on it."

"Okay. I'm happy to still see her, but it's okay we have a babysitter with us for now."

The others smiled at this. Danny had stopped crying and was physically more relaxed. It was time to turn to the requests made by others in the family and to give equal attention to their needs for safety. Barbara guided them back to those earlier requests. Jorgé offered to go with Samantha to get the lock she wanted and said he would put it on the door. Maggie, Lydia, and Samantha all offered to walk to school with Amy. Danny wanted to be included. "Can I come too?" Barbara provided information to Jorgé about restraining orders. The Safehouse advocate had left some printed materials about both temporary and permanent restraining orders and the procedures involved. Barbara indicated that Jorgé might wish to take a look at that information and let her know if he had other questions the next time they met.

The remainder of the middle phase of work took place over the next five months. For the three summer months, Amy and Samantha were with their respective fathers. They talked on the phone to each other at least two times a week and with Lydia, Jorgé, and Danny once a week. Lydia completed her chemotherapy in mid-June and would continue with six-month checkups for the next five years. Barbara assisted Jorgé when some of the negotiations about his medical insurance hit a snag related to Lydia's "preexisting condition." After Jorgé provided some additional paperwork and agreed to an adjustment to his monthly fee for this benefit, his insurance retroactively covered most of the expenses for Lydia's surgery and treatment.

No further incidents occurred with Maria during the remainder of the middle phase. Jorgé continued to take Danny to the agency for the supervised visits, and he continued to send monthly alimony checks to Maria. Maggie returned to England at the end of July. Lydia contacted her former employer and explained her need for part-time work that she could do in her home. She had maintained contact with several of her coworkers during and after her surgery, and now this part of her support network was more than willing to welcome her back as part of their staff. From preparing conference packets, to sending out mass mailings, to preparation of minutes to meetings, to phone calling, she had more than enough to keep her busy. The added income helped relieve Jorgé's stress about financial concerns. But he did accept Barbara's offer to help the two of them work out a simple budget. For the first time since coming to the United States, they started a savings account. The first item on the list for those savings? To take a honeymoon.

The Ending Phase

Lydia and Jorgé had observed in previous years that there was an adaptation phase when Samantha and Amy returned from their summers with their fathers and reintegrated into this, their "other" family. Because of the events that had occurred this year before they left, Jorgé and Lydia had requested that their time with Barbara's support continue at least through the girls' return and the beginning of the school year. As often happens when a family faces traumatic and highly stressful times together and comes through them intact, there was evidence of an even stronger bond as "family" when Amy and Samantha returned. Lydia phoned Barbara before the meeting to tell her "the girls' adjustment to being back is going much better than expected. It's really fine, but we would still like you to come. We were thinking that this might be our last time to see you, at least for working on all our stuff. Could you stay for dinner?" Barbara could easily accept this invitation within the whole context of her work with this family. Many important factors come to bear when social worker and family can share in this way: the symbolism of sharing a meal together carries many relational meanings; it has a simple yet profound capacity to connect people across cultures; it is often used, in all cultures, to fulfill the purpose of acknowledging and celebrating a turning point, a major transition or a rite of passage. In addition, Barbara was familiar with the need expressed by many of the families with whom she had worked, the need to find a way to "give back" at the end of their work. The social worker's only task at those moments is to graciously receive the gift in a manner that reflects the meaning, cultural and relational, that the family places on the gesture.

On the evening of their meeting, Samantha and Amy reported how they had had time to think about what had happened in the spring and how they all had responded as a family.

Samantha's words to Barbara were: "We are all so different, I mean we all come from different backgrounds. You listened to each one of us and made me glad that we are different. I don't think we would have managed all that we went through without all those different ideas about what to do. And that includes Aunt Mag, too. Mom and Dad—Dad Jorgé, that is—talk a lot about how being different is one of the best things going for us as a family. But now I know what they mean. It makes us a lot more interesting than some of the other families I know, too."

Jorgé nodded and commented, "I'm thankful for the work we did with our finances. That's important, but the biggest gain for me is that now we are married! (Hugs Lydia.) And I feel lots closer to Amy and Samantha. We weren't quite sure of each other before, I think, but now we are at a different place. Huh, girls? Do you think so, too?" (They both agree.)

A family's use of the past tense to describe the events related to their distress is one clue that they are moving into the ending phase of the work. The time of distress is being placed in the background rather than the foreground. Sometimes, as in Samantha's case, family members also identify gains realized in the work. These statements can serve as prompts for the social worker to reach for information from the family members about the other key tasks of the ending phase: dealing with the feelings that may arise around the ending, reevaluating the connections with the social/community networks and strengthening those where necessary, and mutually evaluating the work together (Lee 2001).

Lydia commented, "I think in looking back, I'm relieved about the way things turned out with Maria. We could work out a plan that met her needs, but, even more important, it could meet Danny's needs to be with his mom on a regular basis in a safe way, too. We don't have to end up with bad feelings toward her. That makes it easier for all of us, even though we still take it one step at a time."

Lydia's concern for Maria's well-being is a gift to this whole family. Often there are family members, however, who are so centered on the needs of others that they may pass by the opportunity to speak about the gains they have had for themselves. Barbara was alert to what was missing in Lydia's comments in this regard and invited her to consider her own gains as well.

"For me? Well, I have Jorgé and this wonderful family. And Sam, you are so right. We each brought something different to get us to where we are today. You had your experience with your dad and knew to call 911. Amy, you understand Danny in a way that none of the rest of us can. Danny, you are so brave to remind us how special your mum is to you. Jorgé does a great job with all the money stuff, which I am a real doofus with. Little Billy just smiles at everyone and seems to let us know that everything will be fine. And me? Well, I'm alive and, believe me, with my family around me, I am not taking that for granted."

Barbara inquired about the supports they had in place now that could help them maintain what they had accomplished. Separated by huge geographic distances from extended family, this family had had to build connections socially and in their community that could provide support during times of need. The most significant and available of those connections had been not only maintained but actively utilized throughout the work with Barbara. On a feeling level, the Laurencio-Smith family was ready to party.

"So, we are thinking of this as a kind of welcome ending tonight, and we have one of our British-Brazilian feasts for you. We hope you'll enjoy it because we know we could never have done all this without you and we want to say thank you."

And from Danny: "Let's eat cake!"

Reflections Through an Empowerment Lens

Was the purpose of empowerment practice served in Barbara's work with this family? In what ways was the family's sense of well-being sustained, enhanced, created? Guided by the empowerment framework with its principles, actions, and roles, Barbara's work moved through beginning, middle, and ending phases with a balance of assisting and guiding. Integration occurred among and between personal, interpersonal, and social/community levels. In her process analysis and self-evaluation, Barbara states:

This was the first time I had intentionally begun work with a family determined that I would look for their strengths, to *constantly* look for their strengths, and go from there. What a difference! I had the empowerment ideas in the back of my mind so that all I had to do was take the time to see where things were when we got together and pick up what they were saying they needed at that time. "At that time" was important for me. I know I sometimes get too far into the past or too far ahead and then I miss what's going on or it only makes the family confused or we get stuck. Often with the family, I could hear the message in my head, "Just listen. For right now, just listen." They always said or did something that let me know which one of the empowerment ideas was the direction to take, which action to take, what my role was for that moment. The lead comes from the family.

But I give this family so much credit. They are incredible. (I wonder if I won't see what is incredible about every family by looking for strengths instead of focusing on what's going wrong all the time.) It was evident from the start that Lydia and Jorgé had found their own sense of trust, comfort, and stability with each other before all the events of last spring started to happen. I tried to tap into that as much as possible. [Sustaining.] They did face a time, however, when Jorgé was so worried about the finances that he wasn't much comfort for Lydia. Unfortunately, that was at the same time she was so ill from her treatments and she could not be a very strong support for Jorgé either. That was when their family and community supports played such a key role. [Enhancing.] This was a real lesson for me about calling in the network. Lydia's church support group and Maggie, her sister, did what I never could have done on my own. Their presence sure made my work more doable, and Lydia got much better support as well. They could be with her every day cooking meals, helping the kids with homework, doing the food shopping. In the end, the family did seem to arrive at a new understanding of who they are together as a family. [Creating.] They probably would have eventually gotten there without all the turmoil, but maybe not. It was as if their true colors could shine in their response to something that threatened one of their members. I have this awesome respect for who they are and what they did. I'm glad I could be a part of it.

Another aspect of the evaluation of Barbara's work is to revisit the major oppressive forces faced by the family and ask if diminishing those oppressions helped lead to a heightened sense of well-being for the family. The Laurencio-Smiths faced oppressions of violence, major financial stress, the influence of Maria's addiction to alcohol, and for a short time Jorgé wondered about discrimination as a factor in his being overlooked for the job promotion. The threat of violence was addressed with a multifaceted response at personal, interpersonal, and social/community levels. First, Barbara provided a context in which each individual family member could speak about his or her fear and say what was needed to help gain a greater sense of safety. Interpersonally, both Danny and Lydia experienced direct assaults from Maria, and Jorgé was included through frequent verbal assaults. Supervised visits plus a temporary restraining order addressed interpersonal needs for more safety. And, finally, social/community resources were called upon through Barbara, their social worker, through the investigative team at Child Protective Services, the police, and the advocate from Safehouse.

Maria's addiction was addressed through the alcohol awareness classes and later, through her connection with an AA meeting in her community. Jorgé and Lydia, with Barbara's help, began talking with the three older children about how alcohol "can turn a nice person into a mean person" and answered any questions the children had as they tried to gain understanding about Maria's behavior. It was particularly important to let them know that Maria's behavior was not their fault, that they were in no way to blame for what had occurred.

The oppression of the financial situation was addressed through multiple efforts as well. Following through to gain medical insurance benefits, working on a budget and savings plan, providing information about alimony payments and moving forward with the procedures to get that in place, including the contact with Legal Aid, represented the personal, interpersonal, and social/community dimensions of diminishing the worries about the family's financial well-being. Jorgé did speak with his supervisor at work and learned that the job that he had wanted required training in a specific skill that he did not have. His supervisor said that he respected Jorgé's coming to get more information about what had happened, that he was very pleased to know that Jorgé was interested in advancing, and that he would let him know when there was another opening.

Though Lydia's potentially life-threatening illness was not included in the major oppressions of focus, it is important not to overlook its impact on the family, particularly that it was discovered and had to be dealt with at the same time they were facing the other events. The exhaustion, uncertainty, and confusion of families who are thrust into the world of hospitals and medical personnel, plus the length of time during which the illness has a "presence" of its own in the family, can all result in a kind of oppression that holds a family hostage as much as violence and poverty do. Additional needs for coping, information, and the support of others were as much the result of Lydia's illness as they were of the other oppressions.

Multiple oppressions were addressed by this joint work between worker and family. Strengths and resources, resilience, information, coping, and support from others all contributed to diminishing the capacity of those oppressions for interrupting the family's ability to move on with their lives with greater choice and a greater sense of well-being—that is, to be empowered. Sometimes the work to diminish the impact of oppressions lies beyond the reach of the family members.

This was evident in Maria's choice about what to do with her addiction to alcohol. Even so, Jorgé and Lydia can continue to gain information about addictions and make their own choices about how to cope and how to receive support from others facing similar circumstances, thus taking actions that help their family move from oppression to empowerment.

4

The Williams Family: New Lives Beyond Incest

As their twenty-fifth wedding anniversary celebration came to a close, Jane Williams (age 50) had a clear sense that "all was not right" with her family. But she and her husband, John (age 52), and their two daughters, Linda (age 18) and Susan (age 16), still had visiting family and friends to entertain and take care of. Then, the busyness of their middle-class suburban lifestyle took over once again. The moment of clarity passed, but not for long. It was only one month later that the telephone call came from Susan's school social worker with a recommendation that the whole family be seen for professional help. Jane accepted the tone of urgency and seriousness in the social worker's voice, hearing it as a message that confirmed her own disturbing sense just a few weeks earlier.

Personal, Interpersonal, and Social/Community Levels

Personal

The four individuals in this family are Jane, the mother; John, the father; Linda; and Susan (figure 4.1). Jane was the younger of two children in her family of origin; she had had an older brother, also named John, who died in a car accident at the age of 30. Jane was 28 at the time of his death. Jane lost both of her parents when she was very young. Her mother, Nell, died of stomach cancer when Jane was 11; her father, George, of a heart attack when Jane was 13. Jane then went to live with a maternal aunt and uncle, Alice and Jerry, and her two cousins, Jacob and Ray. She lived with this family until she left for college, at the age of 17. Jane experienced great conflict with both her stepmother (her dad remarried five

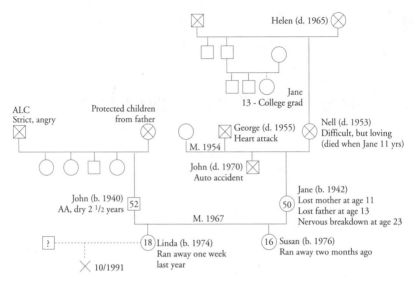

FIGURE 4.1 The genogram of the Williams family.

months after her mother's death) and her aunt, but she found ongoing support, love, and "a deep friendship" with her maternal grandmother, Helen. Jane earned a degree in elementary education and taught second grade for several years before she met John. She stopped working when they married.

John is the youngest of five in his family of origin, all of his siblings still living at the time of the work reported here. The oldest two are Barbara and Joan, then a brother, Nathan, and another sister, Eloise, followed by John. John describes his father as "a strict, angry abuser of alcohol who beat his children" and his mother as "the one who tried to protect us from our father." Both of John's parents had died in the past four years—his father of complications related to multiple sclerosis almost four years ago and his mother after suffering a series of strokes two years ago. John was on speaking terms with his sisters Barbara and Joan; he felt "guilty and inadequate" about his brother, Nathan, who was mentally retarded; and he expressed uncertainty and "confusion" about Eloise and why she did not want him near her children. "I just can't figure her out," he said. With an "I'll show you" attitude, John had put himself through law school, sometimes working three jobs to do so, but his father's words "You'll never amount to anything" were still ringing loudly in his mind.

Linda was attending a junior college in a nearby community, living with friends and making weekly or biweekly visits home. She had "made an intentional choice to hold off on a serious relationship for now, wanting to get my career goals sorted out first." Her major areas of academic interest were microbiology and space aeronautics: "I'd really like to understand what happens to our tiniest life-forms when they are in space." As for hobbies, she "confessed" to a passion for bike riding. In the record from the school social worker, there was a note that Linda had "run away from home for one week" last year, during her senior year in high school.

Susan was a junior in high school. She had difficulty verbalizing during the early sessions with the social worker, so information about her initially came from her parents, Linda, and the report from the school social worker. Susan had always been a strong student, quiet and serious about her work in the classroom but fun-loving and involved with a network of friends she enjoyed. Her sister described her with affection, as "a real whiz on the computer." Jane had become concerned in recent months when there was a marked drop in Susan's grades and she had also run away to a friend's home for a few days. When Jane asked Susan about her reasons for running away, Susan replied, "I just can't talk with you about it right now, Mom" and retreated into silence.

Interpersonal

The picture of the Williams family broadens through the relationships among and between the members of the family: the spouses and parents; the two sisters; and the four parent-to-child dyads—that is, Jane/Linda, Jane/Susan, John/Linda, John/Susan. Extended-family members also contribute to the interpersonal dynamics.

As spouses, Jane and John spoke of the relative separateness of their lives, that it had been more than ten years since they had taken a vacation together, though each individually had an annual vacation with respective groups of friends. They had separate circles of friends and colleagues, separate activities on the weekends, and often spent their evenings at home in different rooms in the house. As parents, they even spent separate time with Linda and Susan and seldom planned activities with all four together. The "impending empty nest" was a theme that came into the conversation on a regular basis, usually introduced by Linda but minimized or avoided by both parents.

Linda assumed a role of "responsible oldest" with Susan and sat with her arm around Susan throughout most of the first session. Linda glanced at Susan frequently, seeming to watch her face for expressions that would give clues to how Susan was doing. When Susan did look up, she looked only in Linda's direction, avoiding eye contact with both parents and social worker.

Jane's relationship with both of her daughters was characterized by concern, a noticeable contrast with John's "apparent disgust" toward them. "Jane physically moved closer to Linda and Susan, seeming to indicate a strengthening of her connection with them." Finally, much still remained unknown about the extended-family members; that would be an area to explore for potential resources and supports.

Social/Community

The Williamses' social/community network included school, workplace, neighbors, friendship and peer groups, and professional organizations. As the story of this family was revealed, additional resources were seen to provide structured environments, information, safety, support, validation, and accountability. Unfortunately, through the actions of certain individuals in those same agencies and institutions, a social/community context existed in which silencing of abuse was perpetuated and enabled for too long before being exposed and reported.

The Beginning Phase

After speaking with Susan's school social worker, Jane Williams immediately phoned the local mental health agency and asked to speak with Liz, a social worker who had been recommended because of her experience and her specialization in working with families. Jane told Liz that her younger daughter's (Susan's) school social worker, Sarah, had strongly recommended that the family seek professional help. Susan had told a friend that she was thinking about running away again, for the second time, and that friend suggested that Susan talk with Sarah first. After talking with Susan, Sarah recommended that the family be seen together at the mental health agency, and she recommended Liz by name. Jane's request for what she hoped to have happen in the work with Liz was "for the family to all get along better." Liz agreed to see the family, and an appointment was scheduled for later that same week. Liz also told Jane that she (Liz) would like to speak with the school social worker (Sarah) at some point after receiving a signed release from Jane and Susan. From Liz's case notes:

> The Williams family arrived at the mental health agency one evening not long after the dinner hour. In meeting the family members for the first time, I noted Mr. Williams's abrupt handshake and angry expression and the red and teary eyes of both daughters, Linda and Susan. Jane, the mother in the family, made the introductions, stating a group preference for first names. John, however, was the one who directed the family into the room and indicated where everyone should sit. I noted how each of the daughters and Jane responded to this directive. Susan sat immediately where her father directed her, but Linda, the older daughter, and Jane glanced at each other, rolled their eyes, and chose different seats than those that John had indicated.
>
> I welcomed the family members individually and asked them what their understanding was about the reasons they had come. Jane commented on the

tension, John said that "this whole thing" was "ridiculous," and both Linda and Susan began to cry. I asked for clarification from John about what he meant by "this whole thing." He responded with a string of accusations toward Jane, and then toward his daughters, calling Linda a "whore."

Seeing the stunned expressions on Jane's, Linda's, and Susan's faces and noting their silence, Liz chose to begin with these responses. She asked if they would be willing to provide background information about the intensity of the emotion in the room. Both daughters and Jane readily agreed. John nodded but continued to stare angrily in Linda's direction.

Even at these early moments in the work, Liz recognized how the family members were coping with the painful information they were carrying. Liz entered her work with this family by setting the stage with the quality of the initial greeting and by taking steps to lower anxiety and ambivalence. She made a mental note of the steps ahead for this initial contact: discovering what help was desired; offering services so they could determine if they were in a place that fit for them; and beginning to approach the work.

Strengths in Response to Oppressions

Working from an empowerment perspective, Liz tuned in to the strengths of the family members from the beginning moments of contact. She was aware of the strong gender alliance between mother and daughters in this family. She saw Jane's openness to facing the reality of her family's situation as one strength that would carry the family through the major distress of what was yet to be revealed. The sibling respect, caring, and concern between Linda and Susan was an additional strength that stood out in this family and a major strength upon which the social worker could build to assist the family. John was credited with being there, making the effort to show up for a meeting that he claimed was "ridiculous." Even though the spousal/parental subsystem looked strained and distant, their presence provided a potential message about the hope that the situation might change. These strengths were readily identified by the social worker in the first session with the Williams family. As is true with all families, however, other strengths continually emerged as the work progressed.

Oppressions

These early transactions with the family gave information about the power and control issues in the family, abuses of power that could lead to an array of oppressions. John used directives, orders, and accusations, behaviors that are all characteristics of verbal abuse. Responses that provided evidence of oppression were visible as well. The silencing and unquestioning "obedience" of Susan, Linda's and Jane's resorting to the indirect communication of rolling their eyes, and the crying as a functional coping choice on the part of both Susan and Linda were all examples of nonverbal behaviors that work hard to communicate messages when the words behind them cannot be spoken without some kind of price to pay. The dynamics of secrecy, threats against speaking out, psychological and emotional violence, age and gender bias, manipulation, and tactics of "power over" were being used to maintain oppressive forces existing in this family.

Also using the empowerment principles, Liz noted multicultural information about the Williams family. Some of it was known or apparent (genders, Linda's and Susan's ages, the use of English, their current geographic location in their community); some was missing (John's and Jane's ages, their preferred religion or spiritual beliefs, differing abilities); and some seemed apparent but were acknowledged as assumptions needing clarification (ethnicity, socioeconomic status, sexual orientation, emotional and chronological developmental stages).

Discovering What Help Is Desired

Liz listened for what it was they said they needed, and she kept mental notes of what she perceived as their needs as well. She had invited the family to take a step back from John's last statement and provide some background so that she could gain a better understanding of what might have led up to where they were in the present. She explained that background information helps identify ways in which the family has dealt with times of distress in the past. Information gathered about family coping skills previously used provides a directly relevant way to *begin with strengths.* They had survived. What had they done to help make that happen? Such information was essential to the work because some of those same skills could be used to relieve current stressors as well. Emphasizing the ways in which the family members had coped with earlier challenges also set the stage for where the work would go during the middle phase. After Liz gave a brief description of the genogram as a visual tool to help her understand what was going on in the family (see figure 4.1), she invited John to tell his story about how he had managed earlier times of distress in his family and how those efforts played a role in the situation they were presently facing.

From Liz's notes:

John, 52 at the time this information was given, initially hesitated to participate and Jane began to provide information about his family. When she "didn't get it right" John spoke for himself. This exchange gave me one picture of how they interact with each other. John is the youngest of five children and, while growing up, faced all that being "youngest" meant in his family of origin: "getting teased, getting left out, getting laughed at." He experienced the deaths of both of his parents; his father's described as "alcohol related" and his mother's as a heart attack. He lived in a family that knew the oppression of addiction, his father an "angry abuser of alcohol." He coped with the uncertainty felt by a child when parents express major conflicts. John also used alcohol as a form of coping, claiming that it helped him "care less about what other people thought" but also meant that his anger got "out of control too many times." He turned to AA as a means of helping him cope with his drinking problem and with "doing a better job with how anger got expressed." His anger, witnessed in the session, was particularly directed toward Jane and Linda. He connected this background with the present, saying that his daughters didn't know how lucky they had it, not having to grow up with a father like his, and that they should be more grateful to him instead of "causing all this trouble."

Jane's coping capacities were revealed in response to an unusually large number of losses: her brother's death in a car accident; her mother's death when she was 11; feeling "shut out" by her stepmother; her father's death; her grandmother's death; and her own suffering what she called a "nervous breakdown" that felt like the loss of her mind. She connected these experiences with the present by pointing to the "impending empty nest" which meant the loss of her daughters from their home. With wise insight, Jane connected this loss with her earlier losses, then turned to her daughters: "But you must know that whatever you need is most important to me."

Liz asked Linda and Susan if they could tell their views of the background that led up to tonight's meeting:

Susan began to cry at the same time Linda began to speak. Linda glanced at Susan and began crying as well but managed to say, "I can't talk with him in the room." I nodded and asked, "Would you like to ask him to wait in the waiting room while we talk for a while?" Both Linda and Susan nodded and indicated that they wanted their mother to stay. There was a brief silence before Linda spoke to me. "Could you do this part for us, asking my dad to go to the other room for right now?" I asked John and he agreed to wait outside.

Still working to discover what help was desired, Liz noted that Linda and Susan had requested a procedure that is frequently recommended at this point in the beginning stage of the work. With "power and control" dynamics evident, the more controlling family member, in this case John, claimed one kind of help while other, less controlling members, Linda and Susan, were required to acquiesce according to roles scripted in the family. There was evidence that they were afraid to speak freely and voice their own viewpoints. Rather, they were speaking according to what they thought John expected. These observations provided valuable information about the use of oppressive communication styles in the family, ones deeply embedded in the family's overall transaction dynamics. Asking members individually, or in subgroups such as the siblings, was one way to allow the Williams family members to discuss the help they were seeking, individually as well as for the family as a whole.

Also from Liz's notes:

> I could sense that a significant shift was about to take place in the work and that even though I was still gathering information from the family, John's leaving the room meant that we were moving to a deeper level somehow. I chose to see this as the start of the middle phase.

At the time of the transition from the beginning phase to the middle phase of the transactions with a family, the focus and the direction of the work are enhanced by the social worker's internal check regarding the actions for empowering practice: what information has been gained so far and what is still needed, by and for both social worker and family members; what coping skills are evident and which additional ones could be helpful to consider; and what forms of participation with others have been identified so far and what possibilities for participation might become part of the work in the next stages. For Liz, information about the history, structure, and emotional climate of the Williams family was coming into clearer focus through observation and the use of the genogram.

In her *role as guide*, she took the work in a direction that could acknowledge the exchange and its emotion while moving to a more neutral path, one of gathering background information about coping resources. The forms and quality of participation with others—extended family, friends, peers, coworkers, supports in school and community—however, were still a big question mark for Liz. She simply made a mental note of this gap as the work moved into the middle phase.

> Linda held Susan's hand as she asked me for reassurance that everything was confidential and that no sound could travel through the door. I informed them of the limits of confidentiality, that if there was any information about harm to self or others or any information about child abuse or neglect, that I would be required to report. Linda nodded, "Yeah, we actually knew that part," and turned to Susan, "Okay, sis, do you still want to do this?" Susan, still crying and unable to speak, nodded for Linda to go ahead, but she pointed to Jane and motioned for her mother to sit beside her.
>
> "Mom, are you prepared to hear some really bad news?" Linda began. Jane shifted slightly then and said she was ready. Linda's story began approximately five years earlier, when she was 13, with the night her dad came into her bedroom and

began the incest. The abuse continued over the next four years with a frequency of one to three times a week. His threats about what he would do if Linda told any-one—"ANYONE!!"—were so convincing that she kept this buried even through the experience of becoming impregnated by her father. A subsequent abortion (ar-ranged by her father) took place just last year, when she was 17. Jane thought Linda had accepted a position as a camp counselor in Vermont, but now the pieces came together into a much different picture. When Jane heard about the abortion, she lowered her head into her hands and began to cry. Linda went on to say that she had the strength after that to refuse her father, but when she asked Susan why she was trying to run away again, and if their dad was doing "anything weird," Susan was able to tell her sister what had happened. John had begun exactly the same behavior with Susan. This was the turning point for Linda. "No more silence, we both agreed on that. No more covering for him. My dad needs help. My sister needs help. Now, after this, our mom needs help. I need help. We all need it."

Breaking the many years of silence was an act of courage and determination for both Susan and Linda. Liz verbally recognized the strength it took for them to take this step. She wondered if and how this violence connected with other op-pressions—addiction, poverty, and discrimination—and what role those factors played in this family's situation. The abuse itself was, without question, defined as a major experience of violence. John had already mentioned his "drinking prob-lem" and his involvement with AA. Information about other addictive behaviors was right around the corner. And Jane's, Linda's, and Susan's financial reliance upon John was about to come to an abrupt end, practically overnight, plunging them to the brink of poverty. John would face not only a drastic change in his monetary income but also what he later came to call "a poverty of my soul." Age and gender discrimination were most visible so far; other areas of discrimination were also possible with this family.

Linda's story of her father's incestuous behavior and the damage that she and her sister felt included familiar responses to trauma: anxiety about the possible recurrence of the event, confusion and memory problems, diminished interest in school and/or work, mood swings and sleep problems, and withdrawal from relationships. Complicating the process for both Linda and Susan was the reality that "traumatic events caused by known and trusted persons or institutions can be far more harmful than those inflicted by strangers or unknown entities, the reason being that they call into question the victim's ability to trust as well as his or her competence in choosing safe persons or institutions" (Everstine and Everstine 1993:39). Liz realized that Susan, and Linda to a different degree, might find it dif-ficult to feel they could trust her. The task of decreasing anxiety and ambivalence, a core task of the beginning stage of empowering practice, continued to be of particular importance.

To accomplish this task Liz explained that their responses were typical and natural, ones that were "built in" for survival purposes, to protect the person's emotional well-being or to serve as part of the healing process. (Providing information.) These comments seemed to be particularly calming for Susan, who said that one of the most difficult things for her had been thinking that all the problems she'd been having meant there was something terribly wrong with her. Liz normalized those behaviors, identifying them as efforts to cope with a terrible experience, lifted Susan's negative self-judgment, and allowed her to restore a degree of trust in her own perceptions.

Linda's story also caused Jane to move, once again, into the beginning steps of the coping response. She stayed in her shock, numbness, and disbelief for only a short time and appeared to have no doubts about what her daughters had expressed. She faced shattered assumptions that no longer described her family, which was clearly not just the "normal suburban family with two kids, a dog, and an SUV." Those assumptions offered little now in the way of accounting for real outcomes. They were recognized, instead, as the facade. What had been seen as a set of "guides to reality" was now "powerfully inadequate and painfully false" (Janoff-Bulman 1999:311).

Letting go of the illusions about the way things had been in the past and moving into an acceptance of the way they were in the aftermath of this information from Linda and Susan was also part of the beginning of coping for Jane and her daughters. Thoughts about themselves and the world around them were different now (Peterson and Moon 1999:270). *Creating* a different set of beliefs and assumptions began. This new set accounted for the traumatic experience in a way that earlier assumptions could not and provided meaning and comfort in ways that were not even necessary with the earlier beliefs. Linda and Susan were also in for a surprise, for events in their mother's life made her much more aware of what they were going through than they had ever imagined:

> Linda and Susan did not have to wait long for their mother's response. "In a moment I want you [to me] to help us with what we need to do. But first, I need to let Linda and Susan know that we three share this experience. I was sexually abused by my uncle Jerry." Now the shock and disbelief were on the faces of Linda and Susan as they moved closer to their mom. Jane's story began when she was 13 and went to live with her aunt, uncle, and cousins after her father died. Her mother had died two years before that, and this uncle who assumed guardianship was her mother's older brother.
>
> From age 13 to 17, the same years as Linda, Jane was sexually abused by her uncle. She got away from him when she left for college. But when she was 23, while attending the funeral of her much-loved grandmother, her uncle "caught her off guard" after the services while she was undressing in her room. His

rape led to her "nervous breakdown." Linda had been aware of her mother's "nervous breakdown." Her father had used it as a way to prevent Linda from telling her mother about his abuse, saying it would "upset her too much and might cause her to have another nervous breakdown." This was the first time both Linda and Susan understood what was at the root of this experience for their mother.

Jane went on: "I should have been able to stop it for Linda and Susan. This is the worst part now." Linda responded to her mom's self-blame. "Oh, Mom. You wouldn't believe how sneaky Dad's been. No one could have stopped him. Please don't blame yourself. You've been through enough. Maybe together, all three of us can get this to stop. We have to. We just have to. He needs help." The three women, Jane with her two daughters, sat and held each other for about ten minutes, crying and nodding but not saying much. The only phrase that they each repeated several times was: "We can make it through this."

Eventually Jane turned to me and asked what the next steps needed to be. I asked if they all understood that I am required by law to report John's actions and that there were a number of possibilities about how that could happen. They all nodded and confirmed that that is what they wanted and Jane offered, "I will report him. I need to do this for the girls." Linda let her mom know that she and Susan had also talked about reporting the abuse. They agreed that the best way was to be there to support each other. Because it was 8:30 in the evening at that time, they agreed to end this first session and to meet again at 8:30 the next morning. Before ending, I explained the procedures of the investigation that would be conducted and asked if they had any other questions.

"What about Dad...I mean, you know, right now?" Linda asked. None of them wanted to see him again that evening. I explained that they could leave by a different exit and that I would meet with John and explain their decision about leaving in that way. They said their good-byes, agreeing to return in the morning.

Jane and Linda had asked for information about next steps. *Providing information* came in the form of procedural information about the reporting of the abuse, when and how it needed to happen, and then, acting as *consultant* and *guide*, assisting Jane, Linda, and Susan to discuss the roles they wished to assume in the step of reporting. Though not included in the above description, another point that Liz also explained was what they could expect to happen in the next week in relation to the investigation, including questions they might be asked. Liz also gave them information in response to Linda's question about how to attend to John, who was still in the waiting room.

Emotion-focused coping and *problem-focused coping* (Snyder 1999) are both evident in Jane's, Linda's, and Susan's responses.[1] Jane voiced her emotional focus on self-blame: "I should have been able to stop it for Linda and Susan." Their pain and resolve were evident through the crying and the determination of the statement: "We can make it through this." Problem-focused coping became evident with questions about what the next steps needed to be. The various steps of problem-focused coping permit structured and manageable action at this stage. They had *explored* the situation with Liz, had explained their *assessment* of what had happened to all three of them, had been clear about their *goals* of what they wanted to have happen, and had made a *plan* together, at least for the immediate next steps that would occur in the few days to follow. The *implementation* of that plan began as they left together, leaving John behind, and it was to continue the following morning with the reporting of his behavior to Child Protective Services. Assessment and *evaluation* of the coping behaviors would occur on an ongoing basis, and the last stage, *termination*, would take place near the end of their work together (Compton and Galaway 1999). For Jane, Linda, and Susan that termination would occur two and a half years later. For the moment, however, picking up where we left off with Liz's work with the family that first evening, we learn more about coping from John's response to the events that followed.

Participation, the third empowering action, also was significant in the interactions with the Williams family up to this point. Linda and Susan had excluded their mom from their secret before that evening's meeting. By including her, and by the joining of the three of them together, they gained a new strength to follow through on their conviction to get the abuse out into the open. The participation between daughters and mother, as well as the social worker, attained a new level. Anticipating possible support needs ahead, Liz also began to think about community support resources that might be helpful, individually or jointly, for each member of this family.

The Middle Phase

Before Liz asked John to return to her office, she noted her own exhaustion, more emotional than physical, from hearing Linda's, Susan's, and Jane's stories. To face the perpetrator of violence upon these two teenagers next would require a mental shift. She recalled his earlier display of anger and prepared herself to become his sounding board. She also turned her thoughts toward his strengths and became curious about the oppressions in John's life. Knowing how often incest occurs across generations, she wondered if John also had experienced sexual abuse at some time during his life. Were these acts of sexual abuse part of an addictive cycle during which he had lost the capacity to control his own behavior? Was alcohol the only addictive substance involved? Initial information indicated his participation in AA, but could he have recently experienced a relapse? What was

John going to need, and how could she assist in integrating support from others? There were potential power differentials between Liz and John that he might call on—in particular those related to gender (male), age (older), wealth (upper class), and profession (lawyer), and Liz would need to watch for ways to equalize that power if and when it became necessary.

When John realized his family was no longer in my office, he sank into the nearest chair. His knees literally collapsed at that moment. He began with a very quiet, shaky voice: "Oh, I see." (Long silence.) "Well, it's over. It's finally over. Oh, my God! The girls must have told you and their mother what I have done to them. It's been so sick, sick, sick. But it's over now. It has to be over. I can't live with myself any longer." (Several deep breaths and a long pause.) "Can you help Jane and the girls get through this?"

This was not the response Liz had expected, and internally she was making yet another shift as she listened to John's words and heard a clear statement of *the help he desired.* She was aware that he was a lawyer himself and therefore he likely knew the procedures that were in his near future. Also, she found that his image in the community as a respected member of the legal profession, the school board, and several other boards of human services agencies as well as a gifted and much sought-after public speaker were "very present in the room" as she shaped her response to the person who sat in front of her "rather than his role." Avoiding the temptation to go with his question, which redirected the focus onto Jane and their daughters and off of him, and also acknowledging her concern about his statement of not being able to live with himself any longer, Liz commented: "I pick up from your words that you have been anticipating this moment for some time. Before I answer your question about your family, would you be willing to talk about what this is like for you right now?" Reaching for his story in "his own voice," John began:

I probably should have my lawyer present, I suppose. Ha. My lawyer. Well, I guess it has finally come to that. Oh, it goes back a long way. My older brother started all this. When he was eighteen and oh so full of himself, I was ten. I worshiped him then, thought the world rotated around him. At least my world did. Well, he used us younger kids, my sister and me. Anyway, I grew up thinking people could somehow tell what he had done to us. Mom was so busy protecting us from my dad, who beat us anytime he wanted to, that I don't think she even knew what Lee was doing. Can't blame her, though. In her own way, she was a saint. She did the best she could.

I just don't know if I can face the music. Hell, I have prosecuted people like me. Not for a while now, but I used to. Have I thought up a plan? Oh, not really. Sometimes in the AA meetings, I would hear other people talk about being sexually abused by their drunk parents and I would wonder if someday Linda or Susan would be in a group saying that about me. But, frankly, I never thought I would get found out, never thought they would speak up. Part of me wants to bribe you for some kind of cover-up like I've done with some people before. But I'm just too tired of this whole thing. I can't do it anymore. At least that's how I feel tonight. Oh God. My life is over. I have been so stupid.

Yeah, you do a good job, asking me about a plan, especially when I'm saying stuff like my life is over. I won't kill myself, not tonight anyway, but I do feel like taking a drink. So what that means is that I will call my sponsor. He even comes and sits with me, keeps me talking, if that's what I need. This is probably one of those times. Think I'll just sleep at the office tonight...bummer, but sure can't go home. If you could let Jane know that, it would be a big help. So when we're done here, I'll use your phone if you don't mind.

Liz described the "contract for life," which she kept for times when people thought they might be a danger to themselves or others. John did agree to sign the contract that evening, pledging to call Liz if he felt like hurting himself or anyone else. They briefly discussed the investigation John could be expecting. (Role of a guide providing information.) Even though he had been familiar with the procedures earlier in his career from the professional side, Liz did not assume that he had that information from the side of a perpetrator. She also asked about the support persons (participation with others) he had, in addition to his AA sponsor, who would be available to him on a more long-term basis. John named his two older sisters and a former partner at his law firm. He did indicate that he could contact all three the following day. Liz asked if John had any questions about her role and what she was required to do in the reporting. Hearing that he had none, Liz summarized, acknowledging John's *strength* to "face the music," as he called it, and to take responsibility now for his actions. She identified the *oppressive* nature of living with his abuses, both the incest with his daughters and his addiction to alcohol. She acknowledged that the next steps in the process were ones familiar to him. These actions and the earlier ones centered around *equalizing the power differential* between them, *assisting* John as he sought to empower himself through this step of truth-telling, inquiring about *his needs* in that immediate moment as well as those to come in the near future, and *integrating the support* needed from others. A few of the details of the follow-up are pertinent to the ongoing nature of the coping behaviors and skills that were *sustained, enhanced,* and *created* as a result of facing this time of major distress in the Williams family.

The next morning Jane, Linda, and Susan did report John to the Child Protective authorities, who conducted an investigation. John pled guilty to the charges and was sentenced to two years in prison to be followed with manda-tory participation in a post-release program for an indefinite length of time to be determined by annual review by his parole officer's recommendation and the decision of the Parole Board. He was required to attend a treatment group for perpetrators of sexual violence against children. Anticipating the loss of his license to practice law, John voluntarily chose not to renew it, hoping to avoid exposure of his actions in his professional circles. He, in essence, ended one life and began a different one as a result of this sentencing and treatment plan.

Jane, Linda, and Susan continued to meet with Liz together on a biweekly basis, individually, or Linda and Susan jointly as needed in alternate weeks for the next two and a half years. Liz chose to stay with practice actions as defined by the empowerment lens, *offering information* and suggesting areas for additional *learning*, inquiring about how coping efforts were working and determining when new *methods of coping* might be helpful, and continuing to encourage forms of *participation* that were relevant to the various stages of the healing and recovery process that they all faced.

Information that Liz provided included choices about how to interact with their father. Linda and Susan did choose to confront John directly about his be-havior, asking for and receiving "a superficial apology" (Linda's words). Confront-ing the oppressor is not indicated in all situations. However, it became evident in the work with Linda and Susan that the decision to ask their father for an apology would be an important step in enabling them to move on with their lives. Liz acted as guide to help them make arrangements to visit their father, to prepare for various responses that might occur, to clarify their expectations of the outcome, and to anticipate the need to let go where necessary. Liz was with them as they spoke with their father and as they listened to his regret. They ended their day by going home to tell Jane what had taken place.

After the reports to Child Protective Services were completed, Jane moved quickly toward her decision to seek a divorce from John. She faced an addi-tional shock, however, soon after reporting the abuse. As she began to gather financial information related to the possibility of divorcing John, she discov-ered that he had emptied their joint savings account and had transferred the investments held jointly to undisclosed locations. Jane had accepted the tra-ditional role stereotype of the woman depending upon the man's income and, as a result, she had not comprehended the importance of having a separate account or credit cards in her name only. At one time earlier in their marriage, when she had requested a checking account in her name, John's rage and his suspicion that she had some kind of "devious plan in the works" caused her to back off and not pursue that option.

Jane had held various part-time jobs on and off throughout their marriage mostly for her own satisfaction or to assist Linda and Susan in reaching various goals. But she was not equipped to face the drastic reduction in income that resulted from John's unemployment and his confiscating of joint funds. The thought of the job interviewing process was initially frightening and overwhelming for her, not only because of her relative lack of a skill base but also because she was aware of age discrimination for someone over 50. When she thought about how important it was to her that Linda and Susan receive the college education they wanted, she cried. She envisioned the three of them "becoming statistics in someone's feminization of poverty research."

I provided information about a class held as part of an outreach program in one of the local banks for women in exactly the kind of situation Jane was facing. Skills in financial planning both during divorce proceedings and following divorce were part of the class agenda. Both Linda and Susan offered to go with Jane to the classes, combining an information-coping-participation empowering response to what had initially seemed an overwhelming task.

As the work of the middle phase continued, Liz responded to the cycles of shock and coping faced by Jane and Susan and, to a lesser degree, Linda. In Liz's words, "All responses were seen as some form of coping." Linda was one of the strongest resources for Jane and Susan, partly because of her assertive character and partly because she had carried an awareness of the abuse longer than Jane or Susan. Also her response of anger was an energizing motivator for her to "move on." "I will NEVER allow this experience to hold me back from what I want to accomplish in my life."

Jane had "anxiety surges" more frequently and to a greater intensity than either Linda or Susan. Hyperventilating, dizziness, intermittent nausea, and intense panic characterized these "surges." Liz interpreted these physical responses as additional forms of coping—that is, the body's way of alerting Jane to potential danger and its way of helping her respond to threatening circumstances. "When I stopped blaming myself for getting so anxious and began believing there was some purpose for it, I paid attention to what was going on. I still had to live through the panic, but it was a lot less scary, it didn't seem to last as long, and I usually had a pretty good idea about what I needed to do next." With Liz's assistance, she *strengthened skills* in managing this anxiety in the moment as well as gradually *gathering information* that could help her determine how she would choose to relate to her anxiety over the longer term. Jane told Linda and Susan what would be most helpful from them (how to *participate*) when she felt her anxiety begin to surge: "Remind me to stop, to move away from what rattles me and toward something to help me calm down." Liz included the option of seeing a physician for anti-anxiety medication as one of Jane's possible choices. Jane chose to "keep that as a last resort."

Linda and Susan both experienced interruptions in their abilities to concentrate. Linda's came primarily with schoolwork: short attention span in the classroom and lack of focus in writing papers. She and Liz worked together for two sessions on *skills for coping* with the distractions—that is, writing them down and setting them aside for later—and on focusing skills, prioritizing and taking one thing at a time, to increase levels of concentration on present tasks.

Of the three, Susan was the one who experienced the greatest vulnerability. She described herself as "shaky, afraid, and not interested in doing anything." These responses fit the scenario of trauma responses, and Liz spoke with Susan in these terms, describing her responses as "just the way we are wired to protect ourselves and to respond when we have been through a traumatic experience." Liz commented (in her process notes and to her supervisor) on her intentional avoidance of the terms *disorder* or *PTSD*. As she said, "That was the last thing Susan needed to hear, because she overheard some kids at school using those terms, thought they were talking about her, and she immediately went back into her shell." Liz *provided information* to Susan about the actions she could take to help her recovery. For example, Liz offered choices and discussed with Susan how she could strengthen her sense of safety; how to tell her mother that she needed to be included in the discussions about money and wanted to understand her own financial base as she thought about leaving home to go to college; how to understand more about what feelings and behaviors to expect with her ongoing recovery from the incest; and, simultaneously, to imagine and begin taking steps toward the life she wanted to create for herself, to "move on" beyond a childhood she presently wanted only to forget.

Together, the *participation* of Jane, Linda, and Susan meant nothing less than a completely new understanding of who they were as a family. Susan was the one who put words to this reality: "Our dad was sick and needed help. He will always be our dad in a biological sense. And what he did will never leave my memory. But my mom and my sister are my true family now in the best sense of what family can be. In a weird sort of way, Dad gave us to each other in a way we might not have known without everything we had to go through. But I know that's me making some kind of meaning that I can live with. So, good for me. Nothing wrong with that, I guess."

A later discussion near the end of the chapter will describe Liz's role in greater detail as it relates to the levels, principles, and purpose of empowerment practice. It can be helpful at this point, however, to summarize the worker's role in this middle phase of the work as well. In particular, it is helpful to look at the interplay between the personal, interpersonal, and community-focused interventions.

Liz prepared for her work with John (individually and interpersonally) by tuning in to potential power differentials that might play a role in their work, and, as a result, she was not diverted when John attempted to move the work away from himself and onto the other family members (interpersonal). She presented the contract for life and provided information about the investigation (community). She inquired about John's support network (interpersonal and community) and acknowledged his strength in saying that he planned to take responsibility for his behaviors and face the consequences. With Jane (individually), Liz offered information about financial planning resources in the community. With Linda (individually), the work on increasing focusing skills and task management skills so Linda could complete her schoolwork (community) was a major focus. And with Susan (individually), information and reassurance about behaviors that were part of her trauma response—"No, you are not losing your mind and what you are experiencing is not a disorder"—plus expectations for the recovery process and enhancing safety were key directions in the work. Liz also served as a guide for concerns that were shared by Jane, Linda, and Susan: assisting them in the process of reporting John's actions; supporting them during the investigation; and inviting and accepting the array of emotions expressed. These selected interventions illustrate the simultaneous emphasis on personal, interpersonal, and community factors, with specific attention to the well-being and respect of persons, relationships, and organizations.

The Ending Phase

Key tasks in the ending phase include dealing with feelings, identifying and consolidating gains, reconnecting with the community if necessary, and evaluating the work that has been done together (Lee 2001). It is rare, however, that every member of the family will be ready to end at the same time. Jane, Linda, and Susan Williams were no exception. Approximately eighteen months after their first meeting, Liz recognized signs that the most empowering next step would be to move toward ending the working relationship with Jane, Linda, and Susan to acknowledge the accomplishments of their work together and to "move on with living" with as much of a sense of well-being as possible. Listening to their voices gave a clear indication that much of their lives in the present no longer focused on the distress of the past that had prompted their initial request for Liz's assistance. Though it would never be completely gone, their reason for coming initially was moving into the background of their day-to-day living.

Liz received mixed responses when she commented on this observation. Linda nodded her agreement that it was time; Susan said a firm, "No, not yet"; and Jane simply looked back and forth between her two daughters. Sometimes family members will choose to end together; other times individual endings at different times is the choice. Liz explained the benefits of each, emphasizing that they could always change their minds at a later time.

Sound reasons and needs accompanied the different responses. Linda knew she was ready to move on and agreed that she would like for this to be her last session with Liz. She spoke of her "determination to move forward" (feeling) and to "not allow the experiences with Dad get in the way of where I want my life to go next" (connections with peers and school/community resources). She also expressed her concern for Susan and the importance of continuing to be a support to her. "I will continue coming here to see you, Liz, anytime Susan wants me to come with her for support." Susan had made this request of Linda. Liz affirmed the importance of this support for Susan and added that she usually invited people to help evaluate their work together at their last session. This involved looking at whether or not their goals had been met, if they felt they had a greater sense of well-being than when they started, and asking whether the other family members had any feedback for Linda and her part in the work. Linda appeared to welcome the chance to put words to her thoughts.

She restated what her goals had been: to get Susan the help she needed; to get their dad to stop the incest; and to tell their mom. Linda felt that each of these had happened, but also that there were "many years ahead still to deal with having all this out in the open." She added that she was glad the conversation had happened with their dad to ask for his apology, even though that had not been one of her goals at the beginning. As she thought about any unmet goals, her sadness was evident: "There's just this big hole. I think I always wanted to believe that my dad was the ideal dad, but I'll never have that. I just have to figure out a way to live with it, and that's not easy. It might take a long time. I hate what he did to us...AND...I'm not going to let it ruin my whole life."

Had the purpose of empowering practice been served? Did Linda have a greater sense of well-being than when they had started? "I feel safer now. You believed us and you believed our story. You helped make telling our mom seem possible. You didn't give up or go away when things got worse for all three of us. So, yes, I do feel safer, for now anyway. When he gets out of jail, well, I don't know about then. Can we come back around that time if we need to?"

Liz assured Linda that this was possible.

The last step of Linda's evaluation was to see if there was any feedback from Jane and Susan. Susan simply said: "Thanks. You're the best sister anyone could want." Jane had one question: "Linnie, you said you would come back with Susan when she needs you to. Would you come with me, too? Because I may need you to help me get through some of this?" Linda answered, "Sure, Mom, sure."

Jane and Susan were not quite as ready for their work with Liz to come to an end. Liz turned to Susan to ask what was telling her she wasn't quite ready.

Liz noted that each of Susan's responses was still accompanied with crying and shaking, but her voice to speak about her experiences was getting clearer. Susan described many post-trauma behaviors: nightmares, memories that intruded into her present and interfered with her concentration, being "jumpy" or hypervigilant, flashbacks, going silent and wanting to withdraw, confused thinking, being overly startled by loud noises or unexpected behaviors around her, and not being able to articulate her thoughts in a way that was clear to others. That day, Liz and Susan set no time limit on their meetings. For the two years following the joint work with her mom and sister, Susan continued to see Liz at least once a week and more when the intensity of her trauma response behaviors became more than she could manage. At the end of those two years, John was released from prison. All of Susan's trauma responses returned and increased in frequency and intensity. Her work with Liz included an increase in protection factors to help Susan feel safer. She installed caller identification on her phone; she went nowhere alone, sometimes "borrowing" her friend's Doberman for additional protection; and she accepted Liz's help with the procedures for a restraining order. This heightened sense of fear and watchfulness diminished somewhat after a year, but one day she stated her stark reality to Liz: "I will live with some of this fear until I know he's dead." At the last report from Liz, Susan was in the sixth year of her recovery work, still seeing Liz but on an "as needed" basis only, approximately once a month.

Jane also found that she was not quite ready to end her work at the same time as Linda. She estimated "maybe another three months or so." In that time, she had three hopes in mind: (1) to explore her own childhood incest; (2) to increase ways of dealing with her "surges of anger and rage toward John"; and (3) to better manage her panic and anxiety, the times when she felt immobilized and depressed, to know when it was grieving and to "let that be, let it happen" and stop blaming herself so much. Jane added that she was in a transition with her relationship to a career and her community. "I think I lack a lot of skills in this department, but I'm not sure. Maybe we could talk some more about that, too." Jane was "empowering herself," actions not lost on Liz. The agenda for the next three months had a clear beginning.

The ending phase began for the Williams family that day with Linda's departure, but upcoming endings for Susan and Jane were also redefined and clarified. The timing of the ending phase, like the timing of other phases of work, is always determined from a place of responsiveness to the needs of the family members, jointly as well as individually. Even though Linda's departure marked the beginning of the ending phase, it would be incorrect to assume that the family sessions had come to an end. The family continues as one of the most important interpersonal arenas for empowerment practice. Even when one person—Jane or Susan, for example—returned to work with Liz, the integration of that person's awareness of the whole family and the need for their ongoing support were still very much a part of the transaction.

Reflections Through an Empowerment Lens

Jane, Linda, Susan, and John all set out to create new lives beyond the oppression of incest. It was just a beginning for all of them, and different degrees of choice existed, with lesser choice available to John. Families who face major distressing events in their lives very seldom experience only one period of time when the need for more information or new learning becomes evident, when their coping skills are stretched to maximum limits, and when the need to be surrounded and supported by others exceeds their norm. Events often push them "to the edge," where they fall short of meeting the demands of present circumstances. Entering practice with these families with an empowerment perspective allows workers to assist in sustaining, enhancing, and creating actions for learning, coping, and support that have worked in the past for the family members. Family members must reach beyond the safety of what is known and trusted to create something new, different, and unknown. Social workers tune in to what actions have been tried but are not working in this situation. They gain a thorough understanding of how each family member learns most effectively so that these methods of learning (auditory, visual, experiential) can be differentially applied to increase the likelihood that each person will be able to learn what is necessary to move forward. Creating new opportunities, meeting challenges in new ways, can be among the most satisfying and rewarding experiences for the family members as well. These acts of creating new directions strengthen self-confidence and self-respect that reach far beyond the challenges of the moment.

Dimensions/Levels of Empowerment

Every member of the Williams family had the opportunity to continue actions begun in their work with Liz to increase self-efficacy, to *develop more positive and potent senses of self,* the personal dimension of empowerment practice (Lee 2001:34). Jane had allowed herself to face her own history of sexual abuse with greater openness and honesty, a use of self that strengthened her truthfulness with herself as well as strengthening the bond with her daughters and their experiences.

Linda had begun her own road to recovery from the incest before the events that led the family to meet with Liz. But she found that her decision to stand up to her father, to hold him accountable for what he was doing to Susan regardless of what the consequences might be, resulted in a renewal of a positive belief in herself as a strong person, "being the kind of big sister to Susan that I truly wanted to be, plus speaking out so that others might have the courage to do the same." Linda had been "surprised by the degree of anger and rage" she felt toward her father when she realized what he was doing to Susan. During her own abuse she had forced herself to deny or suppress that rage. But now she had no reason to suppress it and every reason to give it expression. Linda identified that she was able to direct that anger into a constructive outcome with Liz's assistance even though she had "always worried that it would come out in some enormously destructive way if I ever took the lid off." This, too, she felt, added to her sense of herself as a strong and competent woman.

Susan began her work toward recovery with the help of her sister, her mother, her school social worker, and Liz. Her self-confidence had been profoundly shattered as a result of the incest and the accompanying coercion by her father. For the first few months following the investigation by CPS, Susan chose to work with a tutor in her home rather than to attend school, but several of her friends continued to visit. One of these friends was a confidante for Susan, and she told her story for the first time to someone in her peer group. Much to Susan's surprise, this friend described her own similar experience. She also let Susan know about the group led by the school social worker for incest survivors at Susan's high school. With the help of this friend, Susan began attending the group and continued until the time of her graduation. The work of this group helped Susan to understand that she, as a daughter of a recovering alcoholic, was at higher potential risk for abusing alcohol herself. A further step in her coping process was to ask Linda if she would go to Alateen with her. These meetings expanded their support network even further.

Jane faced a complex array of challenges for strengthening her sense of self. One of the main reasons that the Williams family was selected for this chapter was the ways Jane responded to her situation and the ways those responses served to empower not only her but Linda and Susan as well, in a "ripple effect." Jane had set aside her love of writing thirty years earlier. When Liz discovered this after asking a question about Jane's talents, she went on to explain the healing potential in the writing process (C. Bly 2001; Remen 1996) and asked Jane if she would have any interest in keeping a journal about the transition she was going through. The eight months with no predictable financial income and the struggle to find a job were often frightening for Jane. Her responses included panic and anxiety attacks, immobilization and depression, intense grieving and self-blame, as well as an attempt to parentify Linda and to transfer her previous dependence on John to a similar dependence on her daughters. She began writing about these experiences and discovered parts of herself that had been buried and forgotten, or that were new and previously unrecognized. She looked at her past and worked with her genogram with Liz's assistance on understanding the cross-generational pattern of incest in her family. She accepted that she no longer wanted to be the person in those families, then went through all the steps of grieving the loss of that earlier Jane. She tried on the victim role for a while and used some of the anger she felt to energize an expression of her rage about John's abuses toward Linda and Susan and toward herself as well. She used the information about verbal abuse and her learning about patterns of incest and sexual abuse in families to separate what was her responsibility and what was not. This information convinced her that she had made the right decision to seek the divorce and end that phase of the family as she and "the girls" had known it. Several months into her new job at the hotel, she looked back on these eight months as a "necessary part of the change" and felt "stronger for having faced that time" in her life. Her coping skills covered the array of stress management, trauma recovery, financial management, job skill training, and midlife transition. She redefined her role as parent, support, and friend toward her daughters, and she shaped a new part of her identity related to a career.

John also faced himself in a different way. Liz did not have ongoing contact with him once the investigation and sentencing were over, but she did receive copies of the annual written reports of his progress. One of those documents noted that John had chosen a course of study to become a career counselor and was pursuing that as his new direction. He was cooperating with the cognitively based treatment program, which included hormonal treatment as well, but continued to struggle with setting aside a "false sense of power and intellect" that he had known in his previous life as a lawyer to face the abuses he had committed based upon distortions of "power over" others to satisfy his own needs.

The family also shifted in composition and definition *interpersonally.* As a family facing divorce, they had to develop coping strategies to deal with the cutoff from husband and father. Liz and Jane worked together to include Linda and Susan in the decision about the divorce and how to move through the changes involved so that further trauma could be minimized, especially for Susan, who continued to fear that her father would "come after" her. They worked together on how to inform in-laws and paternal grandparents and other relatives in John's family and supported each other when responses from his family members were angry and rejecting.

Through their experience of working within an empowering framework with Liz, members of this family also came to an *increased comprehension of their social web* (Lee 2001:34). Jane now understood the services of the school social worker and the work of Child Protective Services in a different way. She had experienced new ways of relying on her friendship network, especially as she undertook the daunting task of finding a job "of career proportions" at her age. Linda's web of social influences and supports included a friendship network at college. Susan responded to her sister's and her mother's support, as well as to that of her friends, the school social worker, and the group of incest survivors at her school. John saw a different side of the justice system through the years of his incarceration and group treatment, and he continued his reliance upon his AA sponsor.

Discovering resources and strategies to attain personal and collective goals (Lee 2001:34) can also be seen in this work with the Williams family. Some of those resources are evident in the personal and interpersonal gains and supports mentioned above. Other resources and strategies emerged as Jane, Linda, and Susan came together to brainstorm and plan how they were going to manage given the changes in their financial realities. Since they were not able to afford the cost of maintenance of their home, they agreed to sell it. To avoid rent and mortgage payments, they found a town house that they could purchase with the profit from sale of the house, with some left over to begin a college fund for Linda and Susan. Linda offered to delay going to college while Susan was in high school and to work full time to help meet living expenses and to build up the college fund. She had been attending a local college and living on campus. The family's strategy involved Linda's moving back home temporarily, but this turned out to be something all three of them wanted, given the circumstances, their new sense of connection, and the felt need for mutual support. John's goals had been stated as "stopping the abuse and the need for it" and "finding a new line of work." At last report, Liz saw that both of these goals were still in progress but that he was still headed in that direction.

These personal, interpersonal, and social dimensions of empowerment practice are closely intertwined. Practice that excludes any one of these dimensions is not empowerment practice. Focus on any one of the dimensions will have an impact on the others. The interpersonal sibling relationship between Linda and Susan that supported their decision to report John's behavior had a powerful impact on Jane and John, individually and as a couple. John's individual decision to withhold financial support to Jane, Linda, and Susan had a profound impact on their plans for both the present and the future.

The Seven Principles of Empowerment Practice

The Williams family provides an example of how the complexities of empowerment practice come alive. All seven principles of empowerment practice are evident in Liz's work with this family. This final section will consider the ways in which each of the principles was manifested in the work with this family. In these specific practice behaviors, the potential generalizability of practice using the empowerment lens will be evident. These practice behaviors are not unique to the work with the Williams family; rather, they can be differentially applied with a variety of family structures and situations of distress. A reminder about the unique needs of each family is timely as well.

Building on Strengths, Diminishing Oppression

From the initial telephone call, evidence of the strength of Jane's support for her daughters was visible. When professional help was recommended, Jane sought that help without hesitation. The strength in the connection between the two sisters was also evident from the earliest stages of the work. When the silencing of Susan's voice from oppressive threats was at its most overwhelming, Linda understood the nonverbal messages from Susan's behaviors, and she also served as Susan's voice during those times. With this support and acceptance, Susan regained her capacity to speak using "her own voice." Jane never doubted or diminished the facts as Linda and Susan presented them. She believed them and, in doing so, gave her daughters one of the most strengthening building blocks of their recovery. Liz built upon these strengths by recognizing them openly and by accentuating joint efforts that exceeded the family's capacities to cope individually, such as their cooperation in managing their financial challenges together.

Strengths continued to emerge in the ongoing middle phase of the work, strengths related directly to coping skills. Sustaining coping skills that have been useful in the past, enhancing coping skills that are being used in the present, and helping to create new coping skills where they are needed all serve the purpose of empowerment practice. As such, forms of coping to relieve immediate distress is as important as forms of coping that can serve long-term needs. Relief of the immediate distress was seen in the report to CPS and the immediate ending of John's coercion and abuse of Susan. Coping with the stages of recovery, however, is a long-term process, the length of which can be determined only by Susan, Linda, and Jane individually. Strengths in coping also included personal, interpersonal, and community resources. These will be discussed in greater detail in the section below on the integration of needed support from others.

Oppressions of violence, addiction, poverty, and intrafamilial discrimination were diminished during the course of the work with the Williams family. The violence of the incest reverberated throughout many generations of this family. By breaking the silence around its devastation, family members diminished some of its power, even though the consequences would continue to be felt for many decades.

In the practice setting with Liz, the verbal violence during the first meeting was merely the tip of the iceberg of verbal violence that had been used as an oppressive force in this family in their home life. Liz took specific action to end the verbal violence in the first meeting. John's name-calling toward Linda resulted in an immediate change in the direction of the work. Liz supported the request made by Linda and Susan that John be asked to move to the waiting room. Removing the possibility of his verbal assaults and his oppressive stares enabled them to speak.

Regaining "voice" in the absence of oppressive forces is one indication that empowering actions have occurred.

Addictions control people's lives and are therefore also oppressive forces, forces that remove a person's freedom of choice and action. During the investigation of John's abuse, it was discovered that John had returned to drinking. The oppression of his addiction to alcohol was diminished by the contact with the AA sponsor, who supported John through his trial, sentencing, and incarceration. Patterns and rituals of behavior that defined John's addiction to alcohol had had an effect on the entire family system from the earliest days of John and Jane's marriage. Some similar addictive patterns and rituals were evident in his sexual abuse of Linda and Susan. For example, John would begin planning at midday when he would take his next drink that evening, ensuring that he either had it on hand or had the money with him to purchase it on the way home from work. Likewise, during the years of abuse toward Linda and later Susan, he would begin thinking about the next time of sexual contact around midday and would follow a ritualized mental checklist of the step-by-step preparation, approach, secrecy, and coercion.

The Williams family is also a good example of a family for whom "poverty is not limited to the lack of financial resources alone" (Kilpatrick and Holland 1999:68). "Disease, poverty, alcoholism, chemical dependency, mental deficiency, constitutional inadequacy, parental discord, social isolation, and lack of familial and community support" (Adnopoz, Grigsby, and Nagler 1996:1074) often combine to create ongoing crises for such families. For the Williamses alcoholism and parental discord both played a role in their family dynamics, even though it was primarily the exposure of the incest that led to divorce and Jane's financial poverty. In this family, however, it was more a matter of the allocation of the financial resources that were available than a complete lack of financial resources. Overnight Jane, Linda, and Susan went from an upper-middle-class lifestyle and expectations to poverty. They lived for a period of eight months without knowing when adequate and predictable financial support would be available to them.

Intrafamilial discrimination was evident in the Williams family related to gender discrimination in at least two different ways: first, gender discrimination at the societal, institutional, and individual levels that allows the perpetuation of beliefs around male dominance that results in the horrific choice of a father who subjects his daughter to incest; and second, the perpetuation of myths and stereotypes about "female incompetence" regarding financial astuteness. It is important to recognize Jane's internalized oppression that took the form of acceptance of some of these stereotypes and led her to avoid taking responsibility for her financial well-being at an earlier time in her life.

Diminishing the oppression in Jane's, Linda's, and Susan's lives centered around multiple attempts to access funds, including Jane's preparation to enter the job market and Linda's search for scholarship money and financial assistance at her college. John's lawyers assisted him in delaying court settlements that would have helped, and each month that passed took Susan one step closer to the time when she would no longer be eligible to receive child support payments. When Jane was asked to provide financial records of the past five years, she provided her ineligibility for assistance because all records were in their joint names. She had thought she had no need to develop additional job skills during the previous twenty-five years, so the job-interviewing process was both frustrating and without a positive result for her. Finally, through a lead from a friend, she was hired as a hotel receptionist with on-the-job training and the potential for additional education in hotel management skill training after the first six months. Financial assistance from John came a full year later. Jane looked back on her time of financial need with words that capture her strengths as well as her skill in creating new ways of coping: "I discovered survival skills I never knew I had in me. It was a frightening and horrible time for all three of us in many ways, but I have no doubt that we are better for having gone through it."

Multicultural Respect

Liz considered the multicultural factors in her work with the Williams family. Actions of multicultural respect on the part of the practitioner center around an acceptance of the meaning that family members attribute to factors of ethnicity, gender, age, sexual orientation, religion or spiritual belief, socioeconomic status (class), differing abilities, language, geography, and developmental stage. Empowering practice includes accepting the views of the family members as well as challenging perceptions that may appear to be based upon societal prejudice, discrimination, and stereotype rather than upon individual and family strength. Internalized oppression related to multicultural factors—ageism, sexism, racism, and the like—can be one of the most insidious barriers to a family's empowering strength.

Jane attributed some of her characteristics that helped or hindered her ability to cope to her "stuffy, silent, stoic, never complaining British grandmothers." Both ethnicity and gender played a role here, and as the silence was broken about the incest, Jane commented that these qualities might help in certain ways but this was not one of them. She recognized her own "stoic silence" about her uncle's abuse in Susan's silence about John's behavior. A long lineage of "strong women" was used as a resource throughout the work. A second characteristic recognized by Linda was referred to as part of the "white suburban culture"—how important it was to portray the image of "the Perfect family, with a capital 'P'." Linda felt that this was impressed upon her from a very young age because "Dad was such a public figure in the community and certain things were expected of us as his kids. I hated growing up with a what-will-people-think screen that all of my behavior had to go through."

"Are we poor now, Mom?" was Susan's question that left Jane speechless during one afternoon's joint session. The fluidity of a family's socioeconomic status often goes unrecognized in assumptions of stability when income has been predictable for many years. For the women in the Williams family, financial stability literally disappeared overnight. It took several weeks for them to understand what had happened to the savings and investments, a shorter period of time to move beyond the shock, and then several sessions to work out a plan and begin to get it into place.

Liz also expanded her understanding of the Williams family members when considering their different developmental needs—midlife assessments of both parents; emancipation, work, and relationship needs of the young adult years for Linda; and identity clarification, with sexual identity as a key factor, and anticipation of leaving home for Susan. Liz included her theoretical understanding about the developmental delay that can occur in the face of traumatic experiences. This helped her be aware of the possibility that the chronological ages of Jane, John, Linda, and Susan would likely not match their emotional ages, a factor that has important implications for intervention choices.

Language was an interesting multicultural factor to consider as well when Liz reflected on her work with this family. She was about to move on, thinking issues of language had a minimal influence on the work, until she recalled the many hours spent with Jane's "feeling depleted by all the 'Legalese' as I struggle with the endless documents from John's lawyer." Liz did see this as an issue of language in the work with Jane, especially in light of the confusion and inaction it caused for Jane. She felt silenced, helpless, and "beat." When Liz recognized this, they were able to discuss legal aid resources for Jane and ways that Jane could emotionally remove herself from facing the legal details in moving forward with the divorce.

An example of another multicultural factor came through Liz's respect for the role of sexual orientation. It is common to work with families who protectively shroud all discussion of sexual orientation in secrecy. In empowering practice, a climate of acceptance and safety is naturally extended to sexual orientation. On her list of resources in their community, Liz included groups for lesbians. Linda's comment on her participation in one of the groups opened a conversation about sexual orientation between Linda and Susan. Older sister was once again a source of information and a confidante for younger sister.

Equalizing Power Differentials

The above actions exemplify the practice principle of equalizing power differentials. When working with individuals, this equalization is crucial. When a family is the client, the relationship between the worker and each family member as well as the relationships among and between the family members themselves are included in efforts toward power equalization. Jane and John had been caught in a "power over/ power under" script for many years. It would have been highly unusual for this to change after John moved out of their home. Paralegal assistance obtained through legal aid helped Jane to equalize the power differential that John was attempting to hold over her. Susan sometimes attributed professional power to Liz, that which gets related to a "knowledge is power" belief, and used that to take a "power under" position in her work with Liz. Both "power under" and "power over" distortions need to be addressed to meet the practice principle of equalizing power differentials.

Awareness of Needs, Empowering Themselves, Support from Others, and Use of Cooperative Roles

These illustrations begin to show the interaction of the empowerment principles. Awareness of multicultural factors includes awareness of needs, assistance to family members as they empower themselves, and the worker's role in the integration of support from others. Liz filled cooperative roles of assisting (by providing the safe space) as they empowered themselves, serving as guide and consultant, building on strength, diminishing oppression.

Purpose of Empowering Practice: To Sustain, Enhance, and Create Family Well-being

What did the social worker do in her work with the Williams family to fulfill the purpose of empowerment practice? Was the well-being of the family sustained, enhanced, and created?

When a family has need of social work services, the well-being that they bring with them resides in their strengths. In the midst of the story told by Linda, Susan, and Jane that first evening, Liz listened for and observed coping, decision making, a sense of resolve to no longer remain silent, and the commitment of their relationship to each other. These were a few of the strengths that she realized had brought them to this moment, and she continued to call on them throughout the later work. The strengths visible in each family's story provide a window into understanding their picture of well-being. When sustained and given attention in the work, these same strengths of the family were Liz's foundation for determining her own role each step of the way. When we have a clear picture of the family's strengths, as she did, we can more clearly understand and respect what they can do to empower themselves. In those areas where strengths are less evident, the social worker can gain a more precise view of where the work can benefit from collaboration with a social worker. Through these two actions—actively using the family's strengths and collaborating where the need was evident—Liz provided reassurance that the family had access to familiar ways to make it through this difficult time. The underlying assumption in her approach was that the trauma was only one aspect of what this family faced; it did not define the essence of the family. Liz saw them for who they were beyond the trauma.

Sometimes families also realize through this way of approaching practice via their strengths that the way through to life beyond the turmoil is not something mysterious and unattainable. It is something that has been with them for years, something familiar. Even though they may be learning new information or skills as they go through the process, they will not be called upon to be someone other than who they are. A family's well-being is sustained through supporting and encouraging the ongoing use of their strengths, even as the family structure and the dynamics that enable oppressive violence such as incest are not sustained.

The family as the Williamses had known themselves for twenty-five years came to an end. In that sense, the family was not sustained. Sometimes, when individual or interpersonal well-being is threatened or absent in the family, as it had been for Linda and Susan for many years, the family structure may need to change in order to create or restore a greater sense of well-being. The Williams family teaches us that an important distinction in empowering practice with families is knowing when to support family members when they choose to restructure how they define themselves, even when that means the ending of the family as they have known it. Liz's work relevant to this aspect included supporting their natural grieving of the loss of the former family and their unrealized hopes for it. This took them through expressions of denial, anger, and sadness and eventually allowed them to move on to create a new idea of family—still family but changed. They used words like "safer," "out of the fog," and "scary but freer" to describe where they were when they ended their time with Liz.

John's life was forced to head in a different direction: eliminating the abuse, imprisonment, accountability and serving time, loss of his profession and the financial security that went with it.

Creating lives beyond the incest is a lifetime endeavor for all members of this family, something that occurs day to day and moment by moment. The context for that to happen began, in part, with the work with Liz, their social worker. Jane, Linda, and Susan set out to create new lives for themselves, empowering themselves, beyond the incest they had suffered at the hands of (for Jane) an uncle and (for Linda and Susan) a father. Those lives have not been free of struggles, uncertainty, disappointments, shock, and confusion. But they have each other in a very different way now. In their own words, each of them takes credit for her own strength in transforming a horror of the past into the appreciation for each other in the present. Is this not also one of the truest meanings of empowerment?

Jane, John, Linda, and Susan Williams, the experience of their lives over a period of approximately three years, and their work with Liz, their social worker, have provided an illustration of how empowering practice came to life for one family that faced the enormous distress surrounding father-daughter incest. The major part of the trauma is now in their past, yet it will always serve as the beginning of the strength and resilience that grew from those experiences through courageous choices.

5

The Brown-Wiley Family: Homeless No More

Cynthia Brown left Michigan on her thirtieth birthday in the middle of the night with her two children, Charlie (age 7) and Jessie (age 5), after the worst of her husband's rages. Mike Brown had been beating and verbally abusing her for nine years, since one month after their wedding. Several emergency room visits for a broken nose, two broken ribs, and fear for the safety of their second child during pregnancy strengthened her resolve to leave him as soon as she could figure out how to make it happen. Financial dependence and knowing that he was capable of following through on his threats of hurting her even more severely if she tried to leave kept her physically in the same house with him. Emotionally, however, the distance could not have been greater.

She had tried to leave him four times in the past five years, turning to her parents, cousins, and other extended family for temporary support. Each time they sent her back. At first they said it was because she needed "to work things out with him" or "to live up to your vows" or "the kids need to be with their father" or "the kids are just too much for us." Each time she went back, Mike's fury increased, and the rages became more frequent and more frightening for Cynthia. The last two times she attempted to get away, Mike's threats toward those giving her shelter were so violent that they feared for their own safety. Both of those families asked if she would consider going to a more anonymous place, both for the safety of herself and the children and for the safety of the extended-family members.

A cousin, Danielle, guided her to the nearest crisis hotline, helped her understand the steps to reporting the abuse and how to get a restraining order. Complicating the situation was the fact that Mike was a member of the police force in their small town. Cynthia was so convinced that the system there would work against her and in his favor that she never followed through on any of the options suggested to her. "I grew to believe that I would need to escape to a completely different location if I ever hoped to end this nightmare."

For the past three years she had lived in constant fear that his beating would turn to the children. As Mike's rages increased in intensity, he had started reminding her "in a very calm voice" of the number of guns he had around the house, both for his work and for hunting. The threat alone immobilized her for several weeks, even though he had never pointed a gun at her or at the children. She had been planning her escape, she said, "for months...no, it has actually been years now that I think of it." Three months before the night they got away, Mike had left on a hunting trip for two days and she had stolen the car key to have a copy made while he was away. "How do you steal something that is supposed to be yours to begin with?" In his efforts to control her, Mike made sure that there was only one key to the car and that Cynthia never had access to it unless he gave her an "assignment where to go and what to do and what time to be back."

Just seconds later, after Mike had walked out the door to go hunting and while Cynthia was still holding the key in her hand, she had to quickly shove it to the bottom of the bag of groceries she was unpacking. "He was coming in the back door! He was back!! I couldn't believe it. I thought I had been caught in the act!" But he was returning to pick up another twelve-pack of beer and to "get in one more threat about how I WOULD behave while he was gone, or else..." "Getting that key hidden had been a spur-of-the-moment act for Cynthia, but once that happened, it "started the ball rolling on so much more, on the rest of my life, really."

Two years earlier she had seen a television documentary featuring a shelter for battered women in Colorado. She knew at the time that it would one day be her destination. For two years she hid money in different places, set aside small food items, and packed one small suitcase of clothing and other necessities for herself and the children. Finally, the time to set out for Colorado had come. She got her copy of the car key, and over the next ten weeks made other preparations while the kids were in school. "Everything I did had to follow a certain routine, all directed by Mike, so that nothing raised his suspicion." The mother of one of Charlie's friends was throwing away some maps and gave Cynthia the ones she needed. She knew the exact date Charlie and Jessie would finish school. She purchased a bottle of dark brown hair dye, "because he will come after me. He will describe me to people who would come looking for me, and the first thing he will tell them is about my hair." Her hair color had been blond.

The cross-country trip was filled with uncertainty and doubt. She turned back three times. Fearing that she had made a terrible mistake, not for herself as much as for the children, she almost believed all the "tapes" in her head of Mike's voice telling her that she would never be able to make it without him to take care of her. But each time, another "voice" in her convinced her she was doing the right thing, that she had been planning this for years, and that somehow she would make it work. They slept in the car, usually in rest areas where they could get food from vending machines and have water and bathroom facilities nearby. Several encounters with "do-gooders, truck drivers, drug pushers, and police were the only uncomfortable parts of the trip, plus always looking over my shoulder to see if Mike had caught up with us yet."

Cynthia, Charlie, and Jessie arrived in the town that was their destination on a Tuesday afternoon. Cynthia checked the phone book at a gas station to get the address of the Safehouse Outreach Center and to check the local map for directions. Upon arriving at the center, they were greeted by the outreach worker. "It was a kind welcome, especially after she found out how far we had come, but we did learn that the shelter was full." It would be at least three weeks until space became available for them there, and two other shelters in nearby communities expected about the same waiting period. "I think the outreach worker saw the panic on my face. She assured me that sometimes there were unexpected openings and I could call every couple days to check. She asked if I had any money to pay for a motel room temporarily and told me there was one they recommended for short-term stays. That's what we did the next two nights. She also told me about some help I could get at Emergency Family Assistance."

The third day Cynthia spotted a Help Wanted sign in the window of a self-storage business and decided to see what would be expected for that position. Once again, disappointment. The position had "just been filled," but she noticed the rates for the storage units posted on the wall: $48 a month for a unit about the size of a one-car garage. "It was just quick thinking on my part, but I decided to take one." That evening she had a room, her own "room" in the self-storage unit.

The next day, she decided she might be able to receive some help from someone at the homeless shelter. She hoped this might provide a safe place for Charlie and Jessie for a few hours while she looked for work. The social worker there welcomed her, "gave us the best meal we had had in months and just noticed that I wasn't looking too great for getting a job. I guess I really did look like quite a mess." He watched the children while she showered. After she bathed the children, the conversation "seemed to be going fine, talking about job skills I had and stuff like that when, all of a sudden, something he did with his hand, I can't exactly explain it, but it was just like Mike. I could hardly breathe. All the blood drained out of my face. I just had to get out of there as fast as I could. So I thanked him, said I would keep all these things in mind and I would let him know if I wanted to follow through on them. We were out of there in two minutes!"

That evening, Cynthia realized she would need to tell the young woman who was working the shift at the storage unit what was going on with her. By that time, she had picked up a few more blankets and a folding table, which she had set up in her unit. She wanted to assure the woman, Rhonda, that this was a temporary arrangement for her and the children.

Rhonda heard her story. In fact, Rhonda heard this story or one very much like it several times a month. Single women and men came more frequently than families, but they all came to the "Self-Storage on North Willow" hoping to do exactly what Cynthia was doing, to find temporary shelter. Rhonda knew that with children involved it was important to get in touch with supportive resources in the community as quickly as possible. She had learned from experience that these situations, when poorly handled, could turn against families, setting them up for running away and reducing the likelihood that they would reach out for the necessary help. Lou, a social worker with Emergency Family Assistance, had helped Rhonda define a set of procedures that could meet the requirements of reporting while also maintaining a respectful relationship with the families. Rhonda's first step was to contact Lou.

Lou received Rhonda's message the following morning and made arrangements to see Cynthia and her children that afternoon. Before leaving her office, Lou checked with a colleague at Child Protective Services to see if Cynthia had been reported. The report was there. Required by law to report child neglect and abuse, the social worker at the homeless shelter had submitted information about Cynthia, Charlie, and Jessie. "Potential neglect due to insufficient resources" was the phrasing used on the report. Lou informed the CPS social worker that she had been contacted and was on her way to see the family. Knowing that Cynthia could not be reached by telephone, Lou gave her name and number as the best way to contact the family. She also requested that she be included if an investigation was deemed necessary.

After Rhonda introduced Lou to Cynthia and the children, Lou explained her role as a social worker with Emergency Family Assistance and described the purpose of her visit, as well as the services that were available for Cynthia and the children. Hearing Cynthia's story in her own words was the next step. "For right now, Cynthia, I just want to hear what you have been through to get here and what you would like to happen next. When you are ready, let me know if you would like some help and we can take it from there." Cynthia recounted the experiences of the past week, and Charlie and Jessie also added information about the events that were significant for them. Lou was continually amazed at the resilience, resourcefulness, and sheer stamina of the homeless families she got to know, especially those on the run from violent relationships. Cynthia and her children were no exception.

Following the telling of her story, Lou explained that the social worker at the homeless shelter had reported Cynthia's situation at the Child Protective Services division of the Department of Social Services. "They may send someone to investigate how you are doing. They know that I was coming to see you, and if you are willing to look at some ways we might work together to help improve things for you and the kids, the result should be a favorable one." Cynthia's fear returned momentarily until Lou provided information that helped to calm her anxiety. She explained that the social worker was doing what was required by law, that the purpose of such an investigation was to help access needed resources for the whole family, and that they already knew that Lou would be talking with Cynthia about some of the possibilities.

By the end of the week Lou had checked with the area shelters and discovered that it would be almost a week before a space would be available. When she returned for her next visit, she gave them this information and, with Rhonda, offered the family "a different unit with a better view back near the cottonwoods." Rhonda helped with the move to the new unit, and Lou offered sandwiches for everyone. While they shared lunch, Cynthia continued her story. At one point she paused, then said, "I know I'm lucky to be alive. I know I need help, but I can't go back to that shelter."

From Cynthia's description of the conversation with the social worker at the homeless shelter, Lou knew the importance of following Cynthia's pace. There were many questions in her mind, but she chose to ask just one for the present: "Are you and the children safe?" For the moment, Cynthia said, she thought she was. Her concern was increasing each day, however, because she anticipated that Mike had reported her as a missing person and would probably try to accuse her of kidnapping the children. "As long as he is alive, I will always have to wonder about the answer to that question."

As Cynthia spoke these last words, she rose, walked to the car, and reached for a manila envelope in the glove compartment. She handed the envelope to Lou. "I keep this near me all the time. Please open it. I think it's important for you to see what's in it." Lou glanced at the first page and read the large, bold, handwritten words: "IF I AM FOUND DEAD, ARREST THIS MAN." The next page was a photograph of Mike in his police uniform. Lou nodded, respecting Cynthia's certainty that she and the children needed this kind of protection, and asked, "Would you like for us to make copies and keep one at our office as well as at the shelter when you get a room there?" "Yes, thank you," was Cynthia's response. Lou asked Charlie and Jessie if they understood what their mom had just asked. Both nodded and Charlie offered, "I love my dad, but he scares me sometimes. I miss him and I hope I will get to see him again, but I think it is good that Mom brought us here because he will be SO mad when he gets home and sees that we are not there." Both Cynthia and Jessie nodded in agreement, and Lou and Rhonda could see the anxiety that was raised just from the consideration of this image. What Lou saw on their faces, plus her calculation of the time they had been away from Michigan (about eight days), resulted in an immediate change in her evaluation of need. The Browns' situation jumped to "Urgent."

Lou explained, as calmly as possible, that Cynthia's information helped her to see more clearly that the family's need for protection could not wait. Lou provided crisis line phone numbers and contacts for Cynthia, encouraging her to use 911 if needed. She made temporary arrangements with Rhonda for Cynthia to have a cell phone she could keep with her at all times until she could get one of her own through Emergency Family Assistance. Lou asked Cynthia if she would be willing to take immediate steps to increase her safety and that of the children, given that Mike might be on his way to find her. Cynthia agreed. Lou explained that there were residents in the community who offered temporary, high-security protection in their homes when there was an emergency need. Lou thought that Cynthia and her children would meet the criteria for such a placement, two of which were that no space be available in the local battered women's shelter and that the person had funds to cover the minimal charge for this service. Within half an hour Lou had located a "safe haven" residence, and a short time later she accompanied them to meet Sharon and Linda, the couple who had agreed to take them in.

Lou provided introductions and explained the heightened security, safety, and confidentiality at "safe haven" residences. She briefly described the training Sharon and Linda had received to help them understand situations like the one Cynthia and her children were facing and told Cynthia how that training defined certain roles and functions for them. As Sharon and Linda welcomed the family, showed them where they would be staying, and offered a snack, Lou and Rhonda left, agreeing to return the next morning to discuss next steps.

Personal, Interpersonal, and Social/Community Levels

Once immediate needs had been addressed with the Brown family, Lou took a step back to gain perspective on the three levels of interaction. Cynthia, Mike, Charlie, and Jessie are the individuals whose needs, emotions, and thoughts form the core family dynamic. Interpersonal interactions between the parental/spousal dyad, between brother and sister, and between parents and children shape its climate and character. As the gathering of resources took place, extended-family members, friends, and helping professionals contributed to the social and community layer surrounding this family (figure 5.1).

Personal

At 30, homeless and "with a high fear factor," Cynthia was not where she had hoped to be at this time in her life. "Smart, talented, and ambitious" was the way she described herself at 20, the year before she met Mike. Her younger sister, Jessica, had died in a boating accident when Cynthia was 16, an event that had

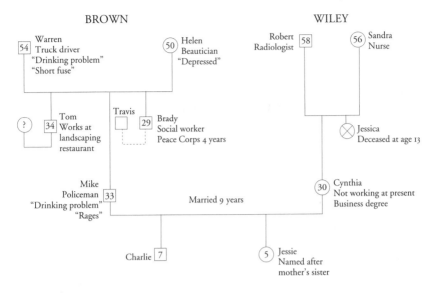

BROWN   WILEY

FIGURE 5.1 The genogram of the Brown-Wiley family.

caused her to "grow up earlier than I might have without that experience, but I decided I would take on life for both of us." Cynthia met regularly with her school social worker following the death of her sister and found her meaning in that tragic event by "making a conscious decision that my life would be a tribute to both of us. It's one reason I named my little Jessie after her."

Mike, at 33, according to Cynthia's description, had a "Jekyll/Hyde" personality. He was "one person publicly and a very different person at home, privately. He had received many awards in his work as a police officer and was respected and admired by his colleagues and charming in his relationships with friends." But at home "he gave his dark side full rein. It was as if he had to hold it in all day, and he thought home was the place to let it fly."

Charlie lived to ride his bike. While they were in Michigan he had developed a pattern of riding as much as possible to "stay away from Dad, to keep out of his way." His expression was animated when talking about the places he liked to go in their neighborhood and how he was planning to get a bigger and better bike someday. But all the light left his face when he was asked to describe what happened between his mom and dad. "He's mean to her. I tried to tell him to leave her alone, but he laughs at me and calls me a stupid little snort." Charlie missed his friends. He and Jessie had no opportunity to say good-bye to their friends, since Cynthia had to make her preparations in secret so that there would be no way for Mike to find out about her plans.

Jessie asked several times a day when they would be going home. She has a favorite stuffed toy—Lily, a koala bear—and never lets it out of her sight. Cynthia explained how she has "learned that Lily is the most important member of Jessie's support system right now. It's all she has of the life we left behind. She will say things to Lily that she would never say to me or Charlie in quite the same way. And Lily seems to have a direct line to Jessie's best friend in Michigan and to her grandma." Lou, their social worker, included Lily in every conversation after that.

Interpersonal

The couple relationship, each parent's relationship with each child, and the relationships with members of the extended family all play significant roles in the interpersonal dynamics of this family. Mike and Cynthia met in college while taking several of the same classes. "Strikingly handsome with a great attitude and a wonderful sense of humor plus so charming. I got pulled in by that charm." She had no idea of his hidden rage and depression until they had been married one month. After they'd moved several large pieces of furniture into their second-floor apartment, Cynthia offered lunch. Mike became furious when he saw that it was a sandwich and nothing more. He "yelled and screamed at me at high volume for ten minutes, waving his arms, then slammed his fist into the table and stomped out, headed for the nearest Burger King. I wasn't quite sure what had just happened, but when he came back, he acted as if nothing was wrong. So I just took a deep breath and hoped I had just imagined it and that it wouldn't happen again. My heart was still pounding, though."

Over the next several years, Mike's control of Cynthia continued to escalate and "oozed its way into every aspect of my life, my work, my friends, my family, everything." She described it as a "cruel and fierce obsession." He expected her to "obey and agree with everything he said. He tried to tell me how I feel and what I think, accusing me of being out to get him in some way. Then he would build his idea of our relationship on his own ideas. I felt totally erased as a person. To him, I was only useful as long as I lived up to his expectation of what a wife should be."

Cynthia described an increase in Mike's violence at two distinct times in their relationship. The first was when Mike was unable to complete the course work for the business degree for which they were both studying. Cynthia successfully completed the requirements and received her bachelor's degree with a major in business. The violent behaviors that increased at that time were Mike's spitting at her and shoving her against the wall. "His use of the 'f' word also increased at that time as in telling me, 'Go f___ yourself.' That's what he told me the morning of my birthday, while I was getting ready to go to my graduation."

Cynthia recalled a noticeable increase in Mike's violent behaviors a second time also, when she was pregnant with their second child. After Jessie was born, Mike made it very clear that he was disappointed that Jessie was not a boy. "This was subtle but violent to Jessie and to my soul, because he made it seem that Charlie could do no wrong while Jessie could do no right. He even said he hated her, that it was her fault that I had stopped taking care of him the way I should."

When I asked Cynthia about her relationship with her children, tears came to her eyes, and it was several minutes before she could speak. "I just hope I got out soon enough for them. They are what keep me going and when I almost turned back, when we were out there on the road, just looking at their faces kept me headed in the right direction." Both children were clinging tightly to their mom. "Charlie is the quiet one, but I'm hoping that won't last too long once we get settled and he has a chance to make some new friends. Jessie is just out there do-ing her thing most of the time. She probably doesn't fully understand what we are doing here, and she does get afraid at night when it's time to go to bed. But two nights ago she thanked me for bringing us here."

Thinking about Mike's relationship with both children, Cynthia reported that Mike continued to treat Charlie as his "favorite." His behavior toward Jessie soft-ened somewhat as she grew older and was able to interact more with him. "But there was one time when he had put her up on a table, she was dancing to music, and several of his friends were all seated around cheering and clapping. I had just walked in from shopping, and I could tell by Jessie's face that she got scared, that she didn't like what was going on but she couldn't figure out a way to get out of there by herself. Just as she was about to start crying, I marched in and got her, making some excuse like I needed her to help me in the kitchen or something. Remembering that whole scene later made me sick to my stomach."

Interpersonal experiences with extended-family members also played a role in the current situation. Cynthia had grown up in a family of origin where education was valued. Both parents were models for her of professionals who balanced work and family life, finding satisfaction in spending time with their two daughters and in their careers. Her father, Robert, was a radiologist, and her mother, Sandra, was a nurse. She and her younger sister, Jessica, were different in many ways, and Cynthia admits fitting the "responsible oldest" stereotype while Jessica "could get away with anything, and did." She describes their relationship as "close most of the time, but we were a pain in the neck for each other at times too, typical sister stuff. I just miss her so much. I think she would have helped me if she could see the fix I'm in right now."

The relationship with her parents changed after Jessica's death. "There was a wall, and they only half looked at me. It's hard to explain but I wondered if it was just too painful to have me around. Jess and I sort of looked alike and I always imagined from their expressions that they would see her when they looked at me and it would bring back all the memories that were just too painful." When asked if she could turn to them for help at this time, Cynthia said that she had gone to her parents when she tried to leave Mike the first time and they convinced her to go back. "I don't think they get what this kind of abuse is all about. They have their own ideas about commitment and going back to work things out. They see only the public, charming side of Mike. He charms them to their face and has only negative things to say about them behind their backs. I don't know. I'm not sure if they even would believe me, and I guess part of me wants to protect them from having to go through too much more pain."

On the interpersonal level, Cynthia's in-laws also played a role in her life and in the lives of the children. Cynthia felt she could trust her mother-in-law, Helen, and her brother-in-law, Brady, to understand her reasons for leaving Mike. Helen was familiar with verbal raging from her husband, Warren, Mike's father. Brady was a social worker and currently worked as an associate director of a victims' assistance program in Arizona. Mike's relationship with his parents mirrored what he seemed to want to create in his family with Cynthia. Mike was the middle son and his father's "favorite." His mother was, as Mike saw it, "obedient to Dad the way wives are supposed to be." Mike's predominant stance toward his brother, Brady, appeared to be one of ridicule or embarrassment as far as Cynthia could see.

Social/Community

The social and community aspects of Cynthia's life had grown narrower and narrower as Mike's abuse increased. His expectation that she would be with him all the time when he was not working or with his friends was intertwined with his rages over believing that her time with her friends was an effort on her part to get away from him. These attitudes gradually eroded most of her friendships. Several friends had tried to help her when they heard about the level of violence, but when she could not respond as they thought she should or when they felt too threatened, they too backed away. "After he broke my nose, he acted like he was embarrassed to be seen in public with me. He tried to order me to stay at home. At first, I laughed that one off. How ridiculous! Then he beat me once after he saw me at the park with my neighbor, Nancy. After that, all he had to do was threaten and I believed him. The brainwashing was intense. Even now, if he were to walk in and hear me telling you all this, I believe he would kill me." Though Mike oppressively confined Cynthia's freedom of movement in her community, he never questioned his own practice of moving freely among his colleagues on the police force and with his hunting and fishing "buddies." In fact, the limiting of people's freedoms, especially those perceived as disobeying "The Law" was simply one part of his job that brought him the accolades and the sense of power he considered essential to "doing his job well."

Now in a completely unfamiliar community, Cynthia described her social and community life by saying, "The only way is up." From her conversation with the social worker at the homeless shelter, she learned that her "antennae were up." She realized that she trusted her intuition in ways that she for many years had thought were lost to her. Renting the storage unit on the spur of the moment was one example she gave. "And look where that brought me. To you." Cynthia spoke of her anticipation that her connections in this new community would increase with time, but her hesitation and uncertainty were also evident at this early stage.

The Beginning Phase

Social Worker Preparation

This was not the first time Rhonda had informed Lou about a homeless family seeking shelter in one of the storage units. Part of Lou's preparation, she realized, was to remember those other families, their stories, and how they had managed to move on. What were the resources they had been able to use? What information had they needed? How had they managed to cope? Who were the people in their support networks? These other stories could provide possibilities and serve her need for anticipatory empathy, yet they could not be expected to necessarily match Cynthia's situation. What would she find this time?

Lou also had a seven-year-old son with whom she was "totally taken in," so she became aware that she might need to watch the balancing of her attention between Charlie and Jessie. She tuned in to the courage and hope plus the grave seriousness related to safety that she always felt every time she heard the story of a person who had survived battering and was in the process of creating a life free from that violence, amazing *strength in response to vicious violence.* Lou wondered how much alcohol (a possible *addiction?*) played a role in this family's oppression, checked again about financial resources, and increased her alertness to any *discrimination* against Cynthia as a transient, as a single mom, or as the spouse of a police officer. Lou had a strong sense that Cynthia was a person who would have no difficulty *empowering herself* and using appropriate *support from others.* She did note, however, that messages of powerlessness were presenting a barrier for Cynthia when she considered using the police as a source of protection in the community. Finding ways to *equalize this power differential* might become part of their work together.

First Meeting

Foremost on Lou's mind when she met Cynthia, Charlie, and Jessie at the storage unit for the first time was their safety and comfort. As she listened to Cynthia's story she could see that the threat of further violence was a constant influence in Cynthia's thinking and decision-making process. When victims of battering need to leave quickly and need to keep their preparations invisible, many of their familiar comforts must be left behind. This was true for the Brown-Wiley family (Cynthia adopted the hyphenated form of her name when she got to her new community). Lou had often found that a tangible contribution to the family's comfort could help provide a sense of safety between social worker and family. Many victims "on the run" feel forced to hide for a time, but as Lou listened to Cynthia's story, she heard that Cynthia was already actively pursuing food, shelter, and employment. Cynthia later confirmed what Lou had suspected: she had been rehearsing in her mind what she would do if she "could get out and start a new life." Cynthia was "still too scared to sit still for long because her imagination would take her to the worst." "And what would that be?" Lou asked. "That he will find us, that he would have one of his guns, that something terrible would happen, that he would try to take the kids, or that I might end up going back there. I will do everything I can to never go back there."

Discussing What Help Is Desired and Contracting for Service

Lou had heard in Cynthia's requests for help, first of all, safety, then food, shelter, and employment. She checked with Cynthia to see if these requests needed to be listed in any other order of importance. Cynthia agreed to the sequence and added that she hoped to have them in place before the beginning of the school year, a couple months away. She wanted to contact a grade school where both children could be enrolled when the time came. Two things were added to her list of desired help: checking with schools regarding registration and enrollment for Charlie and Jessie and cooperating with any mandate that might result from the CPS investigation.

Safety, food, shelter, employment, contact with schools, and response to CPS, then, formed the structure of the contract for service between Lou and Cynthia. These priorities would serve as a guide for their work together initially, and they would regularly review the list to ensure that it continued to fit Cynthia's needs. Lou explained her role as one of assisting Cynthia, providing support and information when needed, and connecting Cynthia to helpful resources in the community. She emphasized the mutuality of the work they would do together.

Taking one thing at a time, and thinking "safety in the choice of shelter," Lou reminded Cynthia of their earlier conversation about the Safehouse shelter for women and their children. Lou remembered that Cynthia had contacted one of these programs when she arrived in town. "Would you like to make the calls yourself to the other shelters? We can do that today if you like." When Cynthia called, the worker remembered her and asked her to come in the next day with the children for an interview, even though space was not yet available. The worker immediately recognized Lou's name when it was mentioned, and she invited Lou to attend the meeting as well. Lou agreed to do so.

Cynthia's financial resources provided the basis to meet needs related to food and employment. Lou clarified exactly what these financial resources were at that time. Cynthia had carefully anticipated various needs. She had calculated a minimum amount to last for at least the summer, two and a half to three months. One thing she had not anticipated, however, was the higher cost of living in her new community. This meant that she would need to find employment or other sources of financial support sooner than she had planned, as soon as possible. To help in the interim, Lou provided information about the town's Cooperative Market and its emergency assistance program for families in transition. Cynthia hoped to find a place to live that would be near the school that Charlie and Jessie would be attending. For that reason, she considered waiting until a later time to contact school personnel about registration.

Strengths in Response to Oppressions

Cynthia's long-term planning, her ability to take significant risks, her awareness of the children's needs, her "I can do this" attitude, and her increasing trust in her own intuition all stood out as strengths in response to the violence she had experienced. That violence in her life was often an overpowering oppression both externally and internally. Externally, she feared a surprise appearance from Mike at any moment, and following closely on the heels of that fear was the constant fear for her life and the lives of the children. Mike had thoroughly convinced her that the "system" would work against her if she ever tried to leave again. She had experienced this with Mike's colleagues in Michigan, and consequently she had internalized this fear. She also experienced the internal oppressive force of a variety of post-trauma responses: exhaustion, confusion, nightmares, startle responses, hypervigilance, self-doubt, insomnia, shaking.

Yet, in the midst of all of these challenges, she pursued an action that seemed at the time to be her "only choice or die. Most of the time I refused to think that I could die, but I had no doubt that my spirit was dying, my will to live was dying. That was enough." Cynthia felt the oppressive force of parents who did not understand what she was facing on a daily basis, who had rigid, traditional beliefs that dictated the way a husband and wife worked out their differences. She had experienced firsthand from her own family what it was like to be the recipient of blame directed at the victim.

For many families this list would have added up to unbeatable odds. Yet the strength of Cynthia's commitment to provide a safer environment for her children plus a strong belief in her capacity to create something better for them and for herself carried her through a transition filled with uncertainty and the need to trust people.

The Middle Phase

When Lou and Rhonda left Cynthia, Charlie, and Jessie at the "safe haven" home with Sharon and Linda, there was a clear sense that the beginning stages of work with this family had come to an end, that Cynthia had agreed to accept services, and that a more detailed understanding of needs, as well as resources to meet those needs, had begun to take shape.

Providing Information

Choices for providing information to Cynthia and her children needed to be closely related to their needs as expressed by Cynthia: safety, food, shelter, employment, the children's education, and the response to a CPS mandate. Lou began by listing possibilities for each of these categories. Safety information, for example, included descriptions of the procedures related to temporary and permanent restraining orders, to self-defense training, to obtaining a protection dog, and to the district attorney's victims' assistance resources. Information related to food included the community food cooperative, food stamps, food banks supported by several local churches and the one at Emergency Family Assistance, and the Community Food Share.

Information related to Cynthia's request for shelter included the regional shelters for battered women and their children. Even though the initial inquiry about vacancies had been unsuccessful, it was still necessary to maintain contact and to follow up periodically. Lou provided information about the "safe haven" home, with the understanding that this arrangement would be temporary; the maximum stay allowed was three weeks. Often family members reach out once they find out what their relatives are facing. In Cynthia's case, however, she had tried this alternative on previous attempts to leave Mike and now felt that she needed to respect her family's request that she make other arrangements. Future possibilities were apartment and trailer rentals in the area. Providing information about comparable costs of living in nearby communities was also on Lou's list.

Lou also considered information relevant to employment: building upon Cynthia's business school training, preparing a résumé that included her goals and her "too rusty" skills, locating short-term courses that would increase her marketability, improving grooming habits and choices of how to dress for job settings, plus some role playing in advance before making contact with a potential employer. Taking a detailed look at Cynthia's budgetary needs and her set of skills could help determine a salary range.

Cynthia also requested information about the children's education. With two months to go before the beginning of the school year and with her financial resources quickly running out, the first step would be finding a new source of income. Her preference was to find a residence close to a school for the children, but it was also desirable that the home be close to her work setting if possible. In the meantime, however, Lou could still provide information about the kinds of schools available and about the quality of educational opportunities for children in the various school systems.

Two days after their first meeting, Lou received a call from the CPS worker, who told Lou that the information received about the Brown-Wiley family did warrant an investigation. Major concerns listed included no residence, violence in the immediate past, lack of a support system since traveling from another state, and lack of financial and other concrete resources. There would be a required visit to the family and a follow-up interview with the Department of Social Services to determine a plan. Lou explained the contract for service that she and Cynthia had discussed and was asked to bring that to the family visit. As planned, Lou was there to support Cynthia during the investigation by the CPS worker. The result was a judge's mandate that mirrored the contract for service and required reports of progress to be submitted at four-week intervals during the summer. There would be a follow-up in September after the children had begun school.

Strengthening Coping Skills

The longer Cynthia was away from Mike, the higher was her stress about the time she would be discovered and would have to face some kind of confrontation. Coping with this daily increase of stress was constantly on her mind. She went through each day with a heightened sense of watchfulness and became even more protective of the children and concerned about their safety. In their work together, Lou and Cynthia began each meeting with issues of safety. Immediate safety needs were addressed first, and a longer-term plan for safety also began to take shape. Responding to immediate needs, Cynthia asked for a "protective shield" at shelters and "safe havens," and she expressed an interest in receiving self-defense training. One aspect of the longer-term plan was how to inform her employer and school authorities that she and the children were at increased risk due to a husband and father with a history of violence. Lou also described a network intervention, a "family group conference," that would invite extended-family members, community service and support personnel including police and Safehouse advocates, colleagues in her workplace, and representatives from the children's school. When Lou first mentioned this option, she could see that this was too much information for Cynthia to grasp at that time, and they agreed to discuss it again later.

Coping choices also grew from Cynthia's expressed needs. Lou would need to find out what skills Cynthia, Charlie, and Jessie already had available to them and what the barriers were to those skills. Cynthia had shown her resourcefulness in providing food while she and the children were making their way across the country. Because she had not been able to build up a reserve of food for the trip, which would have raised Mike's suspicion, she stuffed what she could into the spaces of the small suitcase and then used vending machines along the way to provide additional snacks. She stayed away from restaurants, not wanting "to leave a trail where we would get identified." Once in her new community, she tried for "maximum nutrition at minimum expense" with foods that did not need refrigeration, so at the self-storage unit she had crackers and peanut butter, canned beans, jugs of water, boxes of powdered milk, and bags of sugar. She welcomed Lou's information about bulk foods at the food cooperative as well as how to use food stamps.

To cope with changes in shelter from a three-bedroom home in a suburban community to being homeless, Cynthia used various phrases to help her survive the transition: "It's only temporary." "Little things can make it look like home." "Providing comforts for the kids keeps me going." With assistance from Rhonda and Lou, options for shelter became available that would help her meet her goals of greater safety, comfort, privacy, and eventually self-sufficiency. A back-and-forth process occurred between coping with needs for shelter and coping with the need for employment, each somewhat dependent on the other. Cynthia discovered a four-week evening course in word processing, but to take advantage of it she needed Lou's help with child care and access to a computer. These were arranged through Emergency Family Assistance, and Cynthia overlapped her work in the course with making contacts for jobs that could begin when she finished her course work.

As Cynthia and Lou discussed the children's educational needs during the summer, they became aware of several tasks that could help Charlie and Jessie prepare for school. Before Cynthia and the children had left Michigan, Cynthia read with both children daily. They had not been able to bring any books with them, however, and so Lou provided directions to the local library plus information about children's reading programs there. Additionally, Cynthia wondered if the violence the children had witnessed at home could have set them back in their schoolwork. Knowing that this was a possibility, Lou asked Cynthia if she would like to schedule an evaluation. Cynthia made this call and discovered an evaluation was part of the school's entrance policy and would take place at the school where the children registered.

Participation

Lou also shaped the direction of her work with the Brown-Wiley family on the third empowerment activity of participation, again focusing specifically on the needs requested by Cynthia: safety, food, shelter, employment, the children's education, and the response to the judge's mandate. Needs for safety and shelter came together as Cynthia and Lou discussed options for participation. Lou suggested that it might be important to include Charlie and Jessie in this decision, and Cynthia agreed. Charlie came up with the idea that he would like to live with another family that had kids around his age. He had figured out that this could "make it easier on you, Mom, when you have your classes and when you might need someone to help get our dinner." Cynthia admitted that she had not thought about living with another family and thought it sounded like a good idea but realized "I could not do it with another shelter family." Several weeks of checking the want ads in the newspaper provided no leads, but one day Cynthia saw an advertisement that read, "Housing Helpers. Call This Number." Before calling it, she contacted Lou and requested help in clarifying how she should negotiate for what she wanted and needed. Lou helped her think through questions such as how expenses would be shared, could the children have their own bedroom, were there other children and, if so, what were their ages, were pets allowed, was there a garage for the car (Cynthia wanted to conceal it as much as possible), should she give information about the possibility that her husband might arrive "and cause some serious trouble," and, if so, how much information was necessary? With her questions answered to her satisfaction, Cynthia called the next morning. Of the three possible matches she was given, one interested her more than the others. She called, and she and the children visited the home that afternoon.

Cynthia was encouraged by what she found, both for herself and for Charlie and Jessie, but she asked the Bernards, the couple renting this "apartment over the garage," if they would mind if Cynthia brought the social worker "who has been helping me get established" to take a look and to "bring another pair of eyes and another evaluation." The couple agreed that would be fine. Lou agreed to go with the family the following afternoon, and on the way there she learned that Cynthia's agenda included not only having Lou take a look at the living arrangement but also having her present to support Cynthia when she told the couple about Mike and his rages.

Cynthia was a little surprised when Lou greeted the couple by their first names, but she did not ask about the connection. Lou agreed that everything checked out according to the preferences Cynthia had voiced, they understood that Cynthia was currently interviewing for jobs, and they had an 11-year-old son and a 15-year-old daughter. The only question remaining was whether they would be willing to take Cynthia and the children after they learned about the potential violence.

As Mr. Bernard began putting the pieces together, the name "Mike" with Cynthia's last name, he suddenly asked which police academy Cynthia's husband had attended. He had graduated the year after someone by that same name, but he doubted it was the same person. When Cynthia showed him Mike's picture, all he said was, "This is the same Mike Brown." Mr. Bernard—Sergeant Bernard—took a long look at Cynthia and at Charlie and at Jessie and simply said, "We will do everything we can to make sure you are safe here."

Following the visit with the Bernards, Cynthia and Lou discussed advantages and disadvantages of the living arrangement. Charlie and Jessie were included in these discussions. The conclusion was to stay the maximum time possible with Linda and Sharon with the "safe haven" arrangement and to use the remaining two weeks to continue her search for employment. Cynthia also expressed concern about how many times the children had been moved from place to place and the effects that might have on them. She wanted them to "have a place they can call home before they have to deal with getting used to a new school, too."

Also related to safety and to opportunities for participation, Lou let Cynthia know about the support group offered by the local Safehouse Outreach Center. This group met twice a week and was an open group, so participants were usually different each time, though group members were asked to try to attend at least six times if possible. Education about violence in relationships was combined with group supportive counseling. Cynthia did attend this group for three sessions but decided she would prefer to find support in other ways, since her job search and the time she needed to be with Charlie and Jessie were higher priorities at the time. She told Lou that she wanted to find "ways to move my life forward, rather than looking back."

Considerations for participation also addressed Cynthia's other needs, those for food, employment, the children's education, and the reports to CPS. At first, Lou's question about "sharing food with others" brought some sadness to Cynthia's face. She recalled the vending machines and her experience at the shelter for the homeless. She remembered getting to the bottom of the peanut butter jar. But then she also thought about the lunch Lou had brought the first time they met and about the potluck dinner provided by the food cooperative. Reminiscences about family holiday meals were part of the conversation, and then Cynthia went silent for a moment. "I just realized that I am so afraid to go to the grocery store by myself. Before leaving Michigan, I heard on the news about a woman who was shot by her ex-husband in a parking lot. I'm jumpy about this, and sometimes I do feel like I might faint when I get out of the car. Two days ago I couldn't find a parking place close enough to the front door, so I just left and decided to try later. Is this crazy?" Lou offered reassurance, explaining how this reaction was connected to her reality at this time and briefly telling Cynthia about "hypervigilance" and how it serves a person who is experiencing a response to trauma. Cynthia frequently waited in her car until she saw someone she could follow into the store, and she would walk with others as she left, but going shopping with a group was an idea that had never occurred to her. Lou gave Cynthia contact information for people who provided this service, and she also told Cynthia about the delivery services available through the local food stores.

With regard to employment, Lou told Cynthia about a career workshop that was offered at a local church. Cynthia planned to attend, but she experienced overwhelming panic as she started to leave her apartment and decided to remain at home that evening instead. Mrs. Bernard was taking care of Charlie and Jessie, so Cynthia used the time to contact Lou for support and for guidance on how to cope with the panic. Lou suggested that being with Mrs. Bernard and the kids might be comforting, and Cynthia chose to do that. Later in the week, Cynthia returned to her search for employment and discovered an upcoming job fair advertised in the newspaper.

As the children's education was considered, Cynthia set a goal to contact the school Charlie and Jessie would be attending in the fall for the purpose of scheduling a time for their evaluations. The Bernards introduced Cynthia to other parents with children in that school so that Charlie and Jessie could begin developing friendships with other students before the school year began.

Lou and Cynthia discussed the best way to report the progress of their work to CPS. Well before the expected dates of submission of those reports, they agreed to meet and discuss what had happened during the four weeks to be reported. Lou kept her notes of their contacts, but she suggested that Cynthia might also wish to keep a journal or diary of what was happening in her transition. Cynthia agreed. Her contributions to the monthly reports became invaluable in identifying the steps that she took to move forward with her new life. Also, through her writing, she discovered a way to let go of many of the emotions that often felt overwhelming to her.

Later, Cynthia looked back on the decision to remain with the "safe haven" living arrangement with Linda and Sharon as the "decision that saved my life." The evening after the visit to the Bernards' apartment, Lou received a phone call from Mr. Bernard. He informed her that Mike knew Cynthia was in Colorado and that the "missing persons" list at the police department in town included her name. Mike apparently was not accusing Cynthia of kidnapping the children, "probably because he wants to cover up any report of his violence toward Cynthia, which would bring an abuse charge down on him." Lou contacted Cynthia with this information, and they met shortly after to complete the necessary paperwork for a temporary restraining order. Cynthia mentioned that her cousin, Danielle, had told her about restraining orders earlier. Lou asked, "Would she be available to you if you and the children need a place to stay out of town for a while?"

Danielle was another family member who felt uncomfortable around Mike, so Cynthia hesitated to call on her for further assistance. "Brady, Mike's brother, would probably help, though." Lou handed her the phone. The urgency in Brady's voice was immediately apparent when he heard Cynthia. Mike had told the whole family what Cynthia had done and that he was going to Colorado to look for her and the children to bring them back. "He thinks you are in _____. If that is where you are, get yourself down here [to the town where Brady lived with his partner] right now and we will find a place for you." Cynthia's shaking hands and the look of panic on her face alerted Lou to the need for immediate action. All she heard was, "Brady, we're coming." When Lou heard the offer, she agreed and went with Cynthia to help prepare the children and to inform Sharon and Linda.

The drive to Arizona took twelve hours. Cynthia was "on the run" again. This was not what she wanted for herself or for the children, yet she knew that their safety was more important now than ever before. She had received enough information in the last two weeks to know that the danger from Mike's potential acts was much greater now because of the drastic move she had made to get away. Later she would report that she had made that trip "on adrenaline alone," but it got her to Brady's by midmorning the next day. He welcomed them and told them that there was a room waiting for them at the local women's and children's shelter. "He said he wished we could stay with him but was afraid of what Mike might do if he ever found out."

Lou had arranged with Cynthia that she would use the cell phone she had gotten from Rhonda to call Lou after she and the children had safely arrived at Brady's. When they spoke, Lou had just returned from a meeting on behalf of Cynthia, Charlie, and Jessie. The meeting was attended by a representative from the district attorney's victims assistance program, Sergeant Bernard, Lou, and Mike Brown, Cynthia's husband. The night before, only about three hours after Cynthia had left, Mike had knocked at the front door of Sharon and Linda's home, dressed in uniform, and showed them a picture of the car Cynthia was driving. He asked Linda if she had seen it recently. When she hesitated, Mike announced that he had a warrant to search their home. When Linda asked to see it, however, there was no warrant. Mike began shouting and beating on the side of the house. Sharon, listening from another room, had already recognized who this was from the picture Cynthia had shown them, and she called 911. Police officers arrived within five minutes. They later described Mike's change in manner as "startling, almost like there were two different people there." Mike's "buddy-buddy" act did not deter these officers, though, and he was "respectfully" taken to the police station for "discussion to hear how we can help you find your wife."

When information about Cynthia came on the screen, the temporary restraining order was visible. Lou's name, as advocate and as a social worker at Emergency Family Assistance, also showed up, and she was contacted for a meeting the following morning. It was Lou's idea to ask Sergeant Bernard if he would be willing to be present. Mike seemed aware of the consequences he would face if he attempted to leave town before the meeting. He arrived promptly for the meeting the next morning. In textbook fashion, he tried to place the blame for the recent events on Cynthia, excluding information that might point to his behavior as a factor in her decision to leave. "She has just been acting differently lately. I don't know what has gotten into her. Folks tell me it's amazing what menopause can do to a woman's head. Now I guess I get to see it firsthand." (Smiles.) When Mike was asked if he understood why his wife wanted a restraining order against him, his only response was, "That's the most far-fetched thing I've ever heard of. Where did she ever get such an idea?" Mike did verbally agree to obey the restrictions of the restraining order, and he did not object to Cynthia having the two children with her. "They can all just take a little vacation if they want to" was how he chose to interpret it in front of his colleagues, who were well aware of an abuser's tendency to minimize the violence. The implication was clear that he would be expecting them to return home to Michigan at some time in the future. Mike was informed that his verbal threats against Linda would be recorded and that he was free to go, but there would be a call to his office the next day "just to make sure you get back there okay." Lou expressed her reservations about this "minimal accountability" and reiterated the procedural steps involved in the transition of a temporary restraining order to a permanent restraining order. Sergeant Bernard informed Mike about the stance of officers in this community as a result of their training in domestic violence. "When it's a fellow officer, we get him the help he needs. You may want to think about this when you get back to Michigan." After a few concluding remarks, Mike left, Linda and Sharon were informed of his departure, and Lou returned to respond to Cynthia's message.

Cynthia decided to stay in Arizona for a few days, and with Brady's help she gained more understanding about the importance of ending the relationship with Mike. Brady helped her with ways to protect herself and suggested that she might want to change her name, have an unlisted number, get a large and intimidating but protective dog, take a self-defense course, and continue in a support group for at least a year. Cynthia brought all of these ideas back to Lou, and most of them were in place by the time Cynthia, Charlie, and Jessie moved into their apartment at the Bernards' house. Charlie and Jessie were given the responsibility of choosing the dog at the animal shelter, and they chose a four-year-old Rottweiler named Lucas. As they left to take him home with them, Charlie matter-of-factly told Lucas, "We were in a shelter for a while, too, Lucas, but now we are homeless no more. We have a place. You come with us."

The Ending Phase

Cynthia and Lou continued to work together over the next several months. Cynthia had twelve job interviews before accepting a position in the medical records department of the local hospital. She did change her name. Returning to her original name, she registered at the Social Security office as Cynthia Wiley. She returned the cell phone to Rhonda and got her own unlisted number. She and the children did move into the apartment over the Bernards' garage. She let her hair grow in with its natural chestnut color. She did take one of the local self-defense training courses for women. She found that "the ones that include aggressive tactics are just not for me. The flashbacks I get are just too overwhelming." So she chose a class in aikido, a nonviolent form of self-protection, and she took Lucas with her wherever she went. Some places did not allow dogs to enter, however. So she made a jacket for him and had the words "Protection Dog" stitched on both sides. Charlie and Jessie were evaluated for placement in classes at school. Jessie would remain at her chronological level, but the recommendation was made for Charlie to repeat his previous year, not only because of the trauma he had witnessed at home combined with his attempts to "be the man" in his mom's life but also because the evaluation revealed that Charlie had moderate dyslexia and could benefit from some additional support in reading and study methods.

Two major tasks remained. The first was getting the permanent restraining order in place. The accused has the right to see the accuser at such hearings. Lou helped Cynthia prepare for the possibility that Mike might show up and attempt to plead his case. She assured Cynthia that she, Lou, would be there with her. Lou asked if Cynthia would like to have other supports as well. "I really wish Brady would come. But I'm not sure he would want to take that risk to his own safety. But if Brady and Travis [Brady's partner] come, I think Danielle [Cynthia's cousin] would come too."

Lou saw this as an opportune moment to explain more about family group conferencing (Burford and Hudson 2000). She told Cynthia that the purpose of such a conference was to bring together abusers, survivors, their families, and sufficient supports and protections in the community so that a plan for the safety and well-being of children and adult family members could be devised. The plan included authorizing those resources to carry out the plan for protection of the survivors. "So Mike would never be able to do to us again what he did back in Michigan. Yes, I would like to give it a try." Once Lou and Cynthia knew the date of the hearing for the permanent restraining order, they contacted the members of Cynthia's network.

Sergeant Bernard offered to contact Mike, to explain the importance of his attendance at the court hearing as well as the conference following, and he offered to accompany Mike to the courtroom that morning. Mike initially claimed to be "too busy" and said, "Just let her do what she wants, I'll get to her when I have time." Sergeant Bernard followed through by obtaining a judge's order for Mike to attend. When he called a second time with this information, Mike agreed to cooperate.

Including the Bernards, Cynthia had fourteen people present for the family group conference that followed the permanent restraining order hearing. Brady and Travis drove to Colorado from Arizona. They met Danielle at the airport, and the three of them shared a place to stay. From the community, two other police officers, a Safehouse advocate, two colleagues from Cynthia's job, and two school representatives (one for Charlie and one for Jessie) also agreed to participate. Perhaps most important for Cynthia, however, was the "complete lack of hesitation" in her parents' voices when she asked for their support. They not only came in response to the invitation to participate in the family group conference but they offered to stay for as long as Cynthia would like "to help in any way we can with the kids or whatever you need."

When Mike entered the courtroom with Sergeant Bernard, Cynthia reached out for Danielle, Brady, Charlie, and Jessie. Her father placed a hand on her shoulder. The permanent restraining order was granted, and the judge directed, "Mr. Brown, you will now be escorted to Room 3A by Sergeant Bernard for your family group conference."

Lou, as the coordinator of the process, opened the conference by thanking those in attendance and stating the purpose of the meeting: "to develop and approve a plan to keep Cynthia, Charlie, and Jessie safe." She also noted that the process is one that includes important roles for each person there and what each contributes to the ongoing realization of their purpose and plan. She stated the ground rules of confidentiality, listening respectfully to each speaker, and remaining nonviolent (Burford and Hudson 2000:176–177).

What followed for approximately the next hour began with Cynthia's recounting many of the experiences she and the children had lived through in the past two years. At several points, Mike buried his face in his hands. Then each of Cynthia's extended-family members and the community support representatives spoke about what was available from them personally and from their respective agencies to ensure safety for Cynthia and the children. Each made a plan with Cynthia about how to contact them if she felt threatened by Mike again or if he attempted to take the children. Major issues for discussion included whether Mike would be able to visit the children, how to access services for Mike in Michigan so that he could receive help in addressing his violence, how to respond if Mike showed up at the door of any one of the family members, and how to arrange periodic checks to verify that their plan was working. Brady had prepared a letter to read to Mike in which he acknowledged his intent to have this meeting serve as a turning point in their relationship as brothers, that Brady was there as a support for Mike, too, if he decided to seek help in ending his violence. When no further concerns were raised, each person was asked to make a statement of agreement with the plan. All those in Cynthia's network agreed. Mike had remained silent through much of the meeting, appearing to listen to what each person said. As it came to his turn to agree with the plan, he simply said, "You all have given me a lot to think about. I never want to hurt my kids, so I go along with your plan about that. I grew up hearing from my dad that a man has a right to whip his wife into shape, not only a right but an obligation. I gotta get rid of that one, I know. It all just got out of hand with you, Cynth. I guess I never thought it would come out. You're a stronger woman than I imagined."

Lou summarized the plan that had been agreed upon and indicated that she would type it out and send each person a copy. According to their plan, Brady would check in next month to see how the plan was working and to find out if there were any changes that could strengthen it. Cynthia rose. "I just need to say thank you to everyone. I have no other words to tell you how much this means to me." Sergeant Bernard invited Mike to leave at that time, and he personally drove Mike to the airport to catch a plane back to Michigan. Mrs. Bernard invited all the others to their home, where she and Cynthia had prepared a meal for everyone.

Lou and Cynthia met the next day for follow-up. After recounting several aspects of the meeting, Cynthia moved to one remaining task for which she wanted Lou's help. She knew she was ready to file for divorce and to gain custody of the children. Through a colleague at work Cynthia found a divorce lawyer who could accept the payment plan she needed. Cynthia told Lou she thought she would "forget about child support because every time he has to write the check, it could set off the rage again and I just can't live with that hanging over my head." Lou offered information about the legal obligation of child support and encouraged Cynthia to discuss with the lawyer the methods for receiving payments in a way that could minimize the threats she felt. The lawyer had faced this before and knew that some employers are willing to take the payment directly out of the person's paycheck and have it electronically deposited in the spouse's account. This arrangement was eventually what was set up for Cynthia's payments, and even though the threat was minimized, it never disappeared entirely.

Cynthia discussed with Lou her need to "refuse alimony because a financial tie is an emotional tie and I want to move on, I want to support myself and not live on an inflated income that will disappear later." Regarding this decision, Lou helped Cynthia weigh the positives and negatives, and in the end Cynthia did not receive alimony. The seeming unimportance to Mike of maintaining a connection with Charlie and Jessie set off what Cynthia called "intense grieving." As Lou supported her while she looked back on that relationship, Cynthia realized "he never saw himself as their father, I guess, since he was always competing with them for my attention."

Dealing with Feelings

The panic, the post-trauma responses, the fear, sadness, and grieving related to multiple losses were evident during the ending phase for Cynthia. Lou continued seeing Charlie and Jessie as well. Charlie was verbal about his feelings, but Jessie relied more on her actions to express her feelings. Then, recalling Jessie's stuffed bear, Lou asked, "Where's Lily?" It is not unusual for children to express feelings through visual or experiential modes in combination with verbal expression, rather than through words alone. Jessie was fortunate to have her connections with friends and her grandmother back in Michigan through Lily. Charlie talked through the changes in his life in a similar fashion with Lucas, who was also included as a regular member of their family sessions with Lou. Charlie said: "Mom, Jessie, me, Lily, Lucas, and Mr. and Mrs. Bernard. This is our family here for now. I still think about my dad and my friends back in Michigan, but I like what we have here better."

Consolidating Gains

As Cynthia moved on with her life, the memory of that trip across country, leaving behind so much of what she had known, began to fade. Part of Lou's work was to help her see how far she had come, to consider where she had started, where she was now, and to take credit for all that had happened in between. The consolidation of gains involved surrounding Cynthia with enough of a supportive structure in this new place that a return to earlier, less beneficial, patterns would have no benefit. Her supportive structure at the family group conference included the support group at the Safehouse Outreach Center, her job where she was valued and respected, a school setting that was responsive to the needs of her children, and a growing friendship network. Connections with her brother-in-law and cousin also helped to decrease the isolation that was often the breeding ground for her fears. Her social worker was a constant resource and provided individual support as well as the connections to the web of services available to her in the community. To Lou, Cynthia wrote, "You have been my anchor, a bridge to all that's here that I would have no way of knowing otherwise. You keep me awake, alert. And you're neutral, I mean you just tell me about possibilities and then let me decide what I need next or what I want to do. You believe in me, sometimes even more than I believe in myself. That's what got us my job, our apartment, our dog, our new life."

When enough patterns toward the well-being of the entire family are introduced, the activities surrounding those patterns replace earlier destructive patterns, leaving no time or reason to revert to those earlier patterns. Family members make conscious choices toward their well-being; those choices do not result in new behaviors immediately, but the time is often short before the new behaviors take root. Once families experience these gains, the likelihood of going back is diminished. We serve families well, however, in realizing and acknowledging the power of addictions to pull people back, the immobilizing impact of recurrent and ongoing trauma, the insidious coercion of emotional and physical abuse, the oppressive force of poverty and homelessness, and how long the road to recovery and change can be. Respecting the struggle and at the same time providing that vision of hope in the midst of it are guideposts for those who work with families through these stresses and changes.

Strengthening Connections with Community

Gains are also consolidated through adding connections in the community, continuing those that are already in place, and strengthening some that may not have been used for many years. Some connections may have served a purpose for the family at an earlier time but are no longer helpful and must be let go.

For Cynthia, connections were added through various housing options with which she came into contact: from living out of her car, to two different self-storage units, to the hope for shelter space that was not available, to the "safe haven" residence, and finally to her own apartment. With each contact, she established relationships with people who continued their support after she and the children had left one place and moved on to the next. Her connections with Lou and with Rhonda continued over time, and this continuity added contacts, such as school personnel and lawyers and potential employers. One of the most timely connections was her brother-in-law, Brady, with his immediate response to her needs for safety and a temporary place to stay.

Cynthia's work with Lou included recognizing that, while one whole set of community connections was forming to provide support to her and her children, she was simultaneously letting go of another community back in Michigan. There were gains and there were losses. Family members must give up earlier connections to allow time and space for new ones. When connections maintain, enhance, and help to create the well-being for families, when they are consistent with the purpose of empowerment practice, then it is likely that those connections will be accepted and used and, possibly, become lasting parts of the family's new life.

Evaluation

The ending phase of work also includes taking a look back at where the relationship began, first meeting, where the work stands at the present time, and what the immediate next steps look like—that is, past, present, future. This is the time to consider where the work started and why, how social worker and family interacted together in the middle phase, and whether the goals set at the beginning were reached. Were there milestones in the work and in the relationship between the social worker and the members of the family? We consider both the process over time and the product.

From an empowerment view, we also consider how the work has been integrated at personal, interpersonal, and social/community levels in the family's daily activity. We examine responses to the oppressions the family members have had to face. We evaluate how multicultural respect has helped understand the family's needs. Have we assisted them as they made the choices for next steps? Did we call upon as many resources and supports as possible? How was power used? And, finally, we evaluate ourselves for cooperative roles, ones that include an openness to future contacts if and when needed.

Lou, Cynthia, Charlie, Jessie, Lily, and Lucas all gathered to take a look at their work together approximately ten months after their first meeting. Cynthia knew she was ready for this to be their last time with Lou. "No question I needed this help to get going on a new life here. I appreciate it, but as long as I keep coming, I'll be remembering what I want to leave behind. I've got to move on. And, besides, other people need you and your time more than I do now. And I know where I can find you if I need something again."

As they considered the past, Cynthia retold the story of the night they left Michigan and recalled several experiences of their first weeks in this different community, including the first time they met Lou. She wanted the children to understand, after a few months in this new place, the reasons "why this is our family from now on, without your dad being here." This comparison between what had been "the good and the bad in Michigan and the good and the bad here" helped the children talk about the present and the changes they had faced.

Looking ahead to the future, Charlie wondered, "When I am older, can I have a talk with Dad then, just to see if he still wants to see me now and then?" Cynthia responded, "I don't know, Charlie. It might be possible. When that time comes, we will talk more about that, but, yes, it might happen."

So much had changed on the personal, interpersonal, and social/community levels for the family, "trading one whole set of relationships for a different one," as Cynthia observed. Yet she also recognized the importance of continuity through the transition. "Even though my marriage to Mike has broken apart, others in the family, like Brady and Danielle, have been there for us all the way through. And my mom and dad. I couldn't have done this without their support, even the ones who don't understand what abuse is all about. I didn't even know what it was all about when I decided I would get out. I just knew that if I wanted to have a life and to see the kids have the kind of life I imagined for them, then we had to get away from there." The social/community network was the one level at which Cynthia felt the most change had occurred. In Michigan she had been isolated from social interactions and community involvement because Mike maintained rigid control over what she did and where she went. She knew individuals in the school system and had contact with the children's teachers and some of the other parents, but that was the only interaction Mike allowed her to have outside the home. Now, in their new community, "I have so much going on that I have to be careful not to get overloaded, but it's great. For me and for the children, well, but when I think about it, this is just normal. But when it gets taken away, then you realize just how important it is when you get it back again."

The response to violence included Cynthia's choice to end her silence about Mike's physical violence, his threats, and other forms of verbal and emotional violence against her and the children. It also ended her attempts to reach out to family members for help, to stop expecting that they would know what to do. The threats that abusers use to convince victims that they must tell no one about the abuse can be extremely powerful in controlling the behaviors of family members. The threat of death is the ultimate tool in silencing their voices. Even though Cynthia had not heard the words "I will kill you if you tell," she had received enough indirect messages from Mike and from the guns available to him that she was convinced that her life was in danger. Such threats can mean that the telling of stories of abuse as experienced by the victims, though an act of great courage, may also place them at even greater danger. This is also why actions to ensure the greatest possible safety, even when it means a sudden change in location, as Cynthia experienced, will be the response of choice.

Simultaneously maintaining and enhancing the sense of well-being in this family accompanied efforts toward creating new ways for them to gain well-being in their new situation. In the midst of experiences of escaping, eating vending machine meals, changing hair color, having flashbacks in the presence of well-meaning homeless shelter workers, calling a storage unit "home," getting a jar of peanut butter to perform like the loaves-and-fishes parable, taking risks of accepting help from strangers as well as family members, and protecting two very frightened yet courageous children, the fundamental well-being in the loving relationship between mother and children carried Cynthia Wiley and her family forward. This is where well-being was maintained. Well-being was enhanced as it built upon that foundation and was further created through the new experiences in location, friendships, and a community that could reach out and support the needs of this family. In Cynthia's words: "Every time I look at Lucas, this dog of ours, I hear Charlie telling him that, just like us, he is homeless no more."

Part III

Helping Families

6

The Phases and Actions of Empowering Practice

The three phases of helping—beginning, middle, and ending—can aid the social worker in conceptualizing the progression of the work. It is useful for the worker to know the generalities about each phase, but the specific shape that each phase takes for an individual family can be determined only in the moment-by-moment transactions with that family. Each phase is characterized by a context, by developmental needs (of the family unit, of the individuals in the family, of the work itself), by a complex web of multicultural factors, by different qualities in the relationship between worker and the family system and subsystems, and by tasks specific to the work of that phase. Individual family members are likely to be in different phases at the same time. While some are ready to end the whole process after ten minutes, others may never leave the trust-building of the beginning phase. Even when a family reaches an active and involved middle phase of work, common post-trauma responses, such as intrusive memories or flashbacks, may enter the working relationship. In these instances, tasks specific to the beginning phase may need to be revisited. Avoidance of a "flight into health" that would prematurely end the work may need to be explained.

Sometimes families are self-referred, such as the Laurencio-Smith family. Sometimes they are mandated to receive services by a court decision, such as Cynthia Brown-Wiley and her children. And sometimes there is a combination of both self-referred and mandated requests for services, as in the Williams family. Many families include at least one reluctant member at some point in the work. Often these members voice their wish not to participate, and that wish is refused. Therefore, this insistence on their participation against their wishes becomes a kind of internal mandate, occurring as part of the family dynamics rather than coming from an external source. These dynamics of both formal and informal mandates have a marked influence on all phases of the work.

Variation exists in the middle and ending phases as well. In highly distressed families for whom chaos and complexity are the norm, rapid change is a given. It is extremely unlikely that such families will be able to follow a treatment plan smoothly from beginning to end. Therefore workers need skills in the middle phase that are consistent with managing rapid change, that enable them to stay with the family from one moment to the next, assisting with actions that are familiar and doable in the moment.

Highly distressed families frequently end their work with social workers prematurely, suddenly moving to other locations or simply deciding to end the work without informing the social worker. When it is difficult to access services, the sheer effort involved in gathering the family together may be too overwhelming to continue. Family members may also leave the work emotionally but still attend physically.

These variations call for us to look at practice in phase-specific ways, discarding rigidity about how and when each phase occurs or "should" occur. True to its constant, dynamic nature, the web of relationships is a fluid process. Staying with the family in the movement of their lives while simultaneously helping them to discover empowering choices to "make things happen" toward greater well-being are key skills in every phase of empowering practice.

The Beginning Phase of Work

At the moment a social worker accepts the opportunity to work with a family, processes that use the empowerment approach move into place. Before the initial meeting with the family, several steps shape the plan: (1) setting the stage; (2) holding the "meeting" before the meeting; (3) approaching initial information about the family with discretion related to the source of that information; (4) exercising professional awareness about strengths-based language and deficit-based language; and (5) acknowledging anticipatory empathy. In turn, the quality of the initial greeting, discovering what help is desired, making a "clear offer of service, and lowering anxiety and ambivalence" set the stage for the work to begin (Lee 2001:69). The central commitment of the empowerment approach—hearing their voices—accompanies every step of this beginning work.

When we work with families, hearing their voices involves a three-pronged focus: hearing individual voices, hearing the transactions between individuals, and hearing the "family voice," the messages that carry the identity of the family history and character. Hearing individual voices includes hearing those who are often treated as invisible—children, elders, or the "quiet ones." Hearing what happens in the interactions between people in the family includes hearing the voices of spouse to spouse, partner to partner, parent to child, and child to child as well as the interactions with extended-family members. Examples of the "family voice" are "We are a family who hangs together when the going is tough," "Blood is thicker than water," and "I left my biological family when I was fifteen and never looked back. My family now is my family of choice, the friends I have chosen to surround me." We also heard similar messages from both the Williams family and the Brown-Wiley family as they defined themselves in new configurations of what "family" meant to them after significant transitions. Hearing their voices also means hearing the context of their experiences and reaching for the meaning behind the words.

These processes and tasks combine to create an empowering base from which to begin practice with families. There is no given order. They are intertwined and simultaneous. A reciprocal influence is observable where each process has an ongoing effect on the others, and these create subsequent effects. The foundation for all later work is built upon the specifics of the beginning phase. It is in specificity that we gain the trust of others (Cameron 1998). In generalities we risk losing that trust. "Although we seldom view it this way, specificity is freedom. In the act of naming things precisely as they appear to us, we free our work from misunderstandings, from ambiguity, from vagueness" (54).

The Worker's Preparation

Our practice is only as effective as the preparation that precedes it. The culprit in struggles or stuck places in practice often lurks in the preparation. It is impossible to anticipate every nuance of meeting, joining, working with, and ending our experiences with highly complex families who face highly distressing events. There are surprises. There are secrets. The unexpected is always just around the corner. And still, the responsiveness of our actions will come from the foundation of our preparation.

Two steps are recommended as preparation for practice with families from an empowering perspective: (1) completing the Family Power Analysis (appendix B) through self-reflection and through feedback with colleagues, a supervisor, or both and (2) using the seven principles for empowering practice as guidelines to assess professional and personal qualities that may influence the work with each family. Review of these steps during the ongoing work with each family can also be beneficial.

The Family Power Analysis

Careful analysis of the worker's own family has long been promoted as one of the most important pieces of work in which professionals in training participate. "Engaging in a power analysis of the situation, another important technique for empowerment practice, first involves analyzing how conditions of powerlessness contribute to the situation. Identifying sources of potential power represents a second step" (Gutiérrez and Lewis 1999:19).

An in-depth analysis using the family genogram includes recognition of themes, patterns, cross-generational repetitions, cultural strengths, resources, and coping styles, as well as choices of behaviors left with past generations and those continued into the present. This tool sets the stage for the Family Power Analysis. The next step is to focus on the power relationships in the worker's family and the meaning given to those relationships by the worker.

One gives meanings to uses of power in one's family of origin and extended family. Those meanings go with social workers into their work with client families. "Power lines" define experiences of power under, power over, and power with. In "power under" experiences, consideration is given to forms of oppression, including internalized oppression, that existed and currently exist in our own families and within ourselves—sexism, ageism, adultism, heterosexism, classism, and discrimination related to ethnicity, differing abilities, religious and spiritual beliefs, education, language and the use of language. Identifying oppressive forces and refusing the "one down" position define and shape understanding of "power under" issues.

In "power over" experiences, the same multicultural categories apply, but they are used when recalling examples of when we found ourselves in the position of "unearned authority," perhaps even in an oppressive role. In the role of social worker, clients may confer "perceived authority" on the worker. Empowering practice means equalizing this power differential, using a "power with" approach, one that acknowledges mutuality of roles. We shift away from a deficit model and toward a family-strengths model as a way to view each family. In the process of self-examination, filtered through a culturally alert lens, "one critical step . . . is the acknowledgment of diversity as a strength rather than a problem" (Dupper and Poertner 1997:420).

A worker's ability to access her or his own strengths in the personal, interpersonal, and social/community arenas enhances preparation. Connections are made between worker empowerment and family empowerment. Connections occur between these levels of awareness and the purpose that guides empowering practice: to promote experiences that sustain, enhance, and create the lives we choose to live.

As helping professionals, we understand that all life experiences that lead from distress to strength provide useful information for empowering practice with families. Such experiences are part of the background. They give clarity about why it is important to begin from a place of compassion, humility, mutuality, and respect for the complexity of the work ahead of us.

The social worker's past experiences of power and powerlessness influence interactions with client families (Pinderhughes 1989). Workers must look at the use of power in their own families, both past and present, to avoid running the risk of "using it to meet their own needs" (110). "Power which intends to bolster the image of the therapist is perhaps the most infamous of therapy abuses" (Heller 1985:161). "Vigilance is essential to guard against the helper's normal vulnerability to reinforce the...client's sense of powerlessness and subordinance. Vigilance ensures that helpers learn ways of thinking and behaving that enable them to effectively use empowerment strategies with their clients. Understanding one's own experiences, feelings, attitudes, and behaviors related to having or lacking power is an important step in the attainment of such vigilance" (Pinderhughes 1989:111).

It is not necessary that all power issues from one's past be completely resolved before working with families. It is an ethical responsibility, however, to be as informed as possible about such issues, to continue to work toward their resolution or neutralization, and to have done what we can to have them in their proper place before we meet with client families..

The second tool for worker preparation is the use of the seven principles for empowering practice as guidelines to assess professional and personal qualities that may influence the work with each family.

Self-analysis Using the Empowerment Principles

The following questions can help to direct this self-reflective part of a worker's preparation before meeting a family for the first time and in an ongoing manner, as needed, throughout the work.

1. What strengths and resources do I have that will be of help with this family? Is there any aspect of the early information about the family that appears oppressive or diminishing? If so, what can be done before meeting with them? What is the best way to use strengths and resources in the work?

2. Considering all multicultural factors, what do I have in common with this family? Where are our differences? Are there potential barriers regarding these factors? If so, what can be done before meeting with the family? What is the best way to communicate with them about these commonalities and differences?

3. What individual, interpersonal, and community needs of my own may have an impact on my work with this family? What resources do I have on each of these levels that could serve them? What potential barriers might affect the work? What is the best way to communicate these individual, interpersonal, and community needs to them?

4. To empower myself in my work with this family, what are the ways I will continue to strengthen myself as the work progresses? Who are the people who are my resources as I do the work? What information will be helpful to me as I prepare to meet them? Will any extra effort be necessary to take care of myself physically, emotionally, or otherwise?

5. What, specifically, might I need to ask for from those who support me? From family? From coworkers? From friends? Do I anticipate any hesitation about asking for support from them? If so, what is that about and what do I need to do to take care of that work before I meet with this family?

6. With which family members might I be tempted to assume a "power under" stance? With which family members might I be tempted to assume a "power over" stance? If either of these possibilities presents a potential barrier in the work, what do I need to do to take care of that work before I meet with them? What will be the most helpful way to state the stance of "power WITH"—the mutuality of the work together?

7. What roles are most helpful given the information I have from this family so far? What is my own comfort level with each of these roles? Do I need more consultation about any of these roles before I begin working with them? If so, with whom and where? Are there any potential unintended consequences if I use these particular roles? What will be the best way to explain these roles to this family?

This set of questions can be completed within ten to fifteen minutes. It is usually most helpful to respond with the first answer that comes to mind. The goal is to use the questions to assist in our preparation to meet one family.

Processes for an Empowering Beginning

Setting the Stage

Workplace demands, overwhelming expectations for caseload management, and the enormous pressures of most social work practice settings require conscious efforts to create an environment in which we can enter the life of a family, and this must be attended to before they arrive for the first contact. Workers reassure family members that their lives and their work are the most important focus for the duration of the designated time frame, and distractions are minimized—computers are shut down, telephone calls are redirected, pagers and cell phones are shut off.

Minimizing distractions can also be part of the beginning of a home visit. It is important to respectfully ask about the family's wishes regarding various distractions. What may seem to be a distraction for the worker may not necessarily be a distraction for the family members. Access to telephone calls may need to be allowed, especially during times of emergency and crisis. A corner or a curb at the homeless shelter may serve the purpose of minimizing distraction in that setting. One worker reported her work with a family while sitting at a picnic table in a nearby park. Setting the stage involves the social worker's training in the use of the environment to maximize the comfort and availability of the family members.

Client families may be either self-referred or mandated. When families are required by a court decision or a judge's mandate to attend sessions with a social worker, the preparation of setting the stage changes. A worker "self-check-in" about problem-oriented, rather than strengths-based, orientations is essential in setting the stage for empowering practice with mandated families. "Practitioners should attempt to identify, acknowledge, and examine their problem orientations and worldviews since these provide a framework for interpreting client interactions and assessment information" (Ivanoff, Blythe, and Tripodi 1994:27–28). A key decision for the worker is determining whether or not problem-based orientations and worldviews would prevent him or her from exercising the full range of empowering principles, possibilities, and options with this family.

Second, workers "acknowledge the involuntary nature of the arrangement" (Ivanoff, Blythe, and Tripodi 1994: 29). Preparation includes an explanation about requirements to comply with the mandate, how and when the meetings will be held, role expectations for both worker and family members, how their interactions and the results of those interactions will be reported, what the responses to noncompliance will be, and what, if any, avenues are available for an earlier ending to the mandated requirements.

Third, it is common for mandated client families to respond with anger or resentment at being forced to participate. These feelings may be communicated through silence, through minimally verbalizing or contradicting each other or the worker, or through ridicule or put-downs. Empowering approaches will emphasize a variety of choices for meeting the requirements of the mandate and the client family's control over what those choices will be and how they would like to use them. Every family member is seen as important in fulfilling a role in the process. From this approach, silence, for example, is respected as one choice that family members have. They may eventually see, however, that it would be a slower route to completing the requirements of their mandate than would other forms of participation.

Whether the family is self-referred or mandated, a review of the principles for empowering practice also set the stage for work with families in distress. What strengths will I discover in this family and how can I build upon them? What oppressive experiences are they facing and how can they be diminished? What role does each of the multicultural factors play in the dynamics of this family, for the members individually as well as in the interactions among and between them? What possible needs and wants may be evident and how can I best assist them in obtaining those needs and wants? What supports can be accessed? How can I equalize any power differentials that arise? And finally, what can be done to enhance our ability to work together in cooperative roles with each other?

The "Meeting" Before the Meeting

In many cases, such questions as those just asked can represent a "meeting" of the family in the mind of the social worker before the actual meeting with the family members in person. This first "meeting" may occur through the words of a referral source, through an intake form, or through the request for service from one family member. This "meeting" before the meeting may occur only minutes before the contact with a family, or several days may elapse between these two contacts.

Impressions immediately begin forming, and possibilities for the work begin to take shape. The worker must take care to *build no intervention action on unverified assumptions* about what is happening and what can be done to help. Assumptions that are not based on evidence that can be seen and heard—that is, empirical evidence—in the presence of the family members themselves must be treated for what they are, merely assumptions awaiting confirming or rejecting evidence. Evidence-based practice encourages workers to use interventions that are based upon thorough observations and practice guidelines that have been shown to be effective using careful evaluation with client families and communities (Gambrill 1999; Jensen 2001). For example, one approach, multi-systemic treatment (MST) is an example of evidence-based practice with families in which the systemic network of family, peer group, schools, workplace, and neighborhoods is engaged in an intervention aimed at the prevention or reduction of delinquent and/or antisocial behaviors among youth (Henggeler et al. 1998).

In the empowering process with families, assessment provides the framework for gathering evidence with which to approach empowerment and strengths-based interventions with families in distress. Accurate assessment information is accessible through the voices of the family members themselves by listening to all of their voices, individually and together. Gaining a perspective of the family context through verbal reporting by the family members and observation of their processes of interaction provides evidence for workers to place themselves in the most effective position possible for beginning the work with each family. This "meeting" on the page or on the phone is, however, only the earliest of the beginnings needed to work with the family in order to take specific action toward an empowering experience.

This "meeting" before the meeting may also be the time when the worker first becomes aware of the stories of horror that have occurred in the lives of the families served. The openness required for an empathetic approach means an openness to realities of violence, cruelty, poverty, incest, homicide, suicide, and the like. Approaching practice through a lens of empowerment and strengths does NOT mean euphemizing or denying the tragic and traumatic events experienced by our clients. These early moments of hearing the family's story are often the times when we face the stark and devastating reality of the concerns they bring to the practice setting. The loss of a family member in terrorist attacks, the diagnosis of pancreatic cancer, the severe battering by a husband resulting in broken bones and a broken spirit, the kidnapping and rape of a teenage daughter, ritualized abuse of four-year-old twins where one is forced to watch as the other one is tortured, a ten-year-old discovering his older brother's body after suicide, a husband in prison for selling drugs in a junior high school, the loss of life savings in a bogus investment scam created by a son, and on. This is only a small sampling of the kinds of horrific stories heard by social workers on a daily basis, but it illustrates the necessity of taking an honest look at our own reactions, responses, and self-care before proceeding to serve in a helping role with families. Remembering that each family is so much more than the distress they are facing enables workers to broaden their perspective when "meeting" the family's distress before meeting the family in person.

After the initial introduction to a family's story, the worker faces a choice—whether to move forward with service to the family or refer the family to another helping professional who might better serve their needs. The empowering principle addressed is the integration of the support needed from others, and the empowering purpose is doing all we can to enhance a family's well-being. Workers call on colleagues who have greater expertise in areas needed by certain families. When Jorgé Laurencio spoke with the crisis line worker about Danny's injuries, he was referred to an intake worker at the Family and Children's Services agency. From intake, the Laurencio-Smith family was referred to their ongoing worker, Barbara. The school social worker for Susan Williams contacted Susan's mother, Jane, and provided a referral to a local mental health agency and to Liz, another worker recommended because of her expertise in the area of need for the Williams family.

Information Sources

Reports forwarded from referring sources provide information about a family and at the same time inform workers about the authors of those reports, which are written using the lenses of the reporting persons. They are likely to represent accurate observations according to the authors of the reports. However, many descriptions of client families are based upon pathology-oriented models of assessment and hierarchical models of intervention rather than upon strengths-based assessments and empowerment models of practice. As we review reports from other sources, it is crucial to identify both empowering and oppressive factors that the family may be bringing with them into their first session.

Another factor is that time passes between the writing of a report and the social worker's reading of it for background information of a family. Much is likely to have happened in the interim. It may be risky to assume that the information will still be accurate at the time the social worker reads the report. Information goes through yet another kind of translation when it must be honed and shaped to fit into an agency form, also designed through the lenses of other persons. Some forms provide limited categories that are unable to catch unique aspects of a family's circumstances. Forms may lack a way to integrate multicultural factors that play key roles in a family's ways of coping and identifying needed resources. Some forms have been created specifically to respond to the needs of the funding source.

All of these issues illustrate the necessity of a critical assessment and interpretation of the sources that we use to gather information about the family before meeting them. Some workers, aware of the potential for bias in reports and other sources of information, choose to meet the family members first, to hear their story in the present and in their own words, to form their own initial impressions through an empowerment and strengths-based lens, and only later to read reports from other sources.

The material that Barbara, the social worker for the Laurencio-Smith family, reviewed before meeting the family for the first time made no mention of the fact that Jorgé and Lydia were not married. Liz, in her preparation for meeting the Williams family, saw these words in the report from the school social worker: "Both Mr. and Mrs. Williams are unaware that Linda has had an abortion." As the story unfolded and it became apparent that that pregnancy was the result of the incest between Linda and her father, questions were raised about how that information had become part of Linda's record in the first place. After some investigation, Barbara learned that Mr. Williams had bribed the social worker to falsify the record. In accepting such a bribe, the social worker placed her license to practice in jeopardy. Her behavior was reported and reviewed by the professional ethical review board in the state where she was practicing. These are just two examples that illustrate the importance of weighing carefully the information found in the reports of referral sources and how it matches with the evidence we gather from the family members themselves.

Strengths-Based Versus Deficit-Based Language

Even though there is now a vastly wider network of professionals working from strengths and resource-based models, the helping professions, many of the agencies and institutions in which we work, and even family members themselves continue to be heavily embedded in our lengthy tradition that emphasizes pathology, problem-oriented approaches, and problem-based learning (Graybeal 2001). The language used on intake forms, for process records, and for referral reporting, for example, may continue to be filled with descriptions that promote the labeling of problems. These may or may not give us an accurate picture of what is happening with this family, what specific behaviors and interactions are involved. In addition to using empowerment thinking, we can benefit from approaching this information with curiosity and with an understanding of the wider context of the language selected.

Because of understandable urgency to address the distress in their lives, family members also may focus exclusively on the deficits of the moment, pushing to the background the assets they have used and all that they have done individually and together to survive and cope with the initial impact of the event. Blaming oneself or others in the family is not uncommon. Jorgé, for example, thought he "should have seen it [the physical abuse] coming." Jane Williams thought she should have been able to stop the incest in her family. Yet, as one continues to listen, it often becomes evident that this is one way in which the family member is attempting to make sense out of what has happened. This, too, is an effort at coping.

The shift from deficit-based language to strengths-based language occurs most effectively by first acknowledging the descriptive terms used by the family. In the paraphrasing of their words, an empowerment frame of reference begins to make the shift from deficit to strength. This use of language identifies competence and growth. It is a language that names opportunity and possibility. Families know their strengths that have emerged as a result of facing adversity. The language of empowerment reaches for what those new discoveries have been and how they are serving the family in the present. An empowering environment creates a context of safety, respect, and possibility. The traumatic event is seen as something that happened to them, not as something that they are or are becoming. As the Laurencio-Smiths, the Williamses, and Cynthia Wiley and her children looked back on months and years of violence, addictions, incest, poverty, threats, hunger, and homelessness, each expressed in his or her own words the conviction that their experiences were in the past, not to be forgotten or denied, that they may even have provided greater awareness in some way, but that as a family they were moving forward now, creating a different kind of living for themselves.

Anticipatory Empathy

Empathy, the ability of the social worker to look with the perceptions of the different family members, is an essential ingredient in creating an empowering process. Before the first meeting with the family, anticipating what some of their thoughts and feelings may be helps the worker empathize after hearing their words. Anticipatory empathy involves four steps: (1) identification, or placing oneself in the context of this particular family, insofar as it is known, imagining what each member of the family sees, hears, feels, and thinks, and also attempting to anticipate what their interactions with each other are like; (2) incorporation, or taking in those imagined experiences as if they were one's own, bringing them to a personal level; (3) reverberation, or finding the commonalities between the anticipated emotions and thoughts of each member of the family and one's own past experiences, for the purpose of drawing even closer to what the day-to-day experience of the family is like; and (4) detaching, stepping back and assuming more of a compassionate and respectful observational stance (Lide 1966).

Mary Lou, 23, had barely begun her first job as a psychiatric social worker when she found herself preparing for an interview with Kevin, a 19-year-old man who allegedly had attempted to murder his 22-year-old wife, Karen. Mary Lou's assigned task was to evaluate whether the marriage should be allowed to continue. Finding this difficult to believe, she read on and learned that Karen, though initially hospitalized for gunshot wounds, had recovered and wished to remain in the marriage. The reasons Karen cited for this decision rested primarily upon her religious beliefs. She believed her answered prayers had brought the two of them together in the first place. Mary Lou found herself searching for experiences that could help her connect with Kevin. What in Mary Lou's own life could help her get closer to what he had been through? She wanted to see Kevin, and not just the labels that others had placed upon him. He had been through a lot since shooting his wife. With that one thought, Mary Lou realized she had discovered her "common ground" with this client. Even though she was now committed to helping, she found herself staring at her own capacity to take a human life. She had made choices not to act in this way, but the capacity was still there—indeed, is there in everyone. Her training in self-awareness told her this was something that she would need to accept in order to work with Kevin. If she rejected this in herself, she increased the likelihood that she would also reject it in others. Acceptance allowed her to welcome Kevin that afternoon as the frightened, shy person she saw, to hear his story, and to assess whether a meeting with Karen would be in his best interest.

Mary Lou's experience is one example of how the possibility of anticipatory empathy may not be readily apparent with some clients. "Practitioners might find it difficult to identify with life circumstances such as poverty, grave injury, racism, homophobia, or job loss if they themselves have not experienced such conditions" (Germain and Gitterman 1996:64). Discovering the capacity for anticipatory empathy at the level of the human condition means broadening our scope to universal human experiences.

Maintaining empathy with client families is an ongoing privilege, not a one-time happening. Signals come from clients as to when empathizing is accurate and when it is not, when it is appreciated and when it is not. "Effective empathy always remains open to additional data and impressions, and avoids stereotypes and preconceptions" (Germain and Gitterman 1996:65). Our responsiveness to additional data and the avoidance of stereotypes are key steps in equalizing the power and creating a more empowering process in this beginning phase.

Once consideration has been given to setting the stage, to the "meeting" before the meeting, to discernment with regard to the sources of initial information about the family, to attentiveness regarding strengths-based and deficit-based uses of language, and to anticipatory empathy, it is time to meet the family.

Tasks for an Empowering Beginning

First impressions can lay the groundwork for the quality of the work to follow. Warmth, genuineness, respect, a sense of calm and competence, and a concern for the comfort of those present are essential qualities conveyed in the first moments of meeting. The components of an empowering beginning are the initial greeting (Lee 2001), friendly conversation (Leigh 1998), discovering what help is desired, making an offer of service, lowering anxiety and ambivalence, and approaching the work (Lee 2001).

The Initial Greeting

Introductions and inviting a family to be seated are different in several ways from welcoming an individual client. A wealth of information is available to us in these two seemingly simple transactions, information that can reveal key dynamics in each family's transactions.

In the United States a common form of greeting is the handshake accompanied by words of welcome and our names. Even though family members may accommodate and politely participate in U.S. forms of greeting, we can show respect by following the lead of the first greeter in the family. In our multiethnic society, we can easily find ourselves greeting one family with a handshake and eye contact, then finding that the next family shows respect through an avoidance of both touching and eye contact. In some ethnic groups, handshakes are gender-specific, reserved for men only. Depending on age, degrees of acculturation, and perceptions of authority, a traditional bow or nod of the head is also a preferred form of greeting by some family members. For example, when the Tong family arrived, Jim, their U.S. Euro-American social worker, bowed to the grandfather, shook hands with the father, nodded to the mother, responded to a "thumbs-up" from the teenage son, and shared a "high five" with the five-year-old son.

Use of title is often seen as a sign of respect, and only with permission are first names used. When Mr. and Mrs., Señor and Señora, Ms. and Ms., Mr. and Mr., or professional titles such as Dr., Rabbi, Reverend, Dean, and others precede a person's name, we set aside familiar usage of first names to rest with the preferences and the timing of our clients. There are exceptions to this in some families in which using titles for some family members and not for others is seen as an indicator of inequality, hierarchy, and a misuse of power that may not have been earned. It is important to show this same consideration to all members of the family, children as well as parents and older adults. With the Tong family mentioned above, the adults and the five-year-old addressed Jim as "Mr. Thomas," but the teenager asked if they could call each other by their first names, seeing "Jim" in a similar role as his Big Brother at the Asian Center, with whom he was on a first-name basis. Jim, with respect for the possibility of a traditional hierarchy of power in the family, asked the teenager if he could check with the adults about this usage. The parents smiled, nodded their heads, and, in English, voiced their understanding of their son's "becoming more a part of the United States culture." They were proud of his accomplishments in this light but reminded him of the importance of always valuing his Chinese roots. Following this comment by the parents, the teenager turned to the social worker and explained, "When my grandfather is present, I will call you Mr. Thomas so that he will hear that in the translation. But when he is not here with us, I would still like to call you Jim." This was agreeable to the parents, and they interpreted for the grandfather that this exchange had involved "clarifying the pronunciation of people's names."

Friendly Conversation

After the initial greeting, the introductory conversation that begins each session with a family can determine the effectiveness of the entire interaction to come. Friendly conversation helps to shape an empowering beginning by identifying common areas of interest and providing the context in which perceived power differentials can be minimized. "The purpose of friendly conversation is to begin the relationship not as a client or as a social worker but essentially as two people coming together to get to know each other" (Leigh 1998:60–61). When beginning work with several family members, it is essential to make a connection with each of them, using one-on-one, individualized comments. Equal respect, acceptance, interest, and value are communicated to each member individually as well. This is the time to "enter the client's world" (Lee 2001:191).

Many families come to their initial contacts with social workers with noticeable levels of anxiety, uncertain about what is expected of them, not knowing if they can trust the social worker to understand and to help. Friendly conversation sets the tone to help minimize some of these anxieties through respect and welcoming while normalizing their questions and concerns. The working alliance begins in the midst of this kind of communication.

The need or the mandate to receive help from someone outside the family, as well as the nature and potential outcomes of the helping process, are all culturally embedded. Friendly conversation is "considered crucial in cross-cultural interview situations" (Leigh 1998:61). It enables the worker to begin to discern how this particular family is "both similar to and different from the larger megaculture, the specific ethnic or cultural subgroup, and to see the unique qualities within their family as well as among and between their individual family members" (Berg-Cross and Takushi Chinen 1995). All four levels—the larger culture, the subgroup, the family group, and the individual family members—must be understood in the family's terms to avoid cultural insensitivity through stereotype and bias.

"The length of time for friendly conversation depends on the interviewer assessing the level of comfort and ease of the other person in the encounter" (Leigh 1998:65). This level of comfort needs to be evident for all family members before proceeding. Friendly conversation provides the structure for "settling into an interview, creating a working alliance, and establishing trust" (Leigh 1998:65). It helps to set the stage for empowering practice through mutual connection, multicultural respect, equalizing power differentials, lowering anxiety, and beginning to get a glimpse of the family's needs.

Discovering What Help Is Desired

Self-referred family members will often shift into telling their story, their reasons for coming, and their hopes for what can happen as the worker brings friendly conversation to a close. Families mandated to receive services from a social worker may direct a similar shift in conversation or they may lengthen the friendly conversation to avoid dealing with the requirements of the mandate. Encouraging choices and clarifying the outcomes of those choices can empower family members, whether self-referred or mandated, to move forward with telling their story and describing the help they desire.

This meeting with their social worker may be the first time family members hear how the parents, siblings, and extended-family members describe the events that resulted in the need for social work services. Three kinds of clarification of the descriptions can help as they move from telling the story as seen by each family member toward discovering options for help: from the general to the specific; from the vague to the clear; and from assumptions to evidence. Jorgé, for example, moved from speaking of "abuse" to describing Danny's specific cuts, bruises, and burns. Jane Williams moved from the vague sense that "all was not right" with her family to hearing the urgency in the school social worker's voice. And Cynthia Brown-Wiley made the transition from talking about a "shelter" to describing a home where she and the children could be assured of safety.

Two questions that help discover what help is desired are "What have you tried so far?" and "What was the result of those attempts?" Both Linda and Susan Williams had tried running to friends' homes to get away from the sexual abuse by their father. The abuse continued. Cynthia Brown-Wiley left her violent husband several times before being able to stay away and gather the resources necessary to hold to that decision. Giving credit for earlier attempts empowers family members to trust their own capacity to empower themselves while calling on needed support from others.

As the descriptions of desired help get more specific, more clear, and are grounded in evidence rather than assumption, and after earlier attempts and outcomes are reviewed, social workers using an empowering framework for practice become curious about how the practice actions—providing information and learning opportunities, enhancing coping skills, offering options for participation and support from others—might fit the family's needs and wishes. These thoughts lead toward making the offer of service. Safety, food, shelter, and employment, for example, were on the "help desired" list of Cynthia Wiley and her children. After clarification, contact with the school system was added. As Lou, her social worker, gathered more evidence about the urgency of this family's safety needs, she made an immediate offer of service.

Making the Offer of Service

The offer of service may occur before contact with families or it may follow the hearing of their stories. Moving forward with the implementation of those services, however, is most effective when it is based directly upon the descriptions of what help family members desire, as well as any mandated services that have been defined. Stories differ and requests for help have individual as well as collective themes. Workers check for accuracy by restating individual needs and requests with each person. They summarize the family's requests, invite corrections or additions, then inform the family which services can be provided by the worker and her or his agency and which requests can best be addressed by others. For example, Cynthia Wiley's social worker was not able to conduct the testing for school placement for Jessie and Charlie herself, but she was able to explain how and where that step would occur. Susan Williams's school social worker could not provide the joint sessions for the whole family. Her colleague had greater expertise in working with families where incest was occurring, so she made the referral.

Making the offer of service often leads to an immediate lowering of anxiety and ambivalence. This is not always the outcome, however. The social worker's offer of service may also increase anxiety, as, for example, when Barbara, Jorgé and Lydia's social worker, informed them about what to expect in the investigation with CPS workers. Cynthia also spoke of her heightened anxiety when Lou, her social worker, first raised the possibility of the family group conference. In the beginning phase of work, two of the most pressing questions for clients, both individually and as a family, are "Will I be heard?" and "Will I be helped?" The first is the relationship question. Will this person not only hear the words I am speaking but also hear what I cannot say or what I am trying to say? Will I be heard for who I am and not as some stereotype of some group of which I may be a part? The second is the question about the worker's skill and experience with other families who have faced similar challenges. Can this person put those skills to work to help in this situation? The work will move forward with a lowering of anxiety and ambivalence only when family members can answer affirmatively to both questions (Anderson 1981).

Approaching the Work

After the family members have accepted the offer of service, a statement describing the empowering approach to practice is needed, especially as it plays out in role, purpose, and function. Clarification of roles places emphasis upon mutuality. Worker and family members alike are consultants, guides, collaborators, colearners, coinvestigators, and cocreators. Emphasis is also placed on the accessibility of these roles—that is, they are ones that family members are familiar with, ones with which they already have experience. This work is not going to ask them to attempt to fill a role with which they have no familiarity.

The purpose of empowering practice—to sustain, enhance, and create family well-being—is best described by delineating the strengths and needs of each family, using their experiences as a point of reference. For example, Barbara, the social worker with Jorgé, Lydia, and their children, immediately recognized the value of the way Jorgé and Lydia gave meaning to their cross-cultural relationship so that it strengthened both of them individually as well as their whole family. This was a quality to *sustain*, to support and call upon, throughout their work. It was also a quality to *enhance* through using it as a resource, one that helped expand options when the possibilities from one perspective seemed limiting. And, finally, it was also a quality that helped them to *create* a new place for themselves. "Our differences saved us."

Functions are the specific tasks for which each family member is needed to make their work reach the desired results. When Lydia and Jorgé needed additional family support during and after Lydia's surgery and treatment, their task was to reach out to Maggie, Lydia's sister. Maggie defined her function in joint conversations with Lydia, Jorgé, and the children. The children were included in the planning. Individually and together, they reached an understanding that Lydia's illness and the time she needed for recovery meant they would not have their usual routine at home for a while. They needed to welcome Maggie and understand that she would be helping take care of them. Jorgé's stressors—added pressures at work, the emotional impact of Lydia's medical needs, and the abuse Danny had suffered at the hands of Maria—would have taken a much larger toll on him had he not had the cooperation and support of Maggie and the children. For the worker, tasks in empowering practice center around the principle of "assisting families as they empower themselves." Knowing when to actively participate with the family's movement toward their goals and when to play a more supportive role is an essential skill for workers using an empowering process. With clarification of role, purpose, and function, the next step is gathering information for a thorough assessment, one that deepens and broadens the initial family story.

Empowering Assessments

An assessment based upon the family's own perceptions begins during and after the initial meeting. "Accurate assessment rests on the collection of relevant information, its systematic organization, and the analysis and synthesis of the data" (Germain and Gitterman 1996:101). An empowering assessment is a competency-based assessment (Lee 2001:73), a strengths-based assessment. The effects of powerlessness are explored "conveying a sense of respect for having the strength and resiliency to withstand oppression" (Robbins, Chatterjee, and Canda 1998:109).

Assessment is ongoing throughout all phases of work. The formal assessments that become part of an agency's documentation capture one or more points in time, valuable as a verbal photograph but unable to provide a picture of the dynamic changes happening moment by moment in every family scenario. Six levels of family assessment have been identified for empowerment practice (Lee 2001:209):

1. *Content:* worldview, stressor, multicultural factors as *resource* and/or *oppression*
2. *Family process:* communication (verbal and nonverbal), alliances, feelings, boundaries, conflict resolution, decision making as *resource* and/or *oppression*
3. *Family structure:* form and organization, roles and rules, gender differences, authority seen as *resource* and/or *oppression*
4. *Family history,* including historical oppression
5. *Individuals:* strengths and resources, stages of development, ways of coping, health status, stressors
6. *Environment:* physical and social factors—that is, financial security or need, use or abuse of substance, and the like—as manifestations of *resource* and/or *oppression*

Two additional assessment factors are information about concrete needs and getting a picture of what the family has done so far to address the stressor (Kaplan and Girard 1994:33). Genograms, ecomaps, and timelines are recommended as assessment tools that encourage participation of all members of the family, help identify generational patterns, and provide visual images of the family's historical progression and of their relationships with the wider web of social systems of which they are a part. These tools help family members see how their actions affect others. The Family Empowerment Scale (Koren, DeChillo, and Friesen 1992) is another assessment instrument. This scale was originally created as an assessment measure to determine degrees of empowerment of the parents and other caregivers of children with emotional disabilities. Thirty-four items help gather information to assess the level and expression of empowerment through behaviors, attitudes, and knowledge.

An empowering context is one connected with the family's wishes for the service they desire in the present. Tools that reach into the family's past are helpful only through their relevance to the present. The process and the outcome of using these tools are both important as we begin with families The relationship that develops as a result of the process, however, will determine the quality of interactions throughout the work, while the information may or may not be used as the work continues.

The Middle Phase

Deepening the Relationship Between Worker and Family Members Through Internal and External Family Transactions

The transition to the middle phase of work occurs in different ways and at different times for each family. Core actions for empowering practice during this phase are (1) to provide information about their situation, (2) to assist in strengthening coping skills, and (3) to expand the possibilities for family members to participate with others who have faced similar circumstances (Gutiérrez and Lewis 1999; Lee 2001). These actions are not exclusive, yet they can be sufficient. They also help to lay a strong foundation for other needed interventions to be effective. These three actions overlap and intertwine rather than functioning as separate steps in the process. They are both concise and capable of addressing great complexity.

Dividing the work into manageable steps contributes to "simplifying the complex into what can be known" (Lee 2001:3) or into what is already known but just needs to be applied. Families seen by social workers commonly live with an overlay of complexity, chaos, challenge, and oppression. Work that simplifies or gets too concise before a thorough understanding of that complexity has been achieved will be shallow and is likely to miss essential contextual ingredients that are necessary for the work to be effective. Work that stays only with the complexity without simplifying to make it manageable runs the risk of losing the clients. The complexity must be known and understood as much as possible before the step toward description that is more concise and usable is taken. Simplifying complex situations is a coping skill usually familiar to families in distress long before they contact social workers. Calling on their earlier experiences can remind them of related strengths they already have in their grasp. This restores confidence in their ability to come through this experience as well.

Skilled practice from the empowerment perspective uses all three core actions during the middle phase. Appropriate timing and specific variations increase responsiveness to the particular needs of each family. The three actions work together, informing and enhancing each other. Gathering relevant *information* plays a part in the content and process of support groups and in the acquisition of coping skills. Enhanced *coping* is connected with new information and observation of other group members. And *participation*, whether with one's own family or with the members of support groups, includes shared information, styles of learning, and methods of coping that might be of help to others.

The middle phase is based upon the assumption that most of the major tasks of the beginning phase have been addressed. The initial greeting will have resulted in a beginning connection with each family member, not just with the parents or the most verbal members. There will have been some preliminary description from the family about what is desired as an outcome of this work. The social worker will have had the opportunity to make an offer of service, informing the family about the services available at the agency or about resources that might better serve this family at other agencies or with other helping professionals. If the family wishes to proceed with this worker, beginning steps approaching the work together will have occurred, directly addressing the stressors that the family faces, those that are internal to the family system and those that are external to it as well.

Before the work of the middle phase begins, it is critical to determine the readiness of family members to participate in the steps that will involve their active participation. The pace of the work is in the hands of the family members. They can request a slower or faster pace at any time and, unless it is mandated otherwise, they can set the frequency of their sessions with the worker. Even when mandated, the choice still remains with the family as to whether or not they will attend and how involved or how distant they will be. They can request an early conclusion to any session or can end the work prematurely. Providing choices serves empowering principles of diminishing a potentially oppressive force, showing an awareness of their needs, equalizing power, and using cooperative roles.

As they tell their story, information at each of the six levels of family assessment is included: the content, the family processes, the family structure, the family history, an idea of the strengths and coping skills of each individual, and the physical and social environment in which the family lives (Lee 2001:209). Additional information about each of these levels continues to emerge over the course of the work together. In the work with Jorgé, Lydia, and Danny, for example, the initial assessment revealed the abuse Danny had suffered. Later, additional information became available about Maria's addictive drinking patterns. In the initial session with the Williams family, Susan's and Linda's experiences of incest by their father were described. Later, their mother also told the story of her similar experiences with an uncle when she was about the same age as Susan.

The worker will have mentally noted the roles that oppression and the uses and abuses of power play at each level of assessment. Oppressive forces find a place in the deepening narrative of the family's life. The worker may observe behaviors that indicate oppressive realities about which the family does not yet seem aware: the silencing of the women in the Williams family, for example, noted by their social worker in the first session; or the developmental delays of Jessie and Charlie Brown-Wiley, observed by Lou, their social worker, and attributed to the impact of having witnessed the violence between their mother and father. These realities, too, become part of the information that can be raised with proper timing in a context of empathy, respect, and relevance to the present situation.

Multicultural factors influence personal, interpersonal, and societal levels. The richness and complexity of this information will have been used in the beginning phase to help identify resources and strengths, interacting dynamics among and between the family members, diverse levels of acculturation, and the like. Emergent themes guide the way into the middle phase of work. Some examples of such themes heard from family members are "We rally together when we need to," "We are survivors," "We will make it through this."

As family members tell their stories and make their requests for help, social workers begin to make connections between the needs heard and the actions that would best fit with this particular family. Many families find that the combination of the three actions—gaining information, enhancing coping skills, and participating with others—is sufficient and that they have received the help they requested. For other families, these actions can provide a foundation, and additional help may extend beyond these approaches. One major value of the three key actions for empowering practice comes in their mutuality of function. This means that the worker participates in the gathering of information as much as the family does; the worker continues to develop her or his coping skill in this process as much as the family does; and the worker benefits from the participation with others (one of which is the family), in colleague networks, and with her or his own family. This mutuality of effort makes these actions empowering ones for worker and family alike. The well-crafted, concise, and simple (parsimonious, not simplistic) response is the one that often leads to the most effective, efficient, and useful result. Concise responses are supported by complexities of historical, theoretical, multicultural, and empirical, evidence-based observation. We may work with families at the tip of the iceberg, but the entire iceberg, visible and invisible, is still part of the awareness that supports intervention.

Promoting an empowering context for families also means that we live in a culture that defines knowledge as power. This places the social worker in the position of making a conscious choice to use knowledge in a "power WITH" relationship with family members. We cannot use our knowledge in a "power over" or "power under" sense and maintain an empowering context for practice.

Helping with Internal Family Transactions

Providing Information Through Education and Learning

This first empowerment action includes the need to be consistent with the diverse ways in which family members learn. "Social workers must attend to the different ways in which people process and learn information" (Gitterman 2001:28). This processing and learning go beyond traditional social learning theory and beyond the role of educator. An empowering learning process with families calls upon the multicultural (developmental stage) recognition that children learn in different ways than adults do, that women learn differently than men do, and that people who have been oppressed take in and process information for learning through a different lens than do those from a dominant status (Brookfield 1995). This learning process acknowledges diverse sensory preferences—that is, that some of us learn primarily from visual input, others predominantly through auditory channels, and still others from experiential participation. Some family members are internal processors of information, those who integrate thoughts before speaking. Others are external processors who need to speak their thoughts and receive feedback from others before they are clear about their position. Finally, distressing events alter the capacity for processing information and for learning. The trauma response brings its own characteristic behaviors, such as confusion and intrusions of traumatic memories, to the learning process. The diversity essential for empowering practice extends to diversity in the ways people learn. Skills for guiding the learning process, include "providing needed information regarding the stressor and coping tasks, clarifying misinformation, offering advice, providing feedback specifying action tasks, and preparing and planning for task completion" (Gitterman 2001:28).

Variations in the ways people learn are of crucial importance in working with families because most families include members of different genders, often of different cultural backgrounds, and always of different ages and developmental stages. The facts about differences in learning styles come, in part, from research in the areas of gender differences in moral development and decision making (Gilligan 1977), multiculturalism (Ponterotto et al. 1995), and brain research (Van der Kolk, McFarlane, and Weisaeth 1996).

The more family members are involved in their own learning, the more they are likely to remember. We remember 10 percent of what we read, 20 percent of what we hear, and 30 percent of what we see. When we combine hearing and seeing, we have the possibility of remembering 50 percent of the content. When we participate through speaking, the percentage can rise to as much as 70 percent remembered. However, it is not until we are actually doing, seeing, hearing, and saying, either through simulation or by doing (such as fieldwork) that we reach the potential of remembering 90 percent of what we have learned (Dale 1985).

Creating an environment in our work with families where seeing, hearing, saying, and doing are all present and available increases possibilities for learning and remembering for each member of the family and for the worker as well.[1] Using the unique learning styles of the members of the family provides a maximum learning environment. Women and men, for example, learn in different ways. Women tend to be well suited for synthesis activities, whereas men tend to be well suited for analysis functions. These differences decline during the forties, and synthesis and analysis functions become more integrated, in part because of a wealth of experiences that have required the interaction of both functions (Van der Kolk, McFarlane, and Weisaeth 1996). When meeting with families, we can use these differences to increase the effectiveness of the work.

Adult learning models work from different assumptions than do learning models used with children. "The two distinguishing characteristics of adult learning... are the adult's autonomy of direction in the act of learning and the use of personal experience as a learning resource" (Brookfield 1986:25).

Adults need to be convinced that they need to learn something before they will participate in learning it. One of the characteristics of entering adulthood is taking responsibility for one's own behavior. Therefore, adults enter a learning experience knowing they are responsible for the decisions made about what they hear coming from their social worker. "They resent and resist situations in which they feel others are imposing their wills on them" (Knowles 1984:56).

Adults bring a wealth of experience into the learning situations with other family members and with social workers. This experience can be both a benefit and a hindrance. It is likely that in the past the adults in the family may have faced similar stressors as the ones they are facing at the present time. Coping in those earlier situations can serve as a resource for coping in the current context. Adults often self-identify using family roles and workplace roles, accomplishments relevant to the current situation, or challenges that may have been faced and overcome. The implication for work with families is "that in any situation in which adults' experience is ignored or devalued, they perceive this as not rejecting just their experience, but rejecting them as persons" (Knowles 1984:58).

The richest resources for learning about what is happening in the family are always the family members themselves. The lessons learned in surviving the violence of battering are lessons that will stay with Cynthia Brown-Wiley the rest of her life. As her social worker listened to Cynthia's story, she heard that "just being believed" had an empowering effect on Cynthia's ability to trust the resources that were taking shape for her and her children in her new community.

Earlier experience can also be a hindrance. Biases may have set in, preventing openness to new and creative alternatives that may be necessary in the face of recent challenges. When we work with families' traumatic experiences, we face the possible reactivation of earlier trauma. Both of these potential hindrances respond to empowering interventions, ones that build on strengths, use experiential simulation of new possibilities, and maximize the potential for learning by being shaped around concrete circumstances. When earlier trauma is reactivated, empowering principles emphasize strengths, coping efforts and skills, and supports from others that were used to move through and beyond the traumatic event.

When Maria's alcoholism reactivated Lydia's memories of her mother's alcoholism, for example, Barbara, her social worker, reminded Lydia that she had survived those years with her mother and had learned some ways to manage Maria's behaviors in the present. Jane Williams's memories of her own incest were reactivated as she heard her daughters tell of their experiences of being victimized by John. Jane had used denial for many years to deal with her experiences. She'd had no one to support her as she tried to make sense out of what had happened. When she realized that her denial had blocked her awareness that her daughters could be facing similar experiences, she made this statement: "I vowed to myself that they would not go through their recovery without support the way I had. I would be their support."

Strengthening Coping Skills

Social workers listen to the stories of families in distress partly for the purpose of answering the question "With what are they coping?" It is important for helping professionals to have an understanding of how the family gives meaning to the events they are facing. Even more important may be the question "*How* are they coping?" Family members experience traumatic events in unique ways. Attention to unique coping behaviors is key in assisting family members, individually and together, to move toward greater strength and empowerment.

What exactly is coping? Scholars from fields as diverse as social work, psychology, psychiatry, sociology, epidemiology, counseling, and communication participate in examining the meaning of coping. One definition that captures subtle variations from these various disciplines and that is useful for work with families from an empowerment perspective is this: "Coping is a response aimed at diminishing the physical, emotional, and psychological burden that is linked to stressful life events and daily hassles" (Snyder and Dinoff 1999:5). Coping is "process-related, not trait-oriented" (Lazarus 1993). Coping starts with two steps: (1) a "primary appraisal" of the challenging situation, which answers such questions as "What is at risk here?" and "Is it serious enough to require action?" and (2) a "secondary appraisal" that answers "What can be done?" (Lazarus and Folkman 1984).

Primary appraisals include the degree of risk involved. How do the family members perceive the level of risk? Is this seen as a minimal, a moderate, or a serious and perhaps dangerous risk? When the worker is aware of information that increases the risk to the safety of any one of the family members, he or she must share that information. However, it is also helpful to respect that what is perceived as a major risk by the social worker may be seen as a minimal risk by the family and vice versa. Manageable degrees of risk, successfully addressed, can increase the family's sense of competence and enhance their trust for each other. Assessment, therefore, includes examining the resources, strengths, and connections that are available for the family to successfully address the risk they are facing.

Primary and secondary appraisals occur in families by individual family members; as a joint effort with other family members; or as a combination of individual understanding and joint discussion. When the Laurencio-Smith family realized that the husband's, Jorgé's, child was being physically abused by Maria, his biological mother and Jorgé's first wife, both Jorgé and his partner, Lydia, answered the primary appraisal question "What is at risk here?" with an unquestioning agreement that the child's life could be at risk and, yes, it was serious enough to require action. However, when they came to the secondary appraisal question, "What can be done?" Jorgé and Lydia, after taking immediate action to ensure the safety of Danny and the other children by reporting the abuse, identified different sources for the difficulty. Jorgé appraised Maria's behavior as a direct result of her addiction to alcohol. Lydia appraised it as behavior related to Maria's childhood abuse, compounded by mental illness in her adult years, plus inadequate supervision when Danny was with her. Danny struggled, from his four-year-old perspective, with the possibility that his mother's abusive behavior was somehow his fault. Their answers to what could be done reflected these different starting points and, with the help of their worker, they explored a multifaceted approach that was inclusive of all of these viewpoints, beginning with assuring Danny that his mother's behaviors were not about him.

Secondary appraisals guided by the question "What can be done?" mobilize coping. This question moves the work from assessment of the situation into the middle phase of work as family members and worker consider actions in response to the stressors being faced. The rebuilding of both internal and external worlds often includes high levels of anxiety. Hyperarousal and hyperactivity are also common emotional responses to having "no road map for daily living" (Janoff-Bulman 1999:312).

After the shock of Maria's unexpected and violent visit, emotions were running high for Lydia, Samantha, Amy, and Danny. (Jorgé and Lydia's sister, Maggie, were away from the home at the time). Billy, their infant son, displayed his own version of hyperarousal by "screaming at the top of his lungs for about half an hour." (Amy speaking.) When Barbara arrived, responding to Lydia's call for help, and Maggie returned from shopping, they found all the children in hyperactive mode, trying to take care of each other and Lydia, who was extremely exhausted after the incident. The family literally had "no road map" with which to face such an event. Emotion-focused coping was most evident at that point. Aware of this, Barbara offered her support until there was a greater sense of calm, then recommended that they rest that evening and meet again the next morning. In the morning meeting, with a little distance from the intense emotions and the benefits of a night's sleep, the family would be more able to engage in decision-focused coping.

"Coping efforts are inherently neutral, and they are neither innately adaptive nor maladaptive" (Snyder 1999:10). Through the empowerment lens, one may ask if behaviors sustain, enhance, and create well-being for the family. Family history, earlier coping attempts, developmental and emotional needs, the influence of all of the multicultural variables, as well as other factors, are key here. Coping behaviors that interfere with the family's well-being and threaten the sustainability of the family unit are part of the complex web of relationships in the family. Such behaviors often indicate unmet needs or devastating secrets. Coping efforts that cause damage are often valiant attempts to communicate a need for help when threats against speaking out have imprisoned those messages in silence.

There is an observable connection between a "breakdown in emotional coping skills" (one outcome of experiencing trauma) and subsequent "problematic coping" behaviors (Salovey et al. 1999:160), such as a decrease in school or work performance, an increase in abuse of chemical substances, or displaced anger directed toward family or friends. Empowerment thinkers interpret these behaviors as distress signals, as actions that "speak" when more direct verbal communication is not available or has in some way been silenced. Such an interpretation recognizes that the individual is facing oppressive circumstances and doing the best she or he can with the resources and the understanding at hand. Experiencing oppression and the trauma that is part of it changes capacities for coping.

This takes us back to the question "With what are families coping?" One key role for social workers is to recognize the signs of trauma. Families and individuals who have recently experienced trauma respond with shock, immobilization, and a numbing of their ability to think clearly. These precursors to the appraisal process give the impression that the individual or family members are "frozen" or emotionally unable to proceed. An empowering interpretation of these behaviors acknowledges the purposeful activity that is occurring internally as a response to trauma. These mechanisms bring the individual or the family to a halt. They can prevent movement toward continued or greater danger, and they create a protective barrier against further trauma.

Important additions to the social worker's knowledge base include major advances over the past decade in understanding trauma, trauma responses, and trauma recovery (Blumenfeld and Schoeps 1993; Everstine and Everstine 1993; Herman 1992; Van der Kolk, McFarlane, and Weisaeth 1996; Waites 1993; Williams and Sommer 1994). The importance of recognizing the trauma response as a response (and not a "disorder") cannot be overemphasized. "The term 'response' is used to connote the nonpathological aspects of what the DSM calls 'disorder.'. . When the reaction to trauma is envisaged as part of a restorative process and not as abnormal behavior, a new incentive to helping the victim recover is gained. It is a simpler task to aid a natural process than to cure a disorder" (Everstine and Everstine 1993:12–14).

Refusing to pathologize a natural response to trauma is consistent with an empowerment perspective grounded in strengths-based practice. Traumatic occurrences are part of existence in the natural, biological, and social worlds. All of Susan Williams's coping behaviors in response to incest were indicators of efforts to "leak" information about a situation in which she was trying to avoid pain while simultaneously sending messages that she needed help in dealing with that pain. When a person cannot be direct in requests for help, it may be because of a clear awareness about the potential price she or he may have to pay if the silence around the trauma is broken. Susan had been told, "No one will believe you and I [John] will make sure no one believes you." This threat, and the fear that resulted from it, effectively stopped Susan's words before she had a chance to form them in thought and before she had an opportunity to verbalize them.

A "new generation" of theorists in victimology, the psychology of coping, and the strengths-based models is challenging earlier views that pathologize trauma responses. We now see an increase in interpreting these behaviors as part of the natural process of coping. Kemp has suggested that professionals who "pathologize their clients or deprive them of self-determination are unlikely to be especially helpful" (1998:132). Therefore, it is essential to have a clear picture of what we are talking about when we refer to trauma responses. Table 6.1 lists some of the most common behaviors that are seen as responses to trauma.

The restorative function of these behaviors is recognized. Anxiety is viewed as an "alarm system" that alerts the person to potential dangers. When a person's internal work is intense, such as after a traumatic experience, external behaviors such as focusing on tasks will appear to be slower or more confused. Separation and withdrawal from too much stimulation is a self-protective mechanism. These responses are accepted as part of a process that leads to healing.

The most helpful action for the social worker immediately following a crisis, when family members may be experiencing shock, is to be present, to allow each person's response to take its course within the bounds of safety, and to give tangible responses to requests for help. Meeting the concrete needs of the moment helps to provide solid footing when it seems as if all supports have disappeared. When information is requested, providing it in brief and clear statements helps

TABLE 6.1 Common Responses to Trauma

Anxiety about the possible recurrence of the event or a similar event

Emotional distress caused by events or objects that remind you of the traumatic event

Confusion, difficulty in concentration, memory problems, or an inability to estimate time accurately

Flashbacks of the event that may be visual or may take the form of reliving the event emotionally

Temporary mood swings, general changes in temperament, irritability

Sleep problems and/or nightmares

Feelings of depression or detachment or estrangement from others

Changes in appetite or eating patterns

Shortness of temper, angry feelings, or impatience with yourself or others

Diminished interest in significant activities (work, social, or family)

Sources: Everstine and Everstine 1993:58; Herman 1992; Van der Kolk, McFarlane, and Weisaeth 1996.

move the process forward. Auditory distortion is common when family members experience shock following a traumatic event. Because of these distortions, it may be difficult for them to hear information the first time, and it can be helpful to repeat the information several times. When acceptance begins to come into awareness, the first step—evaluating the situation—begins the coping process.

Lee's (2001) "interlocking dimensions of empowerment" are themselves coping behaviors: (1) development of a more positive and potent sense of self, (2) construction of knowledge and capacity for critical comprehension of the web of social and political realities of one's environment, and (3) cultivation of resources and strategies, of more functional competence for attainment of personal and collective goals (34).

The relationship between coping and empowerment is a tight-knit one, reciprocal in nature, and successful coping strengthens personal, interpersonal, and situational dimensions of empowerment, while commitment to an empowerment lens centers around the coping actions taken to address a family's distress and struggle. Effective coping is identified in the short term by diminishing of immediate distress and in the long term by actions that contribute to the physical, emotional, and social well-being of the family.

Facilitating Participation with Kin and Intimate Non-kin

"The family circle was the first group I knew" (Lee 2001:21). Family members enter the social worker's presence involved in active (verbal and nonverbal) participation with each other. Dynamics observed in that moment provide clues to patterns of family participation in the past few hours, days, weeks, and months. In addition to the participation that takes place within the family, additional forms of participation play a key role in empowering practice with families: participation with kin and intimate non-kin networks, distant kin and non-kin networks, collateral contacts, mutual aid support groups, participation with the social worker, family group conferencing, and the possibility of engaging the oppressor. Three of these kinds of participation—participation with distant kin and non-kin networks, collateral contacts, and mutual aid support groups—will be discussed further in chapter 7. The following discussion considers each of the other forms of participation, beginning with kin and intimate non-kin and whether or not to engage the oppressor.

Long before the moment of our entrance into the world, we participate. Participation with our birth mother exists through sensing her rhythms, what she ate for breakfast, how much sleep she is getting. We can tell when she's angry, when she's singing, when she's ill. It is a reciprocal transaction. We let her know when we are hungry, restless, growing, and ready to move on out of there. We may have known some threats while in the womb. The empowerment lens examines the impact of major oppressions such as poverty, addictions, violence, and discrimination.

If the birth mother is poor, the child may not receive enough food to ensure proper growth or the prenatal care that promotes health and well-being. If the mother is addicted to a substance, the child manifests that toxicity on newly forming limbs and face, and in the development of organs and mind (e.g., fetal alcohol syndrome). If the mother is subjected to violence while pregnant, the fetus or child in utero is likely to be the target of that violence. "The incidence of battering is increased with pregnancy, and victims of violence have a higher rate of pregnancy. Violence toward the pregnant mother is traumatizing and potentially damaging to the fetus" (Kantor and Strauss 1989; Thomas 1988). Discrimination against women in a patriarchal culture and social environment permits and perpetuates the continuation of these forms of oppression and their impact on the earliest of relationships between child and mother.

When we do arrive, the family circle is the first group we know. When a child is removed at birth for adoption, illness, or other reasons, the assumption that he or she has not yet had the chance to bond with the birth parent could not be further from the truth (Tolman 2001). For the newborn, those previous nine months are the equivalent of an entire lifetime, a lifetime filled with everything that has become familiar—the sounds, the smells, the textures. That "participation" has already begun to define who this person is, what she or he counts on, what expectations are in place as a result of the existing routines between mother and growing child. When the child is born—that is, removed from this environment—the whole process starts again, within another strange and unfamiliar environment, but the overlay of that earliest separation never leaves the child's awareness.

All forms of participation later in life are grounded in our earliest experiences with our families of origin: how we develop friendships and intimate relationships, how we work with others in groups, and how we do our coming and going to and from those groups; how we participate as members of our communities, our workplaces, our religious institutions; how we see ourselves as fitting into the fabric of state, national, and global communities. All reflect our earliest experiences of interaction within a family system.

Participation through the empowerment lens, includes *taking action* and challenges a passive "person-in-environment" configuration. "Person WITH environment," a term that appears more frequently in social work literature, takes practice into additional layers of understanding. As social workers speak about "power WITH" clients and client families, about learning WITH them, about connecting WITH others as a central form of coping, and as we seek to understand how family members use their power WITH each other, the use of "person WITH environment" provides a picture of active transactions and involvement. For illustration, consider the opposite. An older adult can spend the day in the lounge in her assisted-living residence, a person *in* her environment, yet she may experience little or no interaction *with* staff or other residents. It would not be uncommon to find that her family lives at some distance from her residence and is therefore also unable to provide frequent contact. Both "participation" and "with" provide action-oriented views that connect more closely with the cornerstone of action that is part of empowering practice.

The family provides one of the key supports for managing distress. "The family and community are key structures that mediate against the effects of oppression and enable people to cope" (Lee 2001:46). Individuals who have strong support from family members suffer fewer and less severe consequences following traumatic events. Their ability to recover is enhanced, and their capacity to cope with situations that cannot be changed increases. And yet, as we know from working with families in distress, the view is not one-sided but highly complex. This complexity of how families participate together is vast. "They can be a buffer in a harsh world, or they can be an additional source of conflict as they face cruel socioeconomic realities" (Lee 2001:46).

Parents participate with each other and with children, individually and as a group. Siblings participate with each other. Participation occurs around common areas for decision making, mutual planning, maintenance, and support and nurturing. The use of power through participation raises connections depicting "power WITH." Power over and power under, though, have to do with meeting individual or personal needs rather than participating to meet the needs of the family as a whole. John Williams exercised a "power over" position with his two daughters, Linda and Susan, to meet his own personal needs and to create a context in which the incest would continue. The incest came to a halt when Linda and Susan refused the "power under" position. Jane, Linda, and Susan experienced "power with" as they supported each other to face past experiences and to create a new start together.

Engaging the Oppressor? Yes or No?

Horror numbs. Surviving the unbelievable and attempting to go on with one's life as a family may be possible only through denial and suppression of memories. These forms of coping afford an emotional protection that allows family members to go on functioning outwardly, at least for a time. Families who live with oppressions of violence, poverty, addictions, and discrimination are "not passive in confronting the situations in which they live" (Valle Ferrer 1998:486). One research study of 76 Puerto Rican women examined their previous exposure to violence, the severity and frequency of battering, and primary and secondary appraisal and coping strategies.

> All the women participants manifested having been victims/survivors of psychological abuse in their current intimate relationship. Sixty-six percent were victims/survivors of physical abuse, 43% of sexual abuse, and 42% of economic abuse. Forty-three percent of the women had been victims of child abuse in their families of origin, and 61% had witnessed abuse in their families of origin. In 65% of these cases, the father was the aggressor, and in 11% the perpetrator was the stepfather. In 76% of the cases, the participant's mother was the victim of abuse. (Valle Ferrer 1998:493)

These women were actively coping in the battering situations. They were seeking social support and using escape and avoidance methods of coping. They were problem-solving and confronting their oppressors. They selected coping methods according to how the violent situation was assessed with regard to such factors as levels of harm and threat and how much control they thought they had in any given situation. They evaluated environment constraints and resources. They drew strength from their past history and from present resources. "Only the severity of psychological abuse (verbal aggression) in the marriage, rather than physical or sexual abuse, was positively related to the use of more coping strategies in the worst battering situation" (Valle Ferrer 1998:495).

Five factors played key roles in determining if and when the women in this study would be more likely to confront their oppressors: (1) having been victims or witnesses of abuse in childhood; (2) higher frequency of abuse received in childhood; (3) the severity of psychological abuse during intimate relationships; (4) the higher the stakes during the worst battering situation; and (5) feeling in control of the situation during the worst battering situation (Valle Ferrer 1998:508). These findings challenge views of survivors as helpless or passive. When people confront oppressive forces in their lives, they confront the people they love, as well as other family members who lack understanding of the complexity of their situations. They confront stereotypes or simplistic explanations in their communities and among their peers. They face losses of friends, of children, of self-respect, of their own lives. The enormous perseverance, resilience, and strength to go on with their lives are resources that can be integrated into empowering steps toward claiming an environment without violence.

Not all victims/survivors of oppressions will choose to confront their oppressors. The members of the Laurencio-Smith family did choose to confront Maria, Jorgé's former wife, yet young Danny, the victim of her addiction and her violence, could not have done it without the help of the adults in his life. Linda and Susan Williams, with the support of their social worker, did choose to confront their father about the incest. They walked away with a less than satisfying sense that he regretted his actions, yet their having taken control of the situation to that degree represented a new stance with their father and with options for their future. Cynthia Brown-Wiley surrounded herself with the resources represented by those who were present at her family group conference, each person a vivid signal to her husband that he would be held accountable for his violence.

Engaging the oppressor is one possibility for empowering practice with families facing abuse, addiction, poverty, and discrimination. Each family's circumstances are complex and may or may not respond to confrontation with oppressors. Facing one's oppressor alone is never recommended. For some survivors, the oppressor is no longer alive. In these situations, communicating to an "empty chair" or writing a letter to the person can address survivors' needs for engagement. An assessment of whether an engagement with the oppressor is likely to lead to empowering ends is also key. It may be helpful for some family members and not for others. Individual goals and family goals need careful and differential consideration.

Helping with External Family Transactions

Empowering practice embraces possibilities for strengthening families at individual, interpersonal, and community levels. The choices social workers can make are limitless, yet selective according to the specific needs of the family members. Some of the possibilities for helping with external family transactions include connecting with distant kin and non-kin networks, identifying informal support resources, deepening the relationship with the social worker, and directing a family group conference. The first two possibilities—connecting with kin and non-kin networks and identifying informal support resources—will receive further attention in chapter 7. We will turn here to a discussion of the last two—deepening the relationship with the social worker and directing a family group conference.

Deepening the Relationship with the Social Worker

Social workers using empowering practice may need to explain as well as demonstrate this approach to family members, who may be inclined to place their workers in assumed positions of authority. The worker's demonstration of *equalizing power differentials* through *cooperative roles* enhances the environment for effective helping. Family members may come with expectations that the worker will tell them what they need to do to remedy their stressors or what is needed to meet the requirements of their mandate for services. Workers *assisting the family members as they empower themselves* may need to give examples of what this means. "The social worker has particular roles and tasks in the empowerment process. But the client(s) must think about the situation, invest the work with feeling, name the oppression, work toward finding or creating options, decide on the best course…and act on it" (Lee 2001:229).

Participation with the social worker is also defined by the empowering practice roles: consultant, collaborator, guide, colearner, coinvestigator, and cocreator. The cooperative nature of these roles and the mutuality of process involved in their realization may represent new ways of interacting with people in helping roles. As family members have their needs addressed, gain information, and strengthen coping skills, as a greater sense of well-being begins to be recognized through their freedom to make choices and their ability to make things happen so that they can move on with their lives, they will gain the understanding about empowering practice that is the most long-lasting.

Directing a Family Group Conference

"Family Group Conferencing brings together a family group with service providers to come up with a plan to resolve problems in individual and social functioning" (Macgowan and Pennell 2001:67).[2] A family group conference is a "partnership arrangement" between the members of the family and their extended family; members of their community such as neighbors, friends, and other resource and support persons; and persons serving in official capacities such as child welfare workers. The "core idea of a family group conference is a meeting of all…persons involved with the family to plan for the care and protection of [family members] seen to be at risk of abuse and neglect." All persons attending such conferencing are "expected to play an important role in planning and providing services necessary for the well-being of [family members]" (Burford and Hudson 2000:xix). The original scope of family group conferencing focused on children at risk for abuse and neglect. For purposes of empowering practice with families, that scope is broadened to include spouses, elders, and other adults who are at risk in families.

Family group conferencing operates on the belief that family members need to be invited and guided to play an active role in all decisions that affect them. When it has been determined that there is a family member in need of care, families "do better when decisions affecting them have been arrived at by respecting the integrity of the family unit, focusing on strengthening family and community supports, and creating opportunities for parents and other adults, including extended family members, to feel responsible for their [members]" (Burford and Hudson 2000:xx). To marginalize or minimize the contributions offered by family members in creating a plan for safety for all members is to run the risk that other plans will fail and may, at worst, place vulnerable family members at even greater risk. To integrate the contributions of family members, however, is to build upon realistic and available resources that already exist. Such efforts are more likely to continue long after helping professionals have concluded their part of the process. "Conferences widen the circle of people who know what was done in the family, putting responsibility on family members to prepare a safety plan that can then be presented, discussed, modified as necessary, and supported by . . . officials" (Burford and Hudson 2000:xx).

Cynthia Brown-Wiley had never heard of a family group conference before Lou, her social worker, described it to her. She had envisioned living the rest of her life vulnerable to the sporadic and unpredictable violence of her husband. Experience had taught her to mistrust the police as a source of protection, since Mike was a respected member of the local police force. Cynthia's extended-family members had also expressed ambivalence by trying to give her support yet encouraging her to work things out with Mike rather than escaping to their homes for protection. Yet when Lou proposed convening supports in Cynthia's new community and helped her reconsider the roles of certain extended-family members, she told Lou: "This is the first time there has been any hope at all that I might have a life of my own, that there may actually be a way to keep the violence at enough of a distance that I might go through a whole day without wondering when the next attack will come." Through the family group conference and the plan that resulted from that meeting, Cynthia Wiley was able to "create a buffer" around herself and her children. "I never imagined a way that I wouldn't have to go on facing this hell all by myself. I really believed that, unless someone has been through it, they never understand what the violence is all about. I can't forget all the fear and the pain, but at least now I can get on with living a more normal life and I can give a loving home to Jessie and Charlie."

The value of these plans is that they were crafted by the people closest to the need of service. These plans were the result of the collaboration of family, friends, and other community members to bring about change. . . . Once the plan is in place, the family group and service providers are charged with carrying it out. The protective authorities continue to hold their mandate to protect children and other family members; however, now they have a plan in place for working with the family group and community organizations and call periodic family meetings to review the progress and make modifications in the plan. When the plan is not working well or the family has major changes in their circumstances, the coordinator may be asked to re-convene the family group. Usually family group members and service providers welcome this opportunity and require far less preparation. (Pennell and Burford 1995, quoted in Burford and Hudson 2000:176–177)

In the middle phase of empowering practice with families, the major practice actions of providing information, strengthening coping skills, and participating with others shape the transactions between family members and their social workers. As these actions lead families in moving on toward greater well-being, the work moves to the ending phase of practice.

The Ending Phase

Endings occur daily, and they occur as once-in-a-lifetime events. Endings occur after long expectation, and they occur unexpectedly. They occur with elaborate planning and preparation or they occur suddenly, with no time to prepare or plan. Endings occur whether we want them to or not. Endings are part of the natural order of living and dying. Some endings are cause for celebration; others are cause for mourning. Endings are sometimes marked by separation and isolation and sometimes by joining and companionship. Endings provide exits from experiences while simultaneously providing entrances into the experiences that follow. Some endings are surrounded by rituals; others leave scars of devastation and darkness. Endings can be taken in stride with daily routines or they may rearrange the rest of our lives. Each ending brings to mind earlier endings and the meanings given to them.

Endings in the work with families in distress bring into play all of the above plus something more as we use the empowerment lens. Seeds of the ending phase are present in the beginning and middle phases. Empowerment practice approaches this phase of the work by asking questions such as "What can make the quality of this ending one that *sustains* this family unit?" "How can this final stage *enhance* the strengths seen in our time together?" "How can the ending serve the family in how they are *creating* who they are and who they are becoming?"

Endings with families are unique to each family. They are also different from endings with individual clients, and the skills used in endings with individuals are not generalizable to endings with families. The worker invites different meanings for endings by each individual family member, as well as joint family scripts that may play out at these times. Linda Williams, for example, was determined to move forward with her life. At the same time, her sister, Susan, was experiencing emotions and behaviors related to trauma recovery and knew she was far from ready to consider ending the support from her social worker. Their mother, Jane, was aware of going in both directions. One part of her wanted to bolt forward and try to forget some of her recent past, and yet another part of her wanted to explore her own childhood incest, in the belief that doing so would help her strengthen her support for her daughters in the present.

Every ending can raise memories and emotions of earlier endings. Endings from an empowerment perspective will place strengths at the forefront: strengths gained from earlier losses, strengths in the work just completed, strengths in the family's capacity to face this ending, and strengths available to them for what lies ahead. All endings are intricately intertwined with the processes of grieving and loss. There are no shortcuts.

Social workers guide these processes during the ending phases, skillfully working with the parallels between the ending of the work with the social worker and the endings and losses that have been faced by the family during the course of their life experiences together.

How does empowerment practice contribute to empowering endings for families? How can we assist families to experience endings that give their strengths prominence over the oppressions faced, endings that respect and integrate multicultural variation, endings that skillfully respond to their needs?

Key Tasks for Empowering Endings

Five key tasks for endings in empowerment practice have been identified: dealing with feelings, identifying gains in their own voices, consolidating those gains, reunifying with the community, and evaluation (Lee 2001:253–258). In addition, the dimension of time plays a significant role in the process of endings. Responses related to past, present, and future increase the likelihood of empowering endings in our work with families. Issues significant to each dimension are as follows:

- *Past:* personal histories of ending and loss for individual family members and for the family as a whole; the history of the helping relationship, including both its content and its process, its highlights and milestones, its frustrations, and its humor.
- *Present:* how to make this ending one that is empowering for each family member and the family as a whole; talking openly about the tendency to avoid this here-and-now ending; inviting feedback about what was helpful, what was not helpful, and any recommended changes.

- *Future:* how the gains from this experience can be carried forward into the family's future; imagining what skills they will use when faced with another challenge in the future; seeing their social worker in the future for follow-up or in more informal settings; if referral to another worker is part of the plan, introducing that worker to the family members.

These tasks for empowering endings interact with the three time dimensions in ongoing and individualized ways for each family member.

Dealing with Feelings

The ending of the worker's relationship with a family will raise memories of earlier endings from the past, especially endings that may feel unfinished or unresolved. These earlier losses may include the death of a loved one, a rejection in a relationship, an abrupt departure that may have been interpreted as abandonment. Certain family members may hope that raising these earlier issues will create a "detour" to another phase of the work. The skilled social worker will acknowledge that earlier ending and then bring the work back to the present. Often, this is the first time family members hear that there are unresolved issues from earlier endings for some members of the family. It can be empowering for them to continue discussing these issues at home following the closure of this part of their work with the social worker.

Because of earlier, unfinished endings, the ending with the social worker may appear more heavily laden with emotion than seems fitting. When the emotion exceeds the relationship between worker and family, it can be helpful to invite family members to consider past endings and losses. It is a natural part of the process that those feelings would enter their collective memory at this time. As Cynthia Brown-Wiley left the family group conference, hoping it would be the last time she would see her husband, Mike, she recalled her escape from their home in Michigan in the middle of the night that began her trek across the country with their two children. Then she had also hoped she would never see Mike again but feared the day when he would track her down and find her. Now, even with the added safety net of her community supports, she realized that she might see him again. There might always be the sense of an "unfinished end until the day he dies," especially considering the children's relationship with their father.

Feelings related to future endings influence what happens with each ending with family members. Developmental stages provide examples. Families anticipate the exit of children when they are grown, leave home, and are "launched"; when parents decline physically and face their dying; when retirement and loss of spouse or partner occur. Each small ending also brings a "ripple" related to each person's final ending of life. In much of our work with families, this ultimate loss may remain in the background. However, in many other instances, for hospice and AIDS workers, for example, assisting families as one or more members experience the dying process places a family's feelings about this future loss very much in the foreground.

The permanence or temporariness of the ending also brings a set of feelings for family members. The more abrupt and more permanent it is, the more likely it is that the feelings accompanying the ending will be intense. Perhaps the family has contracted for eight weeks with the social worker, or a mandate by the courts has determined the length of time they were together. Sometimes the insurance company determines when the work must end or be reevaluated. Geographic moves also provide a variation on the permanence or temporariness of an ending. Temporary endings may be ones that conclude the agreed-upon number of sessions but plan for a follow-up call at some time in the future. Some families prefer to end with the knowledge that the "door is always open" in the event that other times of distress occur.

Identifying and Consolidating Gains

Gains from an empowerment perspective, "power gains," occur at personal, interpersonal, and social/community levels. Personal power gains are evident in self-efficacy and greater freedom to make choices. Interpersonal power gains are observable in actions taken from a stance of "power with" rather than "power over" or "power under." Social/community power gains are visible through making things happen in the social and community networks that increase family well-being and strengthen their ability to move forward with their lives. Power gains come in response to oppressions faced, both internal and external ones. For a family that faces poverty, getting a job is perceived as an economic power gain and is integrated into the family's life. For one who faces violence, an increase in safety represents a power gain. For those who face addiction, the interruption of the addictive cycle and the elimination of access to addictive substances represent power gains over addictions. For those who face discrimination, gains are seen through asserting positions of justice and claiming one's right to be treated with respect and fairness. Gains from an empowerment perspective are built on resilience and self-respect. Power gains come from challenging stereotypes, managing feelings, and taking pride in one's cultural uniqueness.

The social worker shapes the ending process in a different way for each family. The request to identify gains reflects the strengths the family brought with them before they faced the distress that was the focus of their work together. Gains may be those qualities that were added to those strengths. Gains may have come through increased knowledge or information, new coping skills, meeting new people.

Consolidation of gains occurs, in part, through telling what those gains are "in their own voices." It also involves tangible results. One family whose home had been destroyed by fire brought pictures of the new housing project where they would be living. One family had worked on getting a new elevator for their apartment building. One young father found a new job after two years of unemployment and brought his GED certificate to show his social worker. A couple in their late thirties who had tried to get pregnant for more than ten years brought their newborn son, a "miracle" of artificial insemination. A mother and daughter reconnected after a fifteen-year estrangement. Another mother, joined by her 83-year-old sister, visited the grave of her son for the first time in the eight years since his death. A young college-age woman who had suffered agoraphobia for three years stepped outside and walked to the end of her block.

Sometimes families describe less-tangible gains: higher self-confidence; "this has brought us closer together"; greater peace of mind; "I'll never be cured [of AIDS] but now I feel healed." Less tangible gains also include what family members take away with them to give meaning to the next steps in their lives. "I can see now that I needed to learn how to lean on others for a change." "We can live without all that stuff. We still have each other, and that's what really counts." "Life is hard, and my brother was given more than he could bear. I'll never forget when I found his body, but I can see that he made a choice and it wasn't my fault that I couldn't prevent it. Missing him is just part of the fabric of the life I have to live. Finally, I am glad to be alive again." It is in the meaning-making that each family connects with themes common to other families. And it is in the meaning-making that each family uses distress or trauma to empower themselves to move on with their lives with deeper and broader understanding, strengthened by the experience.

Reunifying with the Community

Another "key task for empowering endings" has been defined as reunifying with the community (Lee 2001; Lum 1986). This statement reflects an apparent assumption that during the course of the work, the family's connection with the community will somehow have been disrupted. Such a disjunction may occur for some families, but it seems unfounded to assume that it happens for all families facing a crisis. As I have defined empowering practice with families in this volume, the resources in their community, invited and welcomed, are included from the first contact. Connections with community resources continue throughout the course of the work. Constant and active interrelatedness among personal, interpersonal, and social/community dimensions is one hallmark of practice from an empowering perspective. Building upon strengths and resources at all three of these levels provides the most empowering starting point for any family facing crisis. Helpful questions include: "With what community resources does the family wish to continue?" "Which ones do they feel ready to let go of, and which ones do they want to add?" "What are the supportive services and agencies of common interest with other families?"

A family's support network does not leave them during a crisis; it may actually respond in greater force. The apparent absence of supports during a family crisis has been linked to an assumption made by some helping professionals. Family support network members report that some professionals appear to believe that their own ideas about what is needed are more accurate than those of the family and their network. Understandably, then, members of the family support network might retreat into the background when the professionals are around and involved (Carling 1995).

When professionals welcome network participation, however, and view the contributions that those resources can make as essential to the well-being of the family, that array of resources can be included in the plan for addressing the family's immediate and ongoing needs. The response is not only more readily accepted by the family from the people they know and trust, but it also alleviates the expectation that the professional would carry the complexity of the family's needs on his or her shoulders alone—an impossible task to begin with (Carling 1995).

Evaluation

Central to evaluation of empowering practice with families is what has been done to diminish the impact of oppressive forces upon the family's well-being and, simultaneously, what has enhanced their individual and collective strength—that is, added resources, coping skills, connectedness, and expanded choices—to sustain that well-being. Many forms of oppression have existed in families for multiple generations. Addictions, for example, are passed from one generation to another, sometimes skipping generations yet still exerting powerful influences on the behaviors of the members of that generation. Many oppressions are so much a part of the "family script" that the family defines itself according to that particular characteristic. Therefore, an evaluation of what has been done to help diminish the impact of oppressive forces in a family is tempered with a realistic attitude. When enhanced coping skills, participation with others, and new information and learning are put in place as responses to the oppression, increases in well-being are greater. When the step of building on strengths is missing, the recurrence of oppressive interactions and behaviors is likely.

Increased awareness about the shifting needs of family members and the skills to address those needs characterize an evaluation of empowering practice. The evaluation will be "ethnosensitive" (Lee 2001:255), it will integrate cultural and ethnic standards for relationship and connection, for rituals of ending and going separate ways, for acknowledging the mutuality and universality of giving and receiving assistance.

Evaluation from an empowerment perspective will not place the individual person in the family as the primary unit of focus. Instead, the relationship of power among and between the family members as well as between the family and the wider community is the unit of focus. Empowering practice is complete only when powerlessness has been transformed at the personal, interpersonal, and social/community levels.

Part IV

A Closer Look at Families WITH Their Communities

7

Empowering Families with Community Resources

The family is our first community. From our earliest days as infants, long before the development of verbal skill, we watchfully experience how transactions occur among and between our family members. We observe and experience nurturing and neglect, strengthening and weakening, empowerment and oppression (personal dimensions). In biological, adoptive, and extended families alike, we hear and are affected by interactions (interpersonal dimensions) of loving and hating, of dominance/submission and equal respect, of power/control and guiding with competence and self-assurance, of frustration and support. Extended-family members are a vital part of this family-as-community as they serve as a bridge between the nuclear family of origin and membership in the wider community. "Though the dynamics of extended family networks can vary, empowerment-based practice recognizes the skills and resourcefulness within each extended family system and the expectations that people have of each other" (Hodges, Burwell, and Ortega 1998).

These dynamics, skills, resources, and expectations transfer to the wider community as well (social/community dimension). Patterns of respect and cooperation first experienced in the family carry over into patterns of respect and cooperation in the workplace, in school and recreational settings, in friendships and intimate relationships. In similar fashion, patterns of dominance and submission learned in the family carry over into responses of dominance and submission in the workplace, in school or recreational settings, in friendships and intimate relationships. Patterns of conflict management, peacemaking, and peacekeeping can be traced to similar origins and outcomes. Dynamics observed at any one level of the system can provide information about similar dynamics at other levels of that system, including the relationship between social workers and their client families.

The flow of these patterned behaviors is circular and multidirectional, rippling throughout the many levels of all human systems that affect individual and family well-being. "Family well-being is closely connected to community well-being" (Hodges, Burwell, and Ortega 1996:161). The degree to which communities function from a base of empowerment principles in providing services will be, in part, the degree to which families can experience an ongoing, empowering sense of family well-being. In this chapter we take a closer look at what an empowering community looks like and especially at the difference that such a community can make as it serves families. Yet even though the word *community* is placed in the limelight, the integration of personal, interpersonal, and social/community levels reaches another level at this point. Individual and interpersonal realities are always part of the social and community levels within which they interact. They remind us that at least a "dual focus" between the family and the environment of neighborhood and community (Turner and MacNair 2003:218), if not a multilevel focus (one that includes units internal to the family as well as those beyond the community, such as state, national, and global influences), is required in order to adequately address the needs of families in distress.

Coordinated resource and networking systems in communities have increased in recent years in response to earlier findings that revealed gaps and duplications in services, contradictory advice given by agencies, and fragmentation, bureaucratic barriers, and biases against people in poverty (Turner and MacNair 2003:222–223). Because these difficulties still persist in the midst of commendable efforts to address them, families in need of service continue to experience unevenness in provision, explanation, implementation, support, and follow-through with necessary and requested resources. Empowerment-based community models are among the community networking systems that are helping to address some of the earlier shortcomings in services to families.

Lessons from Empowerment-Based Community Models

According to the principles of the empowerment model, communities are recognized as empowering when there are visible responses to oppressive forces in the community; when community strengths are acknowledged and built upon; when interactions at individual, family, organizational, and community-wide levels are characterized by persistent and ongoing multicultural respect; when there is an awareness of the needs of families in the community and resources are available to address those needs with immediate, helpful, individualized, and sufficient responses; when personnel of community service organizations are aware of their role of assisting families as they seek to empower themselves; when helping efforts include the integration of support already available as well as support needed from others; when equalization of power differentials is an active part of the work; and when cooperative roles are fostered among and between key players in organizations and other community resource institutions who serve families in distress. These efforts, in turn, will lead to a community that sustains families, enhances their strengths, and supports their creative efforts, which, in circular fashion, contribute to the community. Part of the foundation for empowering community practice with families, therefore, is recognizing the differences between oppressive forces and empowering influences in the community.

Differences Between Oppressive Forces and Empowering Influences in the Community

All communities have both oppressive forces and empowering influences. Therefore, no one community can be characterized as 100 percent "empowering" or totally "oppressing." For some communities, however, the extent of oppressive forces, combined with fewer resources with which to respond, results in an oppressive environment in which empowerment—that is, making choices, making things happen to reach goals, moving forward, and gaining a greater sense of well-being—seems out of reach. One major task for social workers is to find the strengths in the midst of (not instead of or apart from) the oppressions and building upon those strengths in ways that lead to empowering results.

Oppressive forces include lack of access to transportation, employment, education, health care, public safety, and other community resources. They include deteriorated and unsafe housing, delinquency and gang activity, crime, violence, homelessness, decrepit school buildings, high rates of teen pregnancy, lack of neighborhood cohesion, high rates of dropouts in high school, illicit drug sales and use, barriers related to language, and fragmented and disorganized services.

An empowering community is seen as empowering, in part, through the ways in which oppressive forces are confronted directly, not denied or ignored, and through the organizations that are the community's response to these forces. How organizations make resources available to families plays a role in whether the outcome for family members is empowering or not. The Laurencio-Smiths, the Williamses, and the Brown-Wileys all relied upon resources at personal, interpersonal, and community levels. The Laurencio-Smiths received information from the staff of the day care program that their sons attended, from babysitters, and from the social worker who provided information regarding visitation and restraining orders. The Williamses received information from the school social worker, cooperated with Child Protective Services, relied upon their social worker at the mental health center, and called upon friendship and neighborhood groups for additional support in areas such as job interviewing and financial management. The Brown-Wileys were informed by their social worker about how to contact the local Emergency Family Assistance agency and housing programs. They received temporary assistance from a "natural helper" at the storage locker business and from a professional helper at the local shelter for the homeless, as well as support from a group of others who had been in their position and had moved on. The community safe house and its shelter provided several levels of service in response to safety needs, education, new coping skills, and participation in a support group for survivors of domestic violence. The family group conference brought family together with a non-kinship network and community resources.

These community services were empowering in their own ways, yet not intentionally connected in a way that could maximize the possibilities for sustaining, enhancing, and creating the well-being of each family unit. The need for integration of services has been widely recognized at state and national levels and is also supported through grant funding by a variety of foundations. Coordination and integration of services, to be effective, grows from the resources that are available in each community and responds to the needs of each family. Family preservation programs and family resource centers are two ways in which such integration and response are currently happening. In family preservation programs, social workers and other practitioners are placed in the home to provide skills training in specific areas required by the individual family. Family resource centers provide integration and collaboration opportunities for social agencies helping families through coordination efforts with school systems, mutual aid support groups, medical support systems, justice systems, and other systems relevant to the family's needs. A mutual and reciprocal relationship is the foundation for a form of practice that not only helps families but can also help to strengthen an organization's and a community's ability to realize their purpose related to serving families.

Empowerment at the community level includes locality development, social planning, and social action (Rothman 1995:42). Locality development identifies transactions among and between the personal, interpersonal, and community levels of empowerment: "personal mastery within residents, as individual growth in people is considered a component of community building and a goal of practice"; "skills to make decisions that people can agree on and enact together"; and "the gaining of community competence" (42).

Empowerment associated with social planning includes information given by residents and consumers to social planners so that their preferences can be built into plan designs. Public hearings and community surveys are two of the tools used. Individual and family consumers are empowered when they can make informed choices about services to meet their specific needs. That sense of empowerment increases even further when they see their own feedback, from public hearings and surveys, used for creating or enhancing family services in their communities.

Empowerment at the community level is also seen through social action: participation on local agency boards and decision-making bodies and electoral campaigns to promote the needs of a particular group such as the homeless or the mentally ill (Rothman 1995:42). Personal, interpersonal, and community goals are evident in these uses of empowerment. For some family members, years may pass between their time of major distress and their time of contributing in the form of social action. Or it may be only a brief time. Social action is not limited to political or board commitments. Equally as powerful are the social actions about which we never hear a word: the neighbor who brings food for neighbors who are unable to provide their own; the grandmother who sits with the children of the single mom who is trying to find employment; the retired executive who provides free advice for newly arrived immigrants; the volunteer who sits through the night with a young person dying from AIDS; the niece who helps her elderly aunt get to the doctor. All of these actions, and thousands more like them, create the well-being of a community in ways that are immeasurable. The quality of each community's capacity to care for and support its members would be noticeably changed without such contributions. "A caring community is a community that confirms otherness; giving each person and group [including family] a ground of their own, affirmed through encounters that are egalitarian and dedicated to healing and empowerment" (Saleebey 1997:10).

Eight components for an "ideal delivery system for multineed families" are key in understanding how an organization committed to empowerment principles works with families (Garnett 1996:1):

1. The family has a major voice in establishing its goals and objectives and in deciding which services it needs in order to meet its goals.
2. The system provides a variety of services that respond to the needs of the child and the family.
3. The system provides an integration of services.
4. The system continually updates the treatment plans to be responsive to the developmental status of the family.
5. Prevention efforts are ongoing.
6. Workers have flexibility to respond to the family's changing needs and to protect its rights.
7. Services are sensitive to cultural, gender, and racial concerns, and they respect values and traditions as a source of strength.
8. Performance is assessed by improved outcomes for the clients (such as improved school attendance, securing employment, timely immunizations) and not by the total number of clients assisted by the agency.

Principles, roles, and practices consistent with empowerment practice are evident in these components: emphasis on strengths with an eye to diminishing oppression (Components 1 and 7); multicultural respect (Component 7); attention to the family's needs and the changing nature of those needs (Components 1, 2, 4, and 6);

knowledge that families empower themselves and workers assist (Component 1); and integration of support from others, including prevention efforts (Components 3 and 5). Garnett's list can benefit from the empowerment principles by adding further clarity about equalization of power differentials and cooperative roles. The empowerment principles guide workers to seek outcomes that respond to all levels of the system, family and agency alike, rather than ones that might place outcomes for the family as a higher priority than outcomes for the agency. An agency whose needs are unmet in the exchange of serving families may be less likely to set policies and to reach out to serve additional families in the future. Our work is not complete until the needs at all levels of the system are addressed in some way.

Work from community-based empowerment models and empowerment-oriented practitioners addresses social needs such as adequate housing, financial and employment resources, freedom from violence and discrimination (Germain 1991). Strengths of individuals and families reflect strengths of communities. Building on the strengths and resources in the community gives the community a future upon which to build as needs and responses emerge.

For decades the literature focused on the family's part in creating or exacerbating their "problem" or on therapies with "pathological" families. Increasingly in recent years, however, and to the credit of family movement advocates, family members are now viewed as people who face serious challenges and who have the strengths, skills, wisdom, and capacities to support themselves and others (Carling 1995:300). These family strengths are supported by strengths in their communities. Community strengths for empowerment practice with families are mutual aid support groups, collaborative relationships, capacity and asset building, extended-family networks, and non-kinship networks (Hodges, Burwell, and Ortega 1998:149–152).

Mutual Aid Support Groups

"Groups are...the optimum medium for empowerment on all levels" (Lee 2001:291). Participation in a mutual aid support group is "an enterprise in mutual aid, an alliance of individuals who need each other, in varying degrees, to work on certain common problems" (Schwartz 1961:18). Family members who seek mutual aid support groups have an opportunity to participate with others who share common experiences. This step, like no other, often brings relief to family members, with the knowledge that they are not alone with their questions and needs for information and coping options. As the intervention of choice with oppressed clients and those responding to trauma, mutual aid groups influence behavioral, attitudinal, and belief change (Gabriel 1996; Harford 1971; Hopps and Pinderhughes 1999).

One mother of a 14-year-old son who had just attempted suicide phrased it like this: "Before I went to the support group for families with a member who had attempted to kill themselves, I felt as if I had a marathon to run when I barely had enough energy to make it to the end of my driveway. After the first meeting, however, I came home realizing there were others who had started the marathon and, with the help of the others, they were making it through each day. They were finding a way to get from one mile to the next mile, slowly but surely and, most important of all, that we have each other. They understand."

In addition to receiving support, understanding, and practical ideas for managing their distress, families also realize that they have much to give as well. When the distress is turned into something that contributes to the lives of others facing similar circumstances, the empowering step of "taking action" has occurred. Family members notice when their own agony transforms into a meaning beyond their individual experience, deepening relationships with others. "The memory of my abuse will always bring a certain amount of pain. But when I decided how I would use that experience to help others while they were recovering, I gained more purpose in my life than I had ever had before making that decision" (Linda Williams). "Members are viewed as active and having the power to make a difference in the group, as social beings who need to belong and as social learners who help each other in learning. They establish bonds, empathy, and identification. Differences are supported and a balance is sought between the needs of the individual and the needs of the group" (Lee 2001:293).

The potential for mutual aid exists when people facing common challenges are brought together. Mutual aid does not, however, happen automatically. The transactions among and between group members are complex. When a support group includes one's family members, complexity increases. The common concern that brings group members together is part of the dynamic. The process that shapes how that content comes alive for each group member is another part of the dynamic. "Creating a mutual aid group is a difficult process, with members having to overcome many of their stereotypes about people in general, groups, and helping" (Shulman 1999:303). The skill of the family group worker is to take these dynamics and the complexity of transactions and guide a process that is characterized by a sense of safety and mutual respect.

The most empowering strength of a mutual aid group may, however, lie beyond the influence of the worker. The transforming power of empathy, both when it is received and when it is given, is something that family members can do with and for each other in a way that exceeds the skill of the worker. "As group members understand the feelings of the others...they begin to accept their own feelings in new ways" (Shulman 1999:308). These experiences lead to cohesion and the group's attainment of its own power. "Group methods, techniques, and skills that develop the *group's power* while attending to the needs of individual members are empowering in both process and outcomes" (Lee 2001:296).

Collaborative Relationships

Collaborative relationships between practitioner and family members have been identified earlier. As the individuals and the family work collaboratively with social workers at the community level, what are additional opportunities for collaboration? Both practitioners and families "must recognize the wealth of knowledge they bring" (Hodges, Burwell, and Ortega 1998:149) to this effort. All experiences with schools, workplaces, health care institutions, employment agencies, homeless shelters, safe houses, emergency rooms, human service agencies, welfare assistance, child care organizations, support groups for addictions, bereavement, or transitions contribute to a wealth of information. All include the potential for collaboration and empowerment, and, realistically, all carry the potential for quite the opposite.

Characteristics that ensure empowering collaboration include trust, respect (and self-respect), careful listening, openness, commitment to the give-and-take of all relationships, acceptance of each other as equals, mutuality of goals, willingness to do one's part when able, willingness to participate in decision making, and a combined knowledge base to address the situation. How do these collaborative efforts contribute to a family's ability to make choices for their well-being, to the capacity for sustaining, enhancing, and creating family well-being? What does well-being mean for this family? Ideally, "as families and practitioners work in partnership, both gain enhanced creativity, new knowledge and skills, and—most important—the chance for enduring change and growth" (Hodges, Burwell, and Ortega 1998:150). Such "gain" and "change" reach for the ideal. And certainly gains in creativity, knowledge, and skills are possible for many. However, social workers see families inundated with drug addiction, violence, and poverty, where creativity may mean finding a new way to roll the joint, new knowledge may be the knowledge of fear in the wake of a battering and broken bones, and skills may include a mother's ability to apply one more layer of duct tape to the soles of her children's shoes. These are hardly the changes we would wish to see "endure." And yet, from an empowering view, the abilities to create and gain knowledge and develop skills are still there and can be used in other forms and toward other ends as a step along the way toward greater well-being.

The relationship between practitioner and family is one possibility for collaborative support. After contact with a social worker has ended, however, the opportunity for collaborative relationships exists within the family and in relationships external to the family. Enhancing skills of collaborating within the family (parents and partners collaborating on decision making, for example) can mean greater resilience when future challenges arise. Similarly, in interactions external to the family, with support group members, coworkers, friendship networks, and service providers, collaborative efforts ensure that there will be others to turn to when necessary. As coteachers and colearners, workers and family members use collaboration as one of their coping skills: the family learns from the worker what those skills look like, and the worker learns from the family what forms of collaboration are most helpful.

The challenges that families face are multifaceted and require multifaceted responses. Each stressor impacts family members on personal, interpersonal, and social/community levels, and each requires a coordinated response that addresses all levels. Comprehensive community initiatives (CCIs) are one answer. CCIs "contain several or all of the following elements and aim to achieve synergy among them: expansion and improvement of social services and supports, such as child care, youth development, and family support; health care, including mental health care; economic development; housing rehabilitation and/or construction; community planning and organizing; adult education; job training; school reform; and quality-of-life activities such as neighborhood security and recreation programs" (Kubisch et al. 1995:1).

Citizen participation is a hallmark of community initiatives, "yet participation by itself is not necessarily empowering" (Flynn, Ray, and Rider 1994). In one community, for example, seventeen women participated in a micro enterprise development project that "dangled the carrot," as one woman put it, of having her own business. After the first year, however, resources dried up because of lack of funding, and no follow-up services were in place. Fifteen of the seventeen women withdrew from the program.

The Ford Foundation's Neighborhood and Family Initiative (NFI) was created to test comprehensive community development efforts in four locations: Detroit, Memphis, Milwaukee, and Hartford, Connecticut. Residents of the selected neighborhoods were included in the structure of each initiative. Three approaches to the integration of services were identified: "finding opportunities for integration at the project level," linking "projects at a broader strategic level to build from or complement other projects," and seeing "integration as the product of planning guided by a strategic 'lens'" (Chaskin and Chipenda-Dansokho 1997: 439–440). Even though these efforts brought together parties interested in integration of services, the actual implementation of strategies was observed to be more of a parallel process than an integrative one. A major reason appeared to be the "need for greater clarity in defining what comprehensive development means in operational terms" and the need to "negotiate and agree on basic operational issues, such as the range of activities needed, the ways these activities would be implemented, the duration of programmatic activity, how programs (or their effects) are to be linked to one another, the expected outcomes, length of time to produce the outcomes, and how outcomes can be measured" (442).

Clearly, CCIs and NFIs are significant efforts toward strengthening community responsiveness to the needs of families. Expansion in choices of services and their improvements, comprehensiveness options, and ongoing involvement of community members all exemplify the empowering model of community well-being for families.

Capacity and Asset Building

Helping families to empower themselves also includes enhancing existing capacities at the individual, interpersonal, and social/community levels. All communities have resources to help families meet challenges of everyday life. Two assumptions are key. First, families already have multiple capacities and assets. Second, "empowerment based practitioners begin with the premise that all families and communities know what they need to function in a healthy way" (Hodges, Burwell, and Ortega 1994:150). These assumptions guide empowerment-oriented social workers as advocates, consultants, colearners, coinvestigators, and interpreters of agency policies and actions. These roles require mutuality in the work. They ensure an environment in which people can make choices about what they need, from whom they want to receive assistance, and how that assistance is provided (Howie the Harp, in Carling 1995). Being helpful includes knowing how and when to step back to avoid getting in the way of the family members as they empower themselves.

Empowerment-oriented practitioners who assist in capacity and asset building also serve as brokers, linking family needs with available resources in the community. Once the families' needs have been met, the workers connect these families with other families who face similar concerns. Mutual aid from those who have "been there" and survived builds capacity through increased resources. As the family group conference for Cynthia Wiley demonstrated, extended-family networks and non-kinship networks act like spotters at the edge of the trampoline while families experience the ups and downs of building and rebuilding their own capacities.

"Community development programs are built in part on the idea that assets have multiple positive effects on well-being...particularly for people who are economically vulnerable" (Page-Adams and Sherraden 1997:423–424). In this usage, "assets" are defined in terms of property and financial holdings, not to be confused with a broader definition that includes "talents and skills of individuals, organizational capacity, political connections, buildings and facilities, and so on" (Kretzmann and McKnight 1993). This way of thinking about antipoverty strategies has much in common with the strengths perspective in social work practice (Chapin 1995; Saleebey 1997). The "multiple positive effects on well-being" of asset building include personal well-being, children's well-being, and women's status, all related to enhanced empowerment for today's families (Page-Adams and Sherraden 1997:424–432).

Extended-Family Networks and Non-kinship Networks

"Empowerment builds on existing resources" (Hodges, Burwell, and Ortega 1994:151). Every family brings a network of others into their transactions with helping professionals, no matter how isolated they may initially seem. In part, the very act of requesting service or being mandated to service with social workers or others outside the family's natural network implies that something in that natural network is not working to meet the needs of the family. However, it is possible that this assumption is inaccurate and may lead to extended-family members' keeping their distance from service professionals. When professional services become the only support, rather than a backup service, extended-family members tend to back away, and the result is that these natural supports become less available to help the family in need. Another possibility is that chronically underfunded formal service systems may suddenly end services to a family as well, thereby leaving the family both isolated and unsupported (Carling 1995). Therefore, it is important to consider other reasons why this family needs to turn to assistance outside their own network. For example, extended-family members may be far away, as they were for Jorgé and Lydia. Geographic distance is often a factor for immigrant families or families who have recently experienced relocation.

Helping professionals cannot assume that a family's extended-family and non-kinship networks will be available to provide support. Sometimes people in the family's network are viewed as the sources of the oppression that the family seeks to diminish, as was the case in all three of the families discussed earlier: Maria in the Laurencio-Smith family, John in the Williams family, and Mike in the Brown-Wiley family. One of the unfortunate reasons that a battered woman has to leave an average of seven times in order finally to be free of an abusive relationship is that the members of her extended family lack the understanding that "going back to work things out" does not work in these situations. In fact, it can, and often does, lead to an escalation of the violence. And yet most families do exhibit a balance of supports and barriers. Discerning which is which is part of the work between social worker and family.

When a family has strong extended-family and neighborhood connections, friendship and workplace relationships, the available resources can be boundless. Identifying them is one step. Accessing them in the time of the family's need is a second step. An ongoing mutual assessment can address the former; unique and individualized responses to the particular dynamics of each family, the latter.

Technology has added resources for extended-family and non-kinship networks to stay connected. The Wong family, for example, attempting to deal with

Mr. Wong's depression and "homesickness" after a work-related move to the United States, discovered that he could have day-to-day contact with his brother and parents in Shanghai via e-mail. Their encouragement about his work and enthusiasm about their preparations for his return with his wife and child became his lifeline through a two-year assignment. The depression lifted noticeably when he and his wife began making friends in their neighborhood, especially with an older couple, the Baileys, whose son was on a work assignment in Europe. The Baileys decided to "temporarily adopt" the Wongs as surrogate family, non-kinship yet "family of choice." This resulted in frequent spontaneous meals together as well as the Baileys' providing babysitting for the Wongs' son. The Wongs offered to do food shopping for the Baileys and provided transportation at various times. "Families of choice," sometimes referred to as surrogate families, are a vital resource not to be overlooked.

"The neighborhood was a kind of extended family.... In my own home there was also the neighborhood flow, people in and people out" (Daloz Parks et al. 1996:32–33). Flexible boundaries exist between family, extended family, neighborhood, and community. Family members perceive their social interactions with organizations and institutions in different ways. College and high school were major parts of the social environment for Linda and Susan Williams, respectively, while these particular institutions were more in the background for Jane and John. The legal profession and the criminal justice system were professional organizations for John one week and punitive institutions the next. As a result of the transition this family faced, the legal profession as John's work world was in the background rather than the foreground for Jane, Linda, and Susan for many years. However, as the two daughters moved toward confronting their father about sexual abuse, the criminal justice system and related service personnel took on major positions in their lives. The social workers in their community and the skill of those social workers to collaboratively guide this family through the procedures required provided community support during a time of distress and need. These examples highlight the shifting nature of social and community supports. What is a resource one week may become a barrier the next. Resources that are not particularly in the forefront one week may become central to the well-being of the family the next.

Extended-family networks and non-kinship networks are not separate. Collaborative relationships and the capacity and asset building that support them are intertwined and reciprocal. Community-based empowerment practice addresses family needs through an individualized approach with each family and through ongoing, long-term connections with others (Taylor et al. 1987). In the past, service systems have used approaches that are, in large part, impractical for many families. Examples include insisting that treatment is the primary need, more important than home, job, or friends; asking people to move through multiple service environments, learning skills in each that they are then required to transfer to other settings, rather than *starting with* a home, a job, a social network" (Carling 1995, emphasis added).

Here is a clear message to consider "treatment" as a supportive effort but not a primary one. Moving "treatment" to the backseat and home, job, and social network to the front requires a shift in thinking for some helping professionals. For community-based empowerment workers, it means validation for what they have been doing all along.

> [This] does not assert that professional services are unimportant or unnecessary, but rather that to be effective, such services must be controlled by their users...and be organized not primarily to "fix" individuals, but instead to support those key foundations of a healthy life on which all citizens rely: a home, a job, and connections with family, friends, neighbors, and coworkers. Thus, this...does not in any way ignore the nature or severity of a [family's distress]. Rather, it approaches [them] in a fundamentally new way—as equal[s], and as valued "customers" whose growing empowerment, satisfaction, and improved quality of life are the critical outcomes through which we can evaluate the success of a professional's work. And it focuses as much on eliminating societal barriers as it does on individual rehabilitation. (Carling 1995:22)

Carling identifies two additional characteristics of family members' helping to support one of the individuals in the family. First, other family members also deserve substantial support and, second, they should not be blamed for the individual's distress or difficulty but treated with respect, "the same respect that all citizens deserve" (22). Carling's work centers around the community integration approach. Even though his use of this approach is directed toward the reintegration of people with psychiatric disabilities into their communities after hospitalization, many of his ideas are consistent with working with families in distress from an empowerment perspective. Professional services are viewed as "necessary but hardly sufficient" (Carling 1995:51). Emphasis is placed on practical supports, coping strategies, and recovery to well-being; networking and choice are priorities; and relationships that are respectful and reciprocal provide the basis for all phases of the contact (50), in short, a framework of support (Trainor and Church 1984).

The Framework of Support

The "framework of support" is guided by a goal, by core attitudes and skills, and by strengthening a family's "circles of support" (Carling 1995:268). The framework of support offers clear guidelines for the order and the nature of the interactions by which resources are accessed. These guidelines are described below, followed by illustrations of their application to the oppression of poverty.

The Goal of the Framework of Support

The framework of support views families as existing within supportive communities. The goal of this framework sounds much like the purpose of empowerment practice, well-being—that is, "to ensure that people...live rich and fulfilling lives in the community" (Carling 1995:57). Two requirements are, first, the empowerment of families to be in charge of their own lives, making choices about which supports to use and, second, the enlistment of resources available in the community to support families in distress. Workers acknowledge the balance between too much and too little support and the need to identify what quality and quantity of support will be helpful. Too much support can lead to dependency and a loss of self-defined goals. Offering supports that are qualitatively "off base" can result in a sense of "ships passing in the night" as worker and family seem to miss each other. Helpful support is frequently the result of providing specific information about coping and an array of relevant contacts from which the family can choose. Stepping back as family members do their work together, yet simultaneously remaining available, adds helpful support.

Certain actions may block the use of a framework of support, for example, focusing on incapacity; viewing professionally delivered services (rather than those available from peers, family, and others) as primary; and believing that the professional knows best how supports should be provided (Carling 1995:52). To address these potential blocks, an empowerment-based worker brings a strengths perspective, a commitment to mutuality of roles, and a stance of assisting while family members empower themselves. Yet it is still helpful to ask oneself certain questions: "In my work with families, how much do I tend to focus on incapacities?" "Do I believe the services I have to offer are more important, more effective, more valuable, more whatever, than the natural help that is available to the families from their peers, family members, and other support persons?" "Do I sometimes attempt to tell them how their supports should be provided?"

Core Attitudes

Several core attitudes are essential to the framework of support: (1) possibility: seeing the capabilities of each family and each of its members and how to connect them with others; (2) equality: seeing the families we serve as equal to each other in the family and to others outside the family, regardless of their current levels of functioning; (3) equanimity: taking both challenges and successes in stride, not being pulled off course by setbacks or triumphs; and (4) necessity: being convinced that an empowering "circle of support" (Carling 1995:268) is crucial for everyone involved (Reidy 1992).

Each family's "circle of support" consists of all the extended-family members, neighbors, friends, coworkers, and others with whom they have day-to-day contact. This valuable source of assistance, the source most familiar to the family, is the best safeguard against the danger that the family will be isolated from the community during a crisis (Carling 1995:268). These circles of support need to be included from the first contacts with every family. The skilled worker will seek to strengthen the people in these circles as much as seeking to strengthen the family members themselves. One guideline for helping to strengthen circle-of-support members is through the core attitudes mentioned earlier: possibility, equality, equanimity, and necessity. Matching family needs with contributions available in the circle of support can be an effective approach on the part of the social worker. Given the typical workload of a social worker, there is no way one worker alone can meet the needs of a family in crisis on a daily basis for an undetermined length of time. Circles of support are a key component in allowing social workers to do what they are called upon to do from an empowerment framework: assisting the family as they empower themselves.

Core Skills

The core attitudes accompanying the work of the framework of support come alive through skills that help a family stay connected with their supports during times of distress. One who is effective in helping a family through the empowerment framework will (1) be curious about and listen carefully to a person's interests; (2) provide emotional support; (3) create opportunities over and over without giving up; (4) encourage without pressuring; and (5) follow through, attend to details, and know when to stay in the background (Carling 1995:263). Assessments of what participants in various community programs told their social workers revealed these same requests time and time again. In the words of one woman in a job skills program, these actions were "what works if those helpers out there want to help us and not take over and do it *for* us or do what they think we need" (Helen 2000, emphasis added).

Listen Carefully to Interests

Each family member has different interests. It is essential to hear from all family members, to listen carefully in order to discover whether there are common themes bringing their choices together on another level and to see how available they are to working with each other's input.

Provide Emotional Support

As the worker strives to provide emotional support, unresolved authority questions, struggles having to do with inclusion and exclusion, and resentment toward those perceived as "favorites" can arise. One family member, for example, may interpret the worker's behavior as favoritism when emotional support is provided specifically to another family member. The worker must employ skill and sensitivity to recognize these dynamics, to balance the emotional support given to each member, and to emphasize that emotional support is available for the family as a whole.

Create Opportunities Over and Over Without Giving Up

Creating opportunities and doing so repeatedly, even when the family chooses not to follow through with them, is also a core skill. From the commitment to enhance the well-being of the family, workers can envision many opportunities for each family, and it is important to make the family aware of such opportunities, even if they choose not to follow through with the suggestions. Such opportunities are most helpful when they match the family's perception of what is possible at that particular time, providing a clear picture of how they will add to the well-being of the family.

Encourage Without Pressure

This practice acknowledges each family member's capacity to work from her or his own ability. The message is similar to "march to your own drummer." Encouragement without pressure reflects the worker's awareness that there are seasons in a family's life together and seasons for each family member and that family members are the best judges of when it is time to hold steady and when it is time to move forward. Families in distress often respond to their recent crises and trauma with the need to slow down, to draw inward, to take events and decisions at their own pace. Encouraging without pressuring includes normalizing the family experiences as long as those experiences are not harmful to any family member.

Follow Through, Attend to Details, and Know When to Stay in the Background

These three skills create trust and a sense of reliability between worker and family. Following through on tasks may be no problem for those who have a clear sense of goals and the steps required to reach them. Immediately after a major traumatic event, however, any sense of the future is often blocked by confusion, shock, and grief. The capacity to manage details can elude families both during and after the event. Knowing that someone is willing and available to manage those details frees the family to attend to their emotional work.

When Mr. and Mrs. Scranton stood at the bedside of their 17-year-old daughter, Natalie, who had just died from an overdose of sleeping pills taken earlier that evening, they already had the information that their daughter's body would need to be removed from the hospital that night. Noticing the confusion on their faces about what to do and whom to call, the medical social worker, Nan, stepped in and assured them that she would take care of the necessary arrangements. All they needed to do was to be with each other and to be there for Doug, their son and Natalie's brother, when he arrived at the hospital.

As a worker stays tuned in to the family's cognitive and emotional expression, the times when they need each other more than they need an outsider will become obvious. These are the times when it is important for the worker to stay in the background. The arrival of Doug was one such moment for the social worker. Nan had offered to wait by the entrance to the family lounge of the ICU to watch for Doug so that the Scrantons could stay with Natalie's body. When Doug arrived, Nan introduced herself, led Doug to his family, then for the next half hour stayed completely in the background but nearby and alert to the time when the family would be ready for her assistance in helping them take the next steps and make the decisions they would need to make together that night.

Accessing Resources

The framework of support offers clear priorities for the use of resources. Family members, often "family of choice" members, are the first source of support, followed by other extended-family members and friends. Generic community services such as schools, hospitals, religious settings, workplaces, and recreational facilities are third, and specific formal agency services are the fourth, and last, source of support. "Informal caring networks of family, friends and neighbors are major, though often unrecognized resources. Their tangible assistance with day to day living needs, as well as the social and emotional support they often provide, may complement and often lessen the need for . . . formal services" (Pape 1990:3). When families face distress, assistance in strengthening the support network is as much a focus for the work as is assistance in strengthening the family.

Identification of resources is a first step, followed by gaining access to those resources. The closer the resources are to the daily lives of the family members, the more easily accessible they are likely to be and the more likely the family will use them. The reality is that many of these families are consumed with concerns about survival from one moment to the next. Overwhelming circumstances can immobilize family members to the point that even a phone call is too much to manage. The availability of resources, the ease of accessing them, and the capacity of family members to do so are all factors that must be carefully considered during this process of matching resource to need. In the midst of crisis and in its immediate aftermath, one familiar and compassionate face can do more to reassure and stabilize families than all of the community services put together. As time passes, however, those additional resources can prove invaluable as well. This timing in offering services complements the timing of the family's responses to their distress. Sometimes incremental change leads to more lasting change. At other times the family may be in the midst of a large life transition—divorce, birth, death, unemployment—and their readiness to move forward fairly quickly may be more empowering, such as when Jane, Linda, and Susan Williams, as well as Cynthia Brown, were ready to create new lives and a new sense of family. The family always retains the right to turn down any or all of the resources offered; they are less likely to do so if those resources are ones that are familiar to them. If the resources offered are unfamiliar to them, explanation and adjustment will be required. The empowering path in this situation is the family's right to choose after they have received sufficient information.

Poverty as an Example of Oppressive Forces

We will now turn to poverty as an example of the oppressive forces faced by families in distress and look at addressing it through a framework of support. Accessing food, clothing, and shelter without financial resources is a nearly impossible challenge when a family must face delays related to institutional red tape, not to mention the unwanted requirement to "tell the story" several times over. Extended-family members, however, relate stories of "dropping everything to get here." Friends and neighbors bring meals and babysit on a moment's notice. People who are part of such a helping network frequently say that this is "just the thing you do when you hear they are going through a tough time because our time will come and then we may need something in return" (a statement made by one of Jane Williams's neighbors, as reported by Jane). And when the poverty is chronic, with no end in sight, family and neighbor networks are the ones most likely to continue their support long after funding support dries up or staff changes occur in the local agencies.

For the goal of the framework of support—"to ensure that people...live rich and fulfilling lives in the community" (Carling 1995:57)—to be met, families living in poverty must be in charge of their own lives, in the sense that they are the ones to make the choices about which resources are used and which ones are set aside. Cynthia Brown chose to accept the assistance of her social worker at Emergency Family Assistance, and at the same time she was very clear about not returning to the homeless shelter. The second aspect of the goal is to call upon community resources to support families in distress. Together, Cynthia and her social worker called upon supports for temporary housing, supports provided by the local safe house and battered women's shelter, and supports through the school system in its response to the children's educational needs.

Even though Cynthia was experiencing poverty when she first came to the attention of the social workers, they were able to believe in the possibility of her increased financial strength, and thereby they exhibited one of the core attitudes of the framework of support. This belief was grounded in the business degree Cynthia held, even though she lacked experience at that time. Other core attitudes evident in the work with Cynthia were seeing her as an equal in her ability to find answers to the challenges she faced, holding steady with support when she faced the setback of her husband's attacks, and persisting in helping her find her "circle of support" in this community that was initially new and unfamiliar but that became her "family of choice."

All five of the core skills of the framework of support came into play in assisting Cynthia as she faced the realities of poverty day by day to meet the needs of her children as well as herself. When her funds began to diminish more quickly than she had anticipated and she still had no signs of future income, she learned of emergency funds that were available on a temporary basis. Her social workers were genuinely interested in her story, her safety, and her goals for herself and her children. They provided emotional support and encouragement and helped her learn about what resources were available to her in that community, particularly with regard to her fears of future violence. They offered opportunities that fit with Cynthia's goals and had no expectations about whether or not she would choose to pursue those opportunities. They respected her pace and did not require that she move more quickly or more slowly, which was especially important at the time of her job interviews and applications to take night school courses. Opportunities were also offered to the children, and their individual needs were addressed on an equal footing with those of their mother.

In matching available resources with Cynthia's needs, workers were always aware that Cynthia could contact many of those resources on her own, such as the clothing and food banks, and that she could request assistance in contacting others, such as the shelter and a potential employer. When she came up against barriers to accessing resources, such as when she was unsuccessful in opening a bank account, the social workers returned to the bank with her to help explain her plan and the circumstances relevant to her being considered a "good risk."

Families Serving Families

Beyond the family unit and beyond strengthening a family's circle of support, additional community-based empowering actions are available. Some families choose to empower themselves in their communities through serving other families. When families take what they have learned from their distress and recovery and use it to help other families, they participate in a wide variety of contributions to their communities. "Families are the most vital source of knowledge about how services intended to meet family needs should be organized" (Carling 1995:310). Family members who have previously been consumers of helping services are involved in all phases of family service systems: program development, training, delivery of services, creation and change of policies, research, and program planning. Some advocate for change by educating legislators or by serving on committees that create new legislation. Some volunteer as public speakers to help educate the public.

Three phases have been noted as a "transformation of consciousness" that occurs as families move through times of distress and crisis. The first phase is characterized by such messages as "Something wrong has occurred that is not my fault" (angry indignation, helplessness). A statement that reflects the second phase might be "There is something we can do about it—there is strength in our numbers" (hope). And in the third phase members of the family might be at the point of saying "There is a specific contribution I can make" (personal empowerment and responsibility) (Deegan 1992). Each family, of course, moves through these phases at their own pace and in their own way. The workers' role is to increase awareness of this process and to offer supportive assistance. Making choices once again becomes a key factor in the third phase. Workers contribute by offering options from which family members can choose as they decide what contributions they wish to make to their communities.

Some human service systems "are moving toward an explicit goal of 50% consumer membership on planning and policy-making bodies, including agency boards of directors, task forces, study groups, advisory committees, and so forth....Maine is phasing in a new Regional Board structure with 50% consumer and family representation and limited participation by professionals" (Carling 1995:278). Through this level of participation, family members receive the message that their observations and opinions are valued by the service system. When family members are asked for their ideas, they have an opportunity to use their success in surviving a terrible event in their lives in a positive way to make a contribution to their community and to the betterment of other families. What was at one point devastating becomes empowering.

From "family as our first community" to families serving other families in the wider community, empowering opportunities for social workers are numerous. The preceding discussion has considered what an empowering community looks like, including the empowering services that it contains. Lessons from several empowerment-based community models have been summarized and applied to families in particular. Components of an ideal delivery system for families who have multiple needs have been analyzed for similarities and differences with the empowerment approach. Options for community strengths have been identified in collaborative relationships, capacity building, and extended-family and non-kinship networks. The idea of a framework of support has been discussed in greater detail as a guide for implementing an empowering framework for community-based practice with families. And the ways in which social workers assist families in serving other families have been addressed.

It is encouraging to note the growth in the number of empowerment-based community programs existing in the United States and Canada today. Information is available about such programs through the National Empowerment Center and Project Share.[1] The Social Integration Project in Amherst, Massachusetts; the Clustered Apartment Project in Santa Clara County, California; and the Canadian Mental Health Association in Vancouver, British Columbia, are all examples of empowerment-based community programs actively involved at the local and countywide levels. One national interactive teleconference based upon the ideals of empowering practice drew ten thousand attendees for a single telecast. M-POWER, a statewide project based in Boston, comprises individuals and families who live with one or more members with significant psychiatric disabilities. It is completely member run, and the members participate in a critical-thinking process about what has happened to them. They also explore ways to maintain or recover being in charge of their own choices about how to live their lives. Family to Family Education Programs are offered throughout the United States and in two Canadian provinces.[2] Focus Points, a family resource center, is located in the Five Points neighborhood in Denver, Colorado, a community in which 50 percent of the population lives in poverty and "many families live in one of the four homeless shelters, in one of six subsidized housing developments or in transitional long-term housing" (Harris 1995:1). Reflecting the empowerment goal of well-being, the Center for Child and Family Well-being is a newly established program at the Bryn Mawr College Graduate School of Social Work and Social Research.

The remainder of this chapter is devoted to an illustration of one empowerment-based community project, located in Denver, Colorado.

Project WISE (Women's Initiative for Service and Empowerment)

Project WISE was created in 1995 as the result of several forces coming together. First, two social workers, Dr. Jean East and Sue Kenney, M.S.W., who were involved in welfare reform in the Denver area responded to the documented need for counseling and supportive services to women making the transition from welfare to work. The need base for Project WISE is women who do not meet the criteria for mental health services from the public sector. The services are directed toward women and children in single-parent families, female-headed households who are receiving TANF (Temporary Assistance to Needy Families), who have begun work and are receiving welfare-to-work benefits, or who are employed in entry-level jobs with incomes at poverty level and are struggling to keep employment.

A second impetus for the development of this program was the availability, through a local religious community, of seed money for two years of funding. And a third, the empowerment of women and their families through combined efforts of individual, family, and social change, was the foundation of the belief system for both of these social workers. This philosophy gave direction for a mission statement and for two organizational goals. The codirectors define the mission of Project WISE as "the empowerment of women with low incomes through offering opportunities to meet personal, family and economic goals and attain a positive involvement with their community" (East and Kenney 2001:1).

The organizational goals are "(1) to provide services for low-income families in transition from reliance on the welfare system to personal and economic self-sufficiency and (2) to work for system change through dissemination of ongoing research and documentation of issues, collaboration with community advocacy efforts, and providing opportunities for welfare recipients and low-income working persons to gain a voice and to participate in policy and organizational change through community organizing, which includes leadership-development training." Levels of participation are identified in the program description in the following way: "In order for women to attain a sense of empowerment and a healthy interdependence with their community, they must have opportunities to experience change at the personal, interpersonal, and political levels" (East and Kenney 2001:1).

Collaboration with the Department of Human Services TANF programs from two counties in the Denver area, with the Peer Counseling Program of the Community College of Denver, and with educational and support groups in a variety of other area agencies provides recruitment sources. That collaboration continues to be a vital part of the ongoing strength of the program. A contract with the Denver Department of Social Services clarifies the procedures and information necessary for making referrals. Collaborative relationships with community-based agencies offering education and employment training programs also serve Project WISE participants. Although programs for job training were available, the need for personal and family support was also recognized as a key element in maximizing the possibility of the women's success. Economic self-sufficiency and personal self-sufficiency combined as joint goals for Project WISE. In 2001 a community advocacy component was added to help increase skills and linkages between the project participants. Opportunities in advocacy include leadership development, community organization, and research.

Leadership development includes three components. First, participants are asked questions about their experiences and their concerns with the welfare system. This communicates to them that their observations are valued and that they are seen, and can see themselves, as "citizens of the community at large" (East 1999:152). Second, participants join focus groups to help shape programs that are part of the project. The third component, leadership training retreats, provide opportunities for learning and skill building as well as action planning. The retreats, which are overnight experiences for groups of fifteen to twenty women, are led by participants and provide opportunities to learn skills such as facilitating meetings, developing workshops, and raising funds.

For community organizing, participants discuss how to have collective power—power WITH—when advocating on local, state, and national levels for issues that affect their families, their communities, and their lives in general. The opportunities in research offer participants experiences in research-related interviews, focus groups, and groups in which they relate their stories to others so that those experiences can be documented and become part of the knowledge base used in further research, disseminated in professional journal articles, or used to gather data for policy-making efforts.

Demographically, the Project WISE participants range in age from 18 to 50. In terms of ethnic background, 50 percent are Latina, 30 percent are Anglo/Euro-American, 19 percent are African American, and 1 percent are American Indian. As of December 2001, 420 people had received individual counseling, 545 groups with 916 participants had been conducted, 76 people had participated in seven leadership development retreats, with 30 providing the necessary planning hours for those retreats, 53 women had participated in community organizing efforts, 75 were involved in research and advocacy, 57 women had participated in luncheons for businesswomen in the community, and 5 had participated in a focus group to provide information about the implementation of the Family Violence Option of the Welfare Reform Law.

The work of Project WISE comes alive through the experiences of its participants. The following case study illustrates key aspects of the program and how they were used to empower one family.

_____

When Sheila was referred to Project WISE, she was voluntarily off her medications for depression and she had returned to hard-core drug use. This 39-year-old African American woman was under the mandate of her TANF contract to seek counseling. She participated in an employment and training program affiliated with Project WISE about the same time she was referred by her TANF case manager. After the training, she expressed an interest in joining the Project WISE leadership development activities. Both a genogram and an ecogram are used to depict the comparison between internal (to the family system) and external dynamics (figures 7.1 and 7.2).

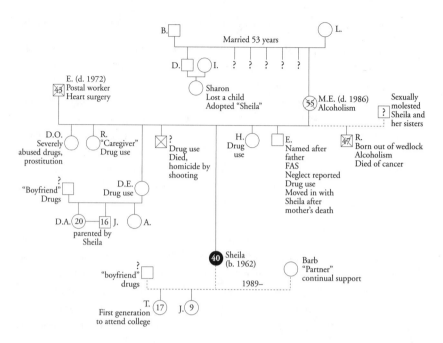

FIGURE 7.1 The genogram of Sheila's family.

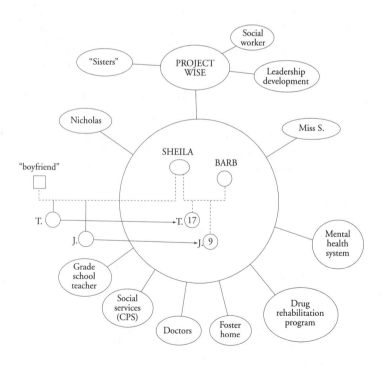

FIGURE 7.2 The ecogram of Sheila's family: circle of support.

Sheila's family of origin includes four sisters and two brothers. Both parents have died; her father when she was 10 from complications related to heart surgery and her mother from alcoholism when Sheila was 24. She described her childhood as chaotic. Her father was the first African American supervisor for the postal service in his area and was described by Sheila as being "like a drill sergeant" who kept her mom "barefoot and pregnant." Her mom was "very good-looking" and had managed a dance club before she married. After marriage, however, she stayed at home and began drinking while her husband was at work. After Sheila was born, her mom's drinking continued, and she also had a relationship with a man who paid her so that he could come to the house and sexually molest Sheila and her sisters. After Sheila's dad died, her mother continued drinking, and 10-year-old Sheila attempted to do what she could to take care of her other siblings. A perceptive teacher at her younger brother's school, however, noticed that his health care was inadequate.

This led to an investigation, and Sheila was removed from her home and placed in a foster home. From the doctors who had evaluated her brother's health, she learned that her brother had fetal alcohol syndrome. This information played a significant role for her later in her own life when she was pregnant with her first daughter.

Sheila "hated" the foster home where she had been placed, and after only a short time there she ran away and returned home. Social Services made no further intervention at that time. At 15, Sheila "escaped from the family" when she met an older man and began dating him. She had already started taking drugs, and she increased her involvement with drugs as part of this relationship. She dropped out of high school when she was 16, got a job, increased her intake of drugs, and was preparing for prostitution when she was in a car wreck. The relationship with her boyfriend continued during her recovery, and soon after she recovered she became pregnant. She thought of her younger brother and all he had gone through and decided that she would be drug-free during her pregnancy so that her children would not have to go through what he had experienced.

Part of Sheila's support network in her community was an older man, Nicholas, whom the family had known. He agreed to allow Sheila and her baby to live with him in his home, and they stayed there for the next eight years. During this time, Sheila continued to work, she gave birth to a second daughter (with the same father as her first daughter), and she was also allowed to take in her youngest brother when her mother died. She and her boyfriend never married, and he continued to supply her with drugs while simultaneously expressing his concern about her. Eventually, Sheila reached a point where she was about to lose her job. Her response was to voluntarily check in to a thirty-day inpatient drug rehabilitation program. That was the beginning of what she describes as "the agencies in Denver helping me to grow up." This help was filled with many ups and downs over the twelve-year period before she came in contact with Project WISE, at a time when she had gone off her medications for depression and had returned to a pattern of drug use.

A major support in Sheila's life is her partner, Barb. They met when Sheila was 27, and Barb has been a continual emotional, and sometimes financial, support since that time.

Their relationship difficulties are sometimes the subject of conversation in her meetings with her social worker at Project WISE but have never been seen as the major focus. Sheila began receiving supportive counseling through Project WISE as a result of a pattern of unpredictable and irregular involvement on the part of the mental health system. She was unable to get consistent care from the health care providers, and that would lead to missed appointments and the choice to go off her medication, which would then lead to a recurrence of her depression. During that time she lost two jobs and seriously considered suicide. Her Project WISE counselor increased her support and continued in the roles of mentor and coach while working with the mental health system for Sheila's medication.

Three areas of focus structured the work with Sheila: her education, integration of the network of services in her life, and advocacy with the mental health system. Supportive counseling was offered on an "as needed" basis. At the time of this writing, Sheila had been participating in the programs at Project WISE for four years. She attributes the consistency of contact by the staff, the trust she developed with her counselor, and the "unconditional support when things fall apart" as the reasons she has been able to stay with the program for this length of time.

Sheila is the only one among her siblings who is not using drugs or alcohol. When crises occur in the family, it is much more difficult for her to stay clean, and her tendency has been to "drop out of sight" and not follow through on some of her commitments. Because of the drug use of her next-oldest sister, Sheila has become the caregiver for a niece and nephew, two of the sister's children. She also continues to take care of her younger brother. The family recently experienced the tragedy of her other brother's death when he was shot. Her commitment to remain drug-free means that she no longer has the numbing effect that the drugs provided. She faces her family challenges and crises "head on." Being drug-free also means that family members expect her to be there for them, to be the strong one, to be the one who can be counted on to come through. Her family bond is very important to her, yet when it all gets too overwhelming, when there seems to be no boundary between where their lives stop and hers begins, she puts her own progress at risk. How can Sheila be present to her family members at important times while also maintaining her own individuality? This is one of the major tasks she works on continually with her social worker. It is part of her skill training, to learn how to define the roles she is willing to assume and those she needs to set aside.

One example came with her younger brother. She took Ernie in to live with her last summer. "The deal was that he had to go to school and if he would complete this program, he could live at my house in the summer. If he asks me to do something, I'm going to do it because he's the baby, I feel responsible. And I can help him get to this next stage. But he can't live with me indefinitely. I'll take him in, but these are my limits." By setting such boundaries, Sheila's social worker acknowledged, Sheila felt "more in control of what often feels like an enmeshed, no boundary, I-have-to-do-it-all type of involvement with her family." She is constantly attending some family event because she feels she needs to be there, she continues to parent her nieces and nephews, and, at the same time, she works hard to avoid getting so depleted that she has nothing left to give. To prevent this, she must stay aware of how easy it has been for her to get caught up in the family drama and instead consciously decide ahead of time what she will do and what she will not do. At the time of her brother's funeral, her words were, "Now I don't want to get caught up in all that. I'll go and I'll be present at the funeral, I'll go and I'll do what I can, but I won't do more than that."

This pull of needing and wanting the connection with family while at the same time needing to have respite from a highly chaotic family environment is a recurring theme among the participants at Project WISE. Sheila puts this into her own words: "As crazy as it feels, it's still my family and it's a sense of history." Another participant, Melanie, realized, "There is something about grandmother and mother that just means you have to be in it, and I really want my son to know his grandmother and his great-grandmother and his aunt and cousins." Even though there are times when these moms and daughters and sisters want nothing more than to get away from their families, they need this connection and the history just as much, if not more in some ways. In a somewhat different way, it is also family, in particular their children, who keep them coming back to their work and their commitments with Project WISE. When Sheila and other participants are asked why they want to change, why they want to make their lives better, responses follow a recognizable pattern: "For my children. I need to change some of the things that went on when I was growing up. I do this so that we can have a stronger family, stronger for them and for me, and so that they never have to live through some of the things I did when I was a kid."

Jean East and Sue Kenney, the codirectors of Project WISE, speak intentionally about their selection of the empowerment model—the personal, interpersonal, and social/community/political framework—to guide how they respond to the unique set of strengths and needs brought by each participant. On the personal level, Sheila had a clear sense of wanting to make her life better for herself and for her family while she worked to stay off of drugs, to stay on the medication that helped her, and to define her boundaries with family members. On the interpersonal level, her partner, Barb, was central to her support system. She also benefited from the relationship with her social worker and their combined perceptions about her relationship with her daughters, with her sisters and brother, with her nieces and nephews, and with the other participants and staff at Project WISE. She relied upon supportive family friends like the male family friend, Nicholas, who welcomed her and her children into his home, and a surrogate mom, "Miss S," someone she wanted nearby when she, Sheila, received an award. On the social/community level, she interacted with teachers, doctors, social workers, foster parents, employers, drug rehabilitation counselors, the people in the mental health system, women leaders in the community, and the people involved in helping her complete her GED.

For each participant Project WISE is concerned with the "whole picture," all three levels of the empowerment model coming together in a "package" that is unique to the skills, resources, strengths, and needs of each person. In Sue Kenney's words, "This is why the empowerment model is really different when one uses the whole model, the whole theory of the personal, the interpersonal, and the political. We have our own boundaries around what we can and cannot do, but it is more than that. It's what adds to our mission as an organization and it's also what fits with empowerment and the participants. We have to ask ourselves if this is something that is going to be empowering for that person and for her family. We're into leadership development but when the leader returns to the family, what happens there? Is it a service to the community to have the leaders out there leading while there's chaos at home? Strengthening families does strengthen the community. So we ask ourselves how we can strengthen families so that the people in those families can get out there and act on behalf of their community."

In addition to practice at all levels of the empowerment model, each one of the empowerment principles was effectively used in the work with Sheila as well. A specific and clear understanding of Sheila's *strengths*, as they emerged in response to the particular *oppressions* in her environment, defined several directions for subsequent work that could be built upon those strengths. For instance, Sheila experienced the consequences of her mother's addiction from the time that she was very young and she witnessed the lifelong challenges that her brother would have because of fetal alcohol syndrome. Her own strength in response to this oppressive environment emerged when she chose to stop her own use of substances during pregnancy.

When social workers hear the earlier experiences of family members' responding to adversity with strength and with conscious decisions to improve upon their lives, they can encourage the family member to call upon these experiences to help them make the decisions that must be faced in the present. "This is nothing new to you. You have done this before. What do we need to do so that you can respond again with strength this time? What do you need so that the outcome this time will also be one that moves your life along in the direction of your goals?" That which is familiar is easier to access as a possibility for change in the face of adversity than that which is unfamiliar. When workers can help to remind family members that they already have skills within themselves to manage the chaos and the sense of feeling overwhelmed, and that they can use those skills "right now," moving through and beyond the turmoil suddenly becomes real. One mother put it this way: "She didn't ask me to trust her...which I didn't; she didn't ask me to learn some highfalutin new techniquey thing...which I had no patience for...and, in fact, she didn't ask me to do anything except what I had already done before. She just heard my story, wondered if what I had done back there when my husband left was something I might be able to do again now and that was it! I was set. I had sort of forgotten how I got through all that, but she helped me see it was worth remembering. If I could do it once, I could certainly do it again. Believing in myself to get through this. That's what she gave me. And I was over at my sister's place that very evening, putting together a plan. What I thought would probably take months took about ten minutes."

Multicultural respect came alive in two ways for Sheila's social worker. First, at one point the worker realized she was getting Sheila's sisters confused. When she began constructing a genogram with Sheila and her family, her four sisters were there, but the participants at Project WISE were "sisters" also. At this moment Sheila was her worker's cultural guide. Another African American woman in a different context described this same use of this status: "It's just the way it is in my culture. I have my sisters and I have my Sisters, capital S." Acknowledging and respecting this inclusivity, that these women were part of her "family of choice," expanded the worker's understanding of the importance of this friendship network and Sheila's connection with "friends who are Sisters in the finest sense of that word."

The second way multicultural respect came alive for Sheila's social worker was through an understanding of what she called the "other mothering" concept. The worker was aware that family means different things to people of different cultures. "I really need to understand what family means to them and what that looks like" (Sue Kenney). After Sheila's mother died, she developed a relationship with a neighbor, an elderly African American woman, Miss S. Over time Miss S. became a vital part of Sheila's non-kinship network. Jean East reports: "She wanted me to meet Miss S. That was really important. And it happened when Sheila received an award and Miss S. also attended that celebration. Now, when other things come up I know when I can say, 'Maybe this is a time when we need Miss S. to fall back on or to call up.' This is just a way of tuning in to their network and their cultural definition of that network and how to tap into it when needed." As I observed the two codirectors of Project WISE, Jean and Sue, the real beauty of a comment like this came through. In their acceptance of Sheila's cultural definition of family, with sisters and mothers reaching far beyond biological roots, they were also illustrating a quality referred to as "something different about Project WISE—we see ourselves as part of people's lives, not just when they are here with us for an hour."

Awareness of needs was illustrated not only in the highly skilled use of "listen, listen, listen" to the voices of the mothers and their children but also in the attention given to preparation for each gathering for groups, for leadership development training, for community organizing efforts, and for story circles and community-building events. Sheila experienced this firsthand when she was asked to collaborate in the preparation for a meeting with two organizers, who remarked, "Well, we don't do food and child care." This was completely unimaginable to Sheila. Having an event right at the dinner hour without feeding them or having child care and not even talking about how that's going to work? Unbelievable! The contrast between this lack of awareness of needs and the usual experience in her own life and at the events at Project WISE plus the resulting chaos of that evening's meeting provided valuable lessons in how attending to needs can make the difference in creating an environment where work can get done or attempting to manage an environment where chaos takes over.

Another very clear statement of awareness of needs from the staff at Project WISE was their response when one of the families is in crisis. "When we first started, the individual was told to call us. But now we don't just wait. When we know there's a crisis in the family, we don't wait for them to make the next appointment. We call them." This kind of outreach shows that the staff at Project WISE are aware of needs that arise in the moments, hours, and days immediately following a traumatic event. Families experiencing behaviors and emotions that are common to post-trauma are often not able to reach out for assistance, even though their need may be enormous.

Sheila had distinct needs for coordination of services when she found herself being "passed around" from one person to another in the mental health system. Contradictions in evaluation, in recommendations for medication, and in length of time for treatment left her baffled, often frustrated, and prone to not showing up for her appointments. Project WISE personnel recognized the need for greater consistency in these services, and they assumed the role of counseling with Sheila while coordination with one person in the mental health system was maintained for the purpose of medication only.

Assisting Families as They Empower Themselves

Sheila knew she wanted to complete her education, but this empowering step forward was filled with procedures, requirements, and paperwork that were all very unfamiliar to her. Family members know what they need and what their choices are about how to improve their lives and their family's sense of well-being. What they often lack, however, is information about how to describe those needs to others, where to begin, to whom they need to speak first, what questions to ask and how to ask them, and what step-by-step procedures they need to take to reach their goals, to make things happen and move forward.

Integrating the Support Needed from Others

Sheila, like so many of the parents in the families who participate at Project WISE, gives an enormous amount of support to other people. It is easy for her to set aside her own needs and "overdo it in being there" for others in her family and community. It has not always been easy for her to ask for support when she needs it or to let others know when she experiences their behaviors toward her as being unsupportive. These issues have become themes in her work with her social worker at Project WISE.

At another level, however, there is evidence that she has welcomed support from the longtime neighbor who invited her to live in his home, from Miss S., who fills a role in her "non-kinship network," and from the groups at Project WISE. As Sheila demonstrated, family members themselves integrate the support they need from others as a natural part of taking care of themselves. In such cases, the worker's task is simply one of meeting these support persons with respect, openness, and appreciation. In other cases, where family members may be isolated from such supports, the worker may play a more active role in providing opportunities for connections to happen, such as the mutually supportive groups and the leadership development program that are part of Project WISE.

Equalizing Power Differentials

Family members carry with them memories of earlier experiences with social workers and other helping professionals. Some of these earlier experiences may have included interactions in which the professionals assumed authoritarian positions or in which personal biases around power were not fully understood before the worker accepted a position of serving the needs of families. Power differentials related to work positions, to providers and recipients of services, to education, to racial majority and minority, to age, to experience, to socioeconomic status, and numerous other categories may all play a role in the first moments of contact and efforts to establish an atmosphere of acceptance, safety, and trust. The social worker who prepares for empowerment practice using the tool of the Family Power Analysis will have understanding about how important it is to free oneself from assumptions. Explicitly stating areas of commonality and similarity in ways that can equalize power and sending the message of "power WITH," which declines acceptance of either "power over" or "power under" stances are crucial communications in the early, as well as the ongoing, phases of practice with all family members.

Project WISE staff equalize the power differentials between themselves and their participants in a variety of ways. Two that are evident in Sheila's story involved both reaching out to her and inviting her to fill a leadership role. Sheila's workers have recognized her tendency to retreat at times when the pressures and stress get to be too great for her to manage. In earlier days, they might have waited for Sheila to contact them for help, but as the awareness of needs at such times grew along with the understanding of the immobilization that can take over, the outreach of Project WISE workers during times of crisis has become a central commitment. Another example of equalizing power differentials occurred when the Project WISE workers requested that Sheila employ her leadership capacities to help plan meetings with other community leaders. Participants in Project WISE also attend recognition ceremonies for women leaders in their communities.

Cooperative Roles

All levels of empowerment practice—personal, interpersonal, and social/community—come into perspective with regard to roles that require cooperation. At the personal level, models of cooperation are used to assist in an individual participant's understanding about herself, her messages of self-esteem, her involvement in her family and community. At the interpersonal level, cooperation among and between individual participants and the Project WISE staff model how such interactions can take place between the participants, as well as the members of their families and networks. At social/community levels, cooperation is used in interactions with agency networks, with potential employers, with child care services and schools, and with informal supports.

The goal, core attitudes, core skills, and accessing of resources that shape the framework of support can also be used for reflection upon Sheila's work at Project WISE. She was actively in *charge of her own life* in her choice to participate at Project WISE, her request for help in obtaining her GED, and her acceptance of the leadership tasks that were suggested. *Resources were called upon,* a particular example being the resources she needed in the mental health system. She was supported with attitudes of *equality, possibility,* and *equanimity,* while her "circle of support"— specifically Miss S. and a supportive neighbor—were included as active and involved members of her support system. *Emotional support and encouragement* were offered while a menu of learning opportunities for enhancing coping skills and for strengthening her base of experience was offered on an ongoing basis.

Qualitative outcomes of Project WISE include linkages to needed resources such as intensive family counseling, psychological evaluations, health services, and educational programs and classes; decreases in post-trauma responses; increases in sources of support; reduction of the effects of depression, stress, and anger; changes in unhelpful behaviors; and preparation for as well as maintenance of employment. Other outcomes specifically related to group participation include naming and building on strengths, lessening of isolation, forming and strengthening supportive relationships, managing conflicts with family and in the group, practicing communication skills, and identifying and working on obstacles to success (East 2002).

And Project WISE continues to grow. The women's leadership program continues to support and assist families in which the female heads of households are making the transition from welfare to stable employment or pursuing their education. In addition, the program is expanding to include a community organizing project that promotes active participation with advocacy efforts in their communities, a mentoring program that partners families receiving TANF with employed women in the community, and a leadership council who serve as role models in their families and their communities. The weekend leadership retreats continue as an experiential component of the program, where the "participant leaders plan, coordinate and facilitate workshops and advocacy training to increase personal support and further community action on the part of participants" (East 2002). Increased family stability, as well as individual stability, continues as a desired goal integrated with leadership skills and system and community change activities.

Project WISE stands as one example of the strength of a community resource serving families that is intentionally built upon the concepts and structures of an empowerment model. Both directors readily admit that it is a process—one that requires continual assessment, evaluation, and listening to what their participants are telling them. With loyalty to the empowerment purpose of integrating services at the personal, interpersonal, and social/community levels plus active involvement in confronting oppressions of poverty, addictions, violence, and discrimination, this project provides a powerful rudder in the storm and chaos of daily life for many of these families. New information and learning combined with group support and sets of skills that will serve them for the rest of their lives provide hopeful pathways toward greater economic independence and self-sufficiency. And, in the truest sense of the definition of empowerment as it is used here, Project WISE provides a context in which its participants have the freedom to choose how they wish to be helped and by whom, and they are respected for the abilities they have to make things happen in their lives so that they can move on with their activities of daily living supported by a greater sense of well-being.

8

Supporting Theories that Empower Social Worker-Family Transactions

Selected theories and perspectives support empowerment practice with families in distress. General system theory, the ecological perspective, the strengths perspective, and the theory of family well-being all contribute to this theoretical foundation. Each theory or perspective has been chosen because of connections to empowerment thinking and to its purpose. Each theoretical choice addresses the complexity of the phenomenon; no one theory, however, can account for all of the factors affecting families who are facing distressing events. Each theory applies directly to the person–environment configuration, the interrelatedness between individuals, the family, and the community. Empowerment thinking includes two other criteria: (1) responsiveness to the voices of the family members and (2) recognition that families are free to choose how to make things happen in a way that will help them to move on with living their lives supported by their own understanding of well-being.

Each theory helps to create a structure as well as a springboard for work with families from an empowerment perspective. Some have withstood the test of time and can be noted in the development of social work knowledge for fifty years or more (general system and ecological theories). Concepts are constantly being added. The general system theory we knew in the 1950s is not the general system theory of today.

Some of these theories are "newer" on the scene of theoretical development in social work. Working with family strengths has long been a factor in social work practice, but moving those strengths to center stage is still in its infancy. Use of the term *well-being* is widespread in the social work literature, with an apparent assumption that readers understand its many meanings. The earlier discussion of these concepts in chapter 1, however, points to the complexity of well-being as a theory and leads to a deeper understanding of its potential for application to work with families in distress. The strengths perspective was discussed in chapter 2, where its applicability has the greatest relevance, with the first of the seven empowering principles: building upon strengths, diminishing oppressions.

The questions answered by these theories barely scratch the surface of tools for helping families. The unknown always far surpasses the known in any human interaction. Our brains and the ways they organize information are "completely mismatched with the environment in which we find ourselves," and "our current ways of thinking are out of step with the world we live in" (Ornstein and Ehrlich 1989). Additionally, the life of the human family is in constant motion. What we know about a family today may be in their distant past by tomorrow. These realities do not prevent us from doing what is possible in the moment, but they do help us stay realistic in our approaches to the work with families and in our expectations for results. Theories can help us organize some of the complexity in our worlds, but they can never do the work for us.

The following discussion of the remaining two theories selected for this work, general system theory and the ecological perspective, includes their origins and some newly discovered information about those origins, plus key principles and characteristics that are relevant to the focus of this book. Criticisms help refine and clarify, and recent advances and newer concepts are outlined. Illustrations and applications to empowerment practice are woven into the discussions using the work with the Laurencio-Smiths, the Williamses, and the Brown-Wileys.

General System Theory

General system theory is a grand theory designed to describe the organization of living systems. Systems are defined as "sets of elements standing in interrelation" (von Bertalanffy 1968:38). The origins of general system theory have commonly been attributed to Ludwig von Bertalanffy. It now appears, however, that von Bertalanffy may have been unaware that a theoretical development very close to his own had occurred in Russia approximately twenty or thirty years before his earliest publications in the 1940s. Alexander Bogdanov, a Russian researcher, philosopher, and economist, developed a system theory with the goal of explaining the principles of organization operating in living and nonliving systems (Capra 1996:43–44).[1] Several of his ideas provide key metaphors for work with distressed families. Bogdanov defined organizational form as "the totality of connections among systemic elements," which is identical to the current definition of pattern of organization. The idea of "totality of connections" immediately places our thinking about families and their individual members rightfully within the reality of overwhelming complexity: "In a group of 4 individuals (ABCD), 6 different two-person relationships (AB, AC, AD, BC, BD, CD) are possible—assuming that A's relation to B is the same as B's relation to A, something that is not always true. Among 10 individuals there are potentially 45 different relationships, and among 30 there are 435" (Ornstein and Ehrlich 1989:61–62). It is not unusual for social workers to work with families of four or with families of ten, especially when extended-family members are invited into the process. When we observe the highly complex interaction of many of the highly distressed families we see, families that are usually engaged with several community agencies, we see that the number of thirty people (435 relationships) is quickly attained.

Bogdanov put forth two other key ideas relevant to organization in social systems and natural systems: (1) formation and (2) regulation (Capra 1996:44). Regarding formation, he emphasized the role of the tension between crisis and transformation as central to the formation of complex systems. In the realm of family systems, this creative tension provides a framework for understanding what family members bring when they seek or are mandated to social work services. Keys to transforming crisis lie within the tension. We must, therefore, stay with that tension long enough to discover where the keys to a family's change are, not where the worker's idea of change or some globally prescribed change is. This, in turn, provides direction for the next steps with the family, and it allows us to see what is done with the crisis. The coping takes priority over the occurrence of the crisis itself, an idea that was also promoted by Satir (1988) many years later.

Jorgé and Lydia, for example, had a unique way of using their different cultural perspectives to get creative in their choices for coping. Many families use differences for conflict or disagreements or reasons for withdrawal of love. This family, though, came together across cultures. Their awareness of differences as "just the way we are" led to perceptions about individual needs when they faced a crisis together.

The "formation of this complex system," in Bogdanov's terms, takes place in the response to crisis. When social workers assist families as they move from crises and oppression to coping and strength, we participate in their creation of who they are becoming as a family. From recognition of the crisis, to staying with the tension, to transformation, Bogdanov delineated the steps of how a complex system defines itself in response to crisis and distress. The work of Jack Lavino, "Transforming Addictions," provides one illustration of this process that is relevant to all four of the families described earlier that depicts the major oppression of addiction as faced by families (figure 8.1).

Recognition of the crisis is seen through the "paths into addiction," with family of origin playing a central role and supported by genetic inheritance as well as cultural beliefs and values. Maria Laurencio, John Williams, Mike Brown, and Sheila all brought their own stories about the interweaving of these factors in their

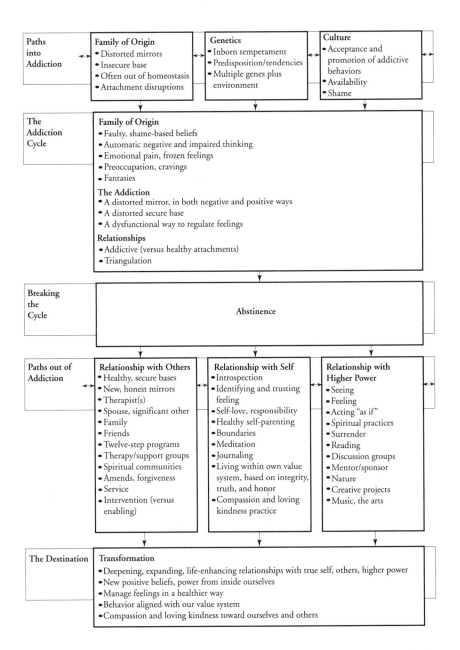

FIGURE 8.1 Transforming addictions: the big picture. (© Jack Lavino. Reprinted with permission)

paths into the addiction cycle. Over time, the addictive substance has the capacity to destroy relationships, to contribute to the physical and mental breakdown of the person, and to affect the financial well-being of addict and family alike. Some recognize the destructive force of the addiction after one or two events, some see it a while later, and for others such recognition may take decades.

Staying with the tension is characterized by the months or years of a person's (and his or her family's) experience with "the addiction cycle." The "complicated web of thoughts and feelings" perpetuates the distortions in beliefs about self, others, the family, and life context. The person's social network, including the immediate and extended-family network, can contribute to the perpetuation of the addiction. Liquor was ritualized for John Williams and his hunting buddies, for example, as part of the interaction on their trips together. Sheila's "boyfriend" was also her supplier, and ending the addiction would mean an end to that relationship as well. To stay with the tension of an addiction long enough results in progressively greater and greater destructive forces in every aspect of the person's life—physically, relationally, socially, financially—until finally some occurrence creates the "breaking point." This leads to the next of Lavino's stages for transformation, "breaking the cycle."

"Breaking the cycle" and the "paths out of addiction" both set the stage for an eventual *transformation* of the addiction. Lavino acknowledges that any decision other than abstinence invites the substance to continue its mind games, deceptions, and distortions. Only when the substance or addictive behavior (e.g., overworking, gambling, overeating, compulsive use of video games) is removed can there be the beginning of an honest relationship with self, others, and one's understanding of a "higher power."

Transformation, then, is viewed as the destination. In Bogdanov's terms, this is the point at which the individual and the family create a new definition of who they are individually and together. The keys to the way each family experiences transformation are in the tension. Transformation does not happen without a response to crisis or change. The crisis itself teaches the need for deeper relationships, strengthening beliefs, expanded possibilities, and compassion.

The second key idea put forth by Bogdanov, regulation, relates specifically to the self-regulation of living systems. Families face processes of regulation that are both internal and external to their family systems. Internal processes of regulation include rules, spoken and unspoken; forms of discipline, teaching, reward and punishment; and the structure of communication patterns. External processes of regulation include the system of law, for example, laws related to child welfare, child and elder and spouse/partner protection, as well as policies that influence family life, such as Temporary Assistance to Needy Families (TANF). The family is self-regulating through responses that sustain them or ones that interrupt the ability to sustain. In overwhelmed and distressed families, self-regulating processes are often missing or inaccessible. Sheila faced a daily struggle to define, or regulate, her boundaries in a way that would not allow the needs of others to overwhelm her. John Williams did not regulate his sexual needs in a way that would not violate his daughters. The possibility of the family being able to sustain itself is then placed at risk.

Von Bertalanffy presented the "concepts of an open system and a general system theory that established systems thinking as a major scientific movement" (Capra 1996:46). He recognized that traditional mechanistic ways of describing the relationships between living organisms and beings were no longer adequate to the phenomena being observed. New ways of thinking were required. His work led to the major criteria of systems approaches as we know them today. Structural and process aspects of these criteria are constantly interacting and intertwined, though here they will be separated for the purpose of discussion. The first two criteria relate to structural and organizational aspects of systems, and the remaining criteria address process aspects: (1) the living world is perceived as a "dynamic world of interrelated events" (Capra 1996:39); (2) the parts of a system can be understood only within the context of the larger whole; (3) "systems thinking is always process thinking" (42); (4) there is an ability to shift attention between systems levels; and (5) relationships are primary and those relationships are embedded in larger networks. Key concepts are italicized.

A Dynamic World of Interrelated Events

Capra (1982, 1996) uses both "dynamic world" and "dynamic web" to describe the living process as constantly in motion, involved with "movement, interaction, and transformation" (87), neither static nor standing still. Early systems thinkers used the term *homeostasis* for the balance maintained by systems over time.[2] But that word's connotations of *stasis* or *static*—that is, unmoving—led theorists soon to recognize that the term was not accurate for the metaphor they were seeking. The term needed was one that could describe an entity that simultaneously maintains certain characteristics over time and is also in constant flux and change. Therefore, the term *homeostasis* was left behind in favor of *dynamic steady state*. Change and movement could be imagined simultaneously with steadiness.

Members of a family are constantly changing with births and deaths, coming home and leaving home, entering and exiting, being a child in one decade, an adolescent the next, and then an adult and later an older adult. When these individual changes occur, the entire *web of relationships* changes in ways that *reflect the events*. When faced with crises, many families respond with available resources and survive to experience the "dynamic steady state" again. Some families, however, experience multiple stressors at the same time or a series of stressors that continue over long periods of time. When coping skills that were reliable in the past are found to be ineffective, the distress in the family can immobilize energy for change. Strengths are still with them but may become overwhelmed by the severity of the stresses faced. *Transformation*, a fundamental change in the structure of the systems, results from being pushed to the limit of the system's ability to maintain steadiness. New ways of coping are discovered. Values, rules, and relationships are restructured in response to the crises. After their experiences, the Laurencio-Smiths, the Williamses, the Brown-Wileys, and Sheila can never return to the way they were before those events took place. Balance takes on different meanings and helps *sustain* the newly shaped configurations of these families as they move through the life course.

This "dynamic world of interrelated events" or "dynamic web" idea is closely related to empowerment thinking through connections in the personal, interpersonal, and social/community layers of influence. The interrelatedness of power and oppression in the family system also connects this concept with empowerment thinking. When we are assisting families to empower themselves, their need for each other and for support from their communities reflects the "dynamic web." With increased complexity, it becomes clear that "no matter how many connections we take into account . . . we will always be forced to leave others out" (Capra 1996:42). We will always be dealing with some approximation of the family before us. We will never have access to an enormous amount of information, yet, at the same time, there is still much that can occur in the helping process with the information that we do have, as, for example, in the family group conference held for Cynthia, Mike, and their children.

Parts Within the Context of the Whole

"Systems thinking is 'contextual' thinking" (Capra 1996:37). There is no way to understand the person apart from the family. The family cannot be fully understood without considering the extended family and the surrounding community, national, and global structures. These structures define the boundaries, limits, and possibilities for each family. The cultural, environmental, political, and economic realities shape the resources and the barriers in efforts to *sustain* the family over time.

A view of the whole is a view that includes all of the relationships, at least all of the ones available, that are occurring among and between the parts. To overlook Cynthia Wiley's cousin and brother-in-law misses important parts of her whole network of extended-family resources. Without Miss S., the picture of Sheila's support network is incomplete. And to exclude Lucas, the Rottweiler, means a huge gap for Charlie. Every part, each with its respective function, is needed to make the whole.

In this "web of nesting levels," the multiple levels of human system interactions are connected with the ongoing flow (depicted by the curving line with arrows)

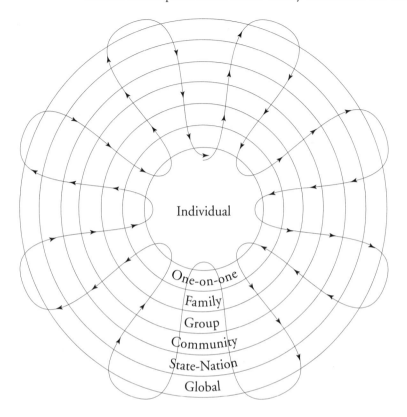

FIGURE 8.2 The web of nesting levels of human systems.

of dynamic transactions among and between the levels (figure 8.2). The concept of a "ripple effect" is visualized. An event at one level has an impact at all levels. A decision at one level has an impact at all levels. A transformation at one level has an impact at all levels.

The *organization* of the multiple levels of the system is also crucial to understanding its structure. Each system is embedded in a larger system (suprasystem) and each system includes smaller systems (subsystems) within itself. Each family is part of the larger system of the neighborhood and the community, and each family includes smaller systems of siblings, parent (single) or parents, partners, parent-child, grandparent to grandchild, aunts and uncles with nieces and nephews, stepparents and stepchildren, and so on. Between suprasystems, focal system (the unit selected for the primary intervention), and subsystem, *boundaries* exist to identify what persons are in a particular system level and what persons are outside that level. Families maintain a boundary, sometimes *flexible* and sometimes *rigid*, between themselves and the outside world. When the boundary is flexible, relationships will be allowed with certain individuals but not with others. When the boundary is rigid, immovable rules are evident, rules that are used regardless of any unique circumstances. Some family members expend great energy to determine who is in and who is out.

Close connections with empowerment thinking are again apparent. An approach committed to "power with" creates an environment within which family members can interact in empowering ways, thus adding to the possibilities for sustaining that family, enhancing their capacity for creating their family life. When the "whole" is oppressive, family members are more likely to respond from positions of power over or power under. Matt, a four-year-old, feeling powerless in his family with older brothers, assumed "power over" behaviors through "bossy" commands with a three-year-old at day care. Matt's father, feeling powerless at work, returned home and engaged in dominant, "power over" behaviors with his spouse and children.

Another interesting connection with empowerment thinking relates to the use of the term *hierarchy*. Even though this term was used by early systems thinkers to describe the relationships between the levels of a system, it was soon recognized that the term carries connotations related to power that were contrary to the description being sought. Hierarchy had been used in organizational systems, for example, in which domination and control were used to transmit information, expectations, and demands from the top down—in short, power over. Typical symbols used to represent a hierarchical structure were the ladder or the pyramid. By contrast, systems in nature, families included, do have observable order in their structures, but the most important functional aspect of the *stratified order* (the term adopted to replace *hierarchy*) was "not the transfer of control but rather the organization of complexity" (Capra 1982:282). Complexity is addressed below in the discussion on newer ideas influencing today's systems thinkers.

Process Thinking

In systems thinking, "every structure is seen as the manifestation of underlying processes" (Capra 1996:42). Two comparisons help to clarify: process and content; process and product. In the communication process, words define content while process helps determine meaning: tone of voice, direction of eye contact, facial expression, hand gestures, and body posture and position, to name a few of the variables. The anticipated outcome is the product; how we get there is the process. Systems thinking is process thinking. Therefore we approach interactions with families by attending to the "how" of each communication and the "what's going on" of each interaction. Once we do this, we are looking for patterns in what we see and hear.

For example, "if-then" and "either-or" thinking patterns are so deeply embedded in the way we structure our knowing that we are often unaware that we are using them. In systems language, this is called linear thinking. For a systems thinker, a process thinker, there is no such thing as an "either-or." There is, instead, "both-and-and-and..." This one shift from linear to process thinking has significant implications for our work with families. Eliminating all "either-or" questions from one's conversations or decision making reveals multiple opportunities and possibilities, as well as their reciprocal influence (an ecological concept). This, in turn, connects with more empowering approaches to practice.

> The process of life is the activity involved in the continual embodiment of the system's *pattern* of organization. Thus, the process criterion is the link between pattern and structure....The structure of a system is the physical embodiment of its *pattern* of organization. Whereas the description of the *pattern* of organization involves an abstract mapping of relationships, the description of the structure involves describing the system's actual physical components. (Capra 1996:158–160, emphasis added)

In the work with families in this volume, the family members were identified (the structure) and abstract mapping of the relationships among and between the family members via genograms and an ecogram was also presented (the process). Patterns were seen as repetitive interactions that help determine the essential characteristics of the system. For example, the pattern of running-away behaviors was seen in the Williams sisters, a pattern that led to an investigation about what they were running away from. Patterns of physical and emotional abuse provided understanding about what Cynthia, Charlie, and Jessie had experienced.

Shifting Attention Between System Levels

When a systems thinker recognizes strengths at one level of the system, it provokes curiosity to find those strengths at other levels of the system. When Barbara heard Jorgé and Lydia's interpretation of their differences as their strength, she was not surprised later when she heard their two daughters, Samantha and Amy, expressing that they liked how their differences made their family "more interesting" than some of the other families they knew. Similarly, when trauma is experienced at one level of the system, it is likely to exist at other levels as well. Discovery of the incest that Linda and Susan had suffered alerted Liz to the possibility of incest in other generations or family units and led to Jane's telling the story of her own incest by her uncle. Systems nest within other systems in the natural world. If we think empowerment and shift attention to all three levels—individual, family, and community—our awareness is expanded to the wider web of interactions. When we observe conflict in a family, we can, for example, see similarities with the process of conflict as it occurs on a playground, in the Senate, and between nations.

Parent behaviors are mirrored in the interactions between the children. Chaos in the home reappears in a teenager's interactions in the classroom or among peers. The parents of that family carry the same chaos into the workplace and notice the boss treating them just like their father did. When incest or alcoholism exists in one generation of a family, there is a likelihood that it exists at other levels of that system. A social worker may realize that a client family is reminding her of a similar dynamic in her own family.

These examples of shifting attention between system levels are reminders of the interaction between the personal, interpersonal, and social/community levels in the use of empowerment thinking. We observe patterns in families that carry over from one level to the others. The poverty they face each day, for example, has an impact on the personal level in how they cope with the exhaustion in moving through another day without financial resources, affects the interpersonal aspects related to the care of children and elders, and also acts upon the community aspects that present barriers to jobs, training in job-related skills, or availability of day care. In like manner, a family's coping, steps toward recovery, resilience, and moving forward with their lives also indicate patterns operating from one level of the system to another.

Relationships, Within Larger Networks, Are Primary

Structure and organization inform us about the relationship of the parts to the whole of a system. The process that occurs between family members, extended-family members, and community is key. Relationships within relationships within still more relationships and wider networks are central to family systems. In our work, there may be only one person sitting in front of us, but the web of transactions that shapes his or her life has an impact on the work that we do together. Social workers and clients alike bring with them families of origin, present and extended families, "families of choice," friendship networks, workplace networks, neighborhood and community relationships. In these multiple interacting networks, no part of the network is more significant than any other part. Every member is an integral part of the family.

In every culture, the family unit is the initial context in which learning about all other relationships occurs. "A family becomes a family when two or more individuals have decided they are a family, that in the intimate, here-and-now environment in which they gather, there is a sharing of emotional needs for closeness, of living space which is deemed 'home,' and of those roles and tasks necessary for meeting the biological, social, and psychological requirements of the individuals involved" (Hartman and Laird 1983:30).

Empowerment thinking is closely connected with the primacy of relationships. There is a definite order, a clear generational stratified structure, in the family, but the empowering uses and oppressive abuses of power, position, or role in that structure are a different matter. For example, the parental subsystem is clearly separated from the sibling subsystem in a structural and generational sense. But when a parent engages a child in a peer-like relationship for emotional, physical, or sexual needs, the abuse of power results in oppression that pervades the entire family system and continues across multiple generations, as was seen with the Williams family. By contrast, a relationship defined by "power with" invites support, nurturing, and growth as seen in the relationships of Jorgé with Lydia, Jane Williams with her two daughters, and Sheila with the participants of Project WISE.

These criteria and key concepts for thinking from the general system theoretical framework have been used in social work scholarship and practice since 1956 when Werner Lutz presented system concepts to the National Association of Social Workers. The system was viewed as central for social work theorizing by Gordon Hearn in 1958. Soon after, system concepts were applied to groups (Schwartz 1961), planned change (Bennis, Benne, and Chin 1961), community equilibrium (Zimbalist 1970), and community social work theory (Warren 1963). In 1968 Germain applied system concepts to casework practice. General system theory was seen as an integrative framework for social work and the application of its concepts to social work practice was encouraged (Hearn 1969).

In the 1970s the influence of a general system approach appeared in social casework (Hartman 1970), social group work (Klein 1972), social policy (Hoos 1972), a new social work (Kahn 1973), application of systems concepts to social work practice (Goldstein 1973; Pincus and Minahan 1973), service networks (Rosenberg and Brody 1974), social work theory (Compton and Galaway 1975), and the systems foundation of human growth indicating the potential for a unified conceptual base for social work practice (Siporin 1975).[3]

Three major criticisms, ones that are important for social work practice with families, are noted about the uses of general system theory:

1. The individual gets lost when the emphasis is placed upon the whole.
2. This theory is too abstract to be usable.
3. Clear distinctions disappear when everything is connected to everything else.

In response to the first criticism, two processes appear to have been at work. First, until someone makes a conscious shift away from "either-or" and hierarchical thinking, there will be a temptation to place one aspect *over* another. In this case, the critics choose emphasis on the whole OR emphasis on the individual, rather than the "both-and …" thinking advocated by general system theory, in which both the whole AND the individual receive emphasis. Second, the critic's reading of the history of general system theory may have bypassed that "the relationship between the parts and the whole has been reversed" (Capra 1996:37). Reversing the relationship between the two is quite different from replacing the focus on the individual with the focus on the system as a whole. Previous belief systems, such as the philosophy of Descartes, lead us to believe that if we analyzed the parts, we would have a complete understanding of the whole. Systems thinking does not set aside the parts but rather states that the only way we can understand them is within their context. This context includes the parts, the environment, and the transactions in the relationships among and between the parts.

The second criticism is extremely helpful in keeping a perspective on what systems thinking can do and what it cannot do. Is systems thinking too abstract to be usable? There is no doubt that the level of ABstraction can be a DIStraction at times. Perhaps the saving grace here is that every concept of systems thinking can be seen in daily activity in people's lives. Moving to an experiential and personal line of thinking can take us from the abstract to the concrete. For example, "I am a system. I move about each day within several different systems, my clients and students are part of multiple systems, so what does this have to do with where I am right now?"

The last criticism reminds us that all knowledge used to understand families in distress is "approximate knowledge" (Capra 1996:41). If we believe all things are connected and continually influenced by others, we could set ourselves up for the impossible task of needing to explain them all in order to explain only one part. Acknowledging that approximate knowledge is valuable and essential contributes to a modest approach about what theories can and cannot do. We can know some things about this complex area, but it will never be possible to know everything. We can only work with what we know.

Seeing knowledge as power has important implications within an empowerment perspective. Knowledge used for "power with" can take us to places in our work with families that are not available when knowledge is used for "power over" or "power under" purposes. This points back to the earlier discussion regarding the roles assumed by social workers from an empowerment perspective: coconsultants, collaborators, guides, coteachers, colearners, coinvestigators, and cocreators.

Recent Advances in Systems Thinking

True to its identity, general system theory has not been standing still during the past half century. New ideas have joined the old, some of them transforming earlier ways of thinking. The metaphors have been applied in a variety of ways, and the feedback has helped advance thinking in numerous directions. Newer concepts that have particular relevance for working with distressed families are (1) complexity, (2) chaos, (3) self-making, and (4) sustainability.

Complexity

Von Bertalanffy's awareness of the complexity of human existence served as the origin for his subsequent development of the core ideas we know as general system theory today. "Society has become so complex that traditional ways and means are not sufficient anymore. Approaches of a holistic or systems nature have to be introduced" (von Bertalanffy 1968:5). Earlier thinkers were at a loss as to how to embrace complexity as a whole. Looking only at the parts of complex systems provided an attainable, yet incomplete, response. No matter how long a social worker speaks with each member of a family separately, the qualities that make this family unique will not materialize until the transactions among its members are understood. "The whole is greater than the sum of its parts" (von Bertalanffy 1968:68).

Complexity is organized in a system through stratified order. "The important aspect of the stratified order in nature is not the transfer of control but rather the organization of complexity" (Capra 1982:282). Complexity is characterized by "richly organized patterns, sometimes stable and sometimes unstable, sometimes finite and sometimes infinite, but always with the fascination of living things" (Gleick 1987:43). Families often enter work with their social workers at a time when they are overwhelmed by the complexities of their daily lives. The opportunity to communicate to the family that their situation can be understood and is of interest to the social worker helps to develop the relationship with the family members.

If social workers hope to embrace even a fraction of the complexity faced by one of today's families, we must acknowledge that we need as many lenses, as many perspectives, as many theories, as much collaboration with colleagues from multiple disciplines as we can gather into our awareness. Systems thinkers recognize the importance of embracing all disciplines. Together, knowledge from all disciplines helps us comprehend realities of human living that would be unattainable if only one discipline was used. Brain research in recent decades, for example, has made it very clear how little we know about the brain's capacity for determining all aspects of behavior (Gazzaniga 1985). One illustration is the research on trauma that shows how it alters the structure of the brain (van der Kolk, McFarlane, and Weisaeth 1996). Because most individuals and families seen by social workers have experienced some form of trauma, this one finding has major implications for assessment, planning, intervention, and evaluation. Many clients face ongoing trauma that results from living with poverty, homelessness, or chronic major illness. Current researchers are seeking to understand the differences of the impact on brain structure between single-event trauma and ongoing, chronic trauma.

Chaos

Closely related to complexity is the idea of chaos, a complex process with an underlying order. Advances in chaos theory cut across disciplines, from the natural sciences to the social and behavioral sciences, and "make strong claims about the universal behavior of complexity" (Gleick 1987:5). Previously, our efforts were considered worthy if we were attempting to create some kind of order out of chaos. Now, with the understanding available to us today through the lens of chaos theory, we see that the order has been there in the midst of the chaos all along. We have simply needed the eyes to see it. Claims are being made that the concepts of chaos theory can now provide those "eyes."

As we approach our work with families, can this mean that we need no longer seek to make some kind of order out of their chaos? This understanding of chaos tells us that the order is already there, the family already has a set of patterns that needs to be seen and understood. In fact, when these patterns—cultural patterns, learning patterns, communication patterns, patterns related to rules and roles, and cross-generational patterns—are used to address the family's distress, the chances for a strengthening result increase. Identification of a pattern, according to Satir and Baldwin (1983), occurs when we observe a behavior at least three times. Our curiosity leads us to notice a behavior for the first time. When we see it a second time, it might still be a coincidence. But by the third time we can usually be assured that we are seeing a behavior pattern. Patterns provide a window into a family's underlying order. Families know their own order. In times of distress, however, their sense of order is often overwhelmed by the chaos of the moment. They may need assistance in making the stabilizing effects of their order overt and usable. Efforts toward helping will not materialize without including the family's order, their foundation, in some way.

Self-making

A creative or self-making process is the response to complexity and chaos in the natural course of living for living systems. As beings of choice, "human beings can choose whether and how to obey a social rule" (Capra 1996; Fleischaker 1992; Mingers 1995). Among the scholars and theorists who move across multiple disciplines, care is taken as these metaphors of systems thinking move from natural sciences to social sciences. German sociologist Niklas Luhmann (1990) is one example. He looks at "self-making" from the social standpoint and says that this occurs through processes of communication.

A family system, for example, can be defined as a network of conversations exhibiting inherent circularities. The results of conversations give rise to further conversations, so that self-amplifying feedback loops are formed. The closure of the network results in a shared system of beliefs, explanations, and values—a context of meaning—that is continually sustained by further conversations.

The communicative acts of the network of conversations include the "self-production" of the roles by which the various family members are defined and of the family system's boundary. Since all these processes take place in the symbolic social domain, the boundary cannot be a physical boundary. It is a boundary of expectations, confidentiality, loyalty, and so on. Both the family roles and boundaries are continually maintained and renegotiated by the auto-poietic (self-making) network of conversations. (Capra 1996:212–213)

All families are self-making. When we observe family members in conversation with each other, they are creating themselves. When we work from an empowerment frame of reference and offer multiple choices, the choices made define the self-creating of the family. The ethical responsibility of the social worker's act of offering a range of choices, rather than choices that may be biased in one direction or another, is significant. The source of change for every family is within that family, not within the professionals who serve the family.

The self-making of every family also serves as a resource upon which to draw in every stage of our work. Families have been creating themselves, sometimes for many decades, before they come into contact with social workers. They have a vast array of experience with decisions that have enhanced who they are and with decisions that have presented barriers. They can let their social workers know what helps and what gets in their way. The self-making history of each family, visually available in part through genograms and ecograms, deserves great respect and can be seen as one of the most significant strengths they bring with them when facing their distress.

Sustainability

It is the nature of living systems, in their cycles of existing and perishing, to sustain the fundamental integrity of the system over time. "From the systemic point of view, the only viable solutions are those that are sustainable. This is the great challenge of our time: to create sustainable communities—that is to say, social and cultural environments in which we can satisfy our needs and aspirations without diminishing the chances of future generations" (Capra 1996:4; Brown 1981). What do social workers need to know about helping families to satisfy their needs and aspirations without diminishing the chances of their children and their children's children to do the same?

In chapter 1, the purpose of empowerment practice with families in distress was defined: to cooperatively *sustain*, enhance, and create family well-being.

And the definition of empowerment, having *the freedom to choose and the ability to make things happen to move on with living supported by a sense of well-being,* reflects a valuing of sustainability, "to move on with living." Choices that sustain families sustain society for future generations. How do living systems, and families in particular, live sustainably? Systems thinkers point to five related concepts: interdependence, the cyclical nature of process, partnership, flexibility, and diversity.

Interdependence

All members are "interconnected in a vast and intricate network or relationships, the web of life. Understanding... interdependence means understanding relationships. A sustainable human community is aware of the multiple relationships among its members. Nourishing the community means nourishing those relationships" (Capra 1996:298). The participants of Project WISE live this interdependence in their daily lives. They have joined with a nurturing and sustaining community program and, in turn, make contributions to their families and communities in ways they had not done previously.

The Cyclical Nature of Process

Respect for the natural cycles of living systems, from birth through stages of living to death that contributes to new life, supports respect for the natural cycles that are part of a family's multigenerational life together. Across the life span from youth through the middle years to the elder years, each stage represents a step in the ongoing, sustaining, cyclical nature of a family of ancestors and progeny.

Partnership

Partnership, the "pervasive cooperation that sustains cyclical exchanges of resources in a system... the tendency to associate, establish links, live inside one another, and cooperate, is one of the hallmarks of life." Cooperative exchanges (also an ecological concept), interactions that promote links among and between family members, sustain those families during times of distress and beyond. "In human communities partnership means democracy and personal empowerment, because each member of the community plays an important role" (Capra 1996:301). Families live sustainably when they recognize that each member of the family plays an important role in who they are as a family.

These first three concepts contribute to the internal conditions of the system, how it is organized to maximize sustainability. Living systems also face changing conditions and disturbances from outside the system. The next two concepts address how a system responds to external conditions in ways that sustain it.

Flexibility

"Lack of flexibility manifests itself as stress. Temporary stress is an essential aspect of life, but prolonged stress is harmful and destructive to the system" (Capra 1996:302). Families facing distress are families facing prolonged stress. Restoring flexibility lowers stress. Rigid thoughts or relationships contradict the fluctuation and change that are part of nature. Increasing possibilities and choices allows the family to move beyond the stressful events. This active participation restores flexibility and increases capacities for coping with major, prolonged stress.

A variety of possibilities and choices were offered in all four families discussed in earlier chapters. The Laurencio-Smiths exercised a choice to change weekend visitation arrangements for Danny's safety. They called upon various options for support from extended-family (Maggie) and community resources (Here in Times of Need Committee). They weighed the possibility of asking their social worker to go with them to speak with Lydia's physician. The Williamses worked with choices and possibilities regarding whether or not to confront their father/husband about the incest. Linda chose to take time off to help her mother with their financial situation. Susan welcomed the option of having time away from her stressful school environment and being able instead to do her work at home, where she felt safer. Cynthia Wiley faced the frightening choice of leaving an abusive and dangerous husband, the choice of when to leave and where to go. She chose schools for her children and a place of employment for herself. Creating opportunities *repeatedly* was identified as one of the core skills in the "framework of support," and it was a vital part of the empowerment of the women in Project WISE.

Diversity

A diverse system is a resilient system because it contains overlapping functions that can replace one another. "In human communities ethnic [diversity] and cultural diversity play this role. Diversity means many different relationships, many different approaches to the same problem. A diverse community is a resilient community, capable of adapting to changing situations" (Capra 1996:303). A simple paraphrase serves to expand the application to families: a diverse family is a resilient family, capable of adapting to changing situations. Diverse viewpoints, diverse suggestions, diverse goals can all enrich the relationships among family members.

These principles for sustainable human communities are, simultaneously, basic principles of ecology. When the principles of ecological systems are understood and used for creating sustainable communities, ecological literacy or "ecoliteracy" informs choices and decisions. "The survival of humanity will depend on our ecological literacy, on our ability to understand these principles of ecology and live accordingly" (Capra 1996:304).

Ecological theory has supported social work theory, research, and practice for many years. The following discussion presents some of the history and development of these ideas, current advances, and relevance to work with families in distress.

The Ecological Perspective

Ernst Haeckel, a German biologist, was the first person to use the term *ecology*, in 1866. He defined it from the Greek *oikos*, meaning "study of the home," as "the science of relations between the organism and the surrounding outer world" (quoted in Maren-Grisebach 1982:30). Later interpretations reflect this same thought: "the study of Earth Household. More precisely it is the study of the relationships that interlink all members of the Earth Household" (Capra 1996:32).

Before 1800, most scientists were viewing individual organisms separately from their natural environments. The turning point came with Charles Darwin's *On the Origin of Species*, published in 1859. Darwin's observations of the mutual adaptation, dependence, and diversity of the species provided the link between the environment and the individual. These thoughts were later presented in his theories of natural selection, genetic drift, and evolutionary development, theories that led to Haeckel's founding of ecology as a field of study and that continue to have a major impact upon our understanding of family life for all species today and upon the growth of knowledge in social work.[4]

Somewhat later, in the early twentieth century, other animal and plant biologists continued to use ecology and its principles for advancing knowledge in their areas of specialization: Jacob von Uexküll used *Umwelt* (environment) at the same time social workers were understanding the importance of work environments and sanitation in new ways; Charles Elton analyzed food chains and food cycles as the central organizing elements of biological communities at the same time social workers were recognizing the ravages of hunger and inaccessibility of food sources for the poor and immigrant populations of the United States; and other ecologists observed functional relationships within animal and plant communities at the same time social workers were identifying the inseparable connections between persons and their environments (Capra 1996:33).

The ecological perspective has contributed to anthropology, psychology, sociology, and human development. In anthropology, Colin Turnbull focused on ecology and culture, while Rene Dubos emphasized the cultural roots of science (1963), the role of adaptation of humans in their natural environments (1968a, 1968b), and the resilience of ecosystems as it relates to environmental restoration

(1978). In psychology, Kurt Lewin encouraged a "holistic view of the individual within the environment" and called it field theory. In sociology, in addition to the work of Darwin mentioned earlier, Robert E. Park of the Chicago Ecological School is known for his work on human ecology, interdependence, and dominance and succession (the orderly succession of changes from a relatively unstable stage to a relatively stable stage) (Robbins, Chatterjee, and Canda 1998:32–33). Parks's colleague, Ernest Burgess, built his work around the central ecological concept of adaptation and believed that social events of all different types were, in some fashion or other, adaptive responses. And in human development, Bronfenbrenner's work included an integration of systems thinking with the ecological perspective as well as a work about the family as a key contextual factor for human development.

In social work, Germain introduced ecological concepts in 1973 with applications of the ecological perspective to casework practice. In 1976 and 1978, respectively, dimensions of time and space were elaborated as key aspects of social work practice. Her "Introduction: Ecology and Social Work" appeared in 1979. In collaboration with Alex Gitterman, Germain went on to derive a model of social work practice based upon ecological concepts, the Life Model of Social Work Practice. The range of applications of ecological concepts to other specializations within social work includes domestic violence (Carlson 1991), school social work (Clancy 1995), home care (Cox 1992), work with elders (Freeman 1984), prevention (Germain 1982), community work (Germain 1985), research (Germain and Gitterman 1986), vulnerable populations (Gitterman 1991), mutual aid groups (Gitterman and Shulman 1994), residential treatment for children (Guterman and Blythe 1986), psychosocial difficulties in children (Hess and Howard 1981), single-parent families (Howard and Johnson 1985), discharge planning (James and Studs 1988), Indian agency development (Kelley, McKay, and Nelson 1985), community mental health (Libassi and Maluccio 1982), and foster care (Milner 1987).

Germain and Gitterman's Life Model of Social Work Practice is not a model in the technical sense of that word. Rather, it is rather intended as a "practice modeled on life processes"(Germain and Gitterman 1995:821). Their use of ecological metaphors expands and enriches our thinking for social work practice and serves a key role in the theoretical structure for empowering practice with families in distress.[5]

In the discussion that follows, original concepts of the Life Model are identified, defined, and illustrated with application to family dynamics. Comparisons and overlap with empowerment and systems theory are noted. Criticisms are reviewed for their potential to refine and specify uses of the ecological perspective. Recent advances in ecological thinking are discussed for application to families in distress. Original ecological concepts include person–environment fit, adaptation, exchanges, life stressors/stress, coping, relatedness, efficacy and competence, self-concept and self-esteem, and self-direction.

Person-Environment Fit

Reciprocal relationships between persons and their environments are central to the ecological perspective. *Person–environment fit* refers to "the actual fit between an individual's or a collective group's needs, rights, goals, and capacities and the qualities and operations…favorable or unfavorable…of their physical and social environments within particular cultural and historical contexts" (Germain and Gitterman 1995:817, 1996:9). With application to families, at least three dimensions consistent with system and subsystem levels provide information for the social worker about person–environment fit: the individual's fit with her or his family, his or her fit with extended-family members, and the family's fit as a whole with the surrounding environment of community and social life. This last level of person–environment fit includes school, workplace, and neighborhood and is congruent with the social/community dimension of the empowerment framework. A supportive, respectful, and nurturing fit between individual and family and between family and the wider social environment can be enhancing and creative for both. From another view, a lack of fit between individual and family and between family and the social/community environment can be damaging and can result in distress for both.

Lack of fit with family, for example, was evident when both Linda and Susan Williams ran away from home and sought an environment of greater safety at the home of friends. Cynthia experienced lack of fit with her extended family when those she turned to for protection, help, and transition instructed her to return to Mike to work things out with him. Sheila also experienced lack of fit with extended family who stepped over her personal boundaries and demanded too much of her emotional time and energy. And lack of fit with a social/community environment was experienced to some degree by Jorgé and Lydia when Jorgé commented on experiencing some exclusion from neighbors because he and Lydia were the only unmarried and cross-cultural couple on their block.

Goodness of fit, however, can be seen with Maggie's presence to assist Lydia following her surgery and with Cynthia's new apartment. Goodness of fit is seen in Sheila's steps toward remaining drug-free, seeking her GED, and pursuing leadership development skills. The experiences of Jorgé and Lydia in coming to the United States offer reminders of the acculturation process faced by immigrant families, the progressive movement from a lack of fit, possibly, in their homeland to a lack of fit in their new country. Goodness of fit with the new location may increase as families learn a new language, as they are welcomed into their new neighborhoods, as jobs and schools become realities. But this gradual process of acculturation is different for each family and for each of the members of a given family. Loyalties to countries of origin, and to family members still residing there, are strong for many. Grieving for those left behind has a powerful influence on the ability to integrate into a new and very different culture. In one sense, acculturation is a type of adaptation.

The refusal of a family member to adapt or acculturate is a decision of theirs that should be greeted with the greatest respect. Each person's meaning and each family's meaning is unique, yet there are themes as well: coming to the different country not by choice but by force; pride in homeland and in the way of life represented there; loyalty to and longing for those who have been left behind; intense fear and panic about any expression of individuality because, in the land from which they just came, such behavior could mean death. Every immigrant family brings their history with them across the generations and across the miles.

> So it is in families. So it is that most of us, if we stop to consider it, can trace who we become to some defining moment within the crucible of the family. This is certainly true for people of African descent, who centuries ago were wrested from our first families by a cruel transatlantic trade. For us, kinship relationships have been critical to our survival, helping us to create entirely new definitions of who we are—and who we might yet become in a world that does not always admit our possibilities or welcome our vision. (Robotham 2003:xx)

Adaptation

Adaptation is defined as "continuous, change-oriented, cognitive, sensory-perceptual, and behavioral processes people use to sustain or raise the level of fit between themselves and their environment" (Germain and Gitterman 1995:817). Families face change on a daily basis, and families in distress are usually facing multiple, significantly challenging stressors simultaneously. Jorgé and Lydia, for example, faced Maria's abuse of Danny, Jorgé's loss of a job promotion, and the major threat to Lydia's health simultaneously. How they responded, both individually and together, gave the worker a view into the family's capacities for adaptation. Consideration of how a family adapts adds to understanding of how the family copes, how they determine what is going on and what kind of action is needed to address the changes taking place in their surroundings. Individual family members do not adapt in the same way or at the same pace. Cultural factors and different developmental stages, for example, play roles in how family members adapt individually and together. One aspect of a social worker's skill in working with a family's different cognitive, sensory, and behavioral adaptations is to look for commonalities around which family members can join as well as to define their differences in adaptation in a way that is supportive and respectful. Some adaptations are strengthening, such as accepting the assistance of others in times of need.

Other adaptations are damaging and create further distress, such as family members' assuming roles that result in perpetuation of a family member's addiction.

Among Linda, Susan, and Jane, Liz recognized different levels of adaptation to the changes in their lives. Each needed different amounts of time and different types of support related to previous skills, impact of the trauma, and the transition, and differing levels of integration of self. For Cynthia, adaptation meant potential threats to her life. Even though she felt a heightened sense of protection after the family group conference, she knew she would continue to live with the reality that Mike could show up at any time with explosive rage. In her words, "As long as he's alive, my guard will be up."

Exchanges

Exchanges are the specific "continuous transactions between people and environments in which each shapes the other over time" (Germain and Gitterman 1996:9). By definition, this looks quite similar to adaptation. Exchanges of communication, verbal or nonverbal, of material or nonmaterial resources, and the like lead to a family's capacity to adapt. Exchanges may be favorable or unfavorable, but to lead to adaptation they must contribute to a family's goal to "sustain or raise the level of fit" between themselves and their environment. For example, the social workers of Project WISE no longer wait to hear from their participants with requests for service during times of crisis and distress. They call. They arrive on the doorstep. They repeatedly offer possibilities, options, and choices.

The shaping of each other over time is a particularly important concept as one views the transactions that take place in a family facing distress. The "ripple" effect comes alive. Family members set examples for each other, examples to emulate or to avoid, in their behaviors and attitudes. These behaviors and attitudes go on to influence the quality of other system transactions and to shape the exchanges, the self-esteem, and the person–environment fit for all in the family system. Sheila sets an example in her family of being the only one who is drug-free. She lives daily with her brother's struggles related to fetal alcohol syndrome because of a mother who did not know what Sheila knows.

Life Stressors/Stress

Life stressors are "life transitions, events, and issues which disturb the level of person:environment fit or a prior state of relative adaptedness." *Stress* is the "internal response to a life stressor." Stress is a given in daily life, neither favorable nor unfavorable in its original form. How people and, in particular, how family members choose to use their stress is a key in understanding "stress response." Creative uses of stress are an active part of the social worker's repertoire when working from an empowerment framework. When family members define their stress in terms of challenge and remain "hopeful and confident and maintain relatedness" (Germain and Gitterman 1995:817), creative use of stress is possible. When a family faces prolonged stress, however, as they do with poverty, addictions, domestic violence, physical and sexual abuse, and discrimination, responses include lowered levels of relatedness and self-confidence and a potentially higher sense of hopelessness.

Coping

Enhancement of coping skills has been identified as one of the core actions for empowering practice and was discussed at greater length in chapter 6. From an ecological perspective, *coping* is defined as "behavioral and cognitive measures used to change some aspect of oneself, the environment, the exchanges between them, or all three, in order to manage the negative feelings aroused" (Germain and Gitterman 1996:14). *Adaptation* and *coping* are similar, yet a subtle difference exists in the connotations of these two terms as well. When a family is called upon to *adapt* to circumstances, for example, the connotation is that they will accommodate to that which is, and possibly to that which cannot be changed. The definition of *coping* given here clearly indicates the possibility of change. When change is possible—in self, the environment, or the exchanges—coping skills play a key role in bringing about that change. Families in distress face many circumstances that cannot be changed, such as the onset of a family member's terminal illness, for example. In these instances, adaptation responses may effectively serve their needs, yet capacities for coping are never far away. The distinction is a very subtle one, though, and unnecessary in the sense that coping and adapting work hand in hand to help empower families, to help them move on with making choices that will increase their sense of well-being. Lydia and Jorgé could have adapted to their lack of information about Lydia's surgery and the expectations of what would occur afterward. Instead, when Barbara, their social worker, offered the option of her accompanying them to their interview with the doctor, they chose to cope in a different way.

Relatedness

Cousin to *interrelatedness* in systems thinking, *relatedness* in ecological thought refers to "attachments, friendships, kin relationships, and a sense of belonging to a supportive social network" (Germain and Gitterman 1995:817). Family is built in to each aspect of this definition. Goodness of fit exists between the person and family or between the family and their social/community life when multiple attachments are present and are characterized by support, acceptance, and nurturing. When the qualities of *friend* in the finest sense of that term are present among and between family members, relatedness serves to strengthen and enhance family life as an environment of choice for its individual members. Family members do much for each other through their patterns of communication and time spent together to shape a network of support that feeds them all. An echo of the importance of participation with others as a key action in empowering practice is heard in this definition of relatedness.

And yet, each of the families also teaches the importance of knowing when to leave certain kinds of relatedness behind. Sheila knew when it was time to leave her boyfriend; Cynthia planned for several years to end her marriage with Mike; Linda, Susan, and Jane severed their relationships with John when they reported the sexual abuse; Jorgé and Lydia created stronger boundaries and rules around their interactions with Maria. Regular contact may end abruptly, but it can take much longer to set aside the influence of emotional ties.

Efficacy and Competence

Efficacy and *competence* refer, respectively, to a "feeling state resulting from a positive experience of having an effect on the environment" and an "inner sense derived from accumulated experiences of efficacy and, at times, associated with the ability to seek and accept help when needed" (Germain and Gitterman 1996:18). From the earliest moments of an infant's cry or laughter, the responses of family and others in the environment begin to build that sense of having an effect on one's environment. If the cries and laughter are met with no response over extended periods of time, the infant can face grave risks to survival. The family support system plays a key role in each family member's earliest messages about efficacy in this way, messages that go on to influence capacities for relatedness, positive exchanges, and the development of a goodness of fit with one's environment. With competence comes an acceptance of the limits of that competence and the knowledge of when outside resources may be necessary as added support. While working on her leadership development skills, Sheila is also aware of when she is feeling pushed to her limit by the expectations of her family and extended family and also of when the outside support of her group at Project WISE is a vital resource for her. Families in distress are often in the midst of attempts to address overwhelming challenges on their own. Defining a family's acceptance of available resources to assist them as a strength, rather than as a weakness, can help them move on to make choices regarding their use of resources and to recover a sense of well-being from those experiences.

Self-concept and Self-esteem

Self-concept is defined as the "totality of a person's thoughts and feelings" about herself or himself. *Self-esteem*, regarded as the most important aspect of a person's self-concept, refers to the "extent to which a person feels capable, significant, and worthy of respect and love" (Germain and Gitterman 1996:18). The levels of empowerment practice—personal, interpersonal, and social/community—are constantly intertwined, and this concept of the ecological perspective reminds us of the importance of the individual dimension. When we begin our work with families in distress with an emphasis on their strengths, we begin with verbalizing observations about how they are individually capable of managing the challenges before them, highly significant in their individual role as each of them contributes to the overall quality of who they are as a family in a way that no other family member can, and worthy of respect and love no matter what "condition of life" they may be facing that is "threatening health and social well-being or imposing enormous adaptive burdens" upon them (Germain 1991:24–25).

Self-esteem is fragile in many distressed family environments. Trauma and crisis shatter self-esteem and self-assurance. Self-doubt, uncertainty, and confusion become pervasive. Individualized, often survival-related, responses are required, and the power of the family bond at these times is often a truly remarkable and courageous response as well. Listening to the voices of each member of the family is the only way to gain an understanding of that person's sense of self-concept and self-esteem. Sometimes family members attempt to speak for each other regarding these characteristics. A context that allows each family member to speak her or his own words regarding these forms of self knowledge is a more empowering context.

Self-direction

Self-direction is defined in the Life Model as "the capacity to take some degree of control over one's life and to accept responsibility for one's decisions and actions while simultaneously respecting the rights and needs of others" (Germain and Gitterman 1995:818). Taking action is key to empowering practice, and this concept of ecological thinking emphasizes an integration with those action steps. The definition captures the balancing of the personal with the interpersonal, taking charge over one's life and at the same time respecting others. Differences of ethnicity, age, gender, sexual orientation, socioeconomic status, religion/spiritual beliefs, language, developmental stage, differing abilities, and geography among family members require differential consideration of self-direction. Families have different ideas about when their members can be expected to assume responsibility for decisions and actions. The family environment often provides the person's first experience with respecting the rights and needs of others. These experiences reiterate the way in which exchanges between family members help to shape who they are individually and together.

Self-direction also implies that creative choice to define oneself, one's family, and one's direction may be available. Oppressions such as poverty, violence, addictions, and discrimination, however, can severely limit or destroy such creative choice. Removing barriers to that choice is the central purpose of working from an empowerment perspective.

Criticisms about the use of ecological metaphors for understanding social work realities include the construing of "adaptation" to be something similar to conformity or accommodation and the relative lack of empirical research to support the use of ecological analysis at multiple systems levels (Robbins, Chatterjee, and Canda 1998:58–59). *Adaptation* comes from biological terminology, the origin and base of ecological jargon. Critics who compare *adaptation, conformity,* and *accommodation* note that all three terms can be used to describe social relationships, yet *adaptation* provides a closer view of the purpose served in the natural order. Learning from transactions in nature to inform transactions in human and social life is the purpose of proposing the bridge of metaphors from ecology to human interaction.

Advances in empirical research related to the use of the ecological framework are occurring at an increasing rate. Empirically based application of ecological theory to the distribution of social problems began twenty-five to thirty years ago (Dunbar 1972; Galaskiewicz 1979; Lenski and Nolan 1984). Competence clarification in the midst of facing "manifestations of the poor fit between people and their environments" has been identified as one subject for empirical research (Compton and Galaway 1999:357). The Family Empowerment Scale is one measure being used increasingly in the attempt to gather quantitative data. Evidence-based research and practice are also acknowledging the natural order, specifically in the relationship between people and their environments, as "evidence" upon which to base conclusions, implications, and recommendations. With focus on the environment, neighborhood poverty rates, evidence of social disorganization, and alienation have been positively related to rates of child abuse and neglect (Coulton et al. 1995).

Recent Advances in Ecological Thinking

New concepts have been added to the ecological perspective in recent years. Three of these— power (including coercive and exploitative power), powerlessness, and pollution—were included in chapter 1's discussion of the uses of power. The remaining newer concepts are "habitat and niche" and "life course" (which serves to replace "life cycle" as the descriptor in models of development).

Habitat and Niche

In ecology, *habitat* refers to "places where the organism can be found" and *niche* refers to "the position occupied by a species within a biotic community—the species' place in the web of life" (Germain and Gitterman 1995:818). From the shelter of tunnels, caves, and cardboard boxes to homeless shelters, safe houses, self-storage units, and foster homes; from one-room apartments with multiple generations to mansions with only two people; from urban to suburban to exurban to rural; and on all continents around the globe, the habitats of families are as varied as the families themselves. Every habitat is defined by culture and class, symbolically representing its inhabitants through the messages it communicates to the wider neighborhood and community. The idea of place is also significant for families, in the sense of where each family member finds his or her own place within the family habitat. Do the parents have a separate room? Do siblings share a room? One child spent the first seven years of his life sleeping under the stairs. What message does this give about his place in that family?

Niche also identifies the place or position occupied by the organism, individual, or family. What is a family's niche in their particular community? What roles do class, culture, occupation, school, religious or spiritual institutions and belief systems play in the identification of a family's niche? Is the family experiencing a "goodness of fit" with where they find themselves in their niche or is there a lack of fit? Is there a certain status, or a sense of degradation, derived from their niche in the community? In the "web" of family life, what is the mother's niche? The father's? The children's? The extended family's? Answers to all of these questions help gain an understanding of how the family members see themselves as a part of the wider systems within which their family is embedded and, in turn, how they live and function in those places and positions.

The impact of oppressive forces upon habitat and niche is crucial for empowering practice with families in distress. Families living with poverty, for example, may face threats of eviction when they are unable to pay rent and may perceive homelessness, loss of habitat, as an ever-present possibility. Family members oppressed by violence in the home think about ways to leave in order to find safety or carefully plan the timing for changing locks on the door to keep the violent person out. Addictions affect habitat and niche in a variety of ways. For the addict, where are the hiding places to keep the substances readily available but out of sight of other family members? Children report that they fear bringing friends home because they never know if a parent or sibling with an addiction will be there and under the influence of the substance at that time. Addictions and violence often go hand in hand, and the home, or one's private niche, can literally be destroyed and broken by such violence. Discrimination, as well, plays a role in assessing a family's habitat and niche, as it did for Lydia and Jorgé when they became aware that some of their neighbors were judgmental about their ethnic backgrounds and their marital status and when Jorgé wondered if discrimination played a role in his being overlooked for a promotion, his work niche.

Transitions from one habitat to another can add enormous stress to a family's overall sense of well-being. Geographic moves are cited as one of the most stressful events in a person's (and family's) life. Loss of support networks, friendship networks, perhaps job and school environments, and, for some, changes in language and customary behaviors can lead to years of adjustment and reconnecting. The resilience of families and their capacity to create new ways to be together and to find themselves strengthened by the adversity are all empowering examples commonly seen regardless of the experiences they have faced.

Life Course

Life course refers to the "unique pathways of development that each human being takes—from conception and birth through old age—in varied environments and through infinitely varied life experiences" (Germain and Gitterman 1996:21). It is meant to replace "life cycle" and "life stage" models, which are seen as embedded in assumptions of sequence, predictability, and being fixed rather than flexible. "The term 'life cycle' is a misnomer, because human development is not cyclical" (21). Each family also follows a family life course that often (but not always) includes the joining of two people as partners or spouses, the birth and growth of children, the exit of children, and the aging and eventual death of the parents. An enormous and creative variation exists across this life course. Families face transitions of births and deaths, possibly divorces and remarriages, restructuring and changing habitats and niches as they expand and contract across the decades and across the generations. No two families progress through the life course in exactly the same way. In that uniqueness and that variation, with all the multiple ways of being family, we find a continuity that shifts and changes with "the multicultural aspects of American society; gender roles in family and work life; and the limitless diversity of individual life experience. The life course conception incorporates difference because it conceives of lifelong development as varying with social change" (Riley 1978).

Social work practice with families and the theories that support that practice evolve together in a spiraling, reciprocal exchange in which each influences the growth of the other. Our practice with families in distress is supported by time-honored theories and theoretical perspectives as well as by theories that represent new ways of seeing familiar forms of human suffering. Guided by what is most effective and most responsive to the needs of the families who open their life struggles to us, the theories presented in this chapter have, first of all, been selected with those families in mind. These theories provide valuable direction not just for families in distress but for all of us who find ourselves taking steps each day, attempting to sustain, enhance, and create the small part of the world around us in our efforts to move from distress to well-being.

Appendix A

Cross-Cultural Counseling Competencies: A Conceptual Framework

Derald Wing Sue, Patricia Arredondo, and Roderick J. McDavis

I. Counselor Awareness of Own Assumptions, Values, and Biases

A. Beliefs and Attitudes

1. Culturally skilled counselors have moved from being culturally unaware to being aware and sensitive to their own cultural heritage and to valuing and respecting differences.
2. Culturally skilled counselors are aware of how their own cultural background and experiences, attitudes, and values and biases influence psychological processes.
3. Culturally skilled counselors are able to recognize the limits of their competencies and expertise.
4. Culturally skilled counselors are comfortable with differences that exist between themselves and clients in terms of race, ethnicity, and beliefs.

B. Knowledge

1. Culturally skilled counselors have specific knowledge about their own racial and cultural heritage and how it personally and professionally affects their definitions and biases of normality-abnormality and the processes of counseling.
2. Culturally skilled counselors possess knowledge and understanding about how oppression, racism, discrimination, and stereotyping affect them personally and in their work. This allows them to acknowledge their own racist attitudes, beliefs, and feel-

Reprinted from Derald W. Sue, Patricia Arredondo, and Roderick J. McDavis, "Multicultural Competencies and Standards: A Call to the Profession," *Journal of Counseling and Development* 70 (1992): 477–486.

ings. Although this standard applies to all groups, for White counselors it may mean that they understand how they may have directly or indirectly benefited from individual, institutional, and cultural racism (White identity development models).

3. Culturally skilled counselors possess knowledge about their social impact upon others. They are knowledgeable about communication style differences, how their style may clash [with] or facilitate the counseling process with minority clients, and how to anticipate the impact it may have on others.

C. Skills

1. Culturally skilled counselors seek out educational, consultative, and training experiences to enrich their understanding and effectiveness in working with culturally different populations. Being able to recognize the limits of their competencies, they (a) seek consultation, (b) seek further training or education, (c) refer out to more qualified individuals or resources, or (d) engage in a combination of these.

2. Culturally skilled counselors are constantly seeking to understand themselves as racial and cultural beings and are actively seeking a nonracist identity.

II. Understanding the Worldview of the Culturally Different Client

A. Beliefs and Attitudes

1. Culturally skilled counselors are aware of their negative emotional reactions toward other racial and ethnic groups that may prove detrimental to their clients in counseling. They are willing to contrast their own beliefs and attitudes with those of their culturally different clients in a nonjudgmental fashion.

2. Culturally skilled counselors are aware of their stereotypes and preconceived notions that they may hold toward other racial and ethnic minority groups.

B. Knowledge

1. Culturally skilled counselors possess specific knowledge and information about the particular group that they are working with. They are aware of the life experiences, cultural heritage, and historical background of their culturally different clients. This particular competency is strongly linked to the "minority identity development models" available in the literature.

2. Culturally skilled counselors understand how race, culture, ethnicity, and so forth may affect personality formation, vocational choices, manifestation of psychological disorders, help-seeking behavior, and the appropriateness or inappropriateness of counseling approaches.

3. Culturally skilled counselors understand and have knowledge about sociopolitical influences that impinge upon the life of racial and ethnic minorities. Integration

issues, poverty, racism, stereotyping and powerlessness all leave major scars that may influence the counseling process.

C. Skills

1. Culturally skilled counselors should familiarize themselves with relevant research and the latest findings regarding mental health and mental disorders of various ethnic and racial groups. They should actively seek out educational experiences that enrich their knowledge, understanding, and cross-cultural skills.

2. Culturally skilled counselors become actively involved with minority individuals outside the counseling setting (community events, social and political functions, celebration, friendships, neighborhood groups, and so forth) so that their perspective of minorities is more than an academic or helping exercise.

III. Developing Appropriate Intervention Strategies and Techniques

A. Beliefs and Attitudes

1. Culturally skilled counselors respect clients' religious and/or spiritual beliefs and values about physical and mental functioning.

2. Culturally skilled counselors respect indigenous helping practices and respect minority community intrinsic help-giving networks.

3. Culturally skilled counselors value bilingualism and do not view another language as an impediment to counseling (monolingualism may be the culprit).

B. Knowledge

1. Culturally skilled counselors have a clear and explicit knowledge and understanding of the generic characteristics of counseling and therapy (culture bound, class bound, and monolingual) and how they may clash with the cultural values of various minority groups.

2. Culturally skilled counselors are aware of institutional barriers that prevent minorities from using mental health services.

3. Culturally skilled counselors have knowledge of the potential bias in assessment instruments and use procedures and interpret findings keeping in mind the cultural and linguistic characteristics of the clients.

4. Culturally skilled counselors have knowledge of minority family structures, hierarchies, values, and beliefs. They are knowledgeable about the community characteristics and the resources in the community as well as the family.

5. Culturally skilled counselors should be aware of relevant discriminatory practices at the social and community level that may be affecting the psychological welfare of the population being served.

C. Skills

1. Culturally skilled counselors are able to engage in a variety of verbal and nonverbal helping responses. They are able to *send* and *receive* both *verbal* and *nonverbal* messages *accurately* and *appropriately.* They are not tied down to only one method or approach to helping but recognize that helping styles and approaches may be culture bound. When they sense that their helping style is limited and potentially inappropriate, they can anticipate and ameliorate its negative impact.

2. Culturally skilled counselors are able to exercise institutional intervention skills on behalf of their clients. They can help clients determine whether a "problem" stems from racism or bias in others (the concept of healthy paranoia) so that clients do not inappropriately blame themselves.

3. Culturally skilled counselors are not averse to seeking consultation with traditional healers or religious and spiritual leaders and practitioners in the treatment of culturally different clients when appropriate.

4. Culturally skilled counselors take responsibility for interacting in the language requested by the client; this may mean appropriate referral to outside resources. A serious problem arises when the linguistic skills of the counselor do not match the language of the client. This being the case, counselors should (a) seek a translator with cultural knowledge and appropriate professional background or (b) refer to a knowledgeable and competent bilingual counselor.

5. Culturally skilled counselors have training and expertise in the use of traditional assessment and testing instruments. They not only understand the technical aspects of the instruments but are also aware of the cultural limitations. This allows them to use these instruments for the welfare of the diverse clients.

6. Culturally skilled counselors should attend to as well as work to eliminate biases, prejudices, and discriminatory practices. They should be cognizant of sociopolitical contexts in conducting evaluations and providing interventions, and should develop sensitivity to issues of oppression, sexism, and racism.

7. Culturally skilled counselors take responsibility in educating their clients to the processes of psychological intervention, such as goals, expectations, legal rights, and the counselor's orientation.

We believe that these cross-cultural competencies represent AMCD's first formal attempt to define the attributes of a culturally skilled counselor. They are not meant to be "the final word" in establishing cross-cultural standards for the profession; rather, they represent what we consider to be very important criteria for counselor practice in working with racial and ethnic minorities. Many will, no doubt, undergo further revision, and other new competencies will be added. We propose these competencies in the spirit of open inquiry and hope they eventually will be adopted into the counseling standards of the profession.

APPENDIX B

The Family Power Analysis

I. Draw a genogram of your family that includes both your family of origin and your current family, one that encompasses at least three generations. Indicate yourself with a double line around the circle or square that represents you. The analysis will be most helpful if you can place yourself in either the second or the third generation.

Second generation   Third generation

II. Choose a time in the life of your family during which experiences of "power WITH," "power over," or "power under" stand out for you. As closely as possible, identify the year during which those experiences took place, then add names, ages, and dates of marriages, commitments, divorces, and deaths, respectively. Use an "X" in the circle or square representing those who have died and include a phrase about the cause of death near that person's symbol. Finally, add three descriptive characteristics next to each person on the genogram.

Add relationship lines for all two-person relationships using the following symbols:

————————	=	close
≡≡≡≡≡≡≡	=	very close
- - - - - - - - -	=	distant
——| |——	=	cut-off
\/\/\/\/\/\	=	conflict

If these symbols do not capture the nature of a relationship as you remember it, create a symbol of your own that is more accurate and explain its meaning in a "Key" below the genogram. If you are uncertain about any one relationship, either use your intuition or guess about what might have happened there. It is important that ALL same-generation and ALL cross-generation relationships are represented with one of these lines indicating the nature of the relationship.

III. List all same-generation relationships by name (marriages, partnerships, divorced couples, siblings, step-siblings, etc.): John and Mary, George and Sam, Lee and Joe, and so on. Next to each pair of names, indicate the relationship line used on the genogram to represent this relationship, then also think about whether "power WITH" or "power over," or "power under" best describes the dynamic between these family members.

| John and Mary | Conflict | Power over/Power under |
| Lee and Joe | Close | Power with |

IV. Taking special note of the relationships of which you are a part, what are the three most important meanings for you related to power from these relationships?

1.

2.

3.

V. List all cross-generational relationships: parent-child (first and second generations); parent-child (second and third generations), grandparents to grandchildren (first to third generations). Create a list similar to the one in part III, one that includes the names, the relationship line used, and the "power with" or "power over/power under" designation. Noting the relationships of which you are a part, list the three most important meanings for you related to power from these relationships.

VI. Observe any power relationships defined by ethnicity, gender, age, socioeconomic status, sexual orientation, religion, different abilities, language, geography, or developmental stage. What are the three most important meanings for you related to power as you consider these relationships?

VII. Based upon these power dynamics in three generations of your family, identify strengths and resources that can be used when working with other families. Identify potential barriers that might appear in your work with other families.

VIII. List three things you can do to maximize the strengths you bring from "power with" relationships in your own family into the work with client families. List three things you can do to minimize the potential barriers from earlier "power over/power under" relationships that might show up in your work with client families.

Notes

3. The Laurencio-Smith Family: Our Differences Saved Us

1. For more specific information about the purpose, benefits, and structure of using the family genogram as a helpful tool in working with family members, see McGoldrick and Gerson (1985).

4. The Williams Family: New Lives Beyond Incest

1. The term *problem-focused coping* is preferred over *problem-solving process.* It is viewed as a more inclusive term and is based upon the understanding that solving problems is only one aspect of coping. A problem, or a series of problems, solved does not necessarily mean that essential ingredients of coping have been addressed. Problem solving is nevertheless viewed as one coping skill, one that serves a key role in the overall process of coping with distress and trauma. This same argument can be applied to "solution-focused" efforts.

6. The Phases and Actions of Empowerment Practice

1. Until recently, the social worker's role of educator has been founded upon the styles and contexts of education found in traditional institutions of higher learning, a role modeled upon a hierarchical relationship between teacher and student rather than a mutual relationship and based upon students' lack of knowledge rather than upon a wealth of experience that informs the process and assures the effectiveness of its outcome. In fact, the shift in training educators from teaching people *how to teach* to understanding *how people learn* has happened only in the last fifty years (Knowles 1977). This shift helps us, in the work with families in distress, to keep their learning needs in the foreground and the worker's need to "teach" in the background.

   Learners, as much as facilitators, have been socialized to view education as an authoritarian-based transmission of information, skills, and attitudinal sets from teacher to student. Under these circumstances, it is hard for educators to avoid the temptation to control the learning encounter. Yet to give in to this temptation is to reaffirm precisely those patterns of dependency that prevent adults from becoming empowered, self-directed learners (Brookfield 1995:296).

Children and adults learn in different ways. Assumptions about how children learn, pedagogy, evolved between the seventh and twelfth centuries in monastic and cathedral schools. The learning process is teacher-directed. The teacher is assigned full responsibility for what is learned, when and how it is learned, and for determining ways of assessing whether learning has taken place. Students are dependent upon their teachers to lead both content and process. For children, the need and capacity to be self-directing is less, though not absent, and as individuals mature, this "need and capacity to be self-directing, to utilize their experience in learning, and to identify their own readiness to learn increases steadily from infancy to preadolescence, and then increases rapidly during adolescence" (Knowles 1977:53). The need to be self-directing continues to develop within the individual whether or not it is promoted in the educational environment. However, if there is a mismatch between the individual's need to become more self-directed and the educational (or helping) environment's need to be teacher-directed (or social worker–directed), stress and tension can result. When we meet with a family as social workers and do not include an understanding of the developmental stages related to learning needs of each family member, we also invite stress and unnecessary misunderstanding.

2. The formalized practice of family group conferencing is traced to New Zealand in the late 1980s, specifically to *Report of the Ministerial Advisory Committee on a Maori Perspective for the Department of Social Welfare* (1986), *Report of the Royal Commission on Social Policy* (1988), and *Maori and the Criminal Justice System* (Jackson 1988). These reports identified "ways in which institutional racism and discriminatory practices operated to disadvantage Maori children and families" and "gave voice to Maori perspectives, critiques, and aspirations as they related to social policy justice, and child and family well-being" (Burford and Hudson 2000:16). Especially significant in this cross-cultural response is the effort of the dominant culture in New Zealand to accurately hear and act upon perspectives that are congruent with the Maori and, in the process, gain wisdom from these perspectives that was later instituted in legislation to serve all families. Concerns about what can be done to ensure family well-being are global concerns. "Service innovations once considered local now find their way rather rapidly into what has become an international discourse on innovative practice" (Burford and Hudson 2000:xi). As a global family and community, we have much we can learn from and with one another. Multicultural practice continually reminds us that there are accomplishments available to us in working together that are out of our grasp individually.

7. Empowering Families with Community Resources

1. The National Empowerment Center is at 29 Ballard Road, Lawrence, Massachusetts 01843-1018. Project Share is at 311 South Juniper Street, Room 902, Philadelphia, Pennsylvania 19107.

2. For information about Family to Family Education Programs, contact the program at 2107 Wilson Boulevard, Suite 300, Arlington, Virginia 22201-3042.

8. Supporting Theories that Empower Social Worker-Family Transactions

1. Bogdanov's work was originally published in three volumes between 1912 and 1917, and a translation in German appeared in 1928. After an attack on his work by Lenin, his writings were banned from public view in the Soviet Union for nearly fifty years. As a result of perestroika, Bogdanov's work at last received the national and international scholarly and philosophical recognition that it so well deserved.

2. The term *homeostasis* was introduced by Walter Cannon from a refinement of the work done by Claude Bernard on the principle of the constancy of an organism's internal environment (Capra 1996:43).

3. By 1975 two other frameworks of thought with very similar names but entirely different conceptual bases came on the scene: the social systems view of Talcott Parsons and a set of concepts called family system theory by Murray Bowen. Neither meets the criteria for being selected for further discussion here. The Parsons model "does not go as far as dynamic systems theory in addressing creative system transformation" (Robbins, Chatterjee, and Canda 1998:36), a key aspect in the shaping of family well-being as it is used in later discussions. And the Bowen model grew out of a medical pathology-oriented base and has since received criticism about its gender bias, both points that present contradictions to the strengths model and the multifocal view promoted here. Some of the criticism about the use of general system theory for social work practice resulted from confusion about the differences among these three areas of knowledge.

4. See, for example, the observation by Germain and Gitterman (1996): "Ecology also rests on an evolutionary, adaptive view of the development of human beings and the characteristics of the species" (6), as well as the discussion "Development and Evolutionary Change" in Miley, O'Melia, and DuBois (2001:33–34).

5. For additional discussion of these concepts, readers are referred to Germaine and Gitterman (1995, 1996).

References

Adnopoz, D. J., R. K. Grigsby, and S. F. Nagler. 1996. "Multiproblem Families and High-Risk Children and Adolescents: Causes and Management." In M. Lewis, ed., *Child and Adolescent Psychiatry: A Comprehensive Textbook*, 1074–1080. 2d ed. Baltimore: Williams and Wilkins.

Allen, D. A., R. Kaur, E. M. Jackson, and K. McLeish. 1993. "Religion." In K. McLeish, ed., *Key Ideas in Human Thought*, 626–627. New York: Facts on File.

Allen, Katherine R., Mark A. Fine, and David H. Demo. 2000. "An Overview of Family Diversity: Controversies, Questions, and Values." In David H. Demo, Katherine R. Allen, and Mark A. Fine, eds., *Handbook of Family Diversity*, 1–14. New York: Oxford University Press.

Allen-Meares, Paula, and Charles Garvin, eds. 2000. *The Handbook of Social Work Direct Practice*. Thousand Oaks, Calif.: Sage.

AmeriStat. 2000. *Families in Poverty: Racial and Ethnic Differences*. AmeriStat Population Reference Bureau and Social Science Data Analysis Network. Washington, D.C.: Department of Commerce, Bureau of the Census.

Anderson, Carol. 1981. "Working with the Resistant Family." Paper presented at conference, October, Bridgeport, Conn.

Angelou, Maya. 2003. "Great Expectations." In Rosemarie Robotham, ed., *Mending the World: Stories of Family by Contemporary Black Writers*. New York: Basic Civitas Books.

Argyle, Michael. 1999. "Causes and Correlates of Happiness." In Daniel Kahneman, Ed Diener, and Norbert Schwarz, eds., *Well-being*, 353–373. New York: Russell Sage Foundation.

Baldwin, Michele, ed. 2000. *The Use of Self in Therapy*. New York: Haworth Press.

Barthel, Joan. 1992a. "Family Preservation, Values and Beliefs." *Youth Policy* 14:32–36.

Barthel, Joan. 1992b. *For Children's Sake: The Promise of Family Preservation*. New York: Annie E. Casey Foundation, Edna McConnell Clark Foundation, Foundation for Child Development, and Skillman Foundation.

Beavers, W. Robert, and Robert B. Hampson. 1990. *Successful Families: Assessment and Intervention*. New York: Norton.

Bennis, Warren, G., Kenneth D. Benne, and Robert Chin, eds. 1961. *The Planning of Change*. New York: Holt, Rinehart and Winston.

Berenbaum, Howard, Chitra Raghavan, Huynh-Nhu Le, Laura Vernon, and Jose Gomez. 1999. "Disturbances in Emotion." In Daniel Kahneman, Ed Diener, and Norbert Schwarz, eds., *Well-being*, 267–287. New York: Russell Sage Foundation.

Berg-Cross, Linda, and Ruby Takushi Chinen. 1995. "Multicultural Training Models and the Person-in-Culture Interview." In Joseph G. Ponterotto, J. Manuel Casas, Lisa A. Suzuki, and Charlene M. Alexander, eds., *Handbook of Multicultural Counseling*, 333–356. Thousand Oaks, Calif.: Sage.

Bernheim, Kayla F., and Anthony F. Lehman. 1985. *Working with Families of the Mentally Ill*. New York: Norton.

Berridge, Kent C. 1999. "Pleasure, Pain, Desire, and Dread: Hidden Core Processes of Emotion." In Daniel Kahneman, Ed Diener, and Norbert Schwarz, eds., *Well-being*, 525–557. New York: Russell Sage Foundation.

Blumenfield, Michael, and Margot Schoeps. 1993. *Psychological Care of the Burn and Trauma Patient*. Baltimore: Williams and Wilkins.

Bly, Carol. 2001. *Beyond the Writers' Workshop: New Ways to Write Creative Nonfiction*. New York: Anchor.

Bograd, M. 1992. "Values in Conflict: Challenges to Family Therapists' Thinking." *Journal of Marital and Family Therapy* 18:245–256.

Bowen, Murray. 1978. *Family Therapy in Clinical Practice*. New York: Aronson.

Braithwaite, J., and K. Daly. 1994. "Masculinities, Violence, and Communication Control." In T. Newburn and E. Stanko, eds., *Just Boys Doing Business? Men, Masculinities, and Crime*, 189–213. London: Routledge.

Bronfenbrenner, Uri. 1979. *The Ecology of Human Development: Experiments by Nature and Design*. Cambridge, Mass.: Harvard University Press.

Bronfenbrenner, Uri. 1986. "Ecology of the Family as a Context for Human Development: Research Perspectives." *Developmental Psychology* 22:723–742.

Brookfield, Stephen. 1995. *Becoming a Critically Reflective Teacher*. San Francisco: Jossey-Bass.

Brown, Lester R. 1981. *Building a Sustainable Society*. New York: Norton.

Brown, Stephanie, and Virginia Lewis. 1999. *The Alcoholic Family in Recovery: A Developmental Model*. New York: Guilford.

Bula, Judith F. 1998. "The Multicultural Matrix." Paper presented at University of Denver Graduate School of Social Work.

Bula, Judith F. 2000. "Use of the Multicultural Self for Effective Practice." In Michele Baldwin, ed., *The Use of Self in Therapy*, 167–189. New York: Haworth Press.

Burford, Gale, and Joe Hudson, eds. 2000. *Family Group Conferencing: New Directions in Community-Centered Child and Family Practice*. New York: Aldine de Gruyter.

Cameron, Julia. 1998. *The Right to Write*. New York: Tarcher/Putnam.

Cantor, Nancy, and Catherine A. Sanderson. 1999. "Life Task Participation and Well-being: The Importance of Taking Part in Daily Life." In Daniel Kahneman, Ed Diener, and Norbert Schwarz, eds., *Well-being*, 230–243. New York: Russell Sage Foundation.

Capra, Fritjof. 1982. *The Turning Point: Science, Society, and the Rising Culture*. New York: Bantam.

Capra, Fritjof. 1996. *The Web of Life: A New Scientific Understanding of Living Systems*. New York: Doubleday.

Carling, Paul J. 1995. *Return to Community: Building Support Systems for People with Psychiatric Disabilities*. New York: Guilford.

Carlson, B. E. 1991. "Causes and Maintenance of Domestic Violence: An Ecological Analysis." *Social Service Review* 58:569–587.

Carter, Betty, and Monica McGoldrick. 1989. *The Changing Family Life Cycle*. Boston: Allyn and Bacon.

Chambers, J. K. 2003. *Sociolinguistic Theory: Linguistic Variation and Its Social Significance*. 2d ed. Malden, Mass.: Blackwell.

Chapin, R. K. 1995. "Social Policy Development: The Strengths Perspective." *Social Work* 40:506–514.

Chaskin, Joseph, and Selma Chipenda-Dansokho. 1997. "Implementing Comprehensive Community Development: Possibilities and Limitations." *Social Work* 42:435–444.

Chasnoff, I. J. 1989. "Drug Use and Women: Establishing a Standard of Care." *Annual of the New York Academy of Science* 56:208.

Chilcoat, Howard D., and Chris-Ellyn Johanson. 1998. "Vulnerability to Cocaine Abuse." In Stephen T. Higgins and Jonathan L. Katz, eds., *Cocaine Abuse: Behavior, Pharmacology, and Clinical Applications*, 313–341. San Diego: Academic Press.

Clancy, J. 1995. "Ecological School Social Work: The Reality and the Vision." *Social Work in Education* 17:40–47.

Cohen, G., N. Fleming, K. Glatter, D. Haghigi, J. Halberstadt, K. McHugh, and A. Wolf. 1996. "Epidemiology of Substance Use." In Lawrence Friedman, Nicholas F. Fleming, David H. Roberts, and Steven F. Hyman, eds., *Source Book of Substance Abuse and Addiction*, 17–40. Baltimore: Williams and Wilkins.

Compton, Beulah, and Burt Galaway, eds. 1975. *Social Work Processes*. Pacific Grove, Calif.: Brooks/Cole.

Compton, Beulah, and Burt Galaway, eds. 1999. *Social Work Processes*. 6th ed. Pacific Grove, Calif.: Brooks/Cole.

Conger, J., and R. Kanungo. 1988. "The Empowerment Process: Integrating Theory and Practice." *Academy of Management Review* 13:471–482.

Corcoran, Mary E., and Ajay Chaudry. 1997. "The Dynamics of Childhood Poverty." *Future of Children* 7:40–54.

Costello, Robert G., ed. 1992. *Random House Webster's College Dictionary*. New York: Random House.

Coulton, C., J. Korbin, M. Su, and J. Chow. 1995. "Community Level Factors and Child Maltreatment Rates." *Child Development* 66:1262–1276.

Cox, C. 1992. "Expanding Social Work's Role in Home Care: An Ecological Perspective." *Social Work* 37:179–183.

Dailey, Dennis. 1997. Personal written communication.

Dale, Edgar. 1985. "Experience and Learning." *Journal of Emergency Medical Services* (June): 61.

Daloz Parks, Laurent A., Cheryl H. Keen, James P. Keen, and Sharon Daloz Parks. 1996. *Common Fire: Leading Lives of Commitment in a Complex World.* Boston: Beacon Press.

Deegan, P. E. 1992. "The Independent Living Movement and People with Psychiatric Disabilities: Taking Back Control of Our Lives." *Psychosocial Rehabilitation Journal* 15:3–19.

Department of Commerce, Bureau of the Census. 1997. *Current Population Reports.* P20–509. Washington, D.C.: Department of Commerce.

Department of Commerce, Bureau of the Census. 1998. *Current Population Reports.* P20–515. Washington, D.C.: Department of Commerce.

Diener, Ed, and Richard E. Lucas. 1999. "Personality and Subjective Well-being." In Daniel Kahneman, Ed Diener, and Norbert Schwarz, eds., *Well-being,* 213–229. New York: Russell Sage Foundation.

Diener, Ed, and Eunkook Mark Suh. 1999. "National Differences in Subjective Well-being." In Daniel Kahneman, Ed Diener, and Norbert Schwarz, eds., *Well-being,* 434–450. New York: Russell Sage Foundation.

Dubos, R. 1963. *The Cultural Roots and the Social Fruits of Science.* Eugene: Oregon State System of Higher Education.

Dubos, R. 1968a. *Man, Medicine, and Environment.* New York: Praeger.

Dubos, R. 1968b. *So Human an Animal.* New York: Scribner.

Dubos, R. 1978. *The Resilience of Ecosystems: An Ecological View of Environmental Restoration.* Boulder: Colorado Associated University Press.

Dunbar, M. J. 1972. "The Ecosystem as a Unit of Natural Selection." *Transactions of the Connecticut Academy of Arts and Sciences* 44:113–130.

Duncan, Greg J., and P. Lindsay Chase-Lansdale, eds. 2002. *For Better and for Worse: Welfare Reform and the Well-being of Children and Families.* New York: Russell Sage Foundation.

Dunst, C. J., C. M. Trivette, and A. G. Deal. 1988. *Enabling and Empowering Families.* Cambridge, Mass.: Brookline Books.

Dupper, David R., and John Poertner. 1997. "Public Schools and the Revitalization of Impoverished Communities: School-Linked Family Resource Centers." *Social Work* 42:415–422.

Dutton, Donald G. 1995. *The Batterer: A Psychological Profile.* New York: Basic Books.

East, Jean. 1999. "An Empowerment Practice Model for Low-Income Women." In W. Shera and L. Wells, eds., *Empowerment Practice in Social Work,* 143–158. New York: Columbia University Press.

East, Jean. 2002. "Grant Application Executive Summary." Typescript.

East, Jean, and Sue Kenney. 2001. "Project WISE: A Women's Initiative for Service and Empowerment." Typescript.

Evans, Patricia. 1992. *The Verbally Abusive Relationship: How to Recognize It and How to Respond.* Holbrook, Mass.: Adams.

Everstine, Diana Sullivan, and Louis Everstine. 1993. *The Trauma Response: Treatment for Emotional Injury.* New York: Norton.

Fabricant, M. 1988. "Empowering the Homeless." *Social Policy* 18:49–55.

Feldman, Harold, and Frances Scherz. 1964. *Family Social Work*. New York: Columbia University Press.

Flagg, Barbara. 1993. "'Was Blind but Now I See': White Race Consciousness and the Requirement of Discriminatory Intent." *Michigan Law Review* 91:953.

Flanagan, J. C. 1978. "A Research Approach to Improving Our Quality of Life." *American Psychologist* 33:138–147.

Fleischaker, Gail Raney. 1992. "Autopoiesis in Systems Analysis: A Debate." *International Journal of General Systems* 21:2.

Flynn, B. C., D. W. Ray, and M. S. Rider. 1994. "Empowering Communities: Action Research Through Healthy Cities." *Health Education Quarterly* 21:395–405.

Fraser, Mark, and David Haapala. 1988. "Home-Based Family Treatment: A Quantitative-Qualitative Assessment." *Journal of Applied Social Sciences* 12: 1–23.

Freeman, E. 1984. "Multiple Losses in the Elderly: An Ecological Approach." *Social Casework* 65:287–296.

Freire, Paulo. 1998. *Pedagogy of the Oppressed*. New York: Continuum.

Frijda, Nico H. 1999. "Emotions and Hedonic Experience." In Daniel Kahneman, Ed Diener, and Norbert Schwarz, eds., *Well-being*, 190–210. New York: Russell Sage Foundation.

Gabriel, Martha A. 1996. *AIDS Trauma and Support Group Therapy*. New York: Free Press.

Galaskiewicz, J. 1979. "The Structure of Community Organization Networks." *Social Forces* 57:1346–1364.

Gambrill, Eileen. 1999. "Evidence-Based Practice: An Alternative to Authority-Based Practice." *Families in Society: The Journal of Contemporary Human Services* 80: 80–94.

Gans, Herbert J. 1995. *The War Against the Poor: The Underclass and Antipoverty Policy*. New York: Basic Books.

Garnett, D. 1996. "Eight Components of the Ideal Delivery System for Multineed Families." Paper presented at Colorado Department of Human Services, January 24.

Gazzaniga, Michael S. 1985. *The Social Brain: Discovering the Networks of the Mind*. New York: Basic Books.

Gee, James Paul. 1996. *Social Linguistics and Literacies: Ideology in Discourses*. 2d ed. Bristol, Pa.: Taylor and Francis.

Gelles, Richard J., and Donileen R. Loseke, eds. 1993. *Current Controversies on Family Violence*. Newbury Park, Calif.: Sage.

Germain, Carel B. 1973. "An Ecological Perspective in Casework Practice." *Social Casework* 54:323–330.

Germain, Carel B. 1976. "Time: An Ecological Variable in Social Work Practice." *Social Casework* 57:419–426.

Germain, Carel B. 1978. "Space: An Ecological Variable in Social Work Practice." *Social Casework* 59:512–522.

Germain, Carel B. 1979. "Introduction: Ecology and Social Work." In C. B. Germain, ed., *Social Work Practice: People and Environments*, 1–22. New York: Columbia University Press.

Germain, Carel B. 1982. "Teaching Primary Prevention in Social Work: An Ecological Perspective." *Journal of Education for Social Work* 18:20–28.

Germain, Carel B. 1985. "The Place of Community Work Within an Ecological Approach to Social Work Practice." In S. H. Taylor and R. W. Roberts, eds., *Theory and Practice of Community Social Work*, 30–55. New York: Columbia University Press.

Germain, Carel B. 1991. *Human Behavior in the Social Environment: An Ecological View.* New York: Columbia University Press.

Germain, Carel, and Alex Gitterman. 1986. "The Life Model of Social Work Practice Revisited." In F. Turner, ed., *Social Work Treatment*, 618–644. New York: Free Press.

Germain, Carel, and Alex Gitterman. 1987. "Ecological Perspective." In A. Minahan, ed.-in-chief, *Encyclopedia of Social Work*, 1:488–499. 18th ed. Silver Spring, Md.: National Association of Social Workers.

Germain, Carel, and Alex Gitterman. 1995. "Ecological Perspective." In R. Edwards, ed.-in-chief, *Encyclopedia of Social Work*, 1:816–824. 19th ed. Washington, D.C.: National Association of Social Workers.

Germain, Carel, and Alex Gitterman. 1996. *The Life Model of Social Work Practice: Advances in Theory and Practice.* 2d ed. New York: Columbia University Press.

Germain, Carel B., and Ann Hartman. 1980. "People and Ideas in the History of Social Work Practice." *Social Casework* 61:323–331.

Giddens, Anthony. 1994. *Beyond Left and Right: The Future of Radical Politics.* Stanford, Calif.: Stanford University Press.

Gilligan, Carol. 1977. "In a Different Voice: Women's Conceptions of Self and Morality." *Harvard Educational Review* 47:481–517.

Gilligan, James. 1996. *Violence: Reflections on a National Epidemic.* New York: Vintage.

Gitterman, Alex. 1991. Introduction to Alex Gitterman, ed., *Handbook of Social Work Practice with Vulnerable Populations*, 1–34. New York: Columbia University Press.

Gitterman, Alex, ed. 2001. *Handbook of Social Work Practice with Vulnerable and Resilient Populations.* 2d ed. New York: Columbia University Press.

Gitterman, Alex, and Lawrence Shulman, eds. 1986. *Mutual Aid Groups and the Life Cycle.* Itasca, Ill.: Peacock.

Gitterman, Alex, and Lawrence Shulman, eds. 1994. *Mutual Aid Groups and the Life Cycle.* 2d ed. New York: Columbia University Press.

Gleick, James. 1987. *Chaos.* New York: Penguin.

Goldstein, H. 1973. *Social Work Practice: A Unitary Approach.* Columbia: University of South Carolina Press.

Gomberg, M. Robert. 1944. "The Specific Nature of Family Casework." In J. Taft, ed., *A Functional Approach to Family Case Work*, 111–147. Philadelphia: University of Pennsylvania Press.

Gomberg, M. Robert, and Francis Levinson. 1951. *Diagnosis and Process in Family Counseling.* New York: Family Service Association of America.

Gray, Sylvia Sims, Ann Hartman, and Ellen S. Saalberg, eds. 1985. *Empowering the Black Family.* Ann Arbor: National Child Welfare Training Center, University of Michigan School of Social Work.

Graybeal, C. 2001. "Strengths-Based Social Work Assessment: Transforming the Dominant Paradigm." *Families in Society: The Journal of Contemporary Human Services* 82:233–242.

Guerin, Philip. 1976. "Family Therapy: The First Twenty-Five Years." In P. Guerin, ed., *Family Therapy: Theory and Practice*, 2–22. New York: Gardner.

Guterman, N., and Betty J. Blythe. 1986. "Toward Ecologically Based Intervention in Residential Treatment for Children." *Social Service Review* 60:633–643.

Gutiérrez, Lorraine M. 1990. "Working with Women of Color: An Empowerment Perspective." *Social Work* 35:149–153.

Gutiérrez, Lorraine and Edith Lewis. 1999. *Empowering Women of Color*. New York: Columbia University Press.

Gutiérrez, Lorraine M., Ruth Parsons, and Enid Cox, eds. 1998. *Empowerment in Social Work Practice: A Sourcebook*. Pacific Grove, Calif.: Brooks/Cole.

Haley, Jay. 1959. "The Family of the Schizophrenic: A Model System." *Journal of Nervous Mental Disorders* 129:357–374.

Hamberger, L. Kevin, and Claire Renzetti, eds. 1996. *Domestic Partner Abuse*. New York: Springer.

Hamilton, Gordon. 1951. *Theory and Practice of Social Casework*. 2d ed. New York: Columbia University Press.

Hansen, M., and M. Harway, eds. 1993. *Battering and Family Therapy: A Feminist Perspective*. Newbury Park, Calif.: Sage.

Hanson, Meredith. 2001. "Alcoholism and Other Drug Addictions." In A. Gitterman, ed., *Handbook of Social Work Practice with Vulnerable and Resilient Populations*, 64–96. New York: Columbia University Press.

Harris, Carolyn. 1995. "Focus Points Family Resource Center." In *Our Children, Our Future: Report of the Denver Task Force on Early Childhood Care and Education*. Denver: JFM Foundation.

Hartford, Margaret. 1971. *Groups in Social Work: Application of Small Group Theory and Research to Social Work Practice*. New York: Columbia University Press.

Hartman, Ann. 1970. "To Think About the Unthinkable." *Social Casework* 51:467–474.

Hartman, Ann, and Joan Laird. 1983. *Family-Centered Social Work Practice*. New York: Free Press.

Hasenfeld, Y. 1987. "Power in Social Work Practice." *Social Service Review* 61:469–483.

Hatfield, Agnes B., and Harriet P. Lefley, eds. 1987. *Families of the Mentally Ill: Coping and Adaptation*. New York: Guilford.

Hawkins, J. David, Richard F. Catalano Jr., and Associates. 1992. *Communities that Care: Action for Drug Abuse Prevention*. San Francisco: Jossey-Bass.

Hearn, Gordon. 1958. *Theory-building in Social Work*. Toronto: University of Toronto Press.

Hearn, Gordon, ed. 1969. *The General System Approach: Contributions Toward an Holistic Conception of Social Work*. New York: Council on Social Work Education.

Hegar, R. L., and J. M. Hunzeker. 1988. "Moving Toward Empowerment-Based Practice in Child Welfare." *Social Work* 33:499–502.

Helen. 2000. Personal communication. [Asked to remain anonymous except for first name]

Heller, D. 1985. *Power in Psychotherapeutic Practice*. New York: Human Services Press.

Henggeler, S. W., S. K. Schoenwald, C. M. Borduin, M. D. Rowland, and P. B. Cunningham. 1998. *Multisystemic Treatment of Antisocial Behavior in Children and Adolescents*. New York: Guilford.

Herman, Judith Lewis. 1992. *Trauma and Recovery: The Aftermath of Violence—from Domestic Abuse to Political Terror.* New York: Basic Books.

Hess, P., and T. Howard. 1981. "An Ecological Model for Assessing Psychosocial Difficulties in Children." *Child Welfare* 60:499–518.

Higgins, E. Tory, Heidi Grant, and James Shah. 1999. "Self-Regulation and Quality of Life: Emotional and Non-emotional Life Experiences." In Daniel Kahneman, Ed Diener, and Norbert Schwarz, eds., *Well-being,* 244–266. New York: Russell Sage Foundation.

Hodges, Vanessa G., Yolanda Burwell, and Debra Ortega. 1998. "Empowering Families." In Lorraine M. Gutiérrez, Ruth J. Parsons, and Enid Opal Cox, eds., *Empowerment in Social Work Practice: A Sourcebook,* 146–162. Pacific Grove, Calif.: Brooks/Cole.

Hollingsworth, L. 1998. "Promoting Same-Race Adoption for Children of Color." *Social Work* 43:104–116.

Hollis, Florence, and Mary E. Woods. 1981. *Casework: A Psychosocial Therapy.* 3d ed. New York: Random House.

Hoos, Ida R. 1972. *Systems Analysis in Public Policy: A Critique.* Berkeley: University of California Press.

Hopps, June G., and Elaine Pinderhughes. 1999. *Groupwork with Overwhelmed Clients.* New York: Free Press.

Horn, James E., and Ellen Y. Matten. 1984. "A New Model for Developing a Community Family Strengths Program." In George Rowe, John DeFrain, Herbert Lingren, Ruth MacDonald, Nick Stinnett, Sally Van Zandt, and Rosanne Williams, eds., *Family Strengths 5: Continuity and Diversity,* 447–456. Newton, Mass.: Education Development Center.

Howard, T. U., and F. C. Johnson. 1985. "An Ecological Approach to Practice with Single-Parent Families." *Social Casework* 66:482–489.

Hurd, Elisabeth Porter, Carolyn Moore, and Randy Rogers. 2001. "Quiet Success: Parenting Strengths Among African Americans." In Joe M. Shriver, ed., *Human Behavior and the Social Environment: Shifting Paradigms in Essential Knowledge for Social Work Practice,* 377–390. Boston: Allyn and Bacon.

Ito, Tiffany A., and John T. Cacioppo. "The Psychophysiology of Utility Appraisals." In Daniel Kahneman, Ed Diener, and Norbert Schwarz, eds., *Well-being,* 470–488. New York: Russell Sage Foundation.

Ivanoff, Andre, Betty J. Blythe, and Tony Tripodi. 1994. *Involuntary Clients in Social Work Practice: A Research-Based Approach.* New York: Aldine de Gruyter.

Jackson, M. 1988. *Maori and the Criminal Justice System: He Whaipaanga Hou. A New Perspective.* Part 2. Wellington, N.Z.: Department of Justice.

Jacobs, Judith B. 1992. "Empowerment Themes for Couples Therapy." In Barbara Jo Brothers, ed., *Equal Partnering: A Feminine Perspective,* 25–40. New York: Haworth Press.

Jacobson, N. S., and J. M. Gottman. 1988. *When Men Batter Women: New Insights into Ending Abusive Relationships.* New York: Simon and Schuster.

James, C. S., and D. S. Studs. 1988. "An Ecological Approach to Defining Discharge Planning in Social Work." *Social Work in Health Care* 12:47–59.

Janoff-Bulman, Ronnie. 1999. "Rebuilding Shattered Assumptions After Traumatic Life Events: Coping Processes and Outcomes." In C. R. Snyder, ed., *Coping: The Psychology of What Works,* 305–323. New York: Oxford University Press.

Jensen, Jeffrey. 2001. "Evidence-Based Practice in Social Work." *Social Work Newsletter, Graduate School of Social Work*, University of Denver.

Kagan, Richard, and Shirley Schlosberg. 1989. *Families in Perpetual Crisis*. New York: Norton.

Kahn, Alfred J. 1973. *Shaping the New Social Work*. New York: Columbia University Press.

Kahneman, Daniel. 1999. "Objective Happiness." In Daniel Kahneman, Ed Diener, and Norbert Schwarz, eds., *Well-being*, 3–25. New York: Russell Sage Foundation.

Kahneman, Daniel. 2001. "Central Capacity Theory." In Nick Lund, ed., *Attention and Pattern Recognition*, 27–29. Philadelphia: Routledge.

Kahneman, Daniel, Ed Diener, and Norbert Schwarz, eds. 1999. *Well-being*. New York: Russell Sage Foundation.

Kantor, G. K., and M. A. Strauss. 1989. "Substance Abuse as a Precipitant of Wife Abuse Victimizations." *American Journal of Drug and Alcohol Abuse* 173:214–230.

Kaplan, Lisa. 1986. *Working with Multiproblem Families*. Lexington, Mass.: Lexington Books.

Kaplan, Lisa, and Judith L. Girard. 1994. *Strengthening High-Risk Families: A Handbook for Practitioners*. New York: Lexington Books.

Katz, J. 1988. "Facing the Challenge of Diversity and Multiculturalism." Working Paper no. 360. Center for Research on Social Organization, University of Michigan, Ann Arbor.

Kaufman, G. 1992. "The Mysterious Disappearance of Battered Women in Family Therapists' Offices: Male Privilege Colluding with Male Violence." *Journal of Marital and Family Therapy* 18:233–243.

Kayser, John. 1999. Personal communication.

Kelley, M. L., S. McKay, and C. H. Nelson. 1985. "Indian Agency Development: An Ecological Approach." *Social Casework* 66:594–602.

Kemp, Alan. 1998. *Abuse in the Family: An Introduction*. Pacific Grove, Calif.: Brooks/Cole.

Kilpatrick, Allie C., and Thomas P. Holland, eds. 1999. *Working with Families: An Integrative Model by Level of Need*. 2d ed. New York: Allyn and Bacon.

Kilpatrick, Allie C., and Thomas P. Holland, eds. 2003. *Working with Families: An Integrative Model by Level of Need*. 3d ed. New York: Allyn and Bacon.

King, Stephen. 2000. *On Writing: A Memoir of the Craft*. New York: Simon and Schuster.

Klein, Alan F. 1972. *Effective Groupwork: An Introduction to Principle and Method*. New York: Association Press.

Klein, David M., and James M. White. 1996. *Family Theories: An Introduction*. Thousand Oaks, Calif.: Sage.

Knowles, Malcolm S. 1977. *The Adult Education Movement in the United States*. 2d ed. Huntington, N.Y.: Kreiger.

Koren, P. E., N. DeChillo, and B. J. Friesen. 1992. "Measuring Empowerment in Families Whose Children Have Emotional Disabilities: A Brief Questionnaire." *Rehabilitation Psychology* 37:305–321.

Kretzmann, J. P., and J. L. McKnight. 1993. *Building Communities from the Inside Out: A Path Toward Finding and Mobilizing a Community's Assets*. Evanston, Ill.: Center for Urban Affairs and Policy Research, Northwestern University.

Kubisch, A. D., C. H. Weiss, L. B. Schorr, and J. P. Connell. 1995. Introduction to J. P. Connell, A. D. Kubisch, L. B. Schorr, and C. H. Weiss, eds., *New Approaches to Evaluating Community Initiatives: Concepts, Methods, and Contexts*. Washington, D.C.: Aspen Institute.

Kubovy, Michael. 1999. "On the Pleasures of the Mind." In Daniel Kahneman, Ed Diener, and Norbert Schwarz, eds., *Well-being*, 134–154. New York: Russell Sage Foundation.

Langston, D. 1995. "Tired of Playing Monopoly?" In M .L. Anderson and P. H. Collins, eds., *Race, Class, and Gender: An Anthology*, 100–110. San Francisco: Wadsworth.

Lazarus, R. S. 1993. "Coping Theory and Research: Past, Present, and Future." *Psychosomatic Medicine* 55:234–247.

Lazarus, R. S., and S. Folkman. 1984. *Stress, Appraisal, and Coping*. New York: Springer.

LeDoux, Joseph, and Jorge Armony. 1999. "Can Neurobiology Tell Us Anything About Human Feelings?" In Daniel Kahneman, Ed Diener, and Norbert Schwarz, eds., *Well-being*, 489–499. New York: Russell Sage Foundation.

Lee, Judith A. B. 1994. *The Empowerment Approach to Social Work Practice*. New York: Columbia University Press.

Lee, Judith A. B. 2001. *The Empowerment Approach to Social Work Practice: Building the Beloved Community*. 2d ed. New York: Columbia University Press.

Leiby, J. 1978. *A History of Social Welfare and Social Work in the United States*. New York: Columbia University Press.

Leigh, James W. 1998. *Communicating for Cultural Competence*. Boston: Allyn and Bacon.

Lenski, G., and P. D. Nolan. 1984. "Trajectories of Development: A Test of Ecological Evolutionary Theory." *Social Forces* 63:1–23.

Lewis, J. M., W. R. Beavers, J. T. Gossett, and V. A. Phillips. 1976. *No Single Thread*. New York: Brunner/Mazel.

Lewit, Eugene M., Donna L. Terman, and Richard E Behrman. 1997. "Children and Poverty: Analysis and Recommendations." *Future of Children* 7:4–24.

Libassi, M. F., and Anthony N. Maluccio. 1982. "Teaching the Use of Ecological Perspective in Community Mental Health." *Journal of Education for Social Work* 18:94–100.

Lide, P. 1966. "Dynamic Mental Representation: An Analysis of the Empathic Process." *Social Casework* 47:146–151.

Longres, John F. 2000. *Human Behavior in the Social Environment*. 3d ed. Itasca, Ill.: Peacock.

Lopez, Ian F. Haney. 1996. *White by Law: The Legal Construction of Race*. New York: New York University Press.

Lubove, Roy. 1977. *The Professional Altruist: The Emergence of Social Work as a Career, 1880–1930*. New York: Atheneum.

Luhmann, Niklas. 1990. "The Autopoiesis of Social Systems." In Niklas Luhmann, *Essays on Self-Reference*, 1–21. New York: Columbia University Press.

Lum, D. 1986. *Social Work Practice and People of Color: A Process-Stage Approach*. Monterey, Calif.: Brooks/Cole.

Lystad, Mary, ed. 1986. *Violence in the Home: Interdisciplinary Perspectives*. New York: Brunner/Mazel.

MacGowan, Mark J., and Joan Pennell. 2001. "Building Social Responsibility Through Family Group Conferencing." *Social Work with Groups* 24:67–87.

Maluccio, Anthony N. 1979. *Learning from Clients: Interpersonal Helping as Viewed by Clients and Social Workers*. New York: Free Press.

Maluccio, Anthony N, ed. 1981. *Promoting Competence in Clients: A New/Old Approach to Social Work Practice*. New York: Free Press.

Marans, S., M. Berkman, and D. Cohen. 1996. "Child Development and Adaptations to Catastrophic Circumstances." In R. Apfel and B. Simon, eds., *Minefields in Their Hearts: The Mental Health of Children in War and Communal Violence*, 104–127. New Haven, Conn.: Yale University Press.

Marcus, E. 1993. *Is It a Choice? Answers to 300 of the Most Frequently Asked Questions About Gays and Lesbians*. San Francisco: Harper.

Maren-Grisebach, Manon. 1982. *Philosophie der Grunen*. Munich: Olzog.

Markee, Numa. 2000. *Conversation Analysis*. Mahwah, N.J.: Erlbaum.

McGoldrick, Monica, and Randy Gerson. 1985. *Genograms in Family Assessment*. New York: Norton.

Middleman, Ruth R., and Gale Goldberg. 1974. *Social Service Delivery: A Structural Approach to Social Work Practice*. New York: Columbia University Press.

Middleman, Ruth R., and Gale Goldberg. 1990. *Skills for Direct Practice Social Work*. New York: Columbia University Press.

Miley, Karla Krogsrud, Michael O'Melia, and Brenda DuBois. 2001. *Generalist Social Work Practice: An Empowering Approach*. Boston: Allyn and Bacon.

Miller, Mary Susan. 1995. *No Visible Wounds: Identifying Nonphysical Abuse of Women by Their Men*. New York: Fawcett Columbine.

Milner, J. L. 1987. "An Ecological Perspective on Duration of Foster Care." *Child Welfare* 66:113–123.

Mingers, John. 1995. *Self-Producing Systems*. New York: Plenum.

Mondros, J., and S. Wilson. 1994. *Organizing for Power and Empowerment*. New York: Columbia University Press.

Morrison, John D., Joy Howard, Casey Johnson, Francisco J. Navarro, Beth Plachetka, and Tony Bell. 1997. "Strengthening Neighborhoods by Developing Community Networks." *Social Work* 42:527–534.

Morton, E. Susan, and R. Kevin Grigsby, eds. 1993. *Advancing Family Preservation Practice*. Newbury Park, Calif.: Sage.

Murphy, Christopher M., and Michele Cascardi. 1993. "Psychological Aggression and Abuse in Marriage." In Thomas P. Gullotta, Gerald R. Adams, Earl H. Potter III, and Roger P. Weissberg, eds., *Family Violence: Prevention and Treatment*, 86–112. Newbury Park, Calif.: Sage.

Myers, David G. 1999. "Close Relationships and Quality of Life." In Daniel Kahneman, Ed Diener, and Norbert Schwarz, eds., *Well-being*, 374–391. New York: Russell Sage Foundation.

National Association of Social Workers. 1996. *NASW Code of Ethics*. Washington, D.C.: NASW.

Nolen-Hoeksema, Susan, and Cheryl L. Rusting. 1999. "Gender Differences in Well-being." In Daniel Kahneman, Ed Diener, and Norbert Schwarz, eds., *Well-being*, 330–350. New York: Russell Sage Foundation.

Nozick, Robert. 1989. *The Examined Life*. New York: Simon and Schuster.

Okun, Barbara F. 1996. *Understanding Diverse Families: What Practitioners Need to Know.* New York: Guilford.

Olson, John T. 1997. *Too Proud to Beg: Self-Empowerment for Today's Dog.* Kansas City, Kans.: Andrews and McMeel.

Ornstein, Robert, and Paul Ehrlich. 1989. *New World, New Mind.* New York: Doubleday.

Our Fight: Parents Tell It Like It Is. 1999. Greenfield, Mass.: Deerfield Valley Publishing. Videotape.

Overton, A., and K. H. Tinker. 1957. *Casework Notebook.* St. Paul, Minn.: Family Centered Project of Greater St. Paul.

Page-Adams, Deborah, and Michael Sherraden. 1997. "Asset Building as a Community Revitalization Strategy." *Social Work* 42:423–434.

Pape, B. 1990. *Building a Framework for Support for People with Mental Disabilities.* CMHA Social Action Series. Toronto: Canadian Mental Health Association.

Payne, Carol, ed. 1991. *Programs to Strengthen Families: A Resource Guide.* Chicago: Family Resource Coalition and Yale University.

Pence, Ellen, and Michael Paymar. 1993. *Education Groups for Men Who Batter: The Duluth Model.* New York: Springer.

Pennell, Joan, and Gale Burford. 1994. "Widening the Circle: The Family Group Decision Making Project." *Journal of Child and Youth Care* 9:1–12.

Pennell, Joan, and Gale Burford. 1995. *Family Group Decision Making: New Roles for "Old" Partners in Resolving Family Violence: Implementation Report.* 2 vols. St. John's: Memorial University of Newfoundland, School of Social Work.

Pennell, Joan, and Gale Burford. 1997. "Communities of Concern for Resolving Child and Adult Abuse: The Family Group Decision Making Project." In G. Burford, ed., *Ties that Bind: An Anthology of Readings on Social Work and Social Welfare in Newfoundland and Labrador,* 280–289. St. John's, N.F.: Jesperson.

Pennell, Joan, and Gale Burford. 1999. *Family Group Decision Making: Communities Stopping Family Violence: Questions and Answers.* Monograph prepared for Health Canada, Family Violence Prevention Division. Hull, Que.: Minister of Public Works and Government Services.

Perlman, Helen H. 1957. *Social Casework.* Chicago: University of Chicago Press.

Peterson, Christopher. 1999. "Personal Control and Well-being." In Daniel Kahneman, Ed Diener, and Norbert Schwarz, eds., *Well-being,* 288–301. New York: Russell Sage Foundation.

Peterson, Christopher, and Christina H. Moon. 1999. "Coping with Catastrophes and Catastrophizing." In C. R. Snyder, ed., *Coping: The Psychology of What Works,* 252–278. New York: Oxford University Press.

Pharr, Suzanne. 1988. *Homophobia: A Weapon of Sexism.* Inverness, Calif.: Chardon Press.

Pieres, P. 2003. "Children's Work: A Multiple Case Study." Ph.D. diss., University of Denver.

Pincus, A., and A. Minahan. 1973. *Social Work Practice: Model and Method.* Itasca, Ill.: Peacock.

Pinderhughes, Elaine. 1983. "Empowerment for Our Clients and for Ourselves." *Social Casework* 64:331–338.

Pinderhughes, Elaine. 1989. *Understanding Race, Ethnicity, and Power: The Key to Efficacy in Clinical Practice.* New York: Free Press.

Ponterotto, Joseph G., J. Manuel Casas, Lisa A. Suzuki, and Charlene Alexander. 1995. *Handbook of Multicultural Counseling.* Thousand Oaks, Calif.: Sage.

Present Time Report to the World Conference. 1981. "Insights About Oppression: The Key Concepts and Insights of Re-evaluation Counseling to Date—Part II." *Present Time,* no. 46, 63–72.

Pressman, B. 1989. "Wife-Abused Couples: The Need for Comprehensive Theoretical Perspectives and Integrated Treatment Models." *Journal of Feminist Family Therapy* 1:23–43.

Pumphrey, R. E., and M. W. Pumphrey. 1961. *The Heritage of American Social Work.* New York: Columbia University Press.

Rainwater, Lee, and Timothy M. Smeeding. 1996. "U.S. Doing Poorly—Compared to Others—Policy Point of View." National Center for Children in Poverty—Child Poverty News and Issues 5 (available at: http: cpmcnet.Columbia.edu/news/childpov/newi0008.html).

Rank, Mark R., and Thomas A. Hirschl. 1999. "The Likelihood of Poverty Across the American Adult Life Span." *Social Work* 44:201–216.

Reid, Jeanne, Peggy Macchetto, and Susan Foster. 1999. *No Safe Haven: Children of Substance-Abusing Parents.* New York: National Center on Addiction and Substance Abuse, Columbia University.

Reidy, D. 1992. "Shattering Illusions of Difference." *Resources* 4:3–6.

Remen, Naomi R. 1996. *Kitchen Table Wisdom: Stories that Heal.* New York: Riverhead Books.

Reynolds, Bertha Capen. 1963. *An Uncharted Journey.* New York: Citadel Press.

Rhodes, Jean I., and Leonard A. Jason. 1988. *Preventing Substance Abuse Among Children and Adolescents.* New York: Pergamon.

Rich, Margaret E. 1956. *A Belief in People: A History of Family Social Work.* New York: Family Service Association of America.

Riley, M. W. 1978. "Aging, Social Change, and the Power of Ideas." *Daedalus* 107:39–52.

Robbins, Susan P., Pranab Chatterjee, and Edward R. Canda. 1998. *Contemporary Human Behavior Theory: A Critical Perspective for Social Workers.* Boston: Allyn and Bacon.

Roberts, Albert R., ed. 1998. *Battered Women and Their Families: Intervention Strategies and Treatment Programs.* 2d ed. New York: Springer.

Roberts, James. 1997. "Long-Term Trends in the Consumption of Alcoholic Beverages." In J. L. Simon, ed., *The State of Humanity,* 114–121. Oxford: Blackwell.

Robotham, Rosemarie, ed. 2003. *Mending the World: Stories of Family by Contemporary Black Writers.* New York: Basic Civitas Books.

Rosenberg, Marvin, and Ralph Brody. 1974. *Systems Serving People: A Breakthrough in Service Delivery.* Cleveland: School of Applied Social Sciences, Case Western Reserve University.

Rothman, Jack. 1995. "Approaches to Community Intervention." In J. Rothman, J. Ehrlich, and J. Tropman, eds., *Strategies of Community Intervention,* 26–63. Itasca, Ill.: Peacock.

Rowe, George, John DeFrain, Herbert Lingren, Ruth MacDonald, Nick Stinnett, Sally Van Zandt, and Rosanne Williams, eds. 1984. *Family Strengths 5: Continuity and Diversity.* Newton, Mass.: Education Development Center.

Ruth, Sheila. 1990. *Issues in Feminism: An Introduction to Women's Studies.* Mountain View, Calif.: Mayfield.

Rutter, Virginia, and Pepper Schwartz. 2000. "Gender, Marriage, and Diverse Possibilities for Cross-Sex and Same-Sex Pairs." In D. H. Demo, K. R. Allen, and M. A. Fine, eds., *Handbook of Family Diversity,* 59–81. New York: Oxford University Press.

Saleebey, Dennis. 1999. "The Strengths Perspective: Principles and Practice." In Beulah R. Compton and Burt Galaway, eds., *Social Work Processes,* 14–23. 6th ed. Pacific Grove, Calif.: Brooks/Cole.

Saleebey, Dennis, ed. 1997. *The Strengths Perspective in Social Work Practice.* 2d ed. New York: Longman.

Salovey, Peter, Brian T. Bedell, Jerusha B. Detweiler, and John D. Mayer. 1999. "Coping Intelligently: Emotional Intelligence and the Coping Process." In C. R. Snyder, ed., *Coping: The Psychology of What Works,* 141–164. New York: Oxford University Press.

Sapolsky, Robert M. 1999. "The Physiology and Pathophysiology of Unhappiness." In Daniel Kahneman, Ed Diener, and Norbert Schwarz, eds., *Well-being,* 453–469. New York: Russell Sage Foundation.

Satir, Virginia. 1967. *Conjoint Family Therapy.* Palo Alto, Calif.: Science and Behavior Books.

Satir, Virginia. 1988. *The New Peoplemaking.* Palo Alto, Calif.: Science and Behavior Books.

Satir, Virginia, and Michele Baldwin. 1983. *Satir Step by Step: A Guide to Creating Change in Families.* Palo Alto, Calif.: Science and Behavior Books.

Satir, Virginia, John Banmen, Jane Gerber, and Maria Gomori. 1991. *The Satir Model: Family Therapy and Beyond.* Palo Alto, Calif.: Science and Behavior Books.

Scanzoni, John. 2000. *Designing Families: The Search for Self and Community in the Information Age.* Thousand Oaks, Calif.: Pine Forge Press.

Schniedewind, N. and Davidson, E. 1997. *Open Minds to Equality: A Sourcebook of Learning Activities to Promote Race, Sex, Class, Age, Language, Ability, Sexual Orientation, and Religious Equality.* Des Moines, Iowa: Allyn and Bacon.

Schorr, Lisbeth B. 1997. *Common Purpose: Strengthening Families and Neighborhoods to Rebuild America.* New York: Anchor.

Schuerman, John R., Tina L. Rzepnicki, and Julia H. Littell. 1994. *Putting Families First: An Experiment in Family Preservation.* New York: Aldine de Gruyter.

Schwartz, William. 1961. "The Social Worker in the Group." In *The Social Welfare Forum: 1961 Proceedings of the National Conference on Social Welfare,* 146–177. New York: Columbia University Press.

Sheffield, Ada Eliot. 1937. *Social Insight in Case Situations.* New York: Appleton-Century.

Shizgal, Peter. 1999. "On the Neural Computation of Utility: Implications from Studies of Brain Stimulation Reward." In Daniel Kahneman, Ed Diener, and Norbert Schwarz, eds., *Well-being,* 500–524. New York: Russell Sage Foundation.

Shriver, Joe M., ed. 2001. *Human Behavior and the Social Environment: Shifting Paradigms in Essential Knowledge for Social Work Practice.* Boston: Allyn and Bacon.

Shulman, Lawrence. 1999. *The Skills of Helping Individuals, Families, Groups, and Communities.* Itasca, Ill.: Peacock.

Silverstein, Brett, and Deborah Perlick. 1995. *The Cost of Competence.* New York: Oxford University Press.

Simon, Barbara L. 1990. "Rethinking Empowerment." *Journal of Progressive Human Services* 1:27–39.

Simon, Barbara. 1994. *The Empowerment Tradition in American Social Work: A History.* New York: Columbia University Press.

Siporin, M. 1970. "Social Treatment: A New-Old Helping Method." *Social Work* 15:13–25.

Siporin, M. 1972. "Situational Assessment and Intervention." *Social Casework* 53:91–109.

Siporin, M. 1975. *Introduction to Social Work Practice.* New York: Macmillan.

Siporin, M. 1980. "Marriage and Family Therapy in Social Work." *Social Casework* 61:11–21.

Smyth, Nancy J. 1998. "Substance Abuse." In John S. Wodarski and Bruce A. Thyer, eds., *Handbook of Empirical Social Work Practice.* Vol. 2, *Social Problems and Practice Issues,* 123–153. New York: Wiley.

Snyder, C. R., ed. 1999. *Coping: The Psychology of What Works.* New York: Oxford University Press.

Snyder, C. R., and Beth L. Dinoff. 1999. "Coping: Where Have You Been?" In C. R. Snyder, ed., *Coping: The Psychology of What Works,* 3–19. New York: Oxford University Press.

Solomon, Barbara B. 1976. *Black Empowerment: Social Work in Oppressed Communities.* New York: Columbia University Press.

Solomon, Barbara B. 1985. "The Roundtable." In Sylvia Sims Gray, Ann Hartman, and Ellen S. Saalberg, eds., *Empowering the Black Family,* 73. Ann Arbor: National Child Welfare Training Center, University of Michigan School of Social Work.

Solomon, Barbara B. 1999. "How Do We Really Empower Families? Strategies for Social Work Practitioners?" In Beulah Compton and Burt Galaway eds., *Social Work Processes,* 351–353. 6th ed. Pacific Grove, Calif.: Brooks/Cole.

Stein, H. 1960. "The Concept of the Social Environment in Social Work Practice." *Smith College Studies in Social Work* 30:187–210.

Stinnett, Nick, John DeFrain, Kay King, Patricia Knaub, and George Rowe, eds. 1981. *Family Strengths 3: Roots of Well-being.* Lincoln: University of Nebraska Press.

Stinnett, Nick, John DeFrain, Kay King, Herbert Lingren, George Rowe, Sally Van Zandt, and Rosanne Williams, eds. 1982. *Family Strengths 4: Positive Support Systems.* Lincoln: University of Nebraska Press.

Stinnett, Nick, Greg Sanders, and John DeFrain. 1981. "Strong Families: A National Study." In Nick Stinnett, John DeFrain, Kay King, Patricia Knaub, and George Rowe, eds., *Family Strengths 3: Roots of Well-being,* 33–41. Lincoln: University of Nebraska Press.

Straussner, Shulamith L. A., and Elizabeth Zelvin, eds. 1997. *Gender and Addictions.* Northvale, N.J.: Aronson.

Sue, Derald W., Patricia Arredondo, and Roderick J. McDavis. 1992. "Multicultural Competencies and Standards: A Call to the Profession." *Journal of Counseling and Development* 70:477–486.

Sue, Derald Wing, Patricia Arredondo, and Roderick J. McDavis. 1995. "Appendix III. Multicultural Counseling Competencies and Standards: A Call to the Profession." In Joseph G. Ponterotto, J. Manuel Casas, Lisa A. Suzuki, and Charlene M. Alexander, eds., *Handbook of Multicultural Counseling*, 624–644. Thousand Oaks, Calif.: Sage.

Surrey, Janet L. 1987. *Relationship and Empowerment*. Wellesley, Mass.: Stone Center for Developmental Services and Studies.

Taylor, S. J., J. Racino, J. Knoll, and A. Lutfiyya. 1987. *The Nonrestrictive Environment: A Resource Manual on Community Integration for People with the Most Severe Disabilities*. New York: Human Policy Press.

Thomas, C. 1988. "Infants of Drug Addicted Mothers." *Australian Pediatric Journal* 24:16.

Tolman, Lani. 2001. "Attachment and Bonding in Young Children." Paper presented at University of Denver.

Trainor, J., and K. Church. 1984. *A Framework for Support for People with Severe Mental Disabilities*. Toronto: Canadien Mental Health Association.

Turner, John B., and Ray H. MacNair. 2003. "The Family in the Community." In Allie C. Kilpatrick and Thomas P. Holland, eds., *Working with Families: An Integrative Model by Level of Need*, 218–229. 3d ed. New York: Allyn and Bacon.

Turner, Sandra. 1997. "Building on Strengths: Risks and Resiliency in the Family, School, and Community." In Elaine Norman, ed., *Drug-Free Youth*, 95–112. New York: Garland.

Valle Ferrer, Diana. 1998. "Validating Coping Strategies and Empowering Latino Bettered Women in Puerto Rico." In Albert R. Roberts, ed., *Battered Women and Their Families: Intervention Strategies and Treatment Programs*, 483–511. New York: Springer.

Van der Kolk, Bessel, Alexander C. McFarlane, and Lars Weisaeth. 1996. *Traumatic Stress: The Effects of Overwhelming Experience on Mind, Body, and Society*. New York: Guilford.

Van Horn, James E., and Ellen Y. Matten. 1984. "A New Model for Developing a Community Family Strengths Program." In George Rowe, John DeFrain, Herbert Lingren, Ruth MacDonald, Nick Stinnett, Sally Van Zandt, and Rosanne Williams, eds., *Family Strengths 5: Continuity and Diversity*, 447–456. Newton, Mass.: Education Development Center.

van Pragg, Bernard M. S., and Paul Frijters. 1999. "The Measurement of Welfare and Well-being: The Leyden Approach." In Daniel Kahneman, Ed Diener, and Norbert Schwarz, eds., *Well-being*, 413–433. New York: Russell Sage Foundation.

von Bertalanffy, Ludwig. 1968. *General System Theory: Foundations, Development, Applications*. New York: Braziller.

Waites, Elizabeth A. 1993. *Post-traumatic and Dissociative Disorders in Women*. New York: Norton.

Walker, Lenore. 1984. *The Battered Woman Syndrome*. New York: Springer.

Walsh, Froma. 1982. *Normal Family Processes*. New York: Guilford..

Walsh, Froma. 1998. *Strengthening Family Resilience*. New York: Guilford.

Warr, Peter. 1999. "Well-being and the Workplace." In Daniel Kahneman, Ed Diener, and Norbert Schwarz, eds., *Well-being*, 392–412. New York: Russell Sage Foundation.

Warren, Roland L. 1963. *The Community in America.* Chicago: Rand McNally.

Waters, D., and E. Lawrence. 1993. *Competence, Courage, and Change: An Approach to Family Therapy.* New York: Norton.

Weick, Ann, and Ronna Chamberlain. 1997. "Putting Problems in Their Place: Further Explorations in the Strengths Perspective." In Dennis Saleebey, ed., *The Strengths Perspective in Social Work Practice*, 39–48. 2d ed. New York: Longman.

Weissberg, Robert. 1999. *The Politics of Empowerment.* Westport, Conn.: Praeger.

Williams, Mary Beth, and John F. Sommer Jr. 1994. *Handbook of Post-traumatic Therapy.* Westport, Conn.: Greenwood.

Williams, T. K. 1992. "Prism Lives: Identity of Binational Amerasians." In M. P. P. Root, ed., *Racially Mixed People in America*, 280–303. Newbury Park, Calif.: Sage.

Williamson, M. 2003. "All Powerlessness Stems from This." *UCC Newsletter.* Boulder, Colo.

Wood, Katherine M., and Ludwig L. Geismar. 1989. *Families at Risk: Treating the Multiproblem Family.* New York: Human Sciences Press.

Young, Iris Marion. 1990. *Justice and the Politics of Difference.* Princeton, N.J.: Princeton University Press.

Zimbalist, Sidney. 1961. *Historical Themes and Landmarks in Social Welfare Research.* New York: Harper & Row.

Index